Vietnam: My War

Five Decades Later

James Ike Schaap, Ph.D.

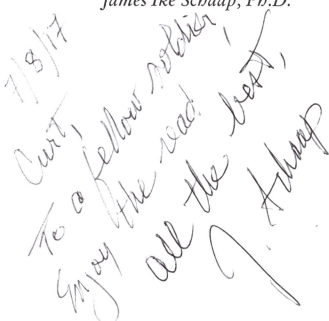

7/8/17
Curt,
To a fellow soldier,
Enjoy the road.
all the best,
J. Schaap

MERRIAM PRESS

HOOSICK FALLS, NEW YORK

2017

First published in 2017 by the Merriam Press

First Edition

ISBN 9781576385609
Library of Congress Control Number: 2017939843

This work was designed, produced, and published in
the United States of America by the

Merriam Press
489 South Street
Hoosick Falls NY 12090

E-mail: ray@merriam-press.com
Web site: merriam-press.com

The Merriam Press publishes new manuscripts on historical subjects, especially military history and with an emphasis on World War II, as well as reprinting previously published works, including reports, documents, manuals, articles and other materials on historical topics.

Contents

Dedication

IN the development and publication of this book, I would like to thank:

My fellow and dedicated Marines and Navy Corpsmen of D (Delta) Company, 1st Battalion, 9th Marines, 3rd Marine Division, FMF. We were tough, dirty, and profane but loveable Gyrenes who battled more for each other than for the reason that landed us in South Vietnam. I am here and grateful to still be alive. Semper Fidelis.

My comrades and stalwart Marines and Navy Corpsmen of M (Mike) Company, 3rd Battalion, 3rd Marines, 3rd Marine Division, FMF, who made this book possible. I am also indebted to these courageous Jarheads. We were resilient and irreverent warriors who also fought more for each other than for the cause in South Vietnam.

All of the other servicemen/women who fought in Vietnam—true American patriots: without your bravery and fervor to keep on going under the most difficult of times, many of us would not be alive.

My lovely, beautiful, creative, patient, supportive, and wonderful wife, Marilyn, of 39 years, who has inspired me, even during her medically challenging times, to write a book about my experiences in the Marines and Vietnam. Thank you—I adore you, and I am very grateful for all your support!

My 34-year-old son, who shared with me his beliefs about all the things wrong about war. For that, I am grateful. Thank you, Joshua—I love you, too—more than you can ever imagine.

My beloved, wonderful, and now deceased parents, Jozua and Mary Schaap who were married for fifty-two years. Thank you Mom and Dad. Shalom Aleichem—peace unto you.

Jennifer R. Mochel and Jean Stoess, for also reading my book and providing their editorial contributions. Also, to Hillar Leetma, M.D., retired physician and internist during the Korean War and a senior consulting editor, for his ability to reorganize my thoughts from a more military perspective.

Ray Merriam (i.e., Merriam Press, Hoosick Falls, New York) for his invaluable assistance. He took a gamble on this project and have done so much to help me make it better.

Introduction

FIRST and foremost, I want to say a special thank you—to the reader—for purchasing my book. I felt and realized that I needed to write a tome about my military experiences in South Vietnam. It was also my objective to help a new age group of readers—young people—possibly relive my story—even if it's in an oblique way. As such, writing this manuscript was my personal healing. To say the least, this was very therapeutic for me. Still, and at times, writing this volume was, periodically, a painful private engagement—I found myself agitated and unfocused after completing a chapter. Nonetheless, it is a true story of my particular viewpoint that I was committed to writing with personal opinions and assumptions interlocked into my message. It is a recollection of war, inescapably evolving from the storehouses of my own memory—other men have their own accounts and their own thoughts as well. I also used the official Marine Corps Command Chronicles, which were declassified in the late 1980s.

Yes, all this senselessness and sometimes stupidity, that you are about to read, really happened. It is a private account and a recollection of my own experiences in the Marine Corps as a youthful rifleman and combat ground warrior, in two different rifle companies, during the early phase of the Vietnam War, from 1965-1966, part of my time in the United States Armed Forces, which was from 1964–1967. Even so, my work does not profess to be history. Therefore, if there are any mistakes in my reporting of this conflict—especially during my direct combat involvements, they are due to the passage of many years—five decades ago, and the responsibility for any errors in writing about these clashes is mine and mine alone.

I have included other worthy information about the war that I hope you find interesting. It was also a time where Vietnam was at the heart of a cultural, social, and partisan change, like no other for the past century in the United States. This is, from what I recall, what happened five decades ago. For the most part, the descriptions of events in this manuscript are from my perspective. At times, those actions were tumultuous. My memory of that experience, of just another American who was sent to war by his country, is also supported by facts and in some cases lots of particulars. Few topics in contemporary history have been studied, analyzed, and debated more than the Vietnam War. The long and bloody struggle, which killed in excess of three million South Vietnamese and wreaked devastation as well as obliteration on huge portions of South Vietnam, has inspired a vast outpouring of books (i.e., even including my manuscript), articles, television documentaries, and Hollywood movies, as well as scholarly conferences and college courses. Nor is there any reason to believe the deluge of words will slow anytime soon, given the war's enormous human and material toll and given its deep—and persisting—resonance in American politics and culture.[1]

Given the resentment that encases the memories of the Vietnam War, even some still today and the extensiveness of my investigation in writing this book, I believe some subjective perspective may be helpful. Knowing this, it is a document about my intimate connection and the memorable events in my life that I am proud of to have experienced. My text, in my humble opinion, does not deliver original thought or dynamic formulation of extant information that might suggest a new perspective on our experiences in Vietnam. It is not unique. Still, my work is my own particular insight and understanding, and is presented in my own unpretentious way.

It is hard to believe that it has been five decades since I stepped on the soil of this bucolic country that was about to be run over by communists from North Vietnam or so I was told.

As Henry Cabot Lodge Jr., who was appointed by President John F. Kennedy, from 1963–1964, as Ambassador to South Vietnam, warned: "If America failed to press the conflict to a satisfactory end, Communism would engulf all Asia and raise the specter of armed confrontation between the United States, the Soviet Union, and the People's Republic of China. Our objective is to help the Republic of Vietnam (RVN, or South Vietnam) achieve and then maintain its independence."

During his time, Lodge spearheaded a military coup to overthrow Ngo Dinh Diem, President of South Vietnam, in a scheme code-named Operation Bravo Two. Lodge further thought that Diem was an eccentric obstructionist who lacked the ability to lead South Vietnam's turbulent population.

As I begin to share my account of what I experienced in Vietnam, here is some general, but very notable, information about the U.S. Marine Corps and the function that it partook in this country. Hopefully, it will provide some added perspective about the role that Marines played in this unpopular and controversial war.

During our preoccupation in the Vietnam War, 14,844 Marines were killed in action. Fifty-seven Marines were bestowed the Medals of Honor (America's highest military decoration for valor, often incorrectly called the Congressional Medal of Honor--refer to Appendix 1, Table XX).

360 Navy Crosses (America's second highest military valor decoration for Marines and Navy personnel) were also awarded to Marines. 2,418 Marines were decorated with the Silver Star (America's third highest military valor decoration). Of course, many other decorations were conferred onto Marines. (Note: The statistics provided above are estimates only. Actual figures may vary.)

---

[1] Fredrik Logevall, *Embers of War—The Fall of an Empire and the Making of America's Vietnam,* p. xv, (Random House Trade Paperbacks, 2013).

Because the fighting in Vietnam was primarily a ground war, the United States Marine Corps played a major role. Next to the U.S. Army, it furnished the majority of the American combat units involved and suffered the majority of the casualties. Instrumental in setting up the South Vietnamese Marine Corps in 1954 and in providing helicopter support for South Vietnamese troops in Vietnam beginning in 1962, U.S. Marine forces were predominant in I Corps from 1965 until 1969. A Marine general commanded the corps-level headquarters there—the III Marine Amphibious Force (MAF).

One of the anomalies of the hostilities, the Marine Corps, which was neither trained nor equipped for sustained defensive operations, ended up defending against cross-border attacks by regular North Vietnamese Army (NVA) units, which historian Allan R. Millett compared to World War I on the Western Front, while the Army's Ninth Infantry Division was being retrained for amphibious operations with the Mobile Riverine Force. This situation developed because in 1965 existing contingency plans in the Pacific Command in Honolulu called for a Marine rather than an Army landing in I Corps for temporary operations. There was a shortage of ports in that area and the Marines were capable of being re-supplied over the beach. When the temporary landing of the Ninth Marine Expeditionary Force in 1965 turned into the long-term commitment of the III MAF, these contingency plans–rather than battlefield protocol–necessitated the commitment.

During the course of the war the Corps deployed one corps-level combat headquarters, two Marine Divisions, two additional Marine regimental landing teams and a reinforced Marine aircraft wing to Vietnam. There were also a number of battalion-size Marine special landing forces afloat with the Seventh Fleet. These combat forces included some twenty-four battalions of infantry, two tank battalions, two antitank battalions, three amphibious tractor battalions, two reconnaissance battalions, ten battalions of artillery, and twenty-six flying squadrons, with about 225 helicopters and 250 fighters and fighter-bombers. In 1975, Marine Corps elements took part in the final evacuation of Cambodia and South Vietnam and the rescue of the *Mayaguez.*[2]

The Vietnam War, also known as the Second Indochina War, began as a conflict between the United States backing the South Vietnamese government and its opponents, which included the South Vietnamese-based communist National Liberation Front (Viet Cong) and the North Vietnamese Army (NVA), also known as the People's Army of Vietnam (PAVN). It began in the late 1950s and lasted, unfortunately, until 1975. Furthermore and according to John Pike, a national security analyst with Global Security, a Washington military think tank organization and leading source of background information and developing news stories in the fields of defense, space, intelligence, WMD, and homeland security, the clash was: The legacy of France's failure to suppress nationalist forces in Indochina as it struggled to restore its

---

[2] Harry G. Summers, Jr., *The Vietnam War Almanac,* pp. 237-238, (Presidio Press, 1985).

colonial dominion after World War II. Led by Ho Chi Minh, a Communist-dominated revolutionary movement. The Viet Minh waged a political and military struggle for Vietnamese independence that frustrated the efforts of the French and resulted ultimately in their ouster from the region. Vietnam had gained its independence from France in 1954. This country, nonetheless, was divided into North Vietnam and South Vietnam. North Vietnam had a Communist government led by Ho Chi Minh. South Vietnam had an anti-Communist government led by Ngo Dinh Diem.

The communist victory in the Chinese Civil War in 1949 and Chinese intervention against the United Nations in Korea made the U.S.-China policy a captive of Cold War politics. Those events also helped to transform American anti-colonialism into support for the French protectorates in Indochina, and later for their non-communist successors. American political and military leaders viewed the Vietnam War as the Chinese doctrine of revolutionary war in action (i.e., using Chinese and Soviet arms, to boot).

The overarching geopolitical aim behind the United States' interest in Vietnam was to contain the spread of communism in Southeast Asia. To accomplish this aim, the United States supported the anti-communist regime of South Vietnam in its fight against a communist takeover from the north. Ho Chi Minh declared independence in Hanoi on September 2, 1940, following the August Revolution, as a provisional government. Preventing South Vietnam from falling to the communists ultimately led the United States to fight a major regional war in Southeast Asia. The North Vietnamese regime, which received outside assistance from the communist great powers, the Soviet Union and the People's Republic of China, proved a formidable adversary. Whether the United States should have heavily committed itself militarily to contain Communism in South Vietnam remains a hotly debated topic. The debate is closely related to the controversy over whether the problems in Southeast Asia were primarily political and economic rather than military. The United States strategy generally proceeded from the premise that the essence of the problem in Vietnam was military, with efforts to win the hearts and minds of the South Vietnamese populace taking second place.

To frustrate North Vietnamese and Viet Cong efforts, and in part to contain China, the United States eventually fielded an army of over 500,000 men and engaged in extensive air and naval warfare against North Vietnam. The American military effort provoked stiff domestic and international opposition, led to strained civil-military relations at home, and called into question many of the assumptions that had dominated U.S. foreign and military policy since 1945, but failed to compel the enemy to do its will. In short, America's strategic culture was fundamentally altered in the jungles of Indochina[3].

The Vietnamese people had struggled for their independence from France during the First Indochina War from 1946–1954. This resulted in the division of Vietnam into North and South Vietnam.

---

[3]   John Pike.

With that prelude, my job in the hamlets/villages, beaches, mountains, and jungles of Vietnam was really simple and straightforward. I took on the role of a combat Marine during those watershed years, when one era was ending in the United States and another was beginning. I was a grunt, a 19-year-old teenager of the 1960s, among many warriors in Vietnam beginning with D (Delta) Company, 1st Battalion, 9th Marines, 3rd Marine Division (1/9/3), FMF, and later with M (Mike) Company, 3rd Battalion, 3rd Marines, 3rd Marine Division (3/3/3), as a Private First Class (PFC), like so many others who also trained to be a small arms expert. A grunt is someone who digs his or her own foxhole, performs front-line tasks, handles live weapons and artillery and duties in combat zones and risks his or her life. In general, Marine grunts are often an insular, standoffish bunch even among other Marines; they pride themselves on being leaner, meaner, and harder. Still, I was just another leatherneck among thousands of spirited and fearless jarheads that routinely conducted short-but-deadly manhunts through jungles and swamps where Viet Cong snipers stalked, harassed, and annoyed us constantly. Booby traps cut us down one by one. I was one of many Marines. We came from all walks of life that scored on the numerous battlefields and partook in a myriad of combat operations all across the northern part of South Vietnam. More important, I was a combat front-liner by trade that went on patrol with a team of other conferred Marines, always looking for the enemy almost every day. I was just one of many grunts who saw their fellow warriors get wounded and killed during the line of duty. These fine young men that I fought with risked their lives for one another, some giving the greatest gift they had—their own life. Some were, without a doubt, heroes, the best that the U.S. Marine Corps could offer.

Without equivocation, I am lucky to be alive. I am even more fortunate to have written this book—*Vietnam: My War—Five Decades Later*—for your knowledge and reading enjoyment. I am also one of the many former members of the Armed Forces who still lives with Vietnam in his day-to-day life, dreams, and nightmares—every day!

While the United States may not have won the war in Vietnam, its servicemen, from what I read and understand, *never* lost a *major* battle. (Note: A major battle or a large-scale search-and-destroy operation is where a battalion or more of its servicemen [i.e., 800–900+ warriors along with supporting Navy personnel] were in direct harm's way with the enemy.) Despite the 'deep' political divisions that brought about our involvement in Vietnam, which were many, most young American men accepted their government's call to arms even though it was difficult and trying, at times, to find sense of this conflict. I know I did!

My story, a self-effacing chronicle, is a ten-month journey, part of a three-year passage of life as a jarhead. It is a simple but detailed description of a young man who was eligible to serve in one of the finest branches of United States Armed Forces, and who accepted his duty, with honor, to his country without hesitation.

My account in the Marines is no more distinguished from the encounters of any other combat serviceman who spent a tour of duty, or two, or even three, in this beautiful country of farmers and serfs. As a naïve kid (i.e., a child of the 1950s and President Kennedy's young loyalists of the early 1960s)— definitely green around the edges, like so many other enlisted youngsters at the time, I was assigned a specific task. I trained with conviction and craving. I quickly became a young man, like so many other young men, sent on a mission, day after day, with clear-cut objectives. My target was simply that to *seek out and destroy my opponents,* an adversary that I never knew or cared to know. Additionally, I hunted for the enemy everywhere—around pagodas, in hamlets, hooches and prostitution huts, caves, rice paddies and sugar cane fields, in front of and behind young children, and throughout the jungle-like wilderness land of South Vietnam. And everywhere we looked for the Viet Cong, we were attacked.

The depiction of archetypal and classic combat experiences of many Marines during the early part of the Vietnam War—also known as the jungle war—was my life. This is how it felt, at least for me, to serve with other Marines in Vietnam.

Despite every account written in my manuscript, I can honestly state that I am honored as well as grateful to have served our country as a United States Marine. Additionally, I am proud and privileged to have fought in Vietnam.

I hope that you will read my work from cover to cover. It is written, on purpose, with very little profanity even though profane words, for the most part, were the order of day, especially during minor skirmishes to major combat operations. Further, my story depicts a very small segment of the war and the things that men do in combat. It is a snapshot of the longest military engagement and struggle, 1965-1975, that America engaged in, at a financial cost to the United States of $111 billion.[4]

I have written this book from the heart, but where there still is no healing—I have yet to be cured from what I experienced in South Vietnam five decades ago. Where possible, it is explanatory and concrete even though I am not a military historian or a diplomatic historian. Still, it is a factual report, as seen by the hundreds of references that I have included, told with no apologies and no memorials. Nevertheless, it is a private story that could *not* have been written at any other time. It is also a narrative of a very average American, born in the Netherlands, who was sent to war by his country, who saw many unexpected things, who also did many perplexing and difficult deeds.

Returning Vietnam veterans like me, some of us just nineteen years of age, still a young person and unable to vote at the time, were scattered throughout the United States, and discovered that, having served God and Country with valor. We were definitely *not* welcomed on our return with approval and praise. I am sorry to say, returning Vietnam veterans, just like

---

4   Stephen Daggett, *Cost of Major U.S. Wars,* p. 2, (Congressional Research Service, June 29, 2010).

me—some of whom were severally disabled, were spat upon, ridiculed, and intensely mocked by resentful protestors when we returned home. As such, the events at home were both startling and baffling. Can you imagine that we were even bullied by deserters—draft dodgers that were afraid to serve their country. Most of these activists were also young people: 18–25 years of age. In fact, and over the time, the ripple effects of these demonstration upheavals spread to the troops serving in Vietnam and added to their burdens.[5] Protests about the war were everywhere, but one of the most serious demonstrations was at Kent State University, Kent, Ohio (i.e., May 4, 1970-- where four students were killed and nine more were wounded) and even in the colleges and universities that I attended at the time–Santa Monica College (SMC), Santa Monica, California, University of California, Los Angeles (UCLA), and California State University, Northridge (CSUN), California. More important, nothing can possibly reimburse me, even though I am compensated monthly, as an 80% service-connected disabled veteran, by the Department of Veterans Affairs, for the physical damage done and the mental pain inflicted during these turbulent, unstable, and very quarrelsome times.

It was the beginning of an era, in 1960, when President Kennedy won the U.S. presidential election against Richard M. Nixon, with a popular percent vote of 49.7% v. 49.6%. Kennedy, in fact, was elected with a lead of only 112,827 votes, or 0.17% of the popular vote, giving him a victory of 303 to 219 in the Electoral College, the closest since 1916. This was the first election in which all fifty of the current United States participated after Hawaii and Alaska became states in 1959.[6] In his inaugural address, President Kennedy pledged to *"pay any price, bear any burden, meet any hardship, support any friend, and oppose any foe, in order to assure the survival and success of liberty.* It was also a period of time when Lyndon B. Johnson, President Kennedy's running mate turned Vice President, was more concerned with his great society and social progressive programs. In fact, he did not consider Vietnam a priority when he took over the presidency after Kennedy's death. Later, however, President Johnson exploited his constitutional discretion, supplemented by supportive resolutions in Congress, to conduct what was said to be called a police action. (From a definitional standpoint, a police action is a euphemism for a military action undertaken without a formal declaration of war.) Still, Johnson and other U.S. officials did not anticipate the scale and scope of the war on which they were embarking[7].

Throughout this book I present numerous snap shots, speech marks, slangs, songs, signs, sayings, as well as other Marine Corps lore that I consider vital to understanding what a Marine was all about. Those I consider especially significant and/or personal favorites are italicized.

---

[5] Robert Tonsetic, *Warriors–an Infantryman's Memoir of Vietnam,* p. viii, (Ballantine Books, 2004).

[6] *United States presidential election, 1960,* Wikipedia.

[7] Joe Allen, *Vietnam: the (last) war the U.S. lost,* p. 203, (Haymarket Books, 2008).

In this day and age there is a good chance that you will not hear words like *courage, bravery, loyalty, commitment, self-discipline, and honor.* They are mentioned throughout my work. Unless you know a former or current combat Marine, Navy Corpsman, Army soldier, or an Air Force pilot, along with all of the other servicemen/women in the Armed Forces, these concepts might not be part of a person's vocabulary—they were, however, mine. Again, Semper Fidelis!

Please note that fictitious names have been used, when needed, to protect the privacy and anonymity of certain persons. Nonetheless, the dates, locations, and Marine Corps operations described in this book are real and documented in the History and Museums Division Headquarters, U.S. Marine Corps, Washington, D.C. Also, please note that this author has relied on a lot of secondary, and hopefully reliable, sources. These references may or may not be credible, or are at least not corroborative with other consensus sources on the war.

Lastly, please note that this author does not portray himself to be a military historian, a diplomatic historian, or even a historian of some discipline. Still, with an earned Doctorate in Philosophy (Ph.D.)—a scholar in the field of strategic management and leadership, and an academician for over thirty-eight years, this author has performed an exhaustive amount of research in the writing of this manuscript.

Chapter 1

Looking Back
Five Decades Ago

URING my extensive research of military history about the Vietnam War, I learned that the ten-year Vietnam War, America's longest "hot" war, was unlike any other conflict the United States ever fought.[8] According to Joe Allen, a long-standing social justice fighter and regular contributor to the International Socialist Review, one who I suppose never served in the U.S. Forces firmly believed that: *"The war in Vietnam resulted in the greatest military defeat ever suffered by the United States"*[9] I do not consider this proclamation to be true. Therefore, please make that determination for yourself once you have read my entire manuscript.

One of the Vietnam War's unique characteristics is that it is difficult to ascertain when the war really began and ended. Further, according to Ronald Frankum and Stephen Maxner, who are affiliated with Texas Tech University's Vietnam Center and Archive: "The Vietnam War was unique in that each country involved in the conflict committed different levels of its nation's resources toward winning the war."[10]

To more than my surprise, our total active participation in Vietnam in 1954 was represented by the arrival of only *one* lone Marine advisor. All the same, its mission, which started in 1950, was when the United States Military Assistance Advisory Group (MAAG), was established in Saigon, the largest city in South Vietnam with a population of over a million people at the time, located near the Mekong Delta. Saigon is now called Ho Chi Minh City, although the name Saigon is still frequently used, particularly by its citizens. The name was changed in July 1976. Incidentally, Saigon served as the capital of the independent state of South Vietnam from 1954 to 1975. Its undertaking, at the time, was to supervise the issuance and employment of $10 million of military equipment to support French legionnaires in their effort to combat Viet Minh forces. The French Foreign Legion is known as an elite military unit whose training focuses not only on traditional military skills but also on its strong *esprit de corps* (i.e., the capacity of a group's member to maintain belief in an institution or goal, particularly in the face of opposition or hardship).

---

[8]   Clark Dougan and Stephen Weiss, *The American Experience in Vietnam*, pp. 92-93 (Boston Publishing Company, 1988).

[9]   Joe Allen, *Vietnam: the (last) war the U.S. lost*, p. 1, (Haymarket Books, 2008).

[10] Ronald B. Frankum, Jr.and Stephen F. Maxner, *The Vietnam War for Dummies*, p. 1, (Wiley Publishing, Inc., 2003).

By 1953, strictly from an economic standpoint, the amount of U.S. military aid had jumped to over $350 million and was spent to replace the badly worn World War II vintage equipment that France, still suffering economically from the devastation of that war, was still using. [11]

Under the leadership of President John F. Kennedy, who had been intrigued by the concept of counter-guerrilla warfare since the rediscovery of the *Marine Small Wars Manual* (written before World War II), Army and Marine advisers were sent to assist the South Vietnamese by as early as 1960. By mid-1962, American military advisers in Vietnam numbered 8,000, by the end of the year over 11,000, and by the time Kennedy's assassination in Dallas, Texas, in November 1963, almost 16,000 advisers were present. [12] President Lyndon B. Johnson, who inherited the entanglement after JFK's assassination in November 1963, escalated the American presence in Vietnam soon after taking office. [13]

Curiously enough and according to Rufus Philips, a former employee of the U.S. Agency for International Development (USAID), this writer stated that:

> At the highest levels we approached the Vietnam conflict with excessive hubris, convinced we knew best how to win, with little understanding of the enemy or of our South Vietnamese allies. We became obsessed with a big-army war when the real war, a people's war—mainly political and psychological in nature—went largely unnoticed. [14]

A few years later, after the Gulf of Tonkin Incident in August 1964, the United States prepared itself to send large numbers of ground forces into Vietnam to fight against the Communist North Vietnamese Army. After 1960 but before 1965, both Presidents' Kennedy and Johnson had sent upwards of twenty thousand military advisers into South Vietnam. The Marines also had a helicopter squadron in Operation Shufly actively supporting the Army of the Republic of Vietnam (ARVN) in the Mekong Delta below Saigon. (Marine Task Unit 79.3.5, code named Shufly, was the first Marine task unit to provide air support during the Vietnam War beginning in 1962. The tasking represented the first large unit commitment of a Marine element to Vietnam during the anti-communist struggle in Southeast Asia.) When North Vietnam attacked the major airfield outside Saigon, destroying many U.S. aircraft, President Johnson ordered the first American ground troops, a Marine Expedi-

---

[11] *U.S. Advisors 1955-1965.*

[12] Fredrik Logevall, *Embers of War–The Fall of an Empire and the Making of America's Vietnam,* p. 705, (Random House Trade Paperbacks, 2013).

[13] Colonel H. Avery Chenoweth, USMCR (Retired), *Semper Fi–The Definitive Illustrated History of the U.S. Marines,* p. 332, (Fall River Press, 2005).

[14] Rufus Phillips, *Why Vietnam Matters,* p. xiii, (Naval Institute Press, 2008).

tionary Brigade (MEB), to land in-country.[15] Johnson's administration chose war because anything less than a total victory would be seen as a defeat. In fact, the President stated earlier (i.e., 1964) that: *"Surrender anywhere threatens defeat everywhere."*[16]

By March 1965, with conventional warfare now taking place, the circumstances that brought about the growth of the Marine Corps' commitment in Vietnam illustrate how deadly a concoction the combination of politics— especially political affairs, war, and victory at any cost can produce. (Note: Conventional warfare is a form of warfare conducted by using conventional weapons and battlefield tactics between two or more states in open confrontation. The forces on each side are well-defined, and fight using weapons that primarily target the opponent's military. It is normally fought using conventional weapons, and not with chemical, biological, or nuclear weapons. Also, the general purpose of conventional warfare is to weaken or destroy the opponent's military, thereby negating its ability to engage in conventional warfare. In forcing capitulation, however, one or both sides may eventually resort to unconventional warfare tactics.[17])

Interestingly enough, the United States' strategy and guiding principle in Vietnam by the early 1960s was, in part, based on the lessons the U.S. learned during battles in the Philippines and World War II. These lessons were applied to Vietnam in anticipation that the victories enjoyed in those two countries would be repeated in South Vietnam. In addition, the United States strategists soon recognized the need for political reform in South Vietnam.

Thinking back to that time, some Americans had to wonder when we would win the war in Vietnam. Did they think it was going to take ten long years? Better yet, did they really want to win this war? Sadly, it was not until the media brought the war into everyone's living room that the American people developed much interest in this war halfway around the world.

It was five decades ago, 1965–1966. It was the time of the counterculture, rock-n-roll, and Woodstock. It was also the beginnings of the Gay Rights Movement. The discord, to say the least, in America was intense. Mini-skirts and bell-bottoms were the dress code of the day. The Green Bay Packers, under the exceptional coaching of Vince Lombardi, won a record third-straight NFL title. Ol' blue-eyes, Frank Sinatra, married Mia Farrow. The unexpected fire in the Apollo test launch killed astronauts Chaffee, Grissom, and White. Walt Disney died. One of my favorite songs, Soul and Inspiration, by the Righteous Brothers, hit "number six on the Billboard Top 10."[18] And the "Soviets launched Kosmos 110 on February 22, 1966, which carried the two-

---

[15] Colonel H. Avery Chenoweth, USMCR (Retired), *Semper Fi–The Definitive Illustrated History of the U.S. Marines*, p. 341, (Fall River Press, 2005).

[16] Joe Allen, *Vietnam: the (last) war the U.S. lost*, p. 39, (Haymarket Books, 2008).

[17] *Conventional warfare*, Wikipedia.

[18] Leo Daugherty, *The Vietnam War–Day by Day*, p. 70, (Chartwell Books, Inc., 2011).

dog crew of Ugolyok (Little Piece of Coal) and Veterok (Breeze) into Earth orbit. It landed on March 16th, after a twenty-two-day flight." [19]

By early 1966, the Vietnam War, conflict that would have been difficult at the best of times, had clearly become an obsession for Lyndon Baines Johnson (LBJ), the 36th President of the United States. He was the President and our Commander-in-Chief from 1963–1969. Johnson was also noticeably gripped and preoccupied with its entire strategic planning and execution. What is more, and as he stated at the Honolulu Conference (January 1 – February 9, 1966, where President Johnson, South Vietnamese General Nguyen Van Thieu, and U.S. General William C. Westmoreland met to discuss the war): "We need to come up with a better military program and a better pacification program, as well as a better peace program." [20] Just before this very meeting, Communist Party Central Committee member Aleksander N. Shelepin visited Hanoi and agreed to increase Soviet military aid to North Vietnam. [21]

Soon, this staunch and devoted democratic president, from Texas, who spent time in the U.S. Navy during World War II—in a non-combat role, began to hear rumbles of dissent from politicians within his own party. They balked at the notion that the President would order even more troops to South Vietnam. He was clearly showing identifiable signs of stress. In fact, the President stated during his 1966 State of the Union message that Vietnam was the center of our concerns. Also that same year, General Westmoreland stated bluntly, as part of his *search and destroy* strategy—simply kill more of them than they kill of us, "we'll just go on bleeding them until Hanoi wakes up to the fact that they have bled their country to the point of national disaster for generations." Though his assertion was prophetic, Westmoreland had no idea when he made it that it would ultimately apply more to the United States than to North Vietnam. [22] Still, this was Westmoreland's envision on the war of attrition. As such *"search and destroy"* was coined as a phrase in 1965 to described missions aimed at flushing the Viet Cong out of hiding in order to deploy air power against them, while the body count was the measuring stick for the success of any operation. Besides this, competitions were held between Army and Marine units for the highest number of Vietnamese killed in action. [23]

President Johnson was so fixated and absorbed on the situation in South Vietnam that he persuaded himself that making any concessions to North Vietnam would provide the Republicans, his political opponents, with the pretext to sabotage his so-called Great Society programs. He reaffirmed his

[19] Ibid, p. 68.
[20] Edward F. Murphy, *Semper Fi Vietnam*, pp.37-38, (Presidio Press, 1997).
[21] Joe Allen, *Vietnam: the (last) war the U.S. lost*, pp. 47-48, (Haymarket Books, 2008).
[22] Stanley Karnow, *Vietnam–A History,* p. 493, (Penguin Books, 1997).
[23] Jack Shulimson, USMC, *U.S. Marines in Vietnam–An Expanding War 1966*, p. 9, (U.S. Government Printing Office, 1982).

pledge to persevere: "We will stay until aggression has stopped because in Asia and around the world are countries whose independence rests, in large measure, on confidence in America's word and in America's protection."[24] Meanwhile, and according to Jack Shulimson, head of the histories section at the Marine Corps Historical Center in Washington, D.C., stated:

> The enemy was increasing at an alarming rate. Allied intelligence estimates of the total enemy strength in South Vietnam had risen from a possible 138,000 people in March 1965 to over 226,000 men by the end of the year. MACV believed that these forces consisted of more than 110,000 guerrillas, 39,000 political cadre, 18,000 combat support troops, and approximately 70,000 men organized in regular formation, including 19 regiments ranging from 2,000 to 2,500 men in strength.[25]

So much for this abbreviated history lesson. Allow me, if I may, to step back in time, five decades ago, to describe what life was like for me and my fellow combat-type of Marines. It was February 1966. At the conclusion of the Honolulu Conference (February 8th), President Johnson, besides he affirming his resolve to stay the course and fight not only the battle of aggression in South Vietnam, he also declared "the battle against both poverty and ignorance there too."[26] As a result, the thought of peace was denied by Hanoi, who responded to American presentation of the issue before the United Nations Security Council by declaring that any resolution by that body would be considered null and void. On top of this, the number of surface-to-air missiles (SAM) sites increased to ninety-three in this month with areas of concentration around Hanoi, Haiphong, Hai Duong, and Kep Air Field (that served as one of the principal air bases for North Vietnamese Soviet-built MiG fighters[27]—all in North Vietnam. At the same time, the North Vietnamese decided to move their military forces south—they sent two NVA divisions across the DMZ (Demilitarized Zone) into Quang Tri Province. Simultaneously, large military units were transferred from Laos across the border into Thua Thien Province, the region just below Quang Tri.

In this month as well, the United States saw the sharpest increase in the wholesale price index since the Korean War. Also, the unmanned Soviet Luna 9 spacecraft, known as Lunik 9, made the first controlled rocket-assisted lunar soft landing on the Moon. It was also able to transmit photographic data back

---

[24] Leo Daugherty, *The Vietnam War–Day by Day,* p. 75, (Chartwell Books, Inc., 2011).

[25] Dr. Spencer C. Tucker, *The Encyclopedia of the Vietnam War, A Political, Social and Military History,* 2nd Edition, Volume 1, A–G, p. 573, (ABC CLIO, 2011).

[26] Ed Gilbert, *The US Marine Corps in the Vietnam War,* p.15, (Osprey Publishing, 2006).

[27] *Donald Cook Medal of Honor,* Wikipedia.

to Earth. In this same month, then again, it was just another of many, or as I liked to call it *boo-coo,* early-morning wake-up calls in South Vietnam. Adrian Cronauer, the fast-talking disc-jockey on Armed Forces radio called out repeatedly: *"Good Morning, Vietnam!"* As seen in the movie, Cronauer was the disc-jockey portrayed by Robin Williams. I thought Williams's portrayal of Cronauer was right on. It was simply another sunrise in Vietnam, or so I thought.

Even though it was overcast, the temperature, at 0700, had already exceeded 95 degrees. The humidity was almost 100%. The scorching sun, in the hot blue sky, created lots of discomfort for my eyes. (Forty years later, I had cataract surgery on both of my eyes. A cataract is a clouding of the eye's natural lens, which lies behind the iris and the pupil.) The weather reminded me of the song *Summer in the City* by the Lovin' Spoonful. Sweat was dripping down my face, and my clothes were thoroughly saturated. I was soaking wet, and the day had barely started. It was miserable. Nevertheless, we Marines, the largest elite fighting force in the world, better trained for this war than most, had a job to do and, as always, we wanted to do it well. We wanted to survive another day. As such, our mission, as commonplace as it may sound, was simply to seek out, control, or destroy the enemy. In particular, our goal, as a Marine doctrine, which stressed achieving both physical and psychological separation of guerrillas from the people by treating non-combatants fairly, was to: "gain decisive results with the least application of force and the consequent minimum loss of life. In addition, the end aim, in Vietnam, was the social, economic, and political development of the people subsequent to the military defeat of the enemy insurgent forces." [28] We hoped that there would be no surprises. We had already survived more than enough ambushes. But every day we remained in this peasant country presented us with another astonishing situation.

To prevent dehydration, I made sure that I had pocketed salt tablets along with two stainless steel M1910 canteens of water. I also carried water purification tablets made of halazone or iodine just in case my water ran out and I had to drink from whatever was available, which was most likely a dirty, bug-infested river. I carted a small first-aid kit along with a standard field dressing. I am sure you can understand why I carried a first-aid kit. And along the rivers were tiger leeches, annoying little critters we had to contend with *all the time.* They would routinely attach themselves to me and increase their size several times over merely by sucking my blood. To get these pesky segmented worms off of me I would have used a lighter and burned them off. Pulling them off would have caused the head of the leech to stay on my skin. (Note: Leeches use an anesthetic they contain while attaching themselves, hence they usually are not noticed.) There also were snakes, such as Spitting Cobra, Bamboo Pit Viper, Malayan Pit Viper, and the Malayan Krait, along the riv-

---

[28]   Colonel H. Avery Chenoweth, USMCR (Retired), *Semper Fi—The Definitive Illustrated History of the U.S. Marines,* pp. 340-341, (Fall River Press, 2005).

ers. They were fairly prevalent, but most of the time they got out of our way. I say this, since I have always been afraid of snakes, especially the venomous ones.

I made sure, as an infantry assaultman or *jungle bunny,* with a MOS (Military Occupation Specialty) of 0351, that my subsistence fighting load consisted of at least 120 rounds of ammunition with one in the chamber of my M14 rifle (an improved version of the M1 Garand, which fired the standardized NATO 7.62 mm cartridge)—a term applied to weapons firing full-power rifle ammunition, "locked and loaded;" 19 in the attached clip; and another 100 bullets, in five metal magazines, strapped to my cartridge belt. Most times, I wore protective body armor, an M69 *flak jacket* made of ballistic nylon and weighing about eight pounds that usually stopped shrapnel but not rifle bullets. In fact, as we later found out, these protective coverings were an ineffective defense against a direct bullet blow. The laminates stitched within the body armor would only slow, not stop, a high-velocity bullet. Most times, too, I wore my M1 issued steel helmet with a single chinstrap, which had been adopted back in 1941. The Vietnam War-era helmets, were different from the World War II/Korean War version by having a lowered, less pronounced dome shape at the top forward section, and were painted a light olive green. I also made certain that at least a couple of M26 fragmentation hand grenades, that looked like a fat egg with an olive drab (OD) smooth steel skin, with four to five-second fuses were well secured to my belt. The M26 grenade, also referred to as a "Mike twenty-six," or a "frag" has a spherical steel body that contains six and one-half ounces of Composition B explosive (a mixture of mostly TNT and cyclonite or hexogen). This grenade weighs approximately 21 ounces, and has a safety clip to prevent the grenade from detonating accidentally. Additionally, I always carried my bayonet knife and scabbard, which was also strapped to my waist belt.

When I did not carry the M14 rifle, I would be supplied with an M20, 3.5-inch rocket launcher or bazooka, and two to three rockets. Originally designed as a so-called tank killer, this shoulder-fired weapon was commonly utilized as a bunker-buster in Vietnam. On a few occasions, I would carry a M79 grenade launcher, also called a blooper (a 40mm single-shot breech-loaded weapon that was introduced in the Vietnam War for close-in fighting, it was more lethal than a sawed-off shotgun), as well as an M1911 pistol. On rare occurrences, I would be assigned the air-cooled, disintegrating metallic link-belt-fed M60, 7.62 machine gun. The standard-issue machine gun during the Vietnam war weighed 23 pounds, was 43 inches in length, and had an effective range of 1,100 yards or over one-half mile. When I hauled the M60, I, as well as my fellow Marines, also carried another 500 rounds of ammunition. These bullets were strapped in a crisscross like manner, as a bandoleer, over my shoulders. They were heavy!

When I knew it was going to rain—and rain it did, I also hauled a 100% waterproof poncho. The OD green poncho is a multi-purpose rectangle of rubberized canvas with a hole in the middle so that the head can be inserted.

It acted as a combination groundsheet, tent, and blanket for most nights on patrol. A patrol usually consisted of walking outside the sight and rifle range of our larger unit and would range anywhere from five to ten kilometers (five to ten "klicks") and easily last up to a full day, depending on the terrain. Almost always, it seemed like I carried an extra fifty pounds of gear, and sometimes more. Most times, I did not bring any food (chow) with me because it was too heavy. Of course, I always wore my dog tags, taped together with black tape so the enemy would not hear the metallic clanking, around my neck. Dogtags were required when we were in the field. A dog tag essentially is the informal name for the identification tags worn by military personnel. The tag is primarily used for the identification of dead and wounded along with providing essential basic medical information for the treatment of the latter such as blood type and history of inoculations. I would also carry my waterproof Geneva Convention Card, which was stored in my breast pocket. The Geneva Convention Card was adopted in 1949, basically for the protection of prisoners of war (POW). One Marine Corps prisoner was Captain Donald Gilbert Cook (December 31, 1964–December 8, 1967), when he served as an advisor to the Vietnamese Marine Division. While wounded and captured, as a POW, he continued to resist the enemy by all means available. He died in a prisoner of war camp from malaria at the age of thirty-three. For his conspicuous gallantry and intrepidity, at the risk of his own life above and well beyond the call of duty, never breaking his indomitable spirit, he eventually earned the Medal of Honor, the highest military decoration awarded by the United States government. [29]

As expected, it was time for us to go out on patrol and find our adversary. We were informed, based on intelligence reports that the Viet Cong were in the area. In this case, hanging around the river (as can be seen in picture 1.1), so we strung out along the trail close to the tributary. The area that we were about to go into this particular morning included a maze of small hamlets or rural villages woven around the river's edge.

Unlike in previous wars the U.S. fought along a so-called front, there was no front in this campaign. There was not even an imaginary border. For us, the so-called frontage or forward-facing enemy lines was everywhere, in all places of South Vietnam because nothing was secure. That said, the Marines were limited to a geographical area in the northern sector of South Vietnam below the Demilitarized Zone. Their battles, like the Army's, became ephemeral, repetitive search-and-destroy missions, with no retention of real estate, but only tallies of enemy body counts. Unlike in earlier conflicts, there was no main line of resistance (MLR). There were only strongpoints and, later, fire-support bases, which had to be defended in 360-degree perimeters called Tactical Areas of Responsibility (TAOR). [30] Knowing this, when the Viet

---

[29] Harry G. Summers, Jr., *The Vietnam War Almanac*, Da Nang, p. 100, (Presidio Press, 1985).
[30] Ibid, p. 136.

Cong were in the vicinity (of which happened only too frequently), they were usually darting in and out of the tree line, and out of tunnels, caves, and bunkers with the specific intent to ambush American patrols.

Since the U.S. Armed Forces far outweighed the Viet Cong in mobility and firepower, if we had any, the VC developed various fighting methods for preventing their forces from being detected and destroyed. Two of their basic military techniques were camouflage, layers of trees and foliage that covered an area, and concealment or underground tunnels and bunker complexes where they stored ammunition, weapons, food, fuel, etc. This meant hiding and using the terrain and jungle, a real tangle, which was clearly in their favor, to mask their movement and activity, which, most of the time, they did very well.

They relied heavily on an assortment of ingenious mines and many different types of booby traps. The command-detonated ones did the most damage. These were made from unexploded bombs, mortars, or grenades, and the VC would rig them up with some type of firing device and explode them when they wanted to, such as when Marines were about to enter a village. Probably the most feared mine was the Bouncing Betty. It is the best-known version of a class of mines known as bounding mines. These concealed explosives would launch into the air at about waist height and explode, propelling shrapnel horizontally at lethal speeds. These mines were also anti-personnel landmines first developed by Germany in the 1930s and used extensively by German forces during World War II. It was designed to be taken advantage of in open areas to attack unshielded infantrymen—guys like us who constantly went out on patrols. The relative simplicity of such explosive devices led to their widespread use by the North Vietnamese and Viet Cong. Grotesquely, these were not designed to kill us, just cut us in half. If we stepped on one, we would probably be paralyzed for life, lose our legs, or our family jewels. Booby traps, some improvised and some imported from China and the USSR (Union of Soviet Socialist Republics), unluckily, accounted for some eleven percent of American deaths and seventeen percent of American wounds in Vietnam, as compared with three to four percent of American deaths and wounds in World War II and the Korean War. [31]

One of the most common types of booby traps was the so-called tiger pit. These were well-camouflaged holes approximately three to four feet in diameter and four to six feet deep. Stakes planted inside the pit would vary from one foot to three and four feet high. Tiger pits usually could be found on a main trail heading into a village. We did not want to fall into one of these pits for it was one hell of a way to die or seriously get injured as impalement would happen immediately.

Still morning, the photograph, as shown in picture 1.2, a specialized type of tractor-like landing vehicle, or amtrac, had just transported a small group of

---

[31] Donald M. Goldstein, Katherine V. Dillon, and J. Michael Wenger, *The Vietnam War*, p. 51, (Brassey's, 1997–Now Potomac Books).

us Marines across a river near the village of La Bong. This amphibian tractor, a lightly armored vehicle, is designed to carry troops and/or cargo from ship to the beach as well as inland.

As we were sitting on the top of the amtrac and moving across the river, we could see the damage that was made from previous fire-fights. The destruction to the thatched huts and pagodas must have been made by previous entanglements with the Viet Cong.

La Bong is in the area of An Trach, about fifteen miles southwest of Da Nang. Da Nang, in the south central coast of Vietnam, was a major commercial port city and later became one of the key command centers for the Armed Forces during the war. For me, though, Da Nang was the place where I had made my initial beachhead landing.

A city in the Quang Nam Province in the northern I Corps, Da Nang was the headquarters for South Vietnamese Army's I Corps and its Third Division. It was also the site of several major U.S. installations during the Vietnam War. A major jet-capable airfield was constructed there. It served at one time or another as the headquarters for the U.S. III Marine Amphibious Force, the U.S. First and Third Marine Divisions and later the U.S. Army's XXIV Corps. Regrettably, it fell during the North Vietnamese Final Offensive in April 1975,[32] and in 1976 South Vietnam officially became the Socialist Republic of Vietnam (SRV).

As we ran from the amtrac, a Viet Cong trip flare went off. That was usually the first indication we were in for another firefight showdown with the enemy. By the way, we called the enemy many different derogatory names. Among them were: Charlie, Victor Charlie, Viet Cong, VC, Slope, Slant, Gook or Dink. We called them every vulgar and grotesque name in the book since they were, without doubt, the enemy. They were small, spindly and haggard, and, at times, starved-looking old men, as seen in picture 1.3.[33] To make matters worse, many times they were young boys, sixteen years of age or younger, who were ready to kill us without fear or concern for their own lives. While many of these teenagers were motivated by idealism, others had been pressured or shamed into joining a cause. As I later found out, some of the local VC guerrillas, who always wore Ho Chi Minh sandals, were given only a basic minimum of infantry training. If they were recruited to a main fighting force unit, they could receive advanced warfare instruction. Additionally, there were dozens of hidden centers all over South Vietnam for squad and platoon leader, weapons, and radio training. To ensure that the guerrillas understood why they were fighting, the training courses included some type of political instruction. Some harbored, however, real doubts about their ability to fight heavily armed and well-trained American soldiers and Marines.

---

[32] Colonel H. Avery Chenoweth, USMCR (Retired), *Semper Fi–The Definitive Illustrated History of the U.S. Marines*, p. 340, (Fall River Press, 2005).
[33] Charles D. Melson, *The Marine Corps in Vietnam*, p. 31, (Osprey Publishing, 1988).

Usually, our encounters with the VC were at the outskirts of a small village. Most of the time, we would approach a hamlet, side-by-side, having first trampled through a rice paddy or other type of vegetable farm. Frequently, we waded through the deep muck of murky water, mud, and rice. Once outside and away from the amtrac, with a flare going off, there would be, as a general rule, a clearing between us and the enemy. In the open farm fields, we would have to walk, run, or even crawl on our bellies. Naturally, this is where the Viet Cong would open fire on us routinely.

The problem was that the VC would quickly pin us down because we could not cross an open field under enemy fire. As the VC shot at us, sometimes with their machine guns, AK-47s, or carbines, we had to scramble our way forward, many times lying in the muck of a rice paddy. Bullets would fly right by our ears. Things would pop and crack in the air. This provoked anxiety. Sometimes, the enemy's rounds would hit the ground right in front of us. That would make us even jumpier. Every now and then, the automatic fire would sound like paper ripping. This was caused by little pieces of copper-jacketed rounds purposely aimed at our heads with the intention to kill us!

We jittery Marines carried on as young men who had come of age very quickly. Though we were curious we were also very worried, yet determined to do our job. Ironically, we were more prepared for death than life. We were a rifle squad, normally thirteen of us, caught in another ambush. We would move at a snail's pace on our stomachs and in the mud, clawing and inching our way through those rice paddies—that were fetid with human fertilizer, typical in Southeast Asia. Often the VC would lace them with booby traps to inflict hideous wounds and infections upon unwary Marines. [34] Blood-sucking leeches clung to our bodies as we made our way through someone's farm. Of course, intolerably high temperatures made it difficult to breathe. On top of this, if it was night time—between 2400 and 0600, we found the tropical nights to be chilling.

There was nothing we could do. We were not about to shoot at the VC while standing up, so we returned fire from behind some type of embankment the instant we could find one. Behind that mound or ridge were usually the muck and mud puddles of rice paddies. Nervously, we would crank off a few rounds. We shot at them at times without being able to aim as well as we should have because of our undesirable positions in the open field. We would move cautiously creating rustling sounds, calling out to one another to stay together. Although the VC, generally group in three to five individuals, were usually no more than fifty yards away, it was difficult to see them as they shot at us from behind a tree, in tall grass, or from a *hooch*. If we stood up, we were sure to be wounded or killed This happened only too often to our Marines.

The best thing we could do in that situation was call in for an air strike. Usually F-4 Phantoms, a two-man fighter/attack aircraft used by the Marines, Navy, and Air Force, that could travel twice the speed of sound and up to

---

[34] Ibid, p. 31.

1,485 mph, would drop 500-pound high-explosive firebombs containing Napalm a substance that pulled the air from the lungs of our foe and turned human flesh to nothing more than ashes. Flying usually at speeds more than 600 miles an hour, many times low to the ground, these twin-engine supersonic jets would drop their "snakes-and-napes." First flown in May 1958, the McDonnell-Douglas F-4 was one of the most commonly operated planes during the war. It was the mainstay of the of the United States Air Force and Navy in the Vietnam conflict where it conducted bombings, combat air patrols and Napalm strikes against the well-hidden enemy.

These two photographs, pictures 1.4 [35] and 1.5, show Napalm bombs being dropped on an enemy target. The picture of the F-4 Phantom shows how the "fins of the bomb opened to delay its flight until the aircraft could get far away to avoid bomb fragments." [36] The other picture (i.e., Picture 1.5), taken by me, shows the actual results of Napalm hitting its target. When it hit its target, it was, for all intents and purposes, gasoline that had been jellied, so that it would adhere to its target as it burned.

We usually knew where the VC hid. More importantly, they certainly were acquainted with our position(s). Calling in for air support made it a lot easier on us for the reason that once the bombs were dropped we were able to advance safely. Our air superiority, nonetheless, could do little to stop the Viet Cong from using their available resources, especially concealment. When they heard our jets come in for a bombing run, the VC would immediately stop their attack on us and head for the nearest tunnel or another hamlet that was close by for cover.

The events just described happened time and time again during my all too many combat experiences in South Vietnam. This was part of our modus operandi. It occurred repeatedly since we could never really liberate an area. In fact, we found ourselves going back again and again to fight the same battles in the same areas with the same disappointing results. After all, this truncated battle scene describes the role that grunts, of the 3rd Marine Division, in the mid-1960s had to carry out routinely during their tour of duty in this God-forsaken place on the planet.

We were fortunate not to sustain any casualties in this particular action, but that was not always the case. Too many times, my fellow Marines would be seriously wounded or killed (i.e., sometimes we called them *blown away*). Occasionally, we would meet enemy forces that were far superior in numbers to us. It was nothing new when we would challenge our foe everywhere and anytime in forbidding and inhospitable conditions such as tunnels, caves, jungles, mountains, valleys, river banks, and in villages that were sometimes miles away from friendly faces.

---

[35] Leo Daugherty, *The Vietnam War–Day by Day*, p. 76, (Chartwell Books, Inc., 2011).

[36] *Battle of Ia Drang*, Wikipedia.

We would do this by hiking through the extreme heat of 100+ degrees with a humidity factor of almost 100%. Looking out over what seemed to be the same iridescent landscape, we would continue on gnawing on salt pills, pulling those blood-sucking leeches from our bodies and watching for booby traps every step along the way. This would result, repeatedly, in immeasurable instances of personal crises, extreme agitation and anxiety beyond imagination. In the end, restlessness coupled with intense excitement eventually ate away on us—especially me, and more serious predicaments that one could possibly envision.

Still it was a conflict between what we, the most advanced American military ever, had to offer versus the oldest kind of warfare—tribal-like guerilla fighting. The Viet Cong, a deadly and destructive enemy, were ubiquitous. They were ever-present, and they thought nothing better than trying to kill us.

During this same month of February 1966, as the war was continuing to intensify, the Marine Corps decided to deploy the First Marine Division from Camp Pendleton, California, for forthcoming combat operations in the I Corps. In fact, Operation New York began (February 27–March 3) when the 2nd Battalion, 1st Marines was alerted that the 1st Battalion, 3rd ARVN Regiment had been ambushed by the Viet Cong's 810th Main Force Battalion northwest of Phu Bai, just north of Da Nang.[37] The unit first established its foreign headquarters at Chu Lai, an area that we, the Third Marine Division, supposedly secured back in August 1965. In truth, at least from my standpoint, it was Operation Starlite, the *"first"* major scuffle of the Vietnam War, before the 1st Cavalry Division of the U.S. Army's skirmish and significant death in the Ia Drang Valley in October 1965. It was one of the largest struggles of the Vietnam War, led by Lieutenant Colonel Harold G. Moore, in which we, allegedly, took control of that general area. The Ia Drang Valley battle inflicted serious defeat on North Vietnamese forces, and was fought exclusively against the North Vietnamese Army regulars. No Viet Cong took part. (Note: The battle derives its name from the Drang River which runs through the valley northwest of Plei Me, in which the engagement took place [Ia means "river" in the local Montagnard language]).[38] That said, in the Ia Drang battle, both sides claimed victory and both sides drew lessons, some of them dangerously deceptive, which echoed and resonated throughout the decade of bloody fighting and bitter sacrifice that was to come.[39]

The success of the Marine Corps's campaign in Chu Lai and the American Army operation in the Ia Drang Valley influenced General Westmoreland's strategy of gnawing away at the enemy was the key to U.S. victo-

---

[37] Lieutenant General Harold G. Moore (Retired) and Joseph L. Galloway, *We Were Soldiers Once ... and Young*, p. xiii, (Random House, 1992).

[38] Harry G. Summers, Jr., *The Vietnam War Almanac*, The Vietnam War: Chronology 1959-1975, p. 36, (Presido Press, 1985).

[39] Jack Murphy, *History of the US Marines*, p. 173 (World Publications Group, 2002).

ry. As such, he ordered the largest search-and-destroy operations of the war in the Iron Triangle, the Communist stronghold in the rural provinces near Saigon. The Iron Triangle is a sixty square mile area in the Binh Duong province of South Vietnam, so named due to it being a stronghold of Viet Minh activity during the war. This operation was intended to find and destroy The National Front for the Liberation of South Viet Nam (NLF) military headquarters. Unfortunately, this campaign failed to wipe out Communist forces from the area. The NLF is an insurgent, partisan organization fighting against the government of the South Vietnam.

My Marine unit, Mike Company, along with other Marine detachments, nonetheless, participated in this first key mêlée called Operation Starlite. Even so, the Ia Drang battle was later made into a major motion picture. It was depicted in the film *We Were Soldiers,* directed by Randall Wallace and starring Mel Gibson. As a side note, a soldier is a person who serves in the Armed Forces for pay. The term *soldier* is usually limited to people who serve in the Army. In fact, we would bristle, figuratively speaking, at being called a soldier.

At the same time, the Senate Foreign Relations Committee, a standing committee of the United States Senate, is charged with leading foreign-policy legislation and debate in the Senate, began televised hearings on the war. President Johnson, while in Honolulu, Hawaii, that same month, "announced renewed emphasis on *The Other War,* the attempt to provide the South Vietnamese rural population with local security and economic and social programs to win their active support." [40]

The conflict that I participated in was considered to be a civil war. It was an effort by a people who had for years been pursuing their freedom from any type of colonial influence. I found that the Vietnamese people, whom we had earnestly tried to mold after our own image, were vehemently reluctant to take up the fight against the threat we were supposedly saving them from. I found that most Vietnamese people ironically did not even know the difference between Communism and democracy. These uneducated villagers, primarily peasants, only wanted to work in rice paddies without helicopters strafing them or Napalm burning their villages and tearing their country apart. They wanted everything to do with the war as long as it would bring them peace and tranquility at that moment. Per se, they practiced the art of survival by siding with whichever military force was present at a particular time, be it the Vietcong, North Vietnamese Army, or American Marines, like us.

Unfortunately, I saw Vietnam ravaged by American bombs as well as by search and destroy missions that I often participated in. These two pictures— 1.6 [41] and 1.7 [42]—with Marines on patrol, show the real life of typical combat

---

[40] Ibid, p.165.
[41] Ed Gilbert, *The US Marine Corps in the Vietnam War,* p.53 (Osprey Publishing, 2006).

warriors in action. A role that I, and my fellow leathernecks, played only too often. Also, I listened while this country tried to blame all of the destruction and devastation on the Viet Cong. Still, I understood why we had to destroy villages like Cam Ne in order to save these people. Furthermore, I saw how America later lost her sense of honor, pride and dignity as she very coolly accepted a tragedy such as My Lai, and instead advocated the image of American soldiers handing out chocolate bars and chewing gum.

I was fortunate enough to hand out some candy and chewing gum, and watch these beautiful little Vietnamese kids play, as kids normally play in the rivers or elsewhere: see picture 1.8. And that, in part, is what this chronicle is all about—*Vietnam: My War–Five Decades Later!*

The legacies and the aftermath left by the Vietnam War changed the way many view conflict and may have influenced the extent to which the United States might become involved in other foreign entanglements. Unlike the First or Second World Wars, the Vietnam War left the United States noticeably divided, and it continues to influence U.S. domestic and foreign policy. Without question, the Vietnam syndrome that emerged after the war's end altered the policies of Presidents Jimmy Carter and Ronald Reagan.

One of the best of many Vietnam War stories is *The First Battle: Operation Starlite and the Beginning of the Blood Debt in Vietnam,* written by Otto J. Lehrack (i.e., a retired Marine Corps infantry officer). The Vietnam War has never been fully understood and probably never will be explained to the satisfaction of those who lived it, directly or indirectly. The account probably will never be fully clarified because the importance, emphasis, and policies of the United States in Vietnam changed several times over the course of the war. Still, at least from a Marine Corps perspective, the initial and frequent Marine strategy for countering the communist guerrillas involved befriending the populace, developing an improved standard of living, and providing security from the VC tax collectors at events like a local market day[43]. It was a conflict calculated to grind down the North Vietnamese Army and the Viet Cong guerrillas. They had factored their human costs into the equation. Instead, the Vietnam War wore out our own military forces and gradually exhausted the patience of the American public. I am sorry to say that this continuous ten-year confrontation became one of the most problematic and convoluted aspect of what was often referred to as the other war or the war of pacification. By the way, pacification was a primary objective of the U.S. war effort in Vietnam. It was formally defined by U.S. Military Assistance Command Vietnam (MACV) in November 1967 as the military, political, economic, and social process of establishing or re-establishing local government responsive to and involving the participation of the people. It includes the provision of sus-

---

[42]   Harry G. Summers, Jr., *The Vietnam War Almanac,* Da Nang, p. 276 (Presidio Press, 1985).

[43]   Ed Gilbert, *The US Marine Corps in the Vietnam War,* p.53 (Osprey Publishing, 2006).

tained, credible territorial security, the destruction of the enemy's underground government, the assertion or reassertion of political control and involvement of the people in government, and the initiation of economic and social activity capable of self-sustenance and expansion. The economic element of appeasement includes the opening of roads and waterways, and the maintenance of lines of communication important to economic and military activity. Pacification was also designed to achieve three basic objectives: (1) to end the war and restore peace, (2) to develop democracy, and (3) to reform their society. [44]

With this in mind, I will try to further explain in plain words, a small part of this struggle and crusade. It was an undertaking, as part of my overall overseas tour of duty, as short as it was for me—July 1965 through April 1966—that will continue to spark debate and disagreements for generations to come. I also hope it will shed some light on the perspective of what war was all about for combat Marines like me five decades ago.

I will share these combat scenarios so that there may be further awareness and possibly appreciation of what warriors like me experienced and live within our minds every single day even now. Yet, my time in Vietnam has already sparked deliberation and considerable differences of opinion with our only son.

---

[44] Harry G. Summers, Jr., *The Vietnam War Almanac*, Da Nang, p. 276, (Presido Press, 1985).

Picture 1.1
Vietnam River
[Author photo]

Picture 1.2
Amtrac with flare
[Author photo]

Picture 1.3
VC soldier
[via Author]

Picture 1.4
F-4 dropping napalm
[via Author]

Picture 1.5
Bombing
[Author photo]

Picture 1.6
Search and destroy
[via Author]

Picture 1.7
Search and destroy
[via Author]

Picture 1.8
Children at the river
[Author photo]

Chapter 2

Vietnam
Da Nang

W HILE The Righteous Brothers were singing *"You've Lost that Lovin' Feelin',"* on June 28, 1965, more men of Delta Company (i.e., me included), 1st Battalion, 9th Marines, 3rd Marine Division, "first in, first out," embarked from Naha, Okinawa, also called The Rock. We headed for the Republic of Vietnam and the region of I Corps sector area of operations. [45] By the way, this battalion, which was formerly the 3rd Battalion, 1st Marines, was formed January 2, 1965. We were also part of the WESTPAC (Western Pacific) Marine group where a unit would be deployed overseas for a thirteen-month tour of duty. It composed of men, like me, fresh out of ITR (Infantry Training Regiment) at Camp Pendleton, California. We also trained at Kin Blue Beach, Okinawa, where we went to Amphibious Raid School. *We were called Marine Raiders.* The purpose of this ship-to-shore combat training and exercises was to potentially penetrate a hostile territory and secure information (usually behind enemy lines), confuse the enemy or destroy installations. Incidentally, I volunteered during these war-like maneuvers to be the scout swimmer for my unit.

About two weeks earlier, the Army had formed an airmobile division at Fort Benning, Georgia (1st Cavalry Division), located southwest of Columbus, to carry out a new concept in warfare called heliborne infantry assaults. Near the end of July, President Johnson announced to the nation that he was ordering that same division to Vietnam. He also alluded: *"We will stand in Vietnam!"* At the time, South Vietnam was administratively divided into forty-four provinces and eleven autonomous cities. These provinces, in turn, were divided into districts, villages, and hamlets. During the Vietnam War, however, four military regions (I Corps, II Corps, III Corps, and IV Corps)—that existed from 1955–1975, which were identical with the country's four Corps Tactical Zones (areas of combat operations), were superimposed over the provinces.

I Corps (refer to I Corps Map 1–2.1 [46]), pronounced "eye," was an area of about 10,700 square miles, including the coastal enclaves of Quang Tri, Hue, Da Nang, Chu Lai, and Quang Ngai. This area, the northern part of South Vietnam, bordered on the DMZ that separates North Vietnam from South

---

[45] Clark Dougan & Stephen Weiss, *The American Experience in Vietnam,* pp. 30-31, (Boston Publishing Company, 1988).

[46] Lawrence C. Vetter, Jr., *Never Without Heroes,* (Ballantine Books, 1996).

Vietnam. It encompassed a population of over 2,500,000 people in five provinces, six cities, and 549 major villages. I had trained intensively for about a year and has recently traveled on two different attack transport ships 9,000 miles to get there.

South of I Corps was II Corps, the largest of the four strategic fighting areas. Next was III Corps, then IV Corps, which was located in the extreme southern part of the country and is made up of river deltas.

Vietnam, shaped somewhat like an upside-down sea horse, a nation that was ruled by the Chinese for roughly 1,000 years, with Laos and Cambodia to the west and North Vietnam and China to the north, with 1,400-miles of S-shaped coastline fronting the China Sea, is located between the Tropic of Cancer and the Equator. It was a country with a rich diversity of flora and fauna.

Approximately forty percent of the landscape was covered by dense forests nourished by prodigious rains. It poured on an ongoing basis, from May to October 1965 and again from November 1965 to February 1966—while I was stationed there. Although beautiful, Vietnam's diverse terrain would soon prove to be menacing and threatening for American soldiers and Marines fighting a counterinsurgency conflict in the countryside. It changed constantly, making it next to impossible to completely understand it. In addition, I felt the terrain was intimidating so we always had to be ready for the unknown.

Even though it was late June, on February 22, 1965, General William C. Westmoreland, U.S.A. Commander, United States Military Assistance Command, Vietnam, had requested two Marine battalions to protect the key air base at Da Nang from the increasing threat by the Viet Cong. What is more, judging that South Vietnam was standing on the verge of defeat—because the Viet Cong controlled most of the countryside, the first set of American combat troops—two battalions of Marines—landed in Vietnam on March 8-9, 1965—with their original orders to protect the U.S. air base. This landing was completed with practically no advance notice to the Vietnamese.[47] When we invaded South Vietnam it was seen as a virtually unshakable power that could impose its will on most of the world through direct military intervention or through the use of its vast economic leverage.[48]

As part of the U.S. Navy's Amphibious Task Force, the 3rd Marine Division splashed ashore with their polished rows of steel bayonets, in four-foot-high waves, at Red Beach II, northwest of the city of Da Nang. The landings, on those days were fortunately unopposed and warmly welcomed by the inhabitants. A perimeter of strongpoints, for internal security for the Americans, was immediately established around the city, and preparations were made for the III Marine Amphibious Force (MAF) headquarters to be set up on the peninsula at the mouth of the harbor. Across the Tourane River, a former French brothel was taken over and turned into the Combat Infor-

---

[47] Rufus Phillips, *Why Vietnam Matters*, p. 247 (Naval Institute Press, 2008).
[48] Joe Allen, *Vietnam: the (last) war the U.S. lost*, p. 204 (Haymarket Books, 2008).

mation Center (CIC), run by the Division of Information from Headquarters Marine Corps. The small cubicles were turned into accommodations specifically for visiting press and VIPs. The CIC had the distinction of being the only air-conditioned bar-restaurant in the area and was also frequented by higher-ranking Marines.[49]

Immediately following the securing of the area, comprised of the 9th Expeditionary Brigade, 3rd Marine Regiment, 3rd Marine Division, two battalions amounting to about 3,500 Marines were deployed to defend the Da Nang Air Base. Later that same month, the 1st Marine Aircraft Wing was deployed from Japan and Okinawa to lend support to the U.S. Marine operations in the I Corps. Also, in March 1965, President Johnson authorized sending an additional 40,000 American troops to Vietnam. This introduction of American conventional ground forces represented the beginning of an ever-expanding ground combat presence in Vietnam. In terms of fighting the war, it meant American troops took increasing amounts of responsibility for engaging the enemy.[50] It was a wonder if these American warriors and soldiers with conventional military training would be able to win a war in Vietnam.

In July of 1965, the Seventh Fleet's Cruiser–Destroyer Group arrived, patrolling the coast on gunfire support duty, while the Navy's Task Force 77 launched air attacks on the North from Yankee Station, 100 miles off the coast of South Vietnam, southeast of Cam Ranh Bay. In fact, during the Vietnam War, the Seventh Fleet, which was first established in 1943, engaged in combat operations against enemy forces through attack carrier air strikes, naval support, amphibious operations, patrol and reconnaissance operations and mine warfare.

In the coming months, over 500 aircraft and ten major military air bases were established in South Vietnam (located at Da Nang, Phu Cat, Pleiku, Tuy Hoa, Nha Trang, Cam Ranh, Phan Rang, Bien Hoa, Tan Son Nhut, and Binh Thy). Tens of thousands of servicemen/women would arrive as the United States began a disputed and contested ten-year effort to keep South Vietnam from collapsing. In the meantime, and on June 28, 1965, as already mentioned, I embarked from Naha, Okinawa (which included the largest amphibious assault by the U.S. and its Allied forces in the Pacific War during World War II, which was also called the Battle of Okinawa) a city on the East China Sea coast of the southern part of the island, the largest of the Okinawa Prefecture where I had been training aggressively for jungle warfare, and the like (mock Vietnamese towns that we had to go to), with full military gear, including my flak jacket. I also carried a sea bag. The sea bag carried my military clothing and a few belongings on board a U.S. attack transport ship. We then headed directly for South Vietnam. Nine days later, the 190th anniversary of the U. S.

[49] Colonel H. Avery Chenoweth, USMCR (Retired), *Semper Fi—The Definitive Illustrated History of the U.S. Marines,* pp. 340-341 (Fall River Press, 2005).
[50] Ronald B. Frankum, Jr. & Stephen F. Maxner, *The Vietnam War for Dummies,* p. 99 (Wiley Publishing, Inc., 2003).

Marine Corps, I was about to get that surreal wake-up call. Reveille was called at 0600, for those who were still asleep. On July 7, 1965, three days after my parents' birthday, I got up, brushed my teeth, and had another wonderful breakfast in the ship's galley. It was my last great meal that I was going to have for a long time. Yes, my parents share the same birthday on July 4th, and also the same year—1913. They were also both born in the same hospital in Amsterdam, Holland.

At about 0800, the USS Bayfield (APA-33), the lead ship in her class of 16,000-ton *attack* troop transport ships, which was built in San Francisco, California, and during the June 1944 Normandy Operation she was the flagship for the Utah Beach landings (as can be seen in picture 2.2), steamed into the harbor of Da Nang, I Corps Tactical Zone, South Vietnam, as can be seen in the I Corps map (picture 2.3).[51] In passing, the Bayfield would be used a month later (August 17, 1965) as an attack troop transport ship for the first major battle of the Vietnam War—Operation Starlite.

It was a hot and slightly overcast day. The temperature must have been over ninety-five degrees with at least the same or higher percentage in humidity, and I was sweating profusely. The sun had already crept out of the Gulf of Tonkin and the Pacific Ocean behind us. The seas were relatively calm with swells averaging between three to four feet, that morning as the renovated World War II assault transport ship (which was also present for the atomic bomb tests at Bikini in the Marshall Islands) moved into position to unload Marines ready for combat. The shoreline was a little over half a mile away. I could see that many anxious servicemen were crowding the ship's railing for a last, quick look at the distant shoreline. I was among them. Even Navy personnel were somewhat apprehensive. They, too, did not know what to anticipate. It was the first trip for most of the sailors to this distant land. It was a place on the globe that would assuredly bring America to war. It was a clash between the newest and the oldest in warfare. In fact, we were told, as we were getting ready to disembark, by our commanding officer (also called *old man or brass*), strangely enough, not to kill Vietnamese people who were not in uniform unless we were fired upon first by them. It was also mentioned that we could/should kill anyone in a North Vietnamese government uniform.

Everyone was quiet but edgy. A few Marines whispered their Hail Mary's. Others murmured prayers. Me, I was in awe as well as befuddled and my *pucker factor* was through the roof. My fellow warriors and I were about to enter a war, and more seriously, a killing zone. I was also full of illusions thinking that the Viet Cong would be quickly defeated and that we were doing something altogether magnanimous and respectable. Nonetheless, I was never prouder to be a Marine for it was also a time that all my military training and skills, and surely my manhood would be tested.

---

[51] Edward Doyle and Samuel Lipsman, *The Vietnam Experience–America Takes Over–1965-67*, War Footing, p. 14, (Boston Publishing Company, 1982).

On pins and needles, we (the Battalion Landing Team [BLT]) collectively checked our weapons and the rest of our gear. We patted each other on our helmets, our silent sign indicating we were ready for action. To say the least, it got frighteningly exciting. To this day, I cannot believe how scared I was. All the while, I was trying to remember everything I learned in boot camp, advanced training in Camp Pendleton, and jungle-warfare and raider preparation on the island of Okinawa only a few months earlier.

I had barely turned nineteen years of age, just losing my youthful clumsiness but had become a hard-charging combat Marine. I was turning into an on-the-ground fully-loaded warrior, ready to destroy the enemy's ability to fight. I guess you could call me a professional (killer). I was definitely not an *ALICE* (All-purpose Lightweight Individual Carrying Equipment).

Whether it was going to be on a jungle ridgeline, in a rice paddy assaulting a tree line, or even village-to-village fighting, this was something I had trained hard for the past year. Everywhere, it meant kill or be killed!

As we climbed down the treacherous nets between stations four and six on the starboard side of the deck of the vessel (as can be seen in picture 2.4), with the waves slapping briskly against the side of the ship, I knew that we were in for a major change. As we loaded into the beach-type landing craft— LSTs (Landing Ship Tank), with our 782 gear (which stands for individual combat/field equipment known, for the most part, by Vietnam-era Marines) at the ready, helmets cocked to one side and cigarettes hanging out of my fellow Marines' mouths, we slowly began to move away from the ship and positioned ourselves ready for an amphibious assault on Da Nang. Lying at the southern end of a horseshoe-shaped bay, it was one of the largest cities in Vietnam and the chief port of the central lowlands. Wave after wave of leathernecks would soon run ashore thinking that the VC would be behind every tree. From what I read in history books, these types of assaults, some twenty years earlier, had been associated with deadly affairs of the French. I thought to myself, was I going to be another statistic that would later be put into a body bag?

About 0900, carrying sixty pound packs and M14 rifles, we jumped off the open amphibious landing crafts, just like what you saw in the movie *Saving Private Ryan*, into knee-deep water and we splashed our way to the shore, as some of our fathers had stormed Normandy on June 6, 1944 (e.g., Omaha, Utah, Gold, Pointe du Hoc, and Juno beaches), or the Pacific atolls during World War II (e.g., The Battle of Kwajalein, Makin, Tarawa, Guadalcanal, Peleliu, Midway, Iwo Jima, Okinawa, etc.), holding our fully loaded weapons (magazines in the rifles) above our heads. We could not have a round in the chamber. As far as we could see to the north and south, there was this beautiful white sand beach and magnificent coastal mountains. Also, all around us was this breathtaking blue-green, awe-inspiring water.

As we moved further ashore in this unforgiving place, directly to the west, I was surprised to find no enemy resistance. I had been told there would probably be many Vietcong taking pot shots at us. Actually, it was a calm assault on the beachhead. I do not believe anything really happened of any major consequence and I was relieved. Thank God. It was quiet because Marines of the 9th Expeditionary Brigade, 3rd Marine Division who landed there in early March, four months earlier, had secured the area, approximately five square miles of relatively unpopulated terrain. This included the airfield and the high ground to the west. The overall responsibility for the defense of the Da Nang area as well as their own bases remained with the ARVNs. I later found out first-hand, as we were fighting side-by-side with the South Vietnamese Army, these ARVN soldiers were poor fighters. More so, they often were left in the dark about the reasons they fought and their nation's politics. In fact, ARVN commanders spent more time fighting one another than engaging the enemy.

Once organized on the coastline, as can be seen in the map of Da Nang (picture 2.13),[52] northwest of the city itself, deuce-and-a-half trucks (M35s) convoyed us quickly on a bumpy road to highly identifiable defensive positions around the Da Nang Air Base, also known as *Rocket City,* as can be seen in picture 2.5.[53] Even though we were moving quite fast, fully armed and ready to fire at the enemy, we could see the broad landscape of rice paddies and its dikes, magnificent palm groves, and misty peaks.

The fortification and other locations around Da Nang later served as the headquarters (also known as an Area of Operations [AO]) for the U.S. III Marine Amphibious Force, the U.S. 1st and 3rd Marine Divisions and later the U.S. Army's XXIV Corps. It fell ten years later to the North Vietnamese during the Final Offensive in March 1975.

Along the way to my first destination, where throngs of children and teen-age boys ran beside the convoy—calling out for a cigarette or candy, we passed through very narrow streets with small shops and thatched houses. These same constricted streets and storefronts later became restaurants, beer parlors, ice shops, laundries, jewelry stores, and brothels for the many American servicemen/women who paraded through the area. Luckily, I never went into town. Good, bad, or indifferent, I never had to worry about what went on in Da Nang itself. Some servicemen would pay a couple of dollars, at most, for a quickie from the local Vietnamese hookers. These were young pathetic-looking girls that were outfitted in Western-style pants usually caught gonorrhea, syphilis, or some other terrible venereal disease.

Notwithstanding, my fellow grunts and I lacking real world combat experience, yet we knew combat in theory and practice only. What is more, we were on very unfamiliar landscape. Anxious and definitely concerned, nervous but eager, not knowing what was about to happen, as contrived as it may sound, I was committed as well as entrusted to the Corps to serve my coun-

---

[52] Harry G. Summers, Jr., *Historical Atlas of the Vietnam War,* p. 99, (Houghton Mifflin Company, 1995).

[53] Jack Shulimson and Major Charles M. Johnson, USMC, *U.S. Marines in Vietnam—the Landing.*

try. I knew I was only one of thousands of dedicated Marines that hit this beautiful beachhead prepared to serve and possibly die for his country.

Even though we just arrived in South Vietnam, ready with our M14s at high port, having assumed that no shore was really friendly, hostilities had already begun. As such, I thought I would share some facts with you about the costs of this war. Sadly enough, we were here for keeps. Among the numerous decorations, awards, and medals that were handed out during the course of this conflict, the following, as mentioned in the introduction section, is only a few that have brought both joy and sadness to my heart:

Fifty-seven Medals of Honor were awarded to U.S. Marines for conspicuous bravery while in Vietnam. I am privileged and honored to say that I knew one of them - Lance Corporal Joe C. Paul*. Of those Marines that were decorated with the country's highest award for heroism, three of them came from the 3rd Battalion, 3rd Marines, 3rd Marine Division—the unit that I served in the longest while in Vietnam.

They are: Corporal Robert E. O'Malley—India Company, August 18, 1965, Lance Corporal William R. Prom—India Company, February 9, 1969*, and Private First Class Ronald L. Coker—Mike Company, March 24, 1969.* [*Denotes that the medal awarded posthumously.]

Regrettably, 58,220 United States Armed Forces personnel died in Vietnam—some of which perished from non-hostile deaths including accidents, illnesses, and self-inflicted wounds. Of that number, 14,844 were Marines who were also killed in action (KIA).

Sadly, 51,392 Marines were wounded (WIA) or injured severely enough to require hospitalization (1964–1972)–(I was one of them). These individuals accounted for over 120,000 battle-related diagnoses of accidents, poisonings, and violence. (Note: The statistics provided above are approximates only. Actual figures may vary.) Most of the wounded Marines were under the age of twenty-five, junior enlisted infantrymen with one year or less of service. The First and Third Marine Divisions accounted for the majority of casualties—I served in the Third Marine Division (which was first organized in 1942, and took part in the amphibious assaults on Bougainville and Guam and in the hard-fighting on Iwo Jima during World War II). Multiple open wounds of the lower limbs were the most common primary diagnoses: bullets, mines, and booby traps were responsible for more than half of the wounds and injuries. [54]

Unfortunately, twenty-five Marines became prisoners of war. Two of them served over eight years in a North Vietnamese prison (1965–1973), while engaged in military operations involving conflict

---

[54] *Prisoner of War Medal*, Wikipedia.

against an opposing foreign force, and while serving with friendly forces engaged in an armed conflict against an opposing armed force to which the United States is not a belligerent; or under circumstances not covered by (the 1985 statute) but which the Secretary concerned finds were comparable to those circumstances under which persons have generally been held captive by enemy armed forces during periods of armed conflict. [55]

Besides our promise of making the world safe for other people, even though some 3,200,000 Vietnamese, on both sides, were killed, according to Marine Corps statements, the Free World served notice that it was answering the Republic of Vietnam's call for help. Our challenge was fourfold:

1. *To defend and provide security to the base area from which our forces operate;*
2. *To find, fight and destroy the Communist main-force units, whether guerrillas or conventional North Vietnamese Army forces;*
3. *To extend the area under positive government control, root out the Viet Cong infrastructure, and provide a screen of security;*
4. *Behind this screen of security, to assist the Vietnamese in an organized program of "Revolutionary Development" or nation-building, the Marine part of which is called a Civic Action.*

As can be seen in picture 2.6, I am here now. Yes, I am really here. Wow, what a weird feeling! Nevertheless, it is hard to describe and put into words. With full combat gear on me and at my side, I am at the far southwest part of the Da Nang fortress, built and occupied by the French, once as a French colony (commonly known as French Indochina) from the mid-nineteenth century until its expulsion in 1954, overlooking a junky and trashy village called Dog Patch (just to the west of my lookout position), you could see the filth and poverty of this hamlet (huts made of thatch), which was the name for the village of dilapidated shacks on the west perimeter of the Da Nang Air Base. More so, you could see the pools of sewage lie in the ditches, and the smell blending with the stench of human and animal excrement. Boney-looking dogs would growl and bark at each other in these filthy streets. I was at that time, what we would call, in the "point" or forward defense sentry position. I was sent here, along with other fine and dedicated warriors from the 9th Marines, to provide internal security for what was now an American compound air base and logistical facility. I was also the FNG—*the fucking new guy.* In fact, we were first confined to about an eight-square mile tactical area of responsibility (TAOR—a geographic area assigned to any unit for which that unit has sole operating authority and responsibility) around the base. On the other hand, our overall mission, as part of the 3rd Marine's Division responsi-

---

[55] *United State Marine Corps 1966*, U.S. Government Printing Office.

bility, was to cover a large area of 257 square miles (south of Da Nang), consisting of twenty-seven villages, 150 hamlets and more than 88,000 Vietnamese civilians. Contiguous to this zone of action was the An Hoa industrial light complex, an area of considerable economic potential to the people of Da Nang and the surrounding Quang Nam Province.

I have never experienced such intolerable heat and humidity in all my life. The temperature frequently exceeded 100 degrees. The humidity consistently hit 95 percent or more. The scorching heat and persistent humidity packed a combined and physically draining punch. For about two weeks, I, along with my fellow grunts, worked under the blazing hot sun and in the dark of the night as a sentinel, providing outer perimeter base security for the air base, where U.S. F-4 Phantom Jets, A-4 Skyhawk light attack bombers and Marine helicopter squadrons were housed. From what I could see, the field in Da Nang was definitely overcrowded with Marine and Air Force squadrons as well as South Vietnamese aviation units and logistics traffic. A few years earlier, however, it served as a provincial airport, with a 10,000-foot runway, for that part of the country. Now it was tasked with being a major military air base in a war zone.

So there I stood watch day and night in a bunker and part of a concrete fortification that was once occupied by French soldiers. It was strange for me. Edward F. Murphy, acclaimed Vietnam War historian whose investigation splendidly fills the gap in the Vietnam War literature, is a writer and researcher who helps account for the key battles, their origins, as well as their aftermath: The Geneva Accords of 1954 ended France's colonial role (in Southeast Asia). The Accords temporarily designated two zones for re-grouping the contending forces pending elections. Essentially, they were re-assigned into a "Communist-supported government north of the seventeenth parallel (governed by the Viet Minh) and an anti-Communist regime to the south (governed by the State of Vietnam, then headed by former emperor Bao Dại). Despite the Accords, Ho Chi Minh, North Vietnam's leader, launched a subversive effort to overthrow the government of South Vietnam and reunite the country." [56]

The basic problem as our platoon saw it at the time was that we did not train for this type of defensive purpose. We did not prepare ourselves, on a regular basis, to be sentries. As such, we made all kinds of grumbling noise about serving security. We were starting to complain. We, on one hand, were trained to be riflemen/combatants and a combat infantry battalion, ready to kill the enemy. On the other hand, we definitely were not a bunch of security guards, and this place surely did not look like a war-torn nation with peaceful rice fields, small villages, and bamboo groves that were located close to the base.

That was an uncertainty that further led to suspicion on our part. We felt that job was for someone else. We were skilled and trained to be hard-

---

[56] Edward F. Murphy, *Semper Fi Vietnam*, p. 2, (Presidio Press, 1997).

charging, offensive fighters adept at hand-to-hand combat and tasked with capturing or killing the enemy, shooting him/her right between the eyes, as necessary. It was gratification when we slew our foe. When we killed the VC, we used words like *greased, offed, lit up, or zapped*. We were further skilled as a lightning-fast amphibious assault unit, hitting the beachhead with all our might and taking full control of the area. Anything else was inappropriate and certainly unacceptable. Nonetheless, the challenge of securing the Da Nang Air Base was part of a larger problem. Defending the entire military region known as I Corps where the air base was located.

In my particular case, as previously mentioned, I was the scout swimmer of our unit, having become quite proficient for these types of amphibious maneuvers back in Kin (Blue) Beach, Okinawa. Also, as a surfer, growing up in Southern California, I could easily hold my own in rough waters. Besides this, I was a small arms expert. I trained, while stationed at Camp Pendleton, California, and Camp Hansen, Okinawa, to handle and use many different types of small-arm, single-person hand-held weapons. Further, I had to deal with the inspection, maintenance, repair, and function of these small arms, including rifles.

We were also taught, during our jungle warfare training in the northern part of Okinawa, also known as the Northern Training Area (NTA), to look out for those deadly booby traps. In spite of this, we were doing exactly the opposite, at least for the time being. We were specifically instructed by our commanding officer (CO) *not* to engage in any day-to-day or evening-to-evening actions against the Vietcong unless we were directly shot at. Unless we were goaded by the enemy, we were to do much of nothing. This was definitely a crappy job. I hated it and it sucked! Again, our overall responsibility, as we were told, was for the immediate defense and security of the Da Nang Air Base.

The upper echelon of the Marine Corps had a distinct notion about their role in Vietnam. Interestingly enough, here is what they had to say at the time:

> Although the deployment of two battalions to Da Nang in March 1965 finally put them in the war, the Marines had misgivings. Trained as assault troops, the Marines at Da Nang found themselves holding static positions and defending territory. That had never been part of their historical mission. Their purpose was to overrun the enemy, take heavy casualties, and evacuate, leaving the army infantry to hold the positions. Premier among the critics was General Victor H. Krulak, one of the few senior military officers convinced that the key to victory was political, not military. For General Krulak, the big engagements between United States, ARVN, Main Force Vietcong, and the North Vietnamese could move to another planet today, and we would still not have won the war because the Vietnamese people

are the prize. Marine Corps Commandant Wallace Green emphatically stated: My boys should not be sitting around on their diddybox. [57]

Even though we were in this country only for a few hours, we felt as if our hands were tied behind our backs. We were soon authorized to play a part in active combat operations. In any case, I was thrilled to get out of guard duty. As uncanny and eerie as it may sound, I was ready to do the job I had trained so hard for the past nine months, especially jungle warfare even though we knew that we would be strangers to this unwelcoming terrain.

In the intervening time, President Johnson adopted the recommendation of General Westmoreland, Commander of America's Armed Forces in Vietnam. He allowed us to take on a different role. And so we did. Combat-ready trained Marines, like me, would later find ourselves conducting deep reconnaissance patrols of the enemy's avenues of approach. Likewise, we would undertake offensive action as a reaction force in coordination with the South Vietnamese soldiers.

So much for being custodians and taking on guard duty at the air base as highly trained jarheads. We would quickly undertake an offensive approach by seeking out and destroying Viet Cong in the Da Nang area. On July 1, 1965, Marines from my unit who were already guarding the air base got their first taste of heavy Viet Cong firepower. A heavily armed and gutsy VC group of about fifteen sappers (specialists) attacked the air base, the world's busiest airport at the time. Using their mortars and light rockets they destroyed a few planes on the ground; one Hercules C-130, four-engine turbo-prop cargo aircraft and two Convair F-102 Delta dagger jets (the world's first supersonic all-weather jet interceptor and the USAF's first operational Delta-wing aircraft). Some of the Marines from Charlie Company headed for the area where the attack started. But the enemy withdrew from the field only too quickly. For the VC, it was simply hit and run, which they did well and only too often. Bravo Company also searched the area. Although some suspects were rounded up, I guess they were not associated with the attack. One Viet Cong, purportedly, was directly involved with the attack. As a result, he was held as a prisoner. As can be seen in picture 2.7, [58] this so-called "dink or gook," a Vietnamese person or possibly a Viet Cong wearing black pajamas was supplied various goods (e.g., weapons, clothes, food, first aid equipment, etc.) by the North Vietnamese. Later, South Vietnamese soldiers found a wounded North Vietnamese officer who expressed to them that the attack had been planned for quite some time.

Having stayed at the air base for only a brief time, what ensued over the next nine months, at least for me, was daily scouting of the enemy's strong-

[57] James S. Olson and Randy Roberts, *Where the Domino Fell–America and Vietnam 1945–1990*, p. 144, (Diane Publishing Company, 1991).
[58] Official USMC photo taken by Sergeant A. J. Cotterell, Combat Information Bureau, 1st Battalion, 1st Marines.

holds. Basically, my mission was to look for, capture, and obliterate, if necessary, the Viet Cong wherever and whenever possible. In other words, my job was to seek and destroy the enemy, and I did that with a great deal of pride and dedication (to the Corps).

Life was interesting during those early days in and around the Da Nang Air Base and around the shanty village of Dog Patch (a so-called average, primitive stone-age community nestled in a bleak valley, between two unassuming hills). As can be seen in picture 2.8, the VC would repeatedly take pot shots at our sentry posts. Between one structure and the next, or in an alley, the Viet Cong would try to take us out. Occasionally, a VC would fire their weapon. Usually, no more than a few rounds were fired at a time. This was definitely a harassment tactic. From what we could tell and rarely see, they shot with old M1 carbines or the War Baby. Baby because it was a three-quarter scale rifle; War Baby since it was the product of an urgently conceived requirement satisfied by Carbine Williams and his colleagues at Winchester. Unfortunately, we could not chase after the Viet Cong. We were specifically told to man our post and hold our position, no exceptions. And that is what we did much to our chagrin. Fortunately, our positions were very well fortified. Auspiciously, the VC, at least in this area, were really poor shots. Thank God. As a result, I do not think anyone in my unit was wounded while I was stationed at the fortress itself and in the outskirts of Da Nang.

The attack of July 1, 1965, and the pot shots by the Viet Cong in the village of Dog Patch set the stage to come. These were only minor skirmishes. and incidental clashes. However, that attack on the Da Nang Air Base generated enough publicity that the Marines' overall role and operations around the air base quickly expanded. In July of that same year, President Johnson asked Robert S. McNamara, Secretary of Defense, whom he called the smartest man he had ever met, to take the conflict, summarize it in a series of policy alternatives, and make a recommendation. McNamara presented his analysis early in July as well. He stated to President Johnson that there appeared to be three options. The first option was advocated by George W. Ball, under Secretary of State, and Mike J. Mansfield, who served under President Kennedy. Mansfield and was sent to Indochina on a fact-finding mission. A second alternative, the one favored by Maxwell E. Taylor, Ambassador to South Vietnam (1964–1965), limited American forces in South Vietnam to 95,000 men fighting an enclave war and preparing ARVN to take over. If that did not work, then the United States should get out. Third, the president could take the advice of Westmoreland (General William Childs Westmoreland, leader of the American military operations in the Vietnam War at its peak from 1964 to 1968, with the Tet Offensive, a military campaign during the Vietnam War that was launched in January 1968 by forces of the Viet Cong and North Vietnam against South Vietnam, the United States, and their allies), and expand the military effort against the Vietcong and North Vietnam until they had to negotiate or be destroyed.

McNamara told President Johnson that the third option was the only way of saving Southeast Asia. He proposed giving Westmoreland his forty-four battalions, mining Haiphong harbor, and sealing off North Vietnam from all external commerce, and bombing to destroy munitions, fuel supplies, railroads, bridges, airfields, missile sites, and war industries. He wanted to call up 225,000 army reservists for active duty. Short of nuclear weapons, McNamara wanted to bring every ounce of American firepower to bear. After consulting with his principal military advisers on the future of American involvement in the ground war, the President appeared frustrated as well as irritated with the inability of the South Vietnamese government to make progress, bewildered at the unresponsiveness of the North to his proposals for negotiations, and skeptical about the usefulness of the dispatch of additional U.S. troops, he agreed with nearly all of the advisers that the costs of a North Vietnam victory was unacceptably high.[59]

Within that strategic fog, Westmoreland tried to fight a war. He was convinced that the confrontation was a military event and that the United States should focus on destroying the enemy, just like what the allies had done to Germany and Japan during World War II. The United States economy was unmatched in its ability to produce and deliver military firepower, and Westmoreland planned to build, in the words of journalist Neil Sheehan, a "killing machine," a huge army backed by the latest in technology and organization. Westmoreland would fight the communists in three stages. In 1965 through early 1966 he would build the infrastructure to support a large, modern army. (Needless to say, the Marines were included in this arrangement.) He estimated it would take one soldier in a logistical support role to maintain each soldier in the field.[60]

Life inside this stronghold, with its 10,000-foot landing strip, was also engaging as well as entertaining. We ate a constant diet of C-rations from 1953, often called C-rats. As a result, we coped with frequent diarrhea. Left over from the Korean War (1950–1953), C-rats were basically a way to fill our stomachs. They were packed in thin cardboard boxes. What passed for food were these boxes that contained cans of sustenance that were also labeled beans and wieners, spicy meatballs, beefsteak and potatoes, spaghetti and meatballs, and ham and lima beans (also called ham and mothers). This package also contained a small can of pound cake, pecan roll, or fruit cake, cheese spread, and thick crackers.

Usually there were eight Marines, clean-shaven, with side-walled haircuts wearing semi spit-shined boots, to a hot and humid encampment, an area without much relief from the constant heat and those pesky malarial mosquitoes (picture 2.9). This would all change only too quickly. Our jungle utilities

[59] Robert D. Schulzinger, *A Time for War–The United States and Vietnam, 1941-1975*, p. 175, (Oxford University Press, 1997).

[60] James S. Olson and Randy Roberts, *Where the Domino Fell–America and Vietnam 1945–1990*, p. 138, (Diane Publishing Company, 1991).

would quickly become frayed and torn. We would, before long, be without the proper military clothing. Some of us would not shave for long periods of time. Our skin color, in time, would become dark from sun exposure and we looked lean and mean. How warriors are supposed to look. Our body odor changed as well. And as time went on, most of us would sustain abscesses (of different types), insect bites, and infected cuts.

In fact, the temperature inside the dusty tent was often oppressive. The air had a strong, unpleasant smell. If a Marine was not on duty, he was most likely back in his tent trying to asleep on his sandy cot. Shut-eye was challenging in the miserable heat. If he was not asleep, he might have been cleaning one of his weapons.

As you can probably tell from that same picture, the area around our grubby tent was one giant very hot sandbox that turned to mud when it rained. And heavy rain did come at times. When it rained we could feel it even if we were inside our tents. It came down with such rage, we could hardly move. When it was not raining, the wind would blow the coarse sand everywhere. It was undoubtedly an environment that created havoc with our weapons. They quickly got dirty, making them difficult to properly function. When our firearms did not work, which sometimes they did not, we were in real trouble.

If we were not doing anything of importance, we might have written a letter to a loved one at home. Or, if we were not in the tent, we might have visited a fellow Marine. Regardless, we were ordered to always keep our boots on so we did. One thing we could not do was walk around outside our tent camp area. We were confined to this sector on the outskirts of the base as part of our temporary duty station, unless we went to our sentry post.

As one who liked to make a few friends, I tried passing the day by visiting other Marines. I had worked and trained closely with Private First Class Rick Martindale, as can be seen in picture 2.10 (Martindale is standing to the left; I am to the right). We trained together in Camp Pendleton and later in Okinawa. We played and drank together. Concurrently, we were both ready for action. I knew his moves, and I am sure he knew mine. Like the rest of the guys in my unit, he was dedicated to making a difference.

I also enjoyed working and training with Private First Class Bill Thompson, as can be seen in picture 2.11 (Thompson is to the right, I am to the left [practice] firing the machine gun). He, too, was a good, well-disciplined warrior. He was a fellow grunt always willing to help and a Marine that you could count on in the heat of battle. I lost contact with him when I transferred—*mounted out*—out of this unit.

You might be interested to know what the large barrel was behind the two of us, as can be seen in the same picture. It was a storage container.

Even though we were well-oiled fighting machines, leathernecks who were ready for the dirty and dangerous tasks at hand, occasionally we needed to clean ourselves. In doing so, that storage tank also became our outdoor shower and aide, as can be seen in picture 2.12. Sadly, this outdoor bathing area was our companion for only a very short time.

As I mentioned before, life was interesting during those early days in Da Nang. Everything was new and more than surprising to us. We did not know what to expect. In fact, the unforeseen became the probable; no matter how prepared we thought we were. I guess we were ready for anything. We were primed, at least in our minds, for the whole shebang as warriors, ready to destroy the enemy's ability to fight.

So there I was, a so-called Devil Dog and a sentry in Delta Company, 1st Battalion, 9th Marines, 3rd Marine Division, ready for the unknown, ready to stop Communist aggression in South Vietnam. Guard duty was on a four-hours-on, four-hours-off basis.

With my "eleven pound, fully loaded, hand-held M14 combat assault rifle, magazine-fed, gas operated, semi-automatic weapon, slung over my right shoulder, with one bullet in the chamber and nineteen rounds in the clip, capable of traveling 2,850 feet per second, and a maximum effective range of 1,509 feet," or 28.4% of a mile, my initial job was to watch for Vietcong snipers taking pot shots at us from the crudely built village of Dog Patch, the outskirts of Da Nang, some 200 feet away.

My M14 was the standard issue U.S. infantry rifle at the beginning of the Vietnam War. It was the only rifle that I used during my time in-country. Because it was too heavy and unwieldy for jungle warfare, even though I felt very comfortable with this weapon, it was replaced in 1966 by the M16 rifle. This high-powered weapon, on the other hand, weighed only 8.79 pounds fully loaded. It used ball and tracer ammunition. The magazine also carried twenty rounds. It was gas-operated and air-cooled. It also had a selector switch that had three positions for firing (safe, semi-automatic, and automatic). The maximum range for the M16 was about 300 yards with a highly effective range of fifty yards or about 150 feet. The rate of fire was 650–700 rounds per minute on full automatic, and 150–200 rounds per minute when reloading twenty-round magazines.

As a sentry, who was constantly on the lookout for the enemy, who might have been hiding between the thatched houses of Dog Patch, here were my eleven general orders, which I learned and memorized in boot camp.

1. *To take charge of this post and all government property in view.*
2. *To walk my post in a military manner, keeping always on the alert and observing everything that takes place within sight or hearing.*
3. *To report all violations of orders I am instructed to enforce.*
4. *To repeat all calls from posts more distant from the guardhouse than my own.*
5. *To quit my post only when properly relieved.*
6. *To receive, obey, and pass on to the sentry who relieves me all orders from the commanding officer, officer of the day, and officers and noncommissioned officers of the guard only.*

7. *To talk to no one except in the line of duty.*
8. *To give the alarm in case of disorder.*
9. *To call the corporal of the guard in any case not covered by instructions.*
10. *To salute all officers and all colors and standards not cased.*
11. *To be especially watchful at night, and during the time for challenging, to challenge all persons on or near my post and to allow no one to pass without proper authority.*

On July 11, 1965, other combat Marines from the 9th Marine infantry unit, my unit, along with men from the 3rd Reconnaissance Battalion were sent out on patrol south of the Da Nang Air Base and across the Cau Do River. Here is a gripping account of what happened, as briefly described by First Lieutenant Bill J. Vankat, the Delta Company commander:

Christ, he no more than got across the river in an area that was supposedly secure, than they got into a world of shit—just across the bridge on Highway One. I took the rest of the company down there to help extract them, and the 9th Marines sent in their 2nd Battalion to help, and they got into a big goddamn row. In a relatively short period of time the entire 9th Marine Regiment was committed to the fight. On the second day of that battle (i.e., July 12, 1965) was when First Lieutenant Frank S. Reasoner was sent with his patrol (from Company A) several miles to the south of us. [61]

That battle, in which there was an estimated 100-man enemy company, regrettably cost the life of Lieutenant Reasoner as he was aiding a wounded warrior. On that day, he led a five-man reconnaissance patrol into enemy-controlled territory. He killed two enemy combatants, and destroyed an automatic weapons position. Sorry to say, numerous other Marines were killed and wounded as they were trying to hold off the VC. For his bravery, Lieutenant Reasoner, born in Spokane, Washington, who was twenty-eight years old at the time, was posthumously awarded the Medal of Honor for his determined fighting spirit, fearless leadership, and unwavering devotion to duty provided the encouragement that was to enable his patrol to complete its mission without further casualties.

During that same fight with the Viet Cong, Corporal B. C. Collins received the Navy Cross, and Second Lieutenant William T. Henderson, Lance Corporal Fred Murray, and Private First Class Thomas Gatlin each received the Silver Star; all for acts of courageousness. In addition, the battalion's command post (CP) at Da Nang was later renamed in honor of Lieutenant Reasoner.

---

[61] Lawrence C. Vetter, Jr., *Never Without Heroes,* pp. 17-18, (Ivy Books, 1996).

VIETNAM: MY WAR

In early August, my company was ordered to leave the air base. We were definitely ready for a new line of (combat) work; jungle warfare that we trained so hard for on the northern island of Okinawa. For almost a month, I had been a sentinel, a protector of the Da Nang Air Base, mostly standing night watch on the outer perimeter of Da Nang, looking and listening to the sights and sounds of the darkness that make for a slow, noisy light show. Also in early August, the Viet Cong destroyed, through constant attacks, well over a million gallons of fuel that was stored in storage tanks near Da Nang. As a result of this horrendous and terrible fuel loss, the U.S. immediately conducted air strikes against the Viet Cong.

We were given the word by villagers who were friendly to our cause that VCs were hanging out in a village not too far away from the base. So, we left our French-built fortress and headed out for Cam Ne, which was made up of several interconnecting smaller hamlets, connected by a commonly farmed rice field, about seven miles southwest of the Da Nang Air Base.[62] It was the same area where another company had been a little earlier and run into some real trouble. This small, but very important, one-day operation was planned in conjunction with the 3rd Marines operation, Blastout I. This was also carried out by an ARVN battalion four miles south of the Cam Ne complex along both banks of the Yen River. The 3rd Marines battalion would provide a blocking force to the south while Delta Company, my company, cleared the Cam Ne complex.

To get to the village, we came up along a river on amtracs and debarked a short distance away. In the meantime, almost daily contact, ironically, was maintained with the village chief, a VC sympathizer, who constantly gave food and refuge to the enemy, in order to obtain information on the civilian population. American as well as Vietnamese intelligence considered Cam Ne to be a well-known VC stronghold.

My group was assigned the lead group. Just as we formed for attack the enemy took us under fire. We still entered the complex. It was a place that lacked young men. Still, the hamlet looked normal. Young women with small children were playing in the area. Older women were working on preparing the meals for that evening. Some would be standing in their thatched doorways, nursing infants and spluttering red streams of betel-nut juice into the dust. (Note: Betel-nut is a mildly euphoric stimulant, attributed to the presence of relatively high levels of psychoactive alkaloids. Chewing it increases the capacity to work and also causes a hot sensation in the body. Chewing betel-nuts is an important and popular cultural activity in many Asian countries.) The older men were working their rice grounds. If they were not working the fields, they were standing by their thatched houses smoking gnarled cheroots. Not surprisingly, they would be staring at us without seeming to

[62] Jack Shulimson and Major Charles M. Johnson, USMC, *U.S. Marines in Vietnam—the Landing and the Buildup 1965*, p. 60, (U.S. Government Printing Office, 1978).

notice us. But there were no young men to be seen. This seemed to be very strange. This was probably a sign that there was going to be trouble.

I was told that Cam Ne, a series of local hamlets, was a place where long-time communist partisans and sympathizers occupied. These bucolic villages acted as a base area for the local VC, where the enemy favored hit-and-run military type of tactics. I can certainly understand that from my own experiences later in Vietnam. Vietcong regulars, as well as local VC, moved with ease and integrated themselves among the uncooperative peasants and village people. A few old men dressed in black pajamas crouched down as they usually did when Marines arrived, in front of their huts while their hostile, silent women stood in the doorways. As we advanced, we constantly took small-arms fire. Several sharp sounds were followed by a number of pops a foot or so above our heads, probably from those missing young men. Further, we thought there were at least 20–50 VC, if not more, in the area. As we took fire while entering the village, we were given the command to overcome and destroy any position, including huts, from which we received fire. We were also ordered to *burn down the hooches.* As young gung-ho Marines, we did so with our Zippo cigarette lighters. We were given a directive and we obeyed. No questions asked! Supposedly but unconfirmed, 150 huts, occupied by various South Vietnamese families, were demolished or burned to the ground as a specific counterinsurgency tactic.

Four Marines from another platoon were wounded during the attack. Another one, however, from my platoon was my squad leader, Corporal Veeney. He, a Marine lifer, was shot right in the butt. As we put him in the helicopter to be evacuated, he softly spoke, *"I am out of here, guys, and I am not coming back."* I never saw this dedicated and would be career grunt ever again.

In the meantime, and as combat actions were taking place: Private First Class Reginald M. Edwards was in an amtrac heading for the village. A helicopter was supposed to have preceded his unit, telling everyone to evacuate. If you remained there you were considered VC. [63]

We were coming into the village and crossing over the hedges. It is like a little ditch, and then you go through these bushes and jump across and start kicking ass, right? Not only did we receive one round, three Marines got wounded right off ... So you know how we felt. [64]

As we left the village, once again we came under sniper fire again, probably from those missing young Vietnamese men. I came away unhurt from this first encounter with the enemy. We were sure we left some dead enemy fighters in our wake. We guessed the death toll to be about seven. The Viet Cong, nonetheless, must have carried off their dead and wounded. Only one small boy was killed, unfortunately, in the crossfire.

---

[63] Marilyn B. Young, *The Vietnam Wars 1945–1990*, p. 143, (HarperPerennial, 1991).
[64] Ibid.

That evening, the American people, back home, and the rest of the world saw the battle of Cam Ne on their television sets, as can be seen in photograph 2.14. I believe that was Private Marion Pride, from our platoon, who lighted the hut with his Zippo. The film and photos of Cam Ne were widely distributed and are among the most famous and important episodes of the entire Vietnam War. To say the least, the images taken by Morley Safer's CBS (Vietnamese) cameraman (Ha Thuc Can) certainly generated a significant amount of controversy in America. I am firmly convinced that Americans saw it differently from what we actually experienced. Also, I do not think most American people knew what the war was about. Information was spoon-fed to them through one journalist's eyes an interpretation of the conflict.

Morley Safer (1931-2016), Canadian born journalist, began his career as a reporter for various newspapers in Canada and England. Later, he joined the Canadian Broadcasting Corporation as a correspondent and producer. As a thirty-three-year old *non-college graduate* reporter at the time, he opened the CBS News bureau in Saigon (an initialism of the network's former name, the Columbia Broadcasting System), one of the first television newsmen to be permanently assigned to the Vietnam War, had been airlifted by a helicopter into Cam Ne, about 400 huts in a cluster of a half-dozen hamlets, along with Major General Lewis W. Walt (commander of III Marine Amphibious Force and 3rd Marine Division in Vietnam) early on the morning of August 3, 1965. They first met with the 1/9 battalion commander—Lieutenant Colonel Verle E. Ludwig. On Walter Cronkite's CBS Evening News, Mr. Safer reported, "... over 150 huts had been burned." He also cited "... two of the Marines had been wounded by friendly fire," and that "... the Marines had taken only one isolated sniper shot after entering the village. If there were Viet Cong in the hamlets they were long gone." Mr. Safer also stated, "... the Marines had been ordered to burn down the entire village if they received any enemy fire, a fact never denied by the Marines and later confirmed by General Walt" Mr. Safer later went on to state: "Old men and women were pleading with the Marines to spare their houses. Their pleas were ignored, and the homes were burned with all the belongings of the people. Pleas to delay the burnings so that belongings could be removed were ignored. All rice stores were burned as well." Mr. Safer even later, in a televised interview by another reporter for the Archive of American Television, went on to say: "There was this atmosphere that the Marines were going in there (Cam Ne) without a real strategic plan."[65] I believe that Mr. Safer's job was *to get the (big) story,* because competition among the journalists' in the field was intense. Also, the U.S. government allowed journalists to wander freely throughout the war zones in Vietnam.

In Vietnam, like everywhere else in Asia, Mr. Safer thought:

[65] Edward Doyle and Samuel Lipsman, *The Vietnam Experience–America Takes Over–1965-67*, War Footing, p. 17, (Boston Publishing Company, 1982).

A home is everything. A man lives with his family on ancestral land. His parents are buried nearby. Their spirit is part of his holding. If there were Vietcong in the hamlet of Cam Ne, they were long gone ... alerted by the roar of the amphibious tractors and a heavy barrage of rocket fire laid down before the troops moved in. The women and the old men who remained will never forget that August afternoon.

There is little doubt that American firepower can win a military victory here. But to a Vietnamese peasant, whose home means a lifetime of back-breaking labor, it will take more than a Presidential promise to convince him we are on his side. [66]

One of Delta Company's platoon commanders, Second Lieutenant Ray G. Snyder, claimed: "Cam Ne was an extensively entrenched and fortified hamlet. Colonel Ludwig explained, "that in many instances burning was the only way to ensure that the house would not become an active military installation after the troops had moved on past it."

As previously stated, General Walt personally accompanied Mr. Safer into the Cam Ne area. Knowing this, here is an interesting statement mentioned by the authors of the book, *U.S. Marines in Vietnam–the Landing and the Buildup 1965*: "In 1977, General Walt remembered that he gave Morley Safer a lift into the Cam Ne area in his personal helicopter on August 3, 1965. According to Walt, he gave permission to the battalion and company commanders 'to burn those thatched houses which hid or camouflaged pill boxes,' and that Mr. Safer heard him give this permission. Walt considered that the television account of the incident was (more than) a misrepresentation of the facts."

Again, I do not think the American public really absorbed, understood, or even captured what transpired at Cam Ne and elsewhere in Vietnam. Yet, they did quickly form disapproving and/or anti-war opinions about the situation with limited information. For example, here comes a reporter to our turf which was held by the Viet Cong. Safer tagged along with us for only one day as we performed a village sweep. Safer observed us burn down village huts. In my opinion, Safer did not realize all the young men who inhabited this village were gone, yet he concluded that we were just a gang of hoodlums. Safer, along with his South Vietnamese cameraman, immediately stereotyped us as the bad guys, ugly Americans, with no empathy for the poor villagers and their families. I am talking *one* day. I am surmising that this was the type of media predisposition that helped us lose the war—at least in the eyes of the public. In fact, earlier or in the spring of 1965, "the White House felt like a besieged fortress. Pennsylvania Avenue was crowded with noisy picketers day and night. Lafayette Park, across the avenue from the White House, had become a virtual campground for taunting protesters. Luci Johnson, the presi-

---

[66] *Saturday Review*, An Invitation to Return to Cam Ne, September 4, p. 16, 1965.

dent's daughter, never forgot the lullaby that kept her awake night after night. Demonstrations outside the White House, the Pentagon, or the U.S. Mission to the United Nations in New York became legion in 1965." [67] Knowing this, you can imagine what the American people saw in Mr. Safer's photo of a Marine burning a hut, with his cigarette lighter, and his accompanying story.

It is also my opinion that Mr. Safer, who passed away on May 19th, 2016, did not realize we had recently been to another nearby village, carelessly wandering around in the bush and skirmishing with snipers, where we lost some Marines because of a similar sniper incident. The correspondent, with no college journalistic education, and self-imposed (Vietnam) war critic most likely did not comprehend it was perhaps the young (missing) farmers in that village that shot at us only hours before. This commentator, in my unassuming opinion, did not grasp that the Viet Cong who shot at us were most likely the same people, the "young farmers by day and the VC by evening." More so, the television report certainly did not understand the magnitude of the problem and the big picture, but he did us a job! Nevertheless, reaction to the Cam Ne report was immediate and especially powerful. CBS, in fact, was inundated with calls and letters critical of this negative portrayal of American military personnel. This is why I feel that Mr. Safer only saw one incident, and his version of the truth. Some say that he was just another reporter trying to get the story. As a result, he was no friend of ours; we certainly did not appreciate his disloyal broadcasting coverage. I do not suppose Rich Tennant did either, as can be seen in cartoon 2.15. [68]

Even though this is not what Safer thought, Cam Ne was actually part of the U.S. strategic hamlet program. Months later, Mr. Safer became aware that it had been picked for eradication by a province chief who wished to discipline the villagers for their tax delinquency.

President Johnson was so infuriated by the report that he accused Mr. Safer and CBS of having *"shat on the flag"* and demanded that Mr. Safer be fired or the White House would expose him as a Communist. In my humble opinion, he should have been dismissed!

Right, wrong or indifferent, whatever happened there, we took an emotional and psychological beating. If nothing else, Cam Ne was put on the map in a long-term detrimental way. Certainly, the anti-war activists deemed what we did was wrong. And while there had been dissent against every other American war, the opposition for this conflict eventually grew to all-time high levels, and I believe the Cam Ne incident certainly did not help matters. Be that as it may, was it wrong what we did? Some activists, as a result of our skirmish with the VC, burned their draft cards. In fact, many people got involved with the antiwar movement that sprang up as a result of the Cam Ne

---

[67] Colonel H. Avery Chenoweth, USMCR (Retired), *Semper Fi–The Definitive Illustrated History of the U.S. Marines,* p. 326, (Fall River Press, 2005).

[68] Edward Doyle and Samuel Lipsman, *The Vietnam Experience–America Takes Over–* 1965-67, War Footing, p. 17, (Boston Publishing Company, 1982).

incident, including students, academics, members of the clergy, pacifists, social activists, civil rights advocates and even government officials, the media, members of Congress, writers, intellectuals, artists and entertainers, as well as radicals from the new left and black power movements. Eventually, it included almost every segment of American society.[69] Furthermore, some early antiwar events were organized by faculty, such as the *teach-in* on April 1, 1965, that future Chancellor William H. Sewell (University of Wisconsin–Madison from 1967–1968) put together. It was the second such teach-in in the nation and came only a few weeks after the first American combat troops arrived in Vietnam. Some teach-ins involved only lectures and discussions; some combined theory with practical steps, such as the 15,000 who marched from the University of California at Berkeley towards the Oakland Army Terminal in October 1965.[70] On April 17, 1965, a month after the first wave of Marines landed in Vietnam, more than 15,000 protesters attended the first antiwar march in Washington, D.C.[71] On May 21–23, a month later, a preceding teach-in antiwar protest was held at UC Berkeley. Organized by the Vietnam Day Committee (VDC), which had been founded by a former graduate student, Jerry Rubin, and Berkeley professor Stephen Smale, among others, it was widely covered by the media and even commercially recorded by Folkways Records. As many as 30,000 students, faculty, and others participated, including child-rearing guru Dr. Benjamin Spock, socialist activist leader Norman Thomas, and novelist Norman Mailer.

Knowing this, ask yourself this: would you have done the same thing if you were in our boots? If you had experienced a similar incident of VC snipers shooting at you with one intention in mind?

Controversy over the war in Vietnam brought the war home, and brought vast changes to the United States in the 1960s. The hostilities, overwhelmingly, affected every institution in American life: universities, Congress, the presidency, the Democratic Party, the Armed Forces, labor unions, religious organizations, and the mass media. By 1968, in spite of what was happening in Vietnam, many thought that the war had become a burden which the country no longer could afford. By this time, I was attending college. Many people, in fact, wanted the United States to decrease its role in Vietnam and reach a negotiated resolution with the North Vietnamese.[72]

By the end of August 1965, President Johnson, who was keenly aware of the anti-war movement, decided to send these pacifists a message. He signed into regulation criminalizing draft card burning. Card burnings became com-

---

[69] Harry G. Summers, Jr., *The Vietnam War Almanac*, Attrition, p. 80, (Presidio Press, 1985).

[70] Mark Atwood Lawrence, *The Vietnam War–A Concise International History*, p. 93, (Oxford University Press, 2008).

[71] Alan Axelrod, *The Real History of the Vietnam War–A New Look at the Past*, p. 156, (Sterling, 2013).

[72] Robert D. Schulzinger, *A Time for War–The United States and Vietnam, 1941-1975*, p. 215-216, (Oxford University Press, 1997).

mon during anti-war rallies and often attracted the attention of the media including Morley Safer.

Even though Cam Ne was a tiny place in South Vietnam, it was a small village where we confronted the enemy. It was a hamlet, like most other thatched huts we entered, where U.S. and Vietnamese casualties occurred in ones and twos, though sometimes more. More vitally, it was a place, like most locations where we patrolled and swept the area, where there was never any remarkable or impressive resistance with the VC, more like a deliberate, constant wearing down from booby traps and sniper fire. To a greater extent, it was a location, in spite of this, that was made clear to the American people that this was unquestionably going to be a different sort of war. In many cases this war was fought by young and old men alike - VC and NVA sympathizers.

Fascinatingly enough, in February 2001, Jon Wiener wrote a piece called *"Whose Vietnam,"* which updated the Safer episode:

> The real heroes of the book, not surprisingly, are the reporters who brought truthful images to Americans. CBS correspondent Morley Safer, for example, did a piece showing film of Marines setting fire to a village of straw huts, in which he declared that American firepower could win victories, but to a Vietnamese peasant whose house meant a lifetime of backbreaking labor, it will take more than presidential promises to convince him that we are on his side. The morning after the story aired on Walter Cronkite's show, Frank Stanton, the president of CBS News, at the time, was awakened by a phone call, and a voice that shouted, 'Frank, are you trying to fuck me?' 'Who is this?' Stanton asked. Lyndon Johnson answered, 'Frank, this is your President, and yesterday your boys shat on the American flag.' It is a story every investigative reporter would love to be the subject of. [73]

College taught me to believe that a journalist is unbiased, fair and balanced and only reports the facts. Further, a reporter is someone who collects, writes, and/or distributes news or other current information in a dispassionate way. As stated earlier, he was at Cam Ne for only *one* day. Mr. Safer witnessed things only that moment in time, and sensationalized the scene for his reporting benefit. His limited awareness of this incident reflected the popular antipathy toward the Vietnam conflict. Is this really a truth-telling image of the war? Nonetheless, he was, in many peoples' eyes, a journalist who collects and disseminates information about current events, people, trends, and issues. But, I certainly do not think so. The correspondent, as mentioned before, did not understand the big picture. All he wanted to do, at least from my perspective, was *"get the (big) story,"* and he did. Regrettably, that is what the Ameri-

---

[73]   *LA Weekly*–Whose Vietnam, February 2-8, 2001.

can people saw, and that is truly a sad commentary, an over-dramatized and certainly overstated account about this conflict.

Earlier in April 1965, Ambassador Maxwell Taylor joined General Westmoreland along with the Secretary of Defense, Robert McNamara, and other VIPs in Honolulu for high-level strategy sessions. They all discussed the need for additional troop deployments to Vietnam. As a result of those meetings, Westmoreland would soon see 40,000 American troops, including additional soldiers from Korea (with whom I later fought) and Australia make their way to this third-world country. Peculiarly enough, on July 8, 1965, Ambassador Taylor submitted his resignation over the employment of more U.S. combat troops in South Vietnam. Former Ambassador Henry Cabot Lodge replaced Taylor. [74]

---

[74] Leo Daugherty, *The Vietnam War–Day by Day,* p. 54, (Chartwell Books, Inc., 2011).

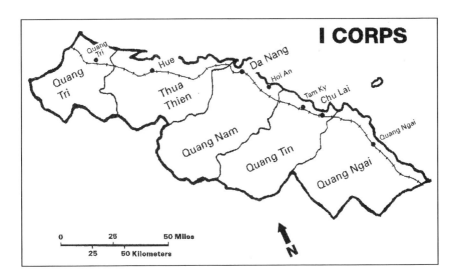

Picture 2.1
Map of I Corps
[via Author]

Picture 2.2
USS Bayfield
[Author photo]

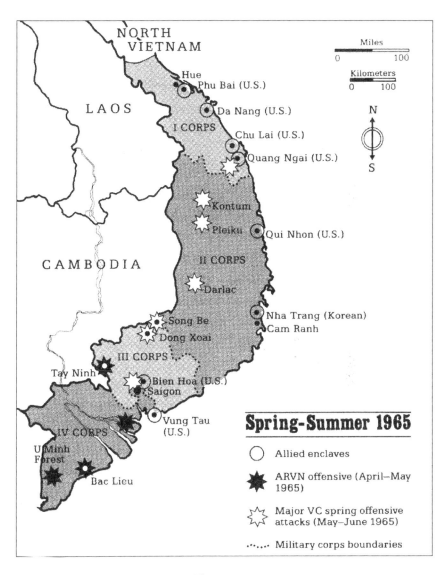

Picture 2.3
Map of I–IV Corps
[via Author]

Picture 2.4
Unloading from ship
[Author photo]

Picture 2.5
Truck into Da Nang air base
[via Author]

Picture 2.6
Author standing at fort
[Author photo]

Picture 2.7
Captured VC
[via Author]

Picture 2.8
Dog Patch
[Author photo]

Picture 2.9
Tent in Da Nang
[Author photo]

Picture 2.10
Martindale and me
[Author photo]

Picture 2.11
Thompson and me
[Author photo]

Picture 2.12
Shower
[Author photo]

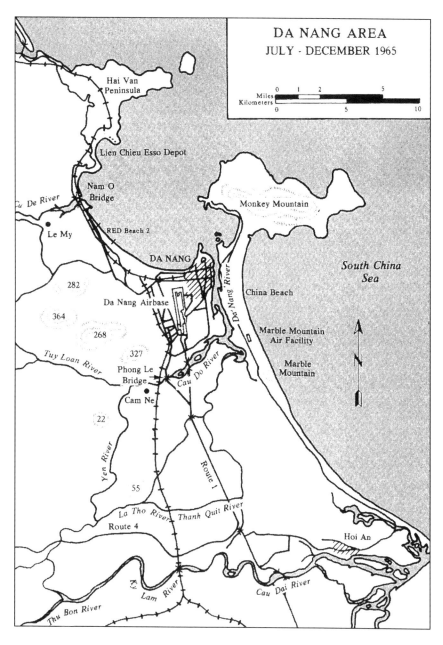

Picture 2.13
Map of Da Nang area
[via Author]

Picture 2.14
Cam Ne burning
[via Author]

Picture 2.15
"Remember men, when you're out there, by ready for the unexpected —
booby traps, snipers, CBS camera crews..."
['The 5th Wave' cartoon series by Rich Tennant; via Author]

Chapter 3

Vietnam
Reassigned to Another Unit

THE buildup in 1965 continued. By mid-summer, Marines had moved outside their cantonment at Da Nang and expanded their area of responsibility to include the Viet Cong-infested villages to the south. Marines later landed at Chu Lai, my next combat duty station, allowing the 1st Wing to expand to their new facilities, home of the Marine Aircraft Group (MAG) 36, while MAG 16 remained at the air base at Da Nang. I was part of that midsummer buildup. [75]

Even though I did not know anything about the transfer, I, along with seven other warriors, including First Sergeant T. P. Trujillo, or "Top" or "First Shirt" as he liked to be called, a decorated (fat-body/salty dog) Marine from the Korean War, also from Delta Company, 1st Battalion, 9th Marines, 3rd Marine Division, were re-assigned to another combat unit. We were sent to various units within the 3rd Battalion, 3rd Marines, 3rd Marine Division–also an infantry battalion, based out of Kaneohe, Hawaii, further known as *"America's Battalion,"* as can be seen in patch–3.1. It even functions out of its home on the island, deploying as needed and directed.

3/3/3 was first activated by the Marine Corps in June of 1942. Later that year, the unit was deployed to American Samoa. In 1943, it was moved to Guadalcanal. It later (i.e., 1944–1945) participated in campaigns in Bougainville (part of Papua New Guinea), Northern Solomon Islands, Guam, and Iwo Jima.

As further stated by *Flashbacks:*

> 3rd Battalion, 3rd Marines was moved from its home in Okinawa to a new airfield that was established along the coast south of Da Nang called Chu Lai. They, commanded by Lieutenant Colonel William D. Hall, landed in Vietnam on May 12, 1965. 3/3/3, from what I was told, replaced another infantry battalion in Okinawa the previous January.
>
> Initial operations were slow-paced and against semi-professional guerrillas, most of whom were armed with outdated weaponry. They were a tough enemy, but not nearly so well-equipped and organized as the NVA, which the battalion encountered later in the war.

---

[75] Associated Press. *Vietnam: The Real War,* p. 106, (Abrams, 2013).

To this day, I do not know why I was transferred so quickly into another battalion. At first, when I left my fellow comrades with whom I had trained so hard with for the past year, I was saddened and disappointed that I had to leave these fine Marines. What was this all about? Why did this have to happen to me? What did I do wrong? These were my combat buddies. These were the young warriors that would take me to the local bars in Okinawa and get drunk or other activities to pass the time. These were the troops that I slept with in the barracks back in Okinawa and even earlier in Camp Pendleton. Now we slept together in eight-man tents. No big deal! These were warriors who revealed to me about their lives back in the states. They enjoyed sharing their trials and tribulations with me.

They were definitely devoted and brave warriors that I could count on and trust in case the shit hit the fan and the going got tough. We were a dedicated team, and we knew it. As can be seen in picture 3.2, we were a close-knit, well-trained group, technically and tactically proficient, and ready for the worst at a moment's notice.

I will never forget the leathernecks of Delta Company, even though today I cannot remember most of their names. They were a part of my life before entering Vietnam and certainly during part of my 10-month stay in Vietnam and my three-year time in the Corps. They were, unequivocally, the *few and the proud;* they were unmistakably dedicated Marines. Guys–Semper Fidelis!

According to Doug Todd, 1997, here is a brief ballad about the men of 1st Battalion, 9th Marines, 3rd Marine Division, as seen through the eyes of one Marine:

> *Here are those who have borne the battle, those, in the crucible of combat, tried.*
>
> *Tempered and turned of the finest mettle, these were the Sons of America's Pride!*
>
> *The First Battalion of the Ninth Marines, hammered and forged in the fires of Hell; built of their blood and their broken dreams, a legend for scribes, unborn, to tell.*
>
> *They fought like Warriors and died like men 'Til their page of history was stained by blood red; and they earned from foe as well as from friend that Honorable title, 'The Walking Dead'!*
>
> *These were the Sons who stepped forward bravely–Courage and Strength and Faith untried; to fight as the Valorous 'Always Faithful.' These are The Sons of America's Pride.*

By the way, the first battalion's nickname, *Walking Dead,* was later earned through many bloody fights with the North Vietnamese along the DMZ under conventional warfare conditions, notably during Operation Buffalo in 1967. In fact, this battalion, during the Vietnam War, sustained the highest killed in action rate in Marine Corps history, especially during the

Battle of July Two. The battalion was engaged in combat for forty-seven months and seven days, from June 15, 1965 to October 1966 and December 11, 1966 to July 14, 1969. Based on a typical battalion strength of 800+ Marines and Navy hospital corpsmen, 93.6% were killed in action and 0.25% were missing in action. [76]

The DMZ was established through the Geneva Conference of 1954 as a result of the First Indochina War. During the Second Indochina War (popularly known as the Vietnam War), it became important as the battleground demarcation separating the North Vietnamese territory from the South Vietnamese territory. The *Geneva Agreements*, which were issued on July 21, 1954, carefully worded the division of northern and southern Vietnam as a "provisional military demarcation line." [77] Still, it did not really separate this country into two states. However, the DMZ was recognized by the 17th parallel, temporarily dividing the country into two geographical areas— Communist North Vietnam and free South Vietnam.

These cruel encounters continued through 1968 as the Marines fought along the DMZ and around Khe Sanh Combat Base. Their grim reputation was earned, as Rock-and-Roll reporter Michael Herr commented, because the belief that one Marine was better than ten Slopes (VC) saw Marine squads fed against known NVA platoons, platoons against companies, and on and on ... [78]

Without further ado, I packed my 782 gear, slung my M14 rifle over my shoulder, and stepped into a helicopter, with a few other grunts, and headed for Chu Lai, in the Quang Nam Province, a hell-hole of a sand box that was too hot to walk on in bare feet during the day, about fifty-six miles southeast of Da Nang. It was also a place where weapons, radios, vehicles, clothing, etc., seemed to be covered with a thin but constant layer of sand. There, I joined the men of M (Mike) Company, 1st Platoon, 3rd Battalion, 3rd Marines, 3rd Marine Division. M Company was a weapons company that provided fire support coordination, medium mortars, anti-armor weapons and heavy machine gun support for the other rifle companies.

Soon I would join a new outfit, another group of Marines; phenomenal and out-of-the-ordinary warriors that I did not even know and did not train with. By the time the 3rd Battalion, 3rd Marines, 3rd Marine Division had landed, the mission of this unit had now become: "1) to establish defensive bases; 2) to conduct deep reconnaissance patrols of the enemy's avenues of approach; 3) to conduct offensive action as a reaction force in coordination with the South Vietnamese; and 4) to intensify offensive operations to fix and destroy the Viet Cong. In accordance with the first of these, their initial task was to assist in securing the Chu Lai area for the construction of an 8,000-foot air-

---

[76] *1st Battalion, 9th Marines,* Wikipedia.
[77] *Geneva Agreements, July 21, 1954,* Wikipedia.
[78] Charles D. Melson, *The Marine Corps in Vietnam,* pp. 15-16, (Osprey Publishing, 1988).

field." [79] In fact, Chu Lai was not even a town until the U.S. Marines constructed a major airfield there. Later, Chu Lai would become a U.S. Marine Corps military base from 1965–1971.

As the month of July 1965 came to a close, with a few skirmishes under my belt, President Johnson announced that he planned to send forty-four battalions to Vietnam, bringing the U.S. military presence to 125,000 men. Monthly draft call-ups were doubled to 35,000. He also said: "I have asked the commanding general, General Westmoreland, what more he needs to meet this mounting aggression. He has told me. And we will meet his needs. We cannot be defeated by force of arms. *We will stand in Vietnam."* Keep in mind, in March, four months earlier, the President authorized sending an additional 40,000 American troops to Vietnam. From the sounds of it, with an ever present aggressive tactic by the communists, sending more troops from North Vietnam to South Vietnam, Johnson decided to meet that force head-on by more men and arms. Besides, after deciding to escalate the war, he refused, during 1965, to call up the National Guard or Army Reserve and chose instead to rely solely on the draft. The draft, though, was initiated by President Franklin D. Roosevelt (FDR), who signed the Selective Training and Service Act of 1940, which created the country's first peacetime draft and officially established the Selective Service System as an independent Federal agency.

From 1948 until 1973, during both peacetime and periods of conflict, men were drafted to fill vacancies in the Armed Forces which could not be filled through voluntary means.

I am sure we could agree that war is ugly. People die. Many times, innocent people die. That, in itself, is a travesty. Sometimes, it does not even make sense. Notwithstanding, with war comes the enemy, a rival who wants to kill you. Knowing this, I want to provide you now with a couple of facts about the meaning of a Viet Cong or VC, the adversary, the enemy of America's war: "Viet Cong was a derogatory term for Vietnamese communists in the south. At the end of the War between the French and the Viet Minh (1946–1954), 90,000 Viet Minh troops in what was to become South Vietnam were to be repatriated to the north. But the Viet Minh left behind an estimated 5,000 to 10,000 soldiers as a fifth column in the south. Instructed by Hanoi to lie low until 1959 (until they scheduled elections), they were then activated by the North Vietnamese Politburo (ruling council) to begin a guerrilla war in the south in an attempt to subvert and overthrow the standing government. Viet Cong forces included 'main force' units organized into companies and battalions, and later into regiments and divisions, and after 1964 reinforced by North Vietnamese regular Army units. There was also what was called the Viet Cong infrastructure, or VCI, which consisted of a party secretary, a finance and supply unit, information and culture, social welfare, and proselytizing sections to gain recruits both from the civilian population and the South

---

[79] Otto J. Lehrack, *No Shining Armor–The Marines at War in Vietnam*, pp. 17-18, (University Press of Kansas, 1992).

Vietnamese military. Search-and-destroy operations by both the U.S. and South Vietnamese units were designed to neutralize the Viet Cong and North Vietnamese Army main force units during clear-and-hold operations. After 1968, the Phoenix program was designed to root out the VCI with interdependent operations." [80]

Early in the war, especially during my tour in Vietnam (1965–1966), the weapon of choice for the Vietcong and North Vietnamese regulars was the AK-47 assault rifle (i.e., Avtomat Kalashnikova–1947). It was an old-fashioned Soviet-made firearm compared to our firearms. It used a 7.62mm bullet, fired either as a single shot or on full automatic at a relatively low velocity. From what I could tell, it was easy to maintain, especially under jungle-like conditions, and simple to operate. Our so-called modern weapon of choice, at the time, was the M14, more formally called the *United States Rifle*. It was quite accurate, especially in short distances.

In their volume, *The American Experience in Vietnam*, Clark Dougan and Stephen Weiss, a comprehensive assessment of the causes, course, and consequences of American involvement in Vietnam from 1941 to 1975, mention the following:

> Unwilling to face the consequences of withdrawal, yet fearful that the war would destroy the domestic reforms of his 'Great Society,' the President determined to do what will be enough, but not too much." The United States would fight in Vietnam, but it would do so with a minimum of domestic disruption. Thus, on a hot day in the summer of 1965, without fanfare or declaration, Lyndon Johnson led the American people into what would become the nation's longest war.
>
> On July 28, 1965, as a Communist offensive threatened to split South Vietnam in two, President Johnson told the American people that their sons and daughters were going to war. "We did not choose to be the guardians at the gate, but there is no one else," declared the President. "We will stand in Vietnam." [81]

So on this day, written by Marilyn B. Young, a historian of American foreign relations and professor of history at New York University, in her book, *The Vietnam Wars: 1945-1990*:

> ... the President decided to go with the majority of his advisers. He would fight this war, but fight it on the side, without asking for an increase in taxes or a declaration of war, or risking a congressional

---

[80] Harry G. Summers, Jr., *The Vietnam War Almanac*, Antiwar Movement, pp. 351-352, (Presidio Press, 1985).

[81] Clark Dougan and Stephen Weiss, *The American Experience in Vietnam*, p. 34, (Boston Publishing Company, 1988).

debate. The country was rich enough for guns and butter, for the Vietnam War and the Great Society: the Tonkin Gulf Resolution would function, in Undersecretary of State Nicholas Katzenbach's words, as the 'functional equivalent' of a declaration of war. Rifle in one hand, ax in the other, Lyndon Baines Johnson went forward, announcing at the end of July that 50,000 more soldiers would be sent to Vietnam, bringing the number of troops there from 75,000 to 125,000. The existing draft call would have to be doubled, but there was no mention of calling up the reserves. The American invasion had begun. [82]

As America's active participation in Vietnam grew during the summer of 1965, so did the antiwar sentiment in the United States. With more and more servicemen being sent to Vietnam each day, more families became personally involved in the war. Many Americans, for the first time, questioned the logic behind the U.S. entanglement in Southeast Asia. In fact, in October of 1964, though, well before ground forces arrived in Vietnam, I was assigned to 1st Squad, "N" Company, 2nd Battalion, 2nd Infantry Training Regiment in Camp Pendleton, California. I was involved with exercises consisting of serving functionally and efficiently in an infantry rifle squad in both assault and protection combat roles. Just as important, our field-related training deployment consisted of participating in security and ambush patrols. Besides, it included cover and concealment strategies. This course of preparation would give us the opportunity to function as a team and a unit, and to learn the intricacies of being a combat Marine in the battlefield. We had to learn the ropes of warfare. Fellowship of Reconciliation (FOR), a pacifist organization founded in England at the start of World War I and came to the United States shortly thereafter, issued the first public statement endorsing draft resistance as a response to the increasing number of Army advisors sent to Vietnam during the Kennedy Administration. [83]

The War Resisters League (WRL), which was founded as the American branch of FOR in 1932, was also a pacifist organization that focused on conscientious objection to the war. Under the leadership of David T. Dellinger, the WRL focused its protests on the expanding U.S. military advisory effort in Vietnam. In May 1964, the WRL sponsored a demonstration in New York City at which twelve men burned their draft cards. In December 1964, the WRL organized the first nationwide demonstration against the Vietnam War. [84]

As more and more young men were sent to Vietnam, and a more conspicuous number of them returned, regrettably, in body bags, the focus of the

---

[82] Marilyn B. Young, *The Vietnam Wars 1945–1990,* p. 160, (HarperPerennial, 1991).
[83] Ronald B. Frankum, Jr. and Stephen F. Maxner, *The Vietnam War for Dummies,* p. 280, (Wiley Publishing, Inc., 2003).
[84] Ibid.

antiwar movement became clearer and its inspiration and enthusiasm for pro-test grew more comprehensible with young people. During 1965 too, more than thirty new antiwar organizations surfaced under the leadership of the National Coordinating Committee (NCC) to end the war in Vietnam. The committee's principle function was receiving and handing out information about antiwar activities throughout the United States. By October of the same year, there had been more than sixty protests against the war across the coun-try involving over 100,000 people. [85]

Once again, and according to Marilyn Young:

> Tom E. Hayden, a University of Michigan student government activist, represented the entire New Left movement to many outsid-ers. This brought plenty of attention to his 'end the war now' cause. Hayden's brand of activism involved organizing mid-1960s university sit-ins against the war on university campuses, and then asking stu-dent followers to the streets in displays of 'people power' outrage. [86]

In fact, on March 24–25, 1965, another source of criticism against the war took the form of "teach-ins" consisting of more than 3,000 students and facul-ty on college campuses. The first occurred at the University of Michigan, Ann Arbor (as an all-night study session involving thousands of students and doz-ens of faculty that began at about 6 p.m. and lasted untill 6 a.m.). The practice spread later to campuses throughout the nation.

Hayden, who was one of the first to go to Hanoi, also worked with the SNCC and served as president of Students for a Democratic Society in 1962 and 1963. He traveled to North Vietnam with other antiwar activists in 1965 and again in 1967—to meet the other side and promote peace talks, journalistic contacts, and American POW releases. He later participated in the student occupation of Columbia University in April 1968. As project director of the National Mobilization Committee (NMC) to end the war in Vietnam, he also organized the antiwar demonstrations outside the Democratic National Con-vention in Chicago.

As a result of his actions, Hayden and seven others were indicted on charges of crossing state lines with intent to riot and conspire to incite a riot. I am glad they got what they deserved. I was certainly glad to hear that he and his draft-dodging numb-nut companions were charged for their cowardly deeds.

Five years after the student occupation at Columbia University, located in New York City, in January 1973, "Hayden married antiwar activist and actress Jane Fonda (the daughter of actor Henry Fonda) and they directed the efforts of the Indochina Peace Campaign toward ending U.S. clandestine in-

---

[85] Joe Allen, *Vietnam: the (last) war the U.S. lost*, p. 113, (Haymarket Books, 2008).

[86] Timothy P. Maga, Ph.D., *The Complete Idiot's Guide To The Vietnam War*, p. 194, (Alpha Books, 2000).

volvement in Vietnam and all U.S. aid to the Thieu government in South Vietnam." [87] Fonda exploited her money and influence at colleges and universities to gather support to advocate communism and encourage rebellion and anarchy against the United States Government.

To better understand the whole pacifist/antiviolence movement, the following information was excerpted from *The Strength Not To Fight: An Oral History of Conscientious Objectors of the Vietnam War:*

> The total number of individuals receiving deferments from the draft as conscientious objectors during the Vietnam War was approximately 170,000. As many as 300,000 other applicants were denied deferments. Nearly 600,000 illegally evaded the draft; about 200,000 were formally accused of draft offenses. Many of these lawbreakers were men who had been denied conscientious objector deferments or who refused to cooperate with the draft on grounds of conscience. Between 30,000 and 50,000 fled to Canada. Another 20,000 fled to other countries or lived underground in America. [88]

In mid-April 1965, the first big manifestation against the Vietnam War was organized by Students for a Democratic Society (SDS), with a march on Washington, D.C. Organizers had predicted a turnout of 10,000 people. Instead, there were somewhere between 15,000 and 25,000. Among the speakers that day—evidence of the antiwar movement's link to the civil rights struggle—was Robert P. Moses, leader of the Student Nonviolent Coordinating Committee [SNCC], who completed a master's in philosophy at Harvard University. [89]

The SDS was a student activist movement in the United States that was one of the main iconic representations of the country's New Left. The organization developed and expanded rapidly in the mid-1960s, especially during the Vietnam War, before dissolving at its last convention in 1969. The number of SDS chapters grew to between 300 and 400 with a membership rising to more than 30,000 by the end of 1966.

Throughout 1965, the antiwar movement became gradually more legitimate as a concern within the political establishment. During this time, more prominent politicians voiced support for the protestors. Also, music performers such as the Animals, Donovan, Crosby, Stills and Nash, Country Joe McDonald, John Lennon, and Bob Dylan, to name only a few, used their melodies to protest the war. Rock and roll music, especially in the late 1960s, served as a unifying and focusing force for members of the antiwar movement.

---

[87] Joe Allen, *Vietnam: the (last) war the U.S. lost,* p. 113, (Haymarket Books, 2008).

[88] Vietnam - *Echoes from the Wall,* p. 76, (Vietnam Veterans Memorial Fund, 1999).

[89] John Prados, *Vietnam: The History of an Unwinnable War,* 1945-1975, p. 127, (University Press of Kansas, 2009).

For the men and women Marines who were serving in Vietnam, like me, morale was high, at least with my unit. We were putting our lives on the front line daily. However, it was a line you could not see or touch. The Viet Cong were everywhere. Hence, the incipient antiwar movement offended us. We were wounded by signs like, "END THE CRUEL WAR NOW," "WE LIKE PEOPLE (SOLDIERS)-WE DON'T LIKE WAR," "I DON'T GIVE A DAMN ABOUT UNCLE SAM-I'M NOT GOING TO VIETNAM," as can be seen in picture 3.3.[90]

Daniel Ellsberg, a person who attended Harvard University, graduating with a Ph.D. in Economics in 1962 described a paradox in decision theory now known as the Ellsberg paradox would soon rise to the ranks of an anti-war activist. Before that, he graduated first in a class of almost 1,100 lieutenants at the Marine Corps Basic School in Quantico, Virginia, and served as an officer for two years. After his discharge, he became an analyst at the RAND Corporation. He also served for two years in Vietnam as a civilian in the State Department. Ellsberg became convinced that the Vietnam War was not winnable, and therefore, he became a full-fledged anti-war protestor. He further considered that nearly everyone in the Defense and State Departments felt, as he did, that the United States had no realistic chance of achieving victory in Vietnam, but that political considerations prevented them from saying so publicly. He specifically wrote intelligence reports for the Department of Defense, and stated: "There was almost total absence of *any* organized popular *support,* or even sympathy for the American-backed regime."[91]

Ellsberg, who was a State Department analyst, leaked important Pentagon Papers in 1971, a secret account of the Vietnam War and its pretexts, to The New York Times. He revealed endemic practices of deception by previous administrations and contributed to the erosion of public support for the war.

The Pentagon Papers revealed the knowledge that the war would not likely be won and that continuing the war would lead to many times more casualties than was admitted publicly. Further, the papers showed a deep cynicism towards the public and a disregard for the loss of life and injury suffered by soldiers and civilians. Ellsberg knew that releasing these papers would most likely result in a conviction and sentence of many years in prison. Throughout 1970, Ellsberg covertly attempted to convince a few sympathetic senators to release the Pentagon Papers on the Senate floor under privilege. When these efforts failed, Ellsberg, with the assistance of Anthony Russo, copied them and leaked them to Neil Sheehan at The New York Times. On June 12, 1971, the Times began publishing the first installment of the 7,000-page document. For fifteen days, the New York Times was prevented from publishing its articles on the orders of the Nixon administration. However, the Supreme Court

---

[90] George Esper and The Associated Press, *The Eyewitness History of the Vietnam War–1961–1975,* p. 59, (Ballantine Books, 1983).

[91] Timothy P. Maga, Ph.D., *The Complete Idiot's Guide To The Vietnam War,* p. 168, (Alpha Books, 2000).

soon ordered publication to resume freely. Ellsberg went underground, and was not caught by the FBI, even though they were under enormous pressure from the Nixon Administration to find him. The Nixon administration also began a campaign to discredit Ellsberg: Nixon's plumbers broke into Ellsberg's psychiatrist's office in an attempt to find damaging information. The revelation of the break-in became part of the Watergate scandal.

On June 28, 1971, Ellsberg publicly surrendered to the U.S. Attorney's Office in Boston, Massachusetts. He was taken into custody believing he would spend the rest of his life in prison; he was charged with theft, conspiracy, and espionage. Due to the gross governmental misconduct, all charges against Ellsberg were eventually dropped. White House counsel Charles (Chuck) W. Colson was later prosecuted and pled no contest for obstruction of justice in the burglary of Ellsberg's psychiatrist's office. Written by Colonel Harry G. Summers, Jr., a soldier, scholar, and a military analyst; one of the most influential military thinkers America has ever produced, *The Vietnam War Almanac*, this writer stated:

> Beginning in about 1965 numerous organizations and peace coalitions were formed to protest the war and some existing organizations began directing their energies to the same purpose: The Spring Mobilization Against the War, Women's Strike for Peace, Clergy and Laity Concerned about Vietnam, Committee for a Sane Nuclear Policy, or SANE, and the Vietnam Day Committee (VDC). Despite their common opposition to the war, there was often disagreement among and within these groups over the proper tactics to be used. Some advocated peaceful means of protest: teach-ins, marches, support of peace candidates, etc. Others pursued more militant tactics, such as attempts to disrupt troop trains. There were exhortations to resist the draft, draft card burnings, attempts to destroy Selective Service files and advice to servicemen to disobey unlawful orders. [92]

This same time period, beginning in 1965 and carrying through the early 1970s, as I later witnessed while attending college (1967–1972), was clearly marked by student activism and social protest/unrest. Everyone, or so it seemed—even though that was not the case, was a pacifist. This was especially the case at UCLA (University of California, Los Angeles), where I spent the first half of my undergraduate education. Angela Y. Davis, a Black Panther member, was also a tenured professor in the History of Consciousness program at the University of California - Santa Cruz. Additionally, she taught at UCLA, but was fired in 1969 when her membership in the Communist Party became known. This resulted in a celebrated First Amendment battle that made Angela Davis a national figure and

---

[92] Harry G. Summers, Jr., *The Vietnam War Almanac, Antiwar Movement*, p. 82, (Presidio Press, 1985).

forced UCLA to hire her back. In 1991, she joined the group Committees of Correspondence, which seeks to unite all radical socialist groups in the United States, and of which, I understand, she remains a member to this day.

I felt it was very difficult to get an education—but *not* from an academic standpoint. Actually, I was enjoying the instructional process. Nonetheless, I had barely survived a war that I participated and trusted in, but there was a feeling alive on campuses throughout America, especially at UCLA, that the system could be changed and that protests could be successful. Antiwar demonstrations, which I saw only too often on campus, were part of academic life. Even though I had been to hell and back, students found the war immoral and unjust for a variety of reasons, and the attractiveness of activism as well as social action contributed to their commitment. Further to this point, they heard arguments that the United States was acting like a colonial power that it was seeking to impose an American solution on a foreign people and it was waging a war with excessive cruelty. It was interfering in what was essentially a civil war and violating international agreements, among other charges. Self-interest was also a motivating factor in student protests. Even though the Johnson Administration had granted college students deferment from the draft, they still faced the threat of the draft upon graduation. [93]

This was also the time the Vietnam War saw the rise of the so-called conscientious objector. Ironically, Muhammad Ali, born as Cassius Marcellus Clay Jr. (1942-2016) in Louisville, Kentucky, was nicknamed "The Greatest." He is considered by many to be the greatest heavyweight boxer of all time, as well as one of the world's most famous individuals protesting the participation in the conflict. Even so, I am proud to say, as an American and Vietnam Veteran that I could never have been a peace lover of this type. It was simply not part of my personality.

A conscientious objector is someone who refuses to serve in the Armed Forces for religious or moral reasons. After 1962, individuals had to prove to their local draft board that their conscientious objection was legitimate. As the Vietnam War escalated, the number of conscientious objectors increased. In 1971, approximately 4,400 military personnel applied for the status. Becoming a conscientious objector did not excuse one from service or participation in the Vietnam War. In fact, many conscientious objectors went to Vietnam as medics and served their country honorably in nonviolent ways. [94]

Even with the whole scene of being a conscientious objector, among the men of my unit serving in Vietnam, support ran high. One thing that is for sure—we were putting our lives on the line each day in service to our country,

---

[93] Ibid, p. 81.
[94] Ronald B. Frankum, Jr. and Stephen F. Maxner, *The Vietnam War for Dummies*, p. 290, (Wiley Publishing, Inc., 2003).

and deeply resented the antiwar movement. Many Marines expressed their resentment and bitterness in angry letters they sent home.

Private First Class Robert Charles Felter, a 23-year-old Marine, wrote to his hometown newspaper in Troy, New York, while serving a tour of duty in Vietnam, July 1965. *Troy Record:*

> I wonder if they (the conscientious objector) have ever been scared? I have been scared and still am scared, whether it is a sweep and clear operation or just a patrol. But I know it has got to be done and I do it. Maybe if they came over here and saw guys blown up by mines, getting hit by mortars or being shot, maybe then it would sink into their thick skulls what we are doing here to keep them free so they can go to college. I am writing this letter beside a candle and I hope you can read it. Thanks for listening. [95]

"Marine and gunner PFC Robert Felter sadly was killed on December 11, 1965, from multiple fragmentation wounds received while engaged under hostile fire in the Quang Nam Province."

Another Marine wrote to the *Oakland Tribune,* Oakland, California, stating: "Some young people at home do not seem to realize why we are here." [96] Lastly, Marine Lance Corporal Henry O. Bacich, the 19-year-old son of a Milwaukee, Wisconsin church janitor, wrote the *Milwaukee Journal* protesting a sympathy march in that city for an Army officer convicted by a court-martial for disobeying orders to join a counter-guerrilla unit in Vietnam: "Do they realize that another man had to take his place? Do they have any sympathy for the others who are out in the jungle acting as advisers for the Vietnamese troops and is there any sympathy for the men who went into the Viet Cong infested territory and lost their lives? I sincerely hope these people will come to realize the importance of us being here and keep this thought in mind: If we do not stop the communists here, where will we stop them? Are these future leaders truly concerned with the actions here in Vietnam, or is it another 'come and go' fad, such as stuffing people into a phone booth or a small foreign car. If they are truly concerned, they would not be holding these foolish demonstrations. All I can say is that if these people would drop by an elementary school and visit a first or second grade classroom, they would hear children giving us more backing than themselves each morning by reciting our Pledge of Allegiance to the flag." [97]

I assumed that none of us liked being there. As I have already mentioned, the days were hot and long, and many times it was quite nerve-racking. We were tense all the time. In my case, I did not know how to relax—I could not!

[95] George Esper and The Associated Press, *The Eyewitness History of the Vietnam War–1961–1975,* p. 59, (Ballantine Books, 1983).

[96] Ibid, p. 59.

[97] Ibid, pp. 60-61.

Although we complained about the conditions, we were there simply to serve a justifiable cause, to help a small country get up off its feet and be free of communist aggression, tyranny, and evil. More significant, I was there to serve my beloved land, a country that I may never see again. Just as important, my fellow Marines and I were there to protect our loved ones and our kids back home. I was there for a very special and personal reason: My beloved Jewish-born parents fled war-torn Holland and the wrath of Nazi occupation, which refers primarily to the principles and practices of the Nazi Party under Adolf Hitler; and the policies adopted by the government of Nazi Germany from 1933 to 1945, a period also known as the Third Reich. The official name of the Nazi party was the National Socialist German Workers' Party. My grandparents and uncle, on my father's side, were not so fortunate. They were *all* exterminated by the Nazis as part of the so-called *Final Solution* that was recommended, under the direction of Adolf Hitler, by Dr. Josef Bühler and urged by Reinhard Heydrich. My parents, with God truly looking over them, came to the Promised Land—the United States of America—to seek a better life for themselves and their only son—me. As contrived or unnatural as it might sound, I wanted to give them something back. More imperative, I wanted to let them know that their dreams for freedom would not die, so I joined the U.S. Marine Corps. I enlisted (March 3, 1964) as a seventeen-year-old teenager. I was in high school at the time as a last semester senior; even though I knew all the while that I could be sent to a war. I was uninformed enough to care that it would become a nationwide tragedy if I, in fact, did go.

In this chapter I provided you with a quick look at what life was like for me in South Vietnam as a 19-year-old combatant. The events took place during most of July and early August 1965. In the next five chapters, I continue to discuss my real-life combat experiences, which take place from the middle of August 1965 through early April 1966.

For now, I ask that you put the Vietnam War aside and take a look at Vietnam, the country, from an entirely different perspective. The tumult and hullabaloo of history that has tested this country and its people has embittered them over the years. All the same, here are fifteen current fascinating facts about this picturesque yet stifling land:

Vietnam ranges from eight to twenty degrees north of the equator and has a climate that varies from steamy tropical in the South to downright chilly in the North.

The Vietnamese think of their country as a house with open doors in each wall. Strong winds may blow through it but cannot blow it down. This is a particularly appropriate analogy for a country that, in the 20th century alone, has survived four major wars within its borders.

The ubiquitous cycles, three-wheeled bicycle taxis–that ply the streets of Vietnam offer a great view of the surroundings because the driver sits behind the passengers. With their leisurely pace, they provide a perfect method of sightseeing but can also cause occasional heart-stopping moments when they negotiate chaotic crossroads.

There are historical differences between South and North. The North takes its influences from China while the South is strongly affected by Indian and the Khmer Krom culture. The name *Vietnam* itself is taken from Chinese characters meaning "far south."

Despite the reverence felt by the Vietnamese for Ho Chi Minh, celebrated as the leader of the nation's independence, the renaming of Saigon as Ho Chi Minh City in 1975 has never caught on. Most people there refer to Vietnam's capital by its former name.

The modern Vietnamese language is the only one in Indochina to use a Roman script. It was invented by a French missionary, Father Alexander-de-Rhodes, in the seventeenth century and employs six vocal tones in the North and five in the South.

Water puppetry is a form of entertainment unique to Vietnam. Developed centuries ago in rural rice paddies, it employs a complex system of underwater rods and pulleys to animate the colorful characters. Satirical skits on universal themes combined with the deft manipulation by the puppeteers make these performances a joy to behold.

Vietnamese currency is known as the dong, and with over 21,000 dong to the dollar (today's exchange rate), it takes a little time for visitors to get used to calculating comparative prices.

The DMZ separated the North from the South until the end of the Vietnam War. It is called the American War by the Vietnamese. It has now become one of the country's top tourist attractions; among a number of exhibits and activities, visitors can crawl through tunnels where the Viet Cong once hid.

Hanoi, principal city of the north, hosted a massive party in 2010, which celebrated its 1,000[th] birthday. The city's colonial architecture, tree-lined boulevards, and fascinating street life make it an endearing destination for travelers.

The áo dài (Vietnamese national costume) worn by women skillfully combines practicality with sensuality. It consists of loose trousers worn under a knee-length tunic that is split up the sides, so that the body is completely covered but with a figure-hugging design.

Buddhism is the main religion of Vietnam, but about two million of the country's seventy-two million inhabitants are followers of the Cao Dai religion, a mix of Buddhism, Catholicism, Islam, and ancestor worship. It was founded in the 1920s, and its saints include Joan of Arc, Victor Hugo, and Napoleon Bonaparte.

Vietnamese cuisine is flavored by a subtle blend of herbs and spices that present infinite opportunities for experimentation. Many dishes are accompanied by a salad, and several require the diner to wrap ingredients into rice paper, offering the chance to balance the fillings according to individual taste.

There are more than fifty different ethnic groups living in Vietnam. Fifty-four are recognized by the Vietnamese government, each with its own language, lifestyle, and cultural heritage and each of which has an elaborate and distinctive form of dress. On market day, groups like the Red Dao and the Flower Hmong form a spectacular sight as they parade in their colorful costumes.

From the second to fourteenth centuries, the Chams (an ethnic group who live in Vietnam, Cambodia, and Thailand), who developed the first written language in Southeast Asia, were one of the most advanced civilizations. The Cham Towers, located from Quang Nam all throughout the coastal provinces and as far south as the Phan Thiet area, were built between the seventh and twelfth centuries and are some of the country's most prized architectural treasures. [98]

As provided by *The World Almanac and Book of Facts 2015*, here are some additional and current data about Vietnam:

Official Name:	Socialist Republic of Vietnam
Population:	93,421,835
Ethnic groups:	Vietnamese or Kinh–86%, Tay–2%, Thai–2% Muong–2%, Khmer, 2%, Mong–1%, Nung–1%.
Principal languages:	Vietnamese (official), English (increasingly favored as the second language), French, Chinese, Khmer.
Chief religions:	Buddhist–9%, Catholic–7%, Hoa Hao–2% Cao Dai–1%, none–81%.
Geography:	127,881 square miles, Southeast Asia, on the east coast of the Indochinese Peninsula.
Topography:	Vietnam is long and narrow, with 1,400 miles of coastline. About 22% of the country is readily arable, including the densely settled Red River valley in the North, narrow coastal plains in the center, and the wide, often marshy Mekong River Delta in the South. The rest consists of semi-arid plateaus

---

[98] Ron Emmons, *Hemispheres Magazine*, pp. 32-33, August 2000.

	and barren mountains, with some stretches of tropical rain forest.
Capital:	Hanoi or Hà Noi
Government type:	Communist state
Head of State:	President Troung Tan San
Local divisions:	58 provinces, 5 municipalities
Defense budget:	$3.8 billion
Active troops:	482,000 [99]

As a footnote, here is some added information about Vietnam that is provided by *The World Almanac and Book of Facts 2015:*

> Vietnam was held by China, 111 BCE-939CE, and was a vassal state during subsequent periods. Conquest by France began in 1858 and ended in 1884 with the protectorates of Tonkin and Annam in the North and the colony of Cochin-China in the South.
>
> Japan occupied Vietnam in 1940. Several groups formed the Vietminh (independence) League, headed by Communist guerrilla leader Ho Chi Minh. In August 1945, the Vietminh forced out Bao Dai, former emperor of Annam and head of a Japan-sponsored regime. France, seeking to reestablish colonial control, unsuccessfully battled Communist and nationalist forces, 1946–1954.
>
> Separate states formed in North and South Vietnam, with communists under Ho Chi Minh (backed by Russia and China) controlling North Vietnam and a non-Communist government (backed by the United States) controlling South Vietnam. North Vietnam aided Vietcong guerillas who south to take over South Vietnam. U.S, troops defended South Vietnam against forces in North Vietnam and border areas of Laos and Cambodia.
>
> A never-implemented cease-fire agreement was signed in Paris January 27, 1973, by the U.S., North and South Vietnam, and the Vietcong. South Vietnam surrendered April 30, 1975. North Vietnam assumed control. The country was officially reunited July 2, 1976.
>
> Among the unstable conditions persisted in the region, heavy fighting with Cambodia took place, 1977–1980. China cut off economic aid when 140,000 ethnic Chinese fled discrimination Vietnam. Reacting to Vietnam's 1979 invasion of Cambodia, China attacked four Vietnamese border provinces, February 1979. [100]

---

[99] *The World Almanac and Book of Facts 2015,* Vietnam (Socialist Republic of Vietnam), p. 851, (World Almanac Books, 2015).

[100] Ibid, p. 851.

Picture 3.1
3/3 Patch
[Author photo]

Picture 3.2
Marines in Da Nang (Author is third from right)
[Author photo]

Picture 3.3
Protesting
[via Author]

Chapter 4

Vietnam
Chu Lai

IT was early August 1965. Ironically, just a few months earlier, on April 7th, the U.S. offered North Vietnam economic aid in exchange for peace, but the offer was rejected. [101], [102] Word spread around our unit that there was a significant build-up of regular North Vietnamese guerrilla fighters (PLAF–People's Liberation Armed Forces, which was formally organized in 1961) heading down the Ho Chi Minh Trail. [103]To the best of my knowledge, they were seeking refuge in the Quang Ngai Province. This can be seen in picture 4.1, which shows the Ho Chi Minh Trail. [104] Quang Ngai was where the Viet Cong could claim control, allowing the main North Vietnamese Army forces to establish a huge base camp in the mountains. Quang Ngai was also a spectacular, striking mixture of stream-cut foothills and mountains, jungle, flat rice paddies bounded by lots of dikes and white sandy beaches along a vastly untarnished shoreline. Directly to the west, however, toward the Laotian border, beyond more hills and mountains, with mountain peaks averaging over 5,000 feet as far as the eye can see, the antediluvian lands of Vietnam stretch into the horizon. The jungle was so thick and treacherous that it was next to impossible to move even a half-mile in one day. Hidden by the massive undergrowth were numerous routes and footpaths that could allow the enemy fairly easy access to the Chu Lai area and provide, if needed, escape routes as well. On top of this, the heat and humidity were like a vise—it could sap the will of the strongest man and put a brave Marine on his knees. Even more, rusted shells of French military vehicles, armored carriers and tanks lay hidden in the bush, overgrown with two decades of weeds and vegetation, dim reminders of the Indochina War, 15 years earlier, and the ultimate defeat of European (French) colonialism. Curiously enough, in 1965, the Central Highlands were the territory of the Green Berets and the U.S. Special Forces. It was also the area of responsibility for Brigadier General Chu Huy Man–The

---

[101] Guidebook Editor, *Guidebook for Marines,* Nineteenth Edition, p. 23, (Marine Corps Association, 2009). Reprinted with permission from Leatherneck magazine on 12/15/15.

[102] George Esper and The Associated Press, *The Eyewitness History of the Vietnam War–1961–1975,* p. 70, (Ballantine Books, 1983).

[103] Edward Doyle and Samuel Lipsman, *The Vietnam Experience–America Takes Over–1965-67,* War Footing, p. 21, (Boston Publishing Company, 1982).

[104] George Esper and The Associated Press, *The Eyewitness History of the Vietnam War–1961–1975,* p. 70, (Ballantine Books, 1983).

People's Army Regiment in North Vietnam. He was in charge of overseeing Viet Cong operations against the U.S. Marines in the Da Nang–Chu Lai region. [105] Before our/their military men arrived and before the French occupied this area, this was the homeland of the many different tribes of Montagnards, or mountain people. [106]

The Ho Chi Minh Trail was essentially a 6,000-mile network of dirt roads, trails, and river crossings stretching, periodically, at least thirty miles wide.

Starting in 1964, the North Vietnamese began transforming the original primitive trails of the area into a more workable road network. The architect of this project was an engineer officer by the name of Colonel Dong Si Nguyen. Nguyen built bridges and roads capable of carrying large trucks. In addition, he set up anti-aircraft defenses against inevitable U.S. air attacks. Hospitals, barracks, fuel depots, and supply warehouses were built in underground facilities, sheltering them from possible U.S. bombings. The communists recruited all sorts of specialists—drivers, mechanics, traffic managers, doctors, and nurses—to be stationed along this roadway. While some 10,000 North Vietnamese moved along the trail in 1964. By 1967 the trail swarmed with as many as 20,000 soldiers a month. [107]

Much of the sheltered trail was covered by a tropical rain forest. It reached southward 200 to 300 miles into Laos, Cambodia, and eventually South Vietnam. The Ho Chi Minh Trail, named after the North Vietnamese president Ho Chi Minh, was so complex that trucks sometimes seemed to suddenly disappear. There were between 1,250 and 1,700 parks and storage areas on the trail. In fact, a single truck rarely ever made the full run; rather, the run was a system of transfers from point to point, using trucks, oxcarts, and human hands. Some supplies, on the other hand, were put in barges and barrels and floated downstream. There were estimates that as many as 75,000 people worked on the trail network, including a coolie force of Laotian tribesmen and villagers. [108]

At some point, the multifaceted route was no longer a collection of tracks and camps but one of roads and bases, called *binh trams* that serviced passing units. Truck convoys replaced bicycles as the standard conveyances. By 1965 Group 559 (559th North Vietnamese Transportation Group under the command of Colonel [later General] Vo Bam to improve and maintain a transportation system to supply the NLF uprising against the South Vietnamese gov-

---

[105] Lieutenant General Harold G. Moore (Retired) and Joseph L. Galloway, *We Were Soldiers Once ... and Young*, p. 16, (Random House, 1992).

[106] Ibid, p. 42.

[107] Donald L. Gilmore and D. M. Giangreco, *Eyewitness Vietnam–Firsthand Accounts from Operation Rolling Thunder to the Fall of Saigon*, pp. 106-106 (Sterling Publishing Company, 2006).

[108] George Esper and The Associated Press, *The Eyewitness History of the Vietnam War–1961–1975*, p. 70, (Ballantine Books, 1983).

ernment [109]) operated six truck battalions, compared with two of bicycles. The *binh trams* were being equipped with vehicle maintenance facilities, anti-aircraft defenses, ground security elements, and many modern appurtenances. Separate anti-aircraft units were also placed at key points, such as the mountain passes where roads crossed from the Democratic Republic of Vietnam into the Laotian domain of the trail. [110]

While U.S. bombing of the Ho Chi Minh Trail grew in intensity during the course of the Vietnam War, most of the North Vietnamese who died while making the long trek were victims of dysentery, malaria and other diseases rather than U.S. bombs. The excruciating march was a ghastly ordeal for many whose job it was to support their VC comrades in the south.

Some of those who marched down the trail looked as non-threatening as this young North Vietnamese woman, with smiles on their faces, as can be seen in picture 4.2. [111] Others looked like young Vietnamese men, who looked like they were going on a camping trip, as can be seen in picture 4.3. [112] These harmless looking hikers, though, were really the enemy. They were North Vietnamese regulars with weapons slung over their shoulders or backs, ready to kill us at a moment's notice, at any chance they had. They were also Viet Cong guerrillas crossing a clearing while on patrol. In addition, they carried submachine guns and rice packed in sacks made, coincidently, of U.S. parachute silk.

It was mid-August 1965. Supposedly and according to the 3rd Marine Division's S-2 Intelligence office, there were three regiments of North Vietnamese soldiers heading our way, supposedly over 2,000 of the enemy. They were evidently coming down from the nearby Annamite Cordillera range, a rugged and overgrown mountain chain that runs along the border between Laos and Vietnam. Hidden by the undergrowth were numerous trails that could allow the adversary fairly easy access to the Chu Lai area and a possible assault on the American air base located in the immediate area.

The enemy's intent, commanded and led by Nguyen Dinh Trong—a veteran of many fights against the French and the South Vietnamese, became clear on August 15, 1965, when a member of the 1st VC Regiment surrendered to the ARVN, and stated that his regiment, numbering almost 1500 men with supporting units, had established its base in the Van Tuong village complex, in the Van Tuong Peninsula, 15 kilometers south of Chu Lai and about two kilometers inland. The attack on Chu Lai (not even a Vietnamese name) would be launched from there. [113]

---

[109] *Ho Chi Minh Trail,* Wikipedia.

[110] John Prados, *Vietnam: The History of an Unwinnable War,* 1945-1975, p. 153, (University Press of Kansas, 2009).

[111] Horst Faas and Tim Page, *REQUIEM–By the Photographers Who Died in Vietnam and Indochina,* p. 101, Random House, 1997).

[112] Julene Fischer, *The Vietnam Experience–Images of War,* p. 81, (Boston Publishing Company, 1986).

[113] Edward F. Murphy, *Semper Fi Vietnam,* p. 17, (Presidio Press, 1997).

The Navy had also been informed of this all-important operation on August 16th. The USS Galveston (CL-93/CLG-3), a guided missile cruiser, the USS Orleck (DD-886), a destroyer, USS Bayfield (APA-33), an attack landing ship dock, a transport vessel that took me from Okinawa to South Vietnam only a month earlier, USS Cabildo (LSD-16), a landing support ship that transports amtracs to the objective area, and the tank landing ship USS Vernon Country (LST- 1161), quickly sprang into action. They all steamed directly toward the Chu Lai area. First, the cruiser USS Galveston and the destroyer USS Orleck, at 0500, bombarded the enemy ashore. Second, the USS Cabildo served as the primary control ship for assault landings. This vessel was also responsible for vectoring all other amphibious crafts to the beach around the targeted hot spot.

To further safeguard security, Vietnamese allies were informed of the operation only at the highest level. Only two Vietnamese generals were told, and they were cautioned to hold the information until the battle actually began.

The operation plan called for 3/3/3 to land I (India) and K (Kilo) companies abreast on Green Beach at 0630 on August 18th. L (Lima) Company was to land in trace as battalion reserve. The radio call sign for this unit was called *Fighting Mad.* My unit, Mike Company, was already positioned on a ridgeline four miles northwest of the landing area, ready to act as a blocking force. Lieutenant Colonel Joseph R. (Bull) Fisher's 2/4/3 was to come into three separate landing zones by helicopter, linking up with 3/3/3 and driving through the Van Tuong village complexes.[114] (Note: Our company commander, Captain Cal M. Morris—skipper, was called in earlier by Lieutenant Colonel Muir, a well-respected, ultra-aggressive, high-energy two-war Marine, and briefed us on our role in this operation. He was given a five-paragraph order—a combat order orally given to Marines for an operation.)

Colonel Fisher was one of the liveliest and most interesting battalion commanders of the Marine Corps. He was a large leatherneck at 6'3" tall and weighing about 220 pounds. He had enlisted in the Marines in 1942 and two-and-a-half years later landed on Iwo Jima as a platoon sergeant. Twice hit by machine-gun bullets, he refused evacuation from the battlefield. He was awarded a Silver Star Medal for his heroism. Later, as a commissioned officer of a rifle company in the legendary Chosin Reservoir campaign (November–December 1950). This was a decisive battle that was fought over some of the roughest terrain during some of the harshest winter weather conditions of the Korean War. He had earned the Navy Cross Medal. By the time Operation Starlite rolled around, Colonel Fisher was balding and aging but was still a tough Marine. In fact, he led a walking skirmish line up a ridge, with every third man firing from the hip. "Come on, you Marines," yelled colorful Fisher as enemy bullets zipped past, "those ain't pinball machines firing at you."

---

[114] Otto J. Lehrack, *No Shining Armor–The Marines at War in Vietnam,* pp. 36-37, (University Press of Kansas, 1992).

Once General Lewis Walt, Commander of the 3rd Marine Division and concurrently commander of the III Marine Amphibious Force, learned of this, he immediately went into action by assembling over 2,500 Marines. Meeting with senior commanders and the like, General Westmoreland finally decided to launch a full-on major offensive move against the 1st VC Regiment. It was a combined air, sea, and ground assault, a three-pronged attack by river crossing, helicopter insertion, and a small amphibious assault [115], using massive firepower, using two battalions of Marines, Phantom and Skyhawk jets, two destroyers (USS Orleck and USS Prichett), one guided missile cruiser (USS Galveston), as well as ground artillery. We were eagerly ready to wage war and that we did! It was known as the Battle of Chu Lai, in the Quang Ngai Province. It was top secret, strictly on a need-to-know basis.

This was *Operation Starlite*, was by far the first, biggest and bloodiest operation in Vietnam to that point. It was the first time Marines, of which many had never tasted combat, would be challenged by a large amount of crack Viet Cong troops, who had been toughened by years of fighting the French. The action was vicious, up close, and gory as Marines fought their way out of ensnares, hot LZs, and fatal crossfire. By the way, Operation Starlite, which would be faced with a bewildering array of threats, both manmade and natural, was originally known as Operation Satellite because NASA was about to launch a Gemini spacecraft the same week as the operation. It, without equivocation, pushed forward the Vietnam War into the main news across the nation and into the hearts and minds of Americans, where it would take up residence for more than ten years. It was also a *blood debt* of a battle that thrust the Vietnam War into the forefront of continuous hostile confrontations. Incidentally, blood debt in Vietnamese (*han tu*) means revenge or hatred, debt of honor or blood owed for blood spilled. Waging this type of war was costly to both sides.

I understand from various sources that we killed over 600 VC and took more than ten prisoners. Most of the enemy were from the 1st VC Regiment—commanded by Nguyen Dinh Trong, 60th and 80th Battalions. Also, a VC company from the immediate area who were engaged in the battle escaped and only a few weapons were ever found.

The high number of VC deaths resulted from their choice to stay and fight. But they were ill-prepared for the immense amounts of armaments the U.S. forces would bring to bear on their locations. As a result and for a time, the 1st VC Regiment ceased to exist. Unfortunately, we lost at least 40 dedicated warriors and suffered 120 wounded. The low number of Americans killed resulted, in part, from the use of Marine helicopters that came in and quickly evacuated the wounded. Of those injured in battle, eight subsequently died of their wounds. One was Lance Corporal Joe Calvin Paul, a fire team leader and a friend of mine from H (Hotel) Company, 2nd Battalion, 4th Marines, 1st Ma-

---

[115]   Colonel H. Avery Chenoweth, USMCR (Retired), *Semper Fi–The Definitive Illustrated History of the U.S. Marines*, p. 341, (Fall River Press, 2005).

rine Division—nicknamed the *"Magnificent Bastards,"* whose motto was *"second to none,"* were originally stationed out of Camp Pendleton. This unit, which landed in Chu Lai on May 7, 1965, as part of the initial landing force, was also called the Magnificent Bastards of the Second Battalion. Joe was somewhat a chubby and diminutive Marine. His former company Gunnery Sergeant, also called *Gunny,* Edward Garr, also disclosed to me that he was a sullen and reserved young grunt that needed, at times, to get his ass kicked. Even so, Ed also said he was a fine, dedicated and gung-ho fighter. A hero and a Medal of Honor recipient, Joe died on August 19, 1965, as he was trying to save other Marines again and again against the enemy positions. He raced across the paddy, placed himself in an uncovered position between other Marine casualties and the Viet Cong, and poured out a constant stream of fire power in order to divert the enemy long enough to permit his fellow wounded Marines to be moved to safety. Unfortunately, he, the quiet and heroic warrior, was mortally wounded before he could return for cover. Born on April 23, 1946, shortly before me, in Williamsburg, Kentucky, he too was, at the time, 19 years old when he enlisted. He was buried at Memorial Park, Dayton, Ohio.

As a real hero, I thought you might be interested in reading about his gallant efforts to save lives of his fellow warriors. The citation, presented by President Johnson, for his courageous test of bravery reads:

> In a violent battle, Lance Corporal Paul's platoon sustained five casualties as it was temporarily pinned down, by devastating mortar, recoilless rifle, automatic weapons, and rifle fire delivered by insurgent Communist Viet Cong forces in well-entrenched positions. The wounded Marines were unable to move from their perilously exposed positions forward of the remainder of their platoon, and were suddenly subjected to a barrage of white phosphorous rifle grenades. Lance Corporal Paul, fully aware that his tactics would almost certainly result in serious injury or death to himself, chose to disregard his own safety and boldly dashed across the fire-swept rice paddies, placed himself between his wounded comrades and the enemy, and delivered effective suppressive fire with his automatic weapon in order to divert the attack long enough to allow the casualties to be evacuated. Although critically wounded during the course of the battle, he resolutely remained in his exposed position and continued to fire his rifle until he collapsed and was evacuated. By his fortitude and gallant spirit of self-sacrifice in the face of almost certain death, he saved the lives of several of his fellow Marines. His heroic action served to inspire all who observed him and reflect the highest credit upon himself, the Marine Corps and the U.S. Naval Service. He gallantly gave his life in the cause of freedom. [116]

---

[116] *Lance Corporal Joe C. Paul,* Wikipedia.

Joe's company landed right in the middle of a Viet Cong battalion (over a 1,000 enemy regulars) around the village of Nam Yen 3. This was a place where many of the huts were actually fortified bunkers. The sides of them dropped down, revealing positions with set fields of fire. His unit found itself completely surrounded. However, the VC let the first wave of helicopters land before opening fire. Once enough Marines were on the ground, the enemy opened up on the group with intensity and fervor. Realizing that there was such a heavy concentration of Viet Cong, the company commander called in an air strike. After fierce fighting, Hotel Company was finally able to take command of the area.

On the first day of battle, among the many Marines wounded during Operation Starlite, on August 18, 1965, there was another Medal of Honor recipient—Corporal Robert (Bobbie) E. O'Malley—the first Marine to receive the Medal of Honor in the Vietnam War. Corporal O'Malley was with India (I) Company, 3rd Battalion, 3rd Marines, 3rd Marine Division. Born on June 3, 1943, he was a native of Woodside, Queens, New York, and was 22 at the time.

I was told that Corporal O'Malley's company, who made an amphibious landing near the village of An Cuong 1, was the hardest hit in this battle. Regrettably, 15 fearless Marines from India Company were killed and another 52 were wounded in this engagement alone. Included in the death toll were their company commander, a Navy Cross recipient, Captain Bruce D. Webb, and a corpsman. As a result of Captain Webb's demise, First Lieutenant Richard M. Purnell immediately assumed command of the unit. Considering that a rifle company had about 216 men, over 30 percent of this unit was bloodied by the enemy. While the lieutenant prepared the company for a full-on assault, Corporal O'Malley spotted a trench that held a small VC unit. With total disregard for his own life, he raced across an open rice paddy that was subjected to a mortar barrage. Facing imminent death from a fanatic and determined enemy, he jumped into a ditch and used his rifle and hand grenades to kill at least eight VC. Corporal O'Malley then returned to his squad, ignoring three serious wounds he received in this action. One was a mortar fragment that he caught in the chest and punctured his lung. This led to the relief of a pinned-down squad that later rejoined the company.

As I stated earlier, waging this type of war was psychologically expensive as well as emotionally draining. It was even more costly for 153 servicemen, including 44 Marines, during 1963–1972, who demonstrated tremendous competence, heroism and gallantry in pursuit of their country's uncertain military goals. All of these brave men exemplified great courage and intrepidness, and regrettably paid the ultimate price. They received the Medal of Honor posthumously. This battle was costly for many spirited and gutsy men` of the 3rd Marine Division. Thus, Operation Starlite, the first major engagement between U.S. and Viet Cong forces, was the combat campaign against which all others were later measured. Without a doubt, the August 1965 battle was a reverberating success for the Marines and a cause for great hopefulness about America's future in Vietnam. Had American forces lost this major battle, which was a definite possibility, given our lack of combat experience, most of us had never come into contact with warfare before, the effects might have been severe indeed.

Once General Westmoreland gave his approval, General Walt now had the authority to go on the offensive. Remember that we were trained and skilled at being offensive warriors. In a gale of strategic planning activities over the next sixty hours, he put together an attack plan that would take five days to complete. In blistering heat, some grunts made an amphibious landing at Green Beach to the south and east of the village of Van Tuong, essentially blocking the VC's southern escape routes. My unit, the battalion's fourth rifle company, would be the first group to move overland from the staging area (as can be seen in picture 4.4—we are now in the staging area). That morning, August 17th, we headed toward Chu Lai to set up a blocking force, the anvil, and we would set in along a ridgeline to the north of the objective area, about two-and-a-half miles northwest of the landing beaches. Luckily, as we traveled, single file, to our blocking position destination, we were not spotted by the enemy. There we dug, ready. An artillery battery of six 107mm mortars from the 3rd Battalion, 12th Marines, 3rd Marine Division, nicknamed *"Warriors of the Pacific,"* also called *cannon cockers,* was helilifted the next morning at dawn into our company's position to provide close artillery support. (Note: 107mm mortars are a hybrid artillery piece consisting of a 4.2" mortar mounted on a howitzer chassis.) Three days earlier we were running combat patrols south of Chu Lai. The map, as seen in picture 4.5 [117], shows the various troop movements.

As shown in picture 4.4, at times we wore long-sleeved uniforms that were used in World War II. Anyhow, they were far too heavy and too hot for the Vietnam weather. Additionally, we wore flak jackets for added chest protection. We also carried one-third of our weight in ammunitions, C-rations, an array of deadly explosives and sometimes junk food (which we called geedunk).

Supporting our assault on the enemy strongholds were Navy A-4 Skyhawks and Marine F-4 Phantom jets (that would leave out of the Chu Lai Air Base). They screamed at speeds over 400 miles an hour at low levels, dropping tons of bombs and gallons of Napalm. When these jets dropped their ammunitions, thick rolls of black smoke filled the air which this made it hard to breathe. For the time being, other Marine companies were heading right into the firefight. We hooked up with Golf Company of our battalion by early afternoon as we searched two hamlets near our rendezvous point, encountering only minor resistance. Nonetheless, it still was a confrontation with our foe. However, Echo Company ran into some heavy resistance as they tried to move onward. As they crept forward toward VC strongholds,

---

[117] Harry G. Summers, Jr., *Historical Atlas of the Vietnam War,* p. 103, (Houghton Mifflin Company, 1995).

they destroyed one enemy bunker after another. After several hours of fierce fighting, we took control of the area. Having set up our blocking positions in the north, the renewed attack commenced the next day. As we moved ahead, through the elephant grass consisting of huge stalks of bamboo-like grass that were sometimes higher than a man's head, we met with stiff resistance from the Viet Cong and the North Vietnamese regulars in the rugged, heavily vegetated, jungle terrain (picture 4.6).

The well-concealed bunkers, trenches, caves, booby traps, and bamboo whips hampered our forward and even our lateral movement. A bamboo whip, which is a spring loaded booby trap (picture 4.7 [118]). At times, we could see sharpened bamboo sticks that rose from the ground.

Finally, we (Mike Company) met up with India Company at An Cuong. This village is about ten miles south of Chu Lai. The enemy fled. In spite of this, we counted over fifty dead VC in the area. After securing this area, we headed for An Thoi.

In his tome, *Semper Fi Vietnam*, Edward F. Murphy, noted U.S. Army veteran of the Vietnam War (where he served with the 4th Military Intelligent Detachment, 4th Infantry Division), further recounted the first major battle of the Vietnam War:

> Operation Starlite continued for five more days because General Walt felt some enemy soldiers remained behind in underground hiding places. Before beginning this mop-up phase, Colonel Oscar 'Peat' F. Peatross, commander of the landing force, released the 2nd Battalion, 4th Marines (2/4/1) and the 3rd Battalion, 3rd Marines (i.e., my unit–3/3/3) on August 20th, replacing them with the 1st Battalion, 7th Marines (1/7/1). The fresh Marines, together with the 3rd Battalion, 7th Marines (3/7/1) and units from the 2nd ARVN Division killed another fifty-four VC before Operation Starlite officially ended on August 24th. In all, 614 VC were killed, nine prisoners were captured, and 109 assorted weapons were confiscated. We Marines suffered forty-five dead and 203 wounded. [119]

Despite some confusion and even some disorder during this encounter, we clearly felt we won the Battle of Chu Lai. It was proclaimed as a significant achievement throughout America's military establishment. Credit not only belonged to us grunts who fought in the hamlets, rice paddies, on hills, and in the caves, but recognition, as well as thanks, was also due to all the supporting arms and magnificent and courageous corpsmen as well. Between close air support (CAS) and constant artillery fire within a few hundred feet or so of our positions, I suspect these actions, at least for the time being, proved deci-

---

[118] Donald M. Goldstein, Katherine V. Dillon, and J. Michael Wenger, *The Vietnam War*, p. 55, (Brassey's, 1997–Now Potomac Books).

[119] Edward F. Murphy, *Semper Fi Vietnam*, p. 25, (Presidio Press, 1997).

sive in breaking the VC's defenses in this area. While this major clash with the Viet Cong and North Vietnamese main forces was significant and vital at the time, it would later be considered an inconclusive battle.

We had already learned that our adversary was far more than a bunch of rebellious peasants wearing coolie hats. They were well-armed, apparently well-led, fanatical, vicious, and certainly brave and capable soldiers. Like us, they were obsessed as well as preoccupied with winning. We were on their land they were trying to reclaim or protect. They took great pride in exploiting every opportunity they could. In fact: "The Viet Cong gave top priority to removing weapons belonging to their casualties from the battlefield for reuse. Second priority was to remove as many bodies of their dead as possible. This was intended to lower Allied estimates of their success." [120]

As we tried to move forward, the VC laid down heavy firepower. It was constant. It appeared that they were not afraid of us and would not be easily beaten. We were fighting on their turf and terrain that they knew only too well. They too were fighting for a cause, one that we could not accept.

Some of us from the 3rd Battalion were not given much notice of the impending operation. According to Sergeant Richard G. Kidwell's story (see below), he too did not know where he was going to go because that was a well-kept secret from everybody. Hence, here is one such incident that put a fellow Marine and many of his men in harm's way in a hurry:

> My job, at the time, was that of right guide for Lima Company. I had just climbed down the starboard side of the nets from the LST (Landing Ship Tank—flat-bottomed, oceangoing vessel capable of hauling troops, tanks, and other heavy equipment). My unit was housed on this ship, parked in the Gulf of Tonkin, at the time. I quickly jumped onboard the moving landing craft that was waiting to take us ashore. The seas were choppy. The word, while in the craft, was suddenly given to us–*lock and load.*
>
> Upon arriving at the beach, the landing craft's front ramp went immediately down. As we hit the shore, half the guys went off to the right. The other half veered to the left. During this time, we laid down a volley of fire. We did so since we were taking heavy enemy fire from the tree line.
>
> It was a frightening feeling. I was so nervous. I stepped off the ramp and into the water that was almost five feet deep. I only weighed 145 lbs. at the time, but I had to carry over 100 lbs. of extra gear and ammunition. When I finally got out of the water, unhurt, I looked like a drowned rat. I was thoroughly soaked from head to toe.

---

[120] Otto J. Lehrack, *No Shining Armor–The Marines at War in Vietnam,* p. 51, (University Press of Kansas, 1992).

Later, as the group was in the thick of it, fighting its way foot-by-foot, I had to help a fellow Marine who had his legs and arms blown to pieces.

We were making a sweep at the end of the beach. I started to move out, and all of a sudden I heard a loud boom. As I looked around, there was my friend lying in a trench. I quickly jumped down in the hollow and pulled him up, and we put him on a stretcher. We then immediately called in a helicopter for a medevac (i.e., medical evacuation). They called back and commented that they would be there soon. Finally, they came. We threw a poncho over the wounded Marine, and as we were carrying the comrade who was drenched in his own blood, his hand fell down. Sadly, the young Marine died in the helicopter on his way to the hospital.

I am telling you, this sickened me to no end. That was the only time I really cried. In fact, this caused me, at least in part, after I left the Marines, to drink for the next fifteen years. It still nauseates me to think that we lost so many fine Marines for nothing! [121]

As a special mention, I feel it is worthy to note that for our actions in Operation Starlite, six Navy Crosses, the second in precedence behind the Medal of Honor, were given to my fellow fearless and courageous Marines. The Navy Cross is awarded to a person who distinguishes himself or herself by extraordinary heroism not justifying the award of the Medal of Honor. To warrant this distinguishing badge of honor, the act or the execution of duty must be performed in the presence of great danger or at great personal risk. Navy Cross recipients, conferred between August 18 and August 23, 1965, include the following names: Private Samuel J. Badnek, Hotel Company, 2/4/3; First Lieutenant Robert F. Cochran Jr. Company A, 1st Amphibian Tractor Battalion, 3rd Marine Division; Lieutenant Colonel Joseph E. Muir, H&S Company 3/3/3; Sergeant James E. Mulloy, H&S Company, 3/3/3; Corporal Ernie W. Wallace, Hotel Company, 2/4/3; and Captain Bruce D. Webb, India Company, 3/3/3.

Two Medals of Honor, as already mentioned, were also awarded, and tragically, one of these was posthumous. Other important medals of bravery and valor were handed out to other warriors as well.

The Battle of Chu Lai, unequivocally, has earned its place in the history books, and became the first major/full-scale confrontation of the Vietnam War. The operation also showed that the crafty and vile Viet Cong could be trodden with American firepower and mobility. It also remained, at least for a very short time, the only proof of what the Marines could do if the enemy stood and engaged. By this time, the number of Marines and other servicemen that were arriving in Vietnam were no longer a dribble but a deluge. Then

---

[121] Former retired Marine, Sergeant Major Richard G. Kidwell, L (Lima) Company 3rd Battalion, 3rd Marines, 3rd Marine Division, 1966.

came the inauspicious decisions in Washington by one man, sitting alone in his office: the President of the United States.

According to Ed Nicholls: "Operation Starlite has earned a place beside other legendary and well-known Marine battles: Tripoli, Belleau Wood, Guadalcanal, Saipan, Okinawa, Tarawa, Iwo Jima, Peleliu, Inchon Beach, and the Frozen Chosin Reservoir. Operation Starlite is now a part of the Marine Corps history, traditions, and lore. It is fitting, for that reason, that we, the survivors of that battle, remember, record, and honor our own that fought and died in it. We intend to personalize the sterile Unit Histories pertaining to this great battle. We do offer this as a tribute to fellow warriors who knew and shared the battle." [122]

Operation Starlite, as problematic and grueling as it was, with so many Marines wounded and killed, was still a major morale booster and psychological lift for us. In fact, there were Pollyanna prognostications of bringing home U.S. troops soon, which, unfortunately, never happened. In fact, the U.S. continued to dispense men and material into the war effort in the belief that Starlite was the beginning of a reversal of fortune in Vietnam.

Operation Starlite clearly demonstrated the effectiveness of U.S. firepower. With a kill ratio of over thirteen to one, this was certainly uplifting for our unit. We had met the VC in a heated clash and defeated them on their own ground with heavy artillery, air strikes, and close-contact fighting with our ground forces. We had passed the first big test of all future battles to come for us, which I participated in including Operation Piranha (September 6–8, 1965), Operation Rice Straw-Golden Fleece (September 10–14, 1965), and Operation Harvest Moon (December 8–20, 1965). God only knows why I came away unscathed. I left there physically unhurt. Even though we were victorious in the Battle of the Chu Lai area, the VC, ironically, would eventually come back and take over this same land.

Operation Starlite was unquestionably a struggle that would later take on an almost mythical importance. Unfortunately, there would be many more battlefield tests. For the moment: "For those Marines who would certainly come later and for whom the landing at Iwo Jima and Inchon Beach were the glory of a past generation, the Battle of Chu Lai was the only evidence of what well-trained warriors could do if the enemy stood and engaged." [123]

As already stated, Operation Starlite, outside of Chu Lai proper, was fought in and around heavily populated villages. Many of the hamlets had been severely damaged, burned or destroyed by Napalm from air strikes, naval gunfire, and us defiant and angry Marines with flame-throwers or by whatever search-and-destroy tactics were available to us at the time. As can be

---

[122] Former retired and disabled Marine Staff Sergeant Ed Wynn Nicholls, Kilo Company, 2nd Platoon, 3rd Battalion, 3rd Marines, 3rd Marine Division, 1965, and the Operation Starlite Survivor's Association.

[123] Edward Doyle and Samuel Lipsman, *The Vietnam Experience–America Takes Over–1965-67*, War Footing, p. 22, (Boston Publishing Company, 1982).

seen in picture 4.8, a hooch is burning from one of our jets that dropped a Napalm bomb.

Our life was constantly on the (front) line. Hard-charging warriors died right and left. More noteworthy, the enemy was within a few feet of our position in the almost impenetrable and dense jungle. We too were always within their range and their direct line of firing sight. All the same, we were surely not about to take it easy or relax during these intense and dangerous times. Our job was to clear, pursue and rescind enemy units, wipe out remaining local guerrillas, and uproot the enemy's secret political infrastructure from populated areas in hopes of preparation for pacification of the region. However, if our adversaries were in our way, and they were only too frequently, we made every attempt to remove them from the scene. Later, General Westmoreland remarked: "Search and destroy was taken to mean aimless searches in the jungle and the random destroying of villages and other property." [124] He later wondered angrily why some friendly critic had not warned him how bad it sounded.

Marilyn B. Young, Professor of U.S. Foreign Relations, New York University, and well-known writer, in her book, *The Vietnam Wars 1945–1990*, stated:

> The approach exemplified by STARLITE and strongly supported by Maxwell Taylor was an enclave strategy, in which major cities and towns and well-placed U.S. military bases, mainly along the coast, would be secured by aggressive patrolling. Whenever the American war seemed to reach a stalemate, the enclave approach would be revived, which would always go slowly, by those who both resisted complete withdrawal of American troops and despaired of the most popular alternative, search and destroy operations. Westmoreland and General Earle G. Wheeler, on the other hand, were impatient of anything that seemed to tie U.S. troops down in a posture of static defense, even one that allowed for offensive patrolling in a fifty-mile radius of any given enclave. They envisaged battles like Ia Drang, finding the enemy and eliminating him; counting the dead bodies in a war of attrition in which U.S. firepower would inevitably win. [125]

Located on the beautiful coastline of the South China Sea, dividing the two southern provinces of Quang Ngai and Quang Tin, Chu Lai, a highly contested area whose control shifted almost daily between the Viet Cong and South Vietnamese forces during the mid-1960s, was not even a developed area when I first arrived. Nothing was there to speak of. Various Marine and Navy units, under the command of Lieutenant General Victor H. Krulak, a gradu-

---

[124] Marilyn B. Young, *The Vietnam Wars 1945–1990*, p. 163, (HarperPerennial, 1991).
[125] Ibid, p. 162.

ate from the U.S. Naval Academy who first saw action in World War II and in the Korean War, selected the area for an airfield and constructed an air base. Later in the war, it became headquarters for the South Vietnamese Army's Second Division, elements of the Marines' First Division, South Korea's Second Marine Brigade, and the Army's Americal Division.

Starting in late August, Chu Lai was where a few of us lived after Operation Starlite ended. As can be seen in picture 4.9, some members of my squad were stationed in the heart of a flea-infested sandy beach. It was reminiscent of my living quarters in Da Nang. In this case, we did not have luxurious heavy-duty eight-man tents for protection from the elements like we did in Da Nang. It was basic survival at its best, truly testing our ability to tolerate the heat, humidity and those lovely creatures: nasty disease-carrying sand flies and other beastly insects that also lived in the area. This was how we endured. About a quarter mile from the shoreline, our tent-like open-space nylon home became an unforgiving and intolerable rest area. This desolate and forbidding place (refer to picture 4.10 [126]) where we walked to the beach so that we could go for a swim and bathe. With weapons at the ready and temperatures easily reaching 110 degrees during the day, the beach became our morbid rest-and-relaxation grounds for the next few days. On top of this, those annoying sand flies and mosquitoes seemed to like being around people, specifically me. These insidious stowaways find human hosts through soil, water, food, or airborne vectors. Following Operation Starlite, our battalion continued to conduct regular sweeps and low-level (small unit) combat operations against the Viet Cong. [127]

As can be seen in picture 4.11, [128] here is another view of the general area where we lived. In this photograph, Marine amphibian tractors are moving across Route 1 (Ham Rong to Hanoi). This so-called highway, which travels north and south, is an all-weather macadam road. It also parallels the South China Sea.

Along with the heat came the giant flies and ants. It was miserable! How much more agony and discomfort could there be? With virtually no protection from the elements, we hung out here, for the most part, during the night. We accustomed ourselves again to those lovely left-over C-rations. They were individually canned, and they could be opened by a P-38. The P-38, first developed in 1942, was a small can opener issued in the canned field rations of the United States Armed Forces from World War II to the 1980s. Also, they were pre-cooked, or prepared wet rations intended to be issued to U.S. military land forces when fresh food (A-Rations) or packaged unprepared food (B-Rations) prepared in mess halls or field kitchens was impractical or not available, and when survival rations (K-rations or D-rations) were insufficient. The-

[126] Associated Press, *Vietnam: The Real War*, p. 95, (Abrams, 2013).

[127] *3rd Battalion, 3rd Marines*, Wikipedia.

[128] Jack Shulimson and Major Charles M. Johnson, USMC, *U.S. Marines in Vietnam– the Landing and the Buildup 1965*, p. 29, (U.S. Government Printing Office, 1978).

se C-rations were from the Korean War; foodstuff that was already a dozen years old, and in many cases, spoiled. To make matters worse, this became our outskirt sentry post while other Marine and Navy personnel (Seabees-engineers) were trying to complete a naval airfield with a portable 4,000 foot runway made with interlocking slats of lightweight metal alloy by the Dung Quat Bay. It was used from 1965–1971, some one and three quarter of a mile away. DC-2s/3s would initially land and unload what few supplies they could. Likewise, AC-47 "Puff, the Magic Dragon" gunships, which were fitted with 7.62mm mini-guns, fired up to 6,000 rounds per minute and the aircraft carried 54,000 rounds, and fly into the area. There was not much of a runway at the time. Few planes came in and out during July 1965; but after a while, it quickly became the home for the Navy's A-4 Skyhawk and the Marine Corps's F-4 Phantom.

The A-4 Skyhawk was originally designed to operate from virtually every carrier in the fleet of the U.S. Navy. Using a Pratt & Whitney jet engine, it could travel at speeds up to 650 miles per hour at sea level. The F-4 Phantom, made by McDonnell Douglas, was maneuvered by a pilot and a radar intercept officer (RIO), was initially designed as an interceptor. It was primarily used in the air-to-ground strike role. In fact, this jet was guided almost entirely by ground radar. It could drop its bombs within 100 yards of a selected target. Thank God they were there for support. We frequently called on these mighty fast flying machines, especially when we knew we were pinned down. Unfortunately, it happened only too often.

As the Chu Lai Air Base grew, so did our back-up military support. Not long after we left Chu Lai for another hot spot, the air base would soon take on a new look. It would be guarded by M48 medium-size tanks (the last U.S. tank to mount the 90mm tank gun), the main U.S. battle tank during the Vietnam War, and self-propelled 106 recoilless rifles (a lightweight, portable armament intended primarily as an anti-tank weapon) mounted on mules, as can be seen in picture 4.11. Mules are jeep-like four-wheel drive vehicles. This equipment and these Marines became our rear echelon support. Although they were not necessarily in the front lines, they were right there behind us. They had the firepower to help us out, even at a long distance, when the going got tough.

During the day, we would head out on patrol. Usually, a dozen of us would go out on patrol for about six to eight hours at a time. Some of the time, a corpsman, who was a medically trained person assigned to us from the Navy (Navy by record only, but Marines by choice), would tag along with us while we headed back into the thick of things in the jungle. Usually, this was about half a mile from our post. All too frequently, we would be without any medical support and devoid of a corpsman. If we were not standing guard at this outer isolated perimeter position, we were in the tropical rain forest.

Operation Starlite was a blood bath for us jarheads—a *blood bath*. It was also very distinctive, in many different ways, to the men who fought in this mêlée. It was also special to the President of the United States, Lyndon Johnson, and the Commander in Chief of the U.S. Pacific Fleet, Admiral Ulysses S. Grant Sharp, Jr. On August 21, 1965, here is what the both of them wrote about this battle:

From: President of the United States

I extend my heartfelt thanks and congratulations—I and those of the American people—to the military units under your command which have achieved clear-cut victory against the first Viet Cong regiment of Chu Lai. This nation is deeply proud of its fearless fighting sons. They have the continued, united, and determined support of their people at home. Our hearts go out to the families and comrades of those who have given their lives.

I know that the men who have won this victory will show the traditional generosity of the American Armed Forces to those whom they have defeated. We must prove all our actions that the path to peace for these adversaries is through return and reconciliation and not through continued aggression. The courage and skill of our men in battle will be matched by their magnanimity when the battle ends, and all American military action in Vietnam will stop as soon as aggression by others is stopped.

From: Commander in Chief, U.S. Pacific Fleet

The results of Operation STARLITE were most gratifying. I join with the President in sending heartfelt thanks and congratulations. The brilliantly planned and coordinated execution of the Operation is a testimonial to the time tested attributes of initiative, coordination, professionalism, and devotion to duty. The officers and men who participated in the Operation can reflect great pride in demonstrating these attributes.

Please convey my compliments "Well Done" to the officers and men who participated in operation STARLITE. "Warm Regards."

Two days later, August 23rd, in a telegram from Admiral Sharp, Honolulu, Hawaii, to the U.S. Joint Chiefs of Staff, here is the message that the Commander in Chief of the Pacific wrote:

The introduction of expanded U.S. air and ground forces and naval support have further compounded the Viet Cong problem as illustrated by the dramatic U.S. operation on the Van Tuong peninsula, south of Chu Lai (i.e., Operation Starlite), where U.S. Marines destroyed the 1st VC regiment. Employment of U.S. forces in the highlands near Pleiku can and will disrupt VC plans for seizure and control of that strategic area. And following Chu Lai, more ground forces will be introduced when the 1st Cavalry Division lands. Hanoi knows that the ROK (Republic of Korea) division and other U.S.

forces will soon be introduced. Employment of B-52's and scheduled deployment of additional U.S. air squadrons will further emphasize U.S. intent. More prisoners are being taken now. More defections are occurring. These rates will rise when augmented U.S. air and ground forces are brought more fully to bear in harassment, attrition, and search and destroy missions.[129]

On the same day, in a telegram from the Saigon Embassy in South Vietnam to the U.S. State Department, here is what Henry Cabot Lodge, Ambassador to South Vietnam at the time, wrote:

> But there is another aspect which gives me pause. I believe we are approaching the point when further public eagerness by U.S. for "negotiations" will harden Hanoi and Peking's resolve and convince them that we are weak internally (however strong we may be at Chu Lai [Operation Starlite]) thus making things harder for our soldiers, tending to prolong the conflict, and sapping the will to win of the GVN (Government of the Republic of South Vietnam) and RVNAF (Republic of Vietnam Armed Forces). [129]

Now, the Battle of Chu Lai (the first major encounter for Marines, for any of the U.S. Armed Forces, and the Vietnam War), was behind us. We were indisputably the lean, mean "Gung-Ho" fighting machines. I felt we were the best-organized and best-led fighting men in the world. We were also the *Brothers of Battle*, and a serious threat to those who spoke against freedom. Without a doubt Operation Starlite was a crusade of wearing the enemy down—at the time. It was also an engagement about death, as mentioned by one U.S. soldier in the volume, *Historical Atlas of the Vietnam War:* "It became a way of life. I did not even know where those shells were going. I did not even know what they were. But every death sound there is, you start to detect it—you know it. You start to know if death is going over you or if it is coming right at you." [130]

Interestingly enough, Newsweek's William "Bill" Tuohy told his story *(The War in Vietnam–A Marine Victory–and 'Optimism')* slightly differently in the August 30, 1965, edition of that publication. By the way, Tuohy served with the Navy in the Pacific in 1940–1946. He won the Pulitzer Prize in 1968 for his Vietnam War reporting on My Lai:

> Whether or not this optimism will prove justified in the long run, there seemed little doubt that Van Truong itself represented an important benchmark in the Vietnam War. For one thing, it marked

---

[129] Ibid.

[130] Harry G. Summers, Jr., *Historical Atlas of the Vietnam War*, p. 102, (Houghton Mifflin Company, 1995).

the first time that the U.S. had been able to apply the immense military power it had assembled in Vietnam as it was designed to be applied. For another, it marked the only occasion so far in which American commanders had succeeded in luring the Viet Cong into a set-piece battle. And the results proved, as U.S. military men had long predicted, that, in a slugging match, U.S. regulars have a big edge over even the toughest guerrillas. Glowed Brigadier General Frederick J. Karch (a veteran of several amphibious campaigns during World War II), assistant commander of the Third Marine Division: "We will probably never know how many Viet Cong we killed. And why they set their neck on the chopping block here, I will never know. [131]

The Battle of Chu Lai, as already stated, was also a means of wearing down and exhausting the enemy. Did we really do that? I mention this for the reason that two months before Operation Starlite, President Johnson expressed serious doubts, especially to Birch E. Bayh, a Democratic senator from Indiana (1963–1981), as to whether America could win the war. Still, on August 4th, the President asked Congress for an additional $1.7 billion for the war effort.

On the other hand, Harry G. Summers Jr., in his book, *The Vietnam War Almanac*, wrote about what weakening the enemy meant:

> Attrition was the primary U.S. military strategy during the Vietnam War. One of the traditional methods of warfare, attrition, aims at wearing down the enemy by killing or disabling so many of its soldiers that its armed forces are destroyed and its will to resist is broken. Sometimes labeled 'the American way of war,' this method plays to America's materiel and technological strengths, and it was such massive use of American firepower that broke the resistance of Germany and Japan in World War II and of North Korea and China during the Korean War. [132]

According to General Nguyen Chi Thanh, a North Vietnamese officer who served as a leading strategist and military commander. As head of the Central Office for South Vietnam (COSVN—the southern headquarters of communist military and political operations), which controlled the Vietcong effort in South Vietnam, as cited by James S. Olson (Distinguished Professor and Chair, Department of History, Sam Houston State University) and Randy W. Roberts (Professor of History at Purdue University), in *Where the Domino Fell–America and Vietnam 1945 to 1990*: "The battle of the Batangan

[131] William Tuohy, *Newsweek*, p. 29, (*Newsweek*, August 30, 1965).
[132] Harry G. Summers, Jr., *The Vietnam War Almanac*, Attrition, p. 91, (Presidio Press, 1985).

Peninsula in August 1965 (Operation Starlite) intensified the debate. To General Thanh, despite the heavy losses, the battle was proof that 'the Southern Liberation Army is fully capable of defeating U.S. troops under any circumstance, even though they have absolute superiority of ... firepower.' Thanh also pointed out that the Americans had withdrawn from the peninsula soon after the battle, and the Vietcong returned in force. Thanh answered Giap's charge that casualties were too high by arguing that the Americans had suffered 250 dead and wounded soldiers and that the United States would be politically unwilling to accept such casualties. [133] Giap, by the way, is General Vo Nguyen Giap.

Thanh joined the Vietminh in 1946 after French troops shot his father. Thanh also argued that the North Vietnamese should engage the United States in big-unit, conventional battles.

Harry G. Summers, Jr., in *The Vietnam War Almanac*, tells us more about General Giap:

> General Giap became Viet Minh's foremost military commander during the war with the French (1946-1954). In 1954 he won lasting fame by directing the Viet Minh siege that overwhelmed the French garrison at Dien Bien Phu, in northwestern Vietnam near the border with Laos, and effectively won Vietnam its independence. Giap became North Vietnam's Minister of Defense, a member of the ruling Politburo and Commander-in-Chief of The North Vietnamese Army (NVA). [134]

According to excerpts written by Dr. George M. Watson, Jr., and Richard O'Neill in *The Vietnam War*: "War was no stranger to Vietnam. For some 2000 years the nation struggled toward independence in the face of civil strife, Chinese incursions and European imperialism. In the 1950s, the nationalist and Communist Viet Minh forces led by Ho Chi Minh and Vo Nguyen Giap destroyed French power in Indochina. Their successes, nevertheless, brought no peace, but resulted in the partition of the Vietnam nation in 1954." [135] Almost ten years later (May 1963), as it looked like Ho Chi Minh and his Viet Minh forces would go to war again—in this case, with the United States— Chinese officials told the president, as mentioned by Mark Philip Bradley (Bernadotte E. Schmitt Professor of International History at The University of Chicago), that: *"we are standing by your side, and if war breaks out, you can*

---

[133] James S. Olson and Randy Roberts, *Where the Domino Fell–America and Vietnam 1945 to 1990*, p. 146, (Diane Publishing Company, 1991).

[134] Harry G. Summers, Jr., *The Vietnam War Almanac*, Giap, Vo Nguyen, pp. 177-178, (Presidio Press, 1985).

[135] Ray Bonds - Editor, *The Vietnam War–The illustrated history of the conflict in Southeast Asia*, p. 46, (Salamander Books, 1999).

regard China as your rear."[136] By June 1965, China's top lieutenants started to send huge quantities of goods—everything from munitions and food to toothpaste and recreational equipment—along with thousands of troops to repair roads and carry out other key tasks. Although China never dispatched combat units, the support troops it sent, peaking at about 170,000 in 1967, freed North Vietnamese regulars to fight below the 17th parallel (DMZ). [137]

The Battle for Chu Lai was finally behind us. Still, few Americans or Vietnamese comprehended it, but Operation Starlite was just the 'first' torrent of what would become a deluge of corpses from Vietnam to the United States. With little going on for the next two weeks, time passed slowly. Then, I got word that I was going to be reassigned to another location (with my same unit)—up and around the Da Nang area (about 56 miles to the northwest). When there was a lull in the fighting, during a time of rest, I got sick. I had a very high fever for a few days, so a corpsman gave me some medication (chloroquine) to bring my temperature down to a normal level. I recall sweating so profusely that I thought I lost ten or more pounds. I had a case of the shivers, which did not go away for a couple of days. As such, I believe I caught a light case of malaria. I suspect it was from those irritating mosquitoes that were living in the area. Such was the life and times of a young combat Marine among his fellow warriors.

There have been a lot of stories written about the Battle for Chu Lai. But what was going on before the major encounter? According to Otto J. Lehrack, who served 24 years as an enlisted man and officer, a historian who also served two tours of duty in Vietnam; the first (1967–1968) in the infantry as a Marine captain and commanding officer of India Company, 3rd Battalion, 3rd Marines and the second (1970–1971) in signals intelligence as a major and operations officer, First Radio Battalion, in his work, *No Shining Armor–The Marines at War in Vietnam*, he presents the following information for your reading enjoyment:

> Before (Operation) Starlite, Marine reports were mentioning the progress they were making in pacifying the civilian population on the Van Tuong Peninsula. Whether this was true or wishful thinking will probably never be known. A great deal of publicity was generated regarding the quantity of materials supplied by the Marines to the Vietnamese, as well as goods contributed by American church and civic organizations. However, this was not accompanied by an objective method of evaluating whether this effort really secured the allegiance of the population. The very nature of the war made relations with the Vietnamese civilians uncertain at best. Members of the same family would take different sides; combatants included women and children;

---

[136] Mark Philip Bradley, *Vietnam at War,* p. 106, (Oxford University Press, 2009).

[137] Mark Atwood Lawrence, *The Vietnam War–A Concise International History,* p. 95, (Oxford University Press, 2008).

and the lack of boundary lines made most areas suspect to the Marines in the field. [138]

From my perspective, I do not believe that this was our role at the time. I was in Vietnam from 1965–1966. It certainly was not in my unit. I personally did not see large quantities of commodities go to the Vietnamese people. On the other hand, I was in a typical combat or infantry unit. Per se, I do not see how we could have performed this distribution task; and if we did, I, too, would have been leery of the situation. All the same, I would not be surprised if this type of activity did happen.

In closing and as an addition to my story about Lance Corporal Joe Paul, which was mentioned in the beginning of this chapter, on June 20, 1970, the USS Paul (FF-1080), a 438-foot anti-submarine medium-sized frigate, equipped with a multi-mode active sonar, named after Joe C. Paul, was christened and launched. It was later commissioned on August 14, 1971, at the Boston Naval Shipyard. And in the later part of 1972: "The USS Paul departed the United States for the Western Pacific, and arrived off the coast of The Republic of Vietnam on November 23rd where she immediately went into action in support of ground troops ashore. One of USS Paul's first gunfire support missions was at Chu Lai, where Lance Corporal Paul died."

On August 14, 1992, the USS Paul was decommissioned in a ceremony at the Naval Station, Mayport, Florida, exactly twenty years after her initial service.

As conceived and refined by Army General William B. Rosson, Operation Oregon, in the heart of the Chu Lai area, was to be executed, in early April 1967, just one and a half years after we supposedly secured the area in three separate phases. By the end of May, with the support of Marine units, as well as an extensive heliborne search and destroy operation, both Army and Marines (from the 1st Marine Division), had succeeded in killing 369 communists and capturing 64. Once again, our soldiers and warriors took control over the former Marine enclave in Chu Lai. [139]

---

[138] Otto J. Lehrack, *No Shining Armor–The Marines at War in Vietnam*, p. 73, (University Press of Kansas, 1992).

[139] Major Gary L. Telfer and Lieutenant Colonel Lane Rogers, USMC, and V. Keith Fleming Jr. *U.S. Marines in Vietnam–Fighting the North Vietnamese 1967*, pp 77-79 (U.S. Government Printing Office, 1984).

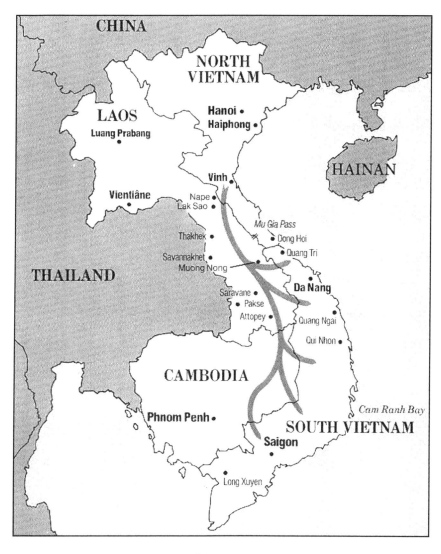

Picture 4.1
Map of Ho Chi Minh Trail
[via Author]

Picture 4.2
VC woman
[via Author]

Picture 4.3
VC men on patrol
[via Author]

Picture 4.4
Staging in Chu Lai
[Author photo]

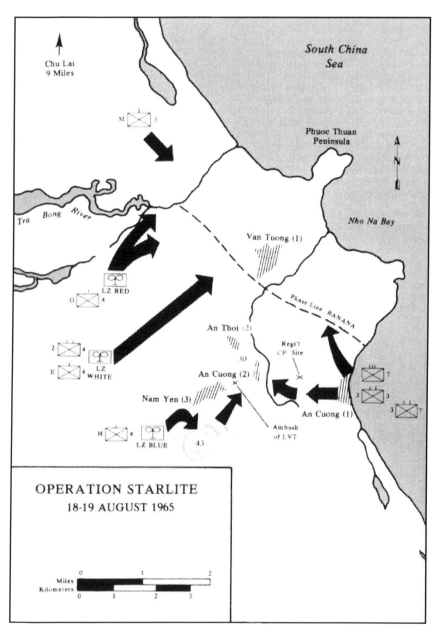

Picture 4.5
Map of Operation Starlite
[via Author]

Picture 4.6
Jungle-like terrain
[Author photo]

Picture 4.7
Bamboo whip
[via Author]

Picture 4.8
Burning hooch
[Author photo]

Picture 4.9
Living in tents in Chu Lai
[Author photo]

Picture 4.10
Walking to the beach to take a swim
[via Author]

Picture 4.11
Highway in Chu Lai
[via Author]

Picture 4.12
Recoilless rifle on Mule
[Author photo]

Chapter 5

Vietnam
Batangan Peninsula ... and More

WE had just completed a successful mission against the enemy in Chu Lai and An Cuong with Operation Starlite—The Battle for Chu Lai. The Viet Cong discovered that they could not defeat us Marines in a full stand-up battle. We had too much military power. In fact, many of these Viet Cong fighters escaped this encounter only to fight another day, elsewhere. As such, this offensive, likewise, forced the Viet Cong away from their bases along the coastline, where they had previously found sanctuary from their enemies. [140]

It was late August 1965. Now it was time to move further south down the coast. Once again, intelligence sources indicated that the rebels had retreated south to the Batangan Peninsula: a notorious Viet Cong iron grip. It was a place of entry for the seaborne infiltration of supplies for the Viet Cong forces in the area—and a horror for allied troops, or Cape Batangan (south of An Cuong but north of Quang Ngai), as can be seen on map 5.1. [141] This area was supposedly another stronghold for the Viet Minh (Vietnamese who fought the French, and forerunner of the Viet Cong), about seven miles south of Van Tuong.

On September 6, 1965, based on the success of Operation Starlite, General Walt planned to continue battering the 1st VC Regiment. Operation Piranha was another regimental-level amphibious-heliborne attack and a joint U.S.-Vietnamese assault on the Batangan Peninsula. A search and destroy follow-up to Operation Starlite, aimed at the remnants of the 1st VC Regiment. Its secondary purpose was to shut down reported places of entry for a VC network of seaborne infiltration. The battle began at 0555, H-hour (the specific hour at which an operation, usually an amphibious landing, is to begin) that day when eight A-4s strafed White Beach on the Batangan Peninsula's north shore for twenty minutes.

At 0635 the first wave of amphibious tractors carrying members of Companies A and C, 1st Battalion, 7th Marines, 1st Marine Division (1/7/1)—another infantry battalion, nicknamed *first of the first,* nosed onto the sand. Within twenty minutes the entire battalion was ashore. The enemy's response

---

[140] Harry G. Summers, Jr., *Historical Atlas of the Vietnam War,* p. 100, (Houghton Mifflin Company, 1995).

[141] Edward Doyle and Samuel Lipsman, *The Vietnam Experience–America Takes Over– 1965-67,* War Footing, p. 18, (Boston Publishing Company, 1982).

was a few badly aimed sniper rounds. The Marines quickly moved inland and established defensive positions. [142]

During Operation Piranha, our company was minimally involved and played a fairly insignificant role. Notwithstanding, we met with enemy resistance. Before we approached a hamlet, we did tell the villagers to evacuate quickly, as can be seen in picture 5.2. [143] To boot, we wanted the locals out of the way so they would not obstruct our field of fire. Nonetheless, not all the peasants heard or followed our call and some stayed in their thatched huts. Most of these provincials did not understand English, therefore, most of the local people did not heed our directions. Not surprisingly, we could not speak Vietnamese. As such, I am sorry to say, some of them paid the ultimate price of being caught between two fighting factions, as can be seen in picture 5.3. [144] Others, especially the women, would scream—loud. Panic-stricken, these inhabitants would run out of the flame and smoke. Sometimes, the livestock such as screeching chickens, yelping pigs and wailing water buffalo would go mad.

When Operation Piranha was over, the allied forces, including soldiers from the 4th ARVN Regiment, claimed another 183 VC killed; this total included 66 men found in a single cave. A VC fully equipped field hospital was also discovered by Marines from 1/7/1. Over 350 enemy or suspects were captured, as can be seen in picture 5.4 [145] with one prisoner taped up. A total of two Marines were killed, with another 14 wounded. I was, once again, spared from any bloodshed. Also, five ARVNs were killed in action and another thirty-three were wounded. Shortly thereafter, my unit headed back to that miserable and unforgiving flee-infested rest hole in Chu Lai. That God-forsaken place would become our rest and relaxation (R & R) grounds for a few more days.

Interestingly enough, General Walt, at the conclusion of Operation Piranha, explained:

> Damned if we do and damned if we don't. Trying to destroy the remainder of the Vietcong 1st Regiment after Operation Starlite, the Marines were met with the stony stares of villagers and the absence of guerrillas. Most of Piranha's 183 enemy killed in action came after the Marines had taken fire from one well-fortified bunker. Another 360

---

[142] Edward F. Murphy, *Semper Fi Vietnam*, p. 26, (Presidio Press, 1997).

[143] *Life–The Blunt Reality of War in Vietnam*, November 26, 1965, Volume 59, Number 22, p. 57, (Time Inc., 1965).

[144] Julene Fischer, *The Vietnam Experience–Images of War*, p. 57, (Boston Publishing Company, 1986).

[145] *Life–The Blunt Reality of War in Vietnam*, November 26, 1965, Volume 59, Number 22, p. 60, (Time Inc., 1965).

became prisoners of war. The victims turned out to be the seriously wounded VC survivors from the earlier Operation Starlite. [146]

In the eyes of the strategists, this particular battle was hardly a success. In spite of this, by questioning the local villagers, we quickly learned that the VC had fled the area several days before the operation even began. I was told that they returned as soon as we left the area. To this point, how could we win a war with this type of strategy? Answer—we could not! Conversely, had we taken on an enitrely different military approach. We could have ended the war within six months (or less). Essentially, had we integrated Sun Tzu's brilliant approach who was a military general, strategist, and tactician, wrote *The Art of War,* the undisputed masterpiece on the philosophy and strategy of combat. The Vietnam War, at least from my perception, could have been over with quickly. I say this, because and according to Tzu's work, this legendary general (circa 512 BC–for King Wu, where for almost two decades the armies of Wu were victorious over their hereditary enemies) stated that:

> War is a matter of life and death, a road either to safety or to ruin. Attack (the enemy) him where he is unprepared, appear where you are not expected, and these military devices, leading to victory, must not be divulged beforehand. And lastly, it is only one who is thoroughly acquainted with the evils of war that can thoroughly understand the profitable way of carrying it on. That is with rapidity. Only one who knows the disastrous effects of a long war can realize the supreme importance of rapidity in bringing it to a close. So, once war is declared, he will not waste precious time in waiting for reinforcements, nor will he turn his army back for fresh supplies, but crosses the enemy's frontier without delay. [147]

This type of tactic, where the Viet Cong return shortly after we leave a secure area, was typical during my fleeting tour of duty in Vietnam in the early phase of the war. They would take a few pot shots at us, wound and/or kill a small number of Marines at a time, and run like the dickens back to their rice-paddy farms and hamlets. There, they would, as peasant agrarians, attend to their crops and family. The Viet Cong were, as I have mentioned before, the farmers by day and enemy fighters by night. Unfortunately, we could not tell the difference. We, in turn, would go on patrol and try to seek them out. We would do this day after day, after day, after day! Going out on patrol, however, was, for the most part, well-orchestrated. Before going out on our watch where we would traverse through various small villages, we would have our briefing and orders, outlining our mission, describing, if pos-

---

[146] Edward Doyle and Samuel Lipsman, *The Vietnam Experience–America Takes Over–1965-67, Search and Destroy,* p. 63, (Boston Publishing Company, 1982).

[147] Sun Tzu, *The Art of War,* pp. 9-15, (Dodder and Stoughton Ltd., 1981).

sible, the weather and terrain, as well as analyzing enemy strength, location, and capabilities.

As unsuccessful as Operation Piranha was in the Batangan Peninsula, this general area would remain an enemy stronghold for many years to come. In fact, on March 16, 1968, two-and-a-half years after my arrival in this area (for Operation Starlite), and almost a year after Operation Oregon, came the site of the infamous and legendary My Lai Massacre—a visceral horror that is undeniable. The slaughter, which was later called "the most shocking episode of the Vietnam War," actually took place in two hamlets of Son My village in the Son Tinh District of the Quang Ngai Province. The villagers, who were getting ready for a market day, at first did not panic or run away, as they were herded into the hamlet's commons. Harry Stanley, a machine gunner from Charlie Company of the 1st Battalion, 20th Infantry Regiment, 11th Brigade of the 23rd (Americal) Infantry Division, said during the U.S. Army Criminal Investigation Division's (CID) inquiry that the killings started without warning. He first observed how a member of the 1st Platoon struck a Vietnamese man with a bayonet. Then, the same individual pushed another villager into a well and threw a grenade down. Further, he saw 15 or 20 people, mainly women and children, kneeling around a temple with burning incense, who were praying and crying. They were all killed by shots in the head. [148] Regrettably, this atrocity was led by 22-year-old Lieutenant William L. Calley, Jr., as can be seen in map [149] of My Lai (picture 5.5).

In the hamlet of My Lai (pronounced "me lie"), a village of about 700 inhabitants, south of Chu Lai, in Son My village, Quang Ngai Province, the Army's Charlie Company, 1st Battalion, 20th Infantry Regiment, 11th Brigade of the 23rd (Americal) Infantry Division conducted a heliborne assault to secure the area. The lieutenant, a platoon leader of that company, moved his men into the village and began rounding up Vietnamese civilians, old men, women, children, babies. Sadly, these villagers were then gunned down in cold blood.

This bloodbath and the physical destruction of My Lai was, inappropriately, not revealed to the American people until November 16, 1969, which can be seen in pictures 5.6 [150] and 5.7. [151] To say the least, the incident prompted global outrage.

What happened at My Lai only came to public light when a U.S. soldier, Paul D. Meadlo, was interviewed on television and admitted to killing "ten of fifteen men, women and children" at My Lai. His admission caused much

---

[148] *My Lai Massacre,* Wikipedia.
[149] Terrence Maitland and Stephen Weis, *The Vietnam Experience–Raising the Stakes, Into the Long Tunnel,* p. 66, (Boston Publishing Company, 1982).
[150] Nick Mills, *The Vietnam Experience–Combat Photographer,* p. 136, (Boston Publishing Company, 1983).
[151] Michael Casey, *The Vietnam Experience–The Army at War,* p. 175, (Boston Publishing Company, 1987).

shock and a great deal of pressure. As a result, the U.S. military launched an investigation. In fact, the U.S. military was already aware of the allegations and had launched an investigation in April 1969, some six months before the public was made aware of what had gone on. It soon became clear that many hundreds of villagers had been killed. The actual number killed was never established but it was officially noted as no less than 175 while it could have been as high as 504. The two most common figures regarding casualties are 347 and 504. The memorial at My Lai itself lists 504 names with ages that range from one to 82 years of age. An official U.S. army investigation came out with the figure of 347.

For his actions, Second Lieutenant William L. Calley, Jr., a former United States Army Officer (Company C, 1st Battalion, 20th Infantry Regiment, 11th Infantry Brigade, 23rd Infantry Division [Americal]), was court-martialed and found guilty of murdering 22 unarmed South Vietnamese civilians by other combat infantry veterans—supposedly his peers. Most of them had served in front-line combat in Vietnam. He was initially sentenced to life imprisonment with hard labor. After a lengthy review process in both military and civilian courts, his sentence was reduced to ten years. After serving part of his sentence, he was released on parole in 1974 and given a dishonorable discharge, which is a punitive discharge rather than an administrative discharge. Dishonorable discharges are handed down for what the military considers the most dishonorable of conduct. This type of discharge may be rendered only by conviction at a general court-martial for offenses such as desertion, rape, or murder, calling for dishonorable discharge as part of the sentence.

I was attending college when I heard about the carnage. I did not know what to expect from the public and my friends. Feelings about this occurrence ran high among combat infantry veterans of the Vietnam War. At the time, I was the social committee chairman for my local Vietnam Veterans Club in Santa Monica, California, where we talked about this slaughter with (more than) mixed feelings. A common reaction among college activists was that those who actually committed the inhumanities and the senior officers who covered up the affair merited the harshest discipline. That opinion, on the other hand, was not widely shared among those of us who had served in Vietnam.

Those students, who seemed to be on the left or liberal side of the political scale, theorized that the My Lai brutalities supported their charges that the Vietnam War was illegal, evil and certainly unfair. Many on the right of the political spectrum (conservatives) saw Lieutenant Calley as the human sacrifice of the anti-war movement in the United States.

So much for sharing some information about the My Lai incident. During my two days of involvement with Operation Piranha, I was quickly taken by helicopter to a converted aircraft carrier in the South China Sea. I, once again, boarded an old and rickety Sikorsky UH-34D medium helicopter. It was also known as a Sea Horse or Choctaw. With that usual deafening and overpowering roar (a sound that I have not forgotten), the helo took us airborne.

At that time, the helicopter, with a gross weight of 13,000 lbs., was the workhorse for the Marines in Vietnam. It was originally designed for general-purpose duties, but it was specifically intended for antisubmarine-warfare missions because it carried sophisticated sonar equipment that was utilized by the Navy. Its performance was unquestionably impressive. It could achieve speeds at almost 150 miles per hour and carry about 15 troops.

We used the Sikorsky UH-34D gunships, old reliables, mainly for assault missions, in which the movement of troops from ship to shore was easily and quickly accomplished. A pilot and co-pilot, sometimes called Peter Pilot, flew the helo. In the belly of the helicopter was a Marine gunner, armed with an M60 machine gun.

Once onboard the helo, my platoon headed directly for the South China Sea. Waiting for us off the coastline and in the Gulf of Tonkin, along with some other ships, was the USS Princeton, LPH stands for Landing Platform Helicopter or Commando Carrier. It was originally named the Valley Forge, a converted and modified 888-foot aircraft carrier (reclassified in 1959 as an amphibious assault ship) designed to transport Marine Corps troops and their thirty helicopter transports. This ship was part of a group of vessels of the Navy's Seventh Fleet Amphibious Ready Group. The USS Princeton was also part of the Essex class of ships, which was originally an escort carrier that was later reconstructed and converted so that they could transport helicopters exclusively for use by the Marine Corps [152] (as can be seen in picture 5.8. [153]). I arrived on the carrier about midday.

My squad was the first to land topside on the LPH. As we touched down on the deck and debarked from the helicopters, sailors escorted us to our living quarters. In this area was a series of four bunks, lined one on top of the other, where we spent the night. That evening, the ship steamed north to Da Nang.

This place was a floating paradise. We were in heaven. For the first time in a long time, we were able to take a nice long hot shower. More important, we could take a crap with peace of mind. Until now, we had to take a dump when the VC were not shooting at us. And when they did, we sometimes shit or peed in our pants. We gorged ourselves with a good old-fashioned hot meal in the ship's mess hall. Sadly, hot meals were not part of my regular diet on land. In fact, they came few and far between. I could only recall a few hot meals during my entire time in Vietnam—maybe two or three times at the most. We were also able to write to our loved ones. Most important, we were able to get a good night's sleep.

---

[152] Colonel H. Avery Chenoweth, USMCR (Retired), *Semper FI–The Definitive Illustrated History of the U.S. Marines*, p. 328, (Fall River Press, 2005).

[153] Jack Shulimson and Major Charles M. Johnson, USMC, *U.S. Marines in Vietnam–the Landing and the Buildup, 1965*, p. 195, (U.S. Government Printing Office, 1978).

Immediately after Operation Piranha was over, I participated in another skirmish with the VC. It was called Operation Rice Straw-Golden Fleece. This operation came about as a result of us trying to help preserve and protect the autumn harvesting of rice by the local farmers. But not all subsequent Golden Fleece operations, which happened each fall, proved successful. They were not always triumphant because every now and then ARVN troops pilfered from the crop they were assigned to protect. The technique became a standard component of military operations conducted at harvest time for the Vietnamese farmers.

On September 10, 1965, the beginning of the monsoon season, our unit, already aboard the LPH Princeton, was sent to the Da Nang area. At first, the showers fell only at night and in the early morning, heavy rains carried by winds that came off the sea and out of the mountains. As time went on, it seemed like it rained non-stop. They did not blow away in a day or so. Monsoon rains are robust, constant, and oppressive. Meanwhile, our encounter with the Viet Cong was supposed to last about five days yet it continued through the end of October 1965.

> With the dispatch for which Marines have become known as the *First to Fight* in several wars, 3rd Battalion, 3rd Marines picked up and moved to the Da Nang area rapidly by fixed-wing aircraft and helicopters. Orders came at 1145 on September 10th. Movement commenced at 1231, and the first units became airborne at 1325. The entire battalion was in place in its assigned position by 1800 the same day.
>
> An hour and five minutes later, a Marine from Lima Company was killed when he stepped on a 155-mm howitzer shell rigged as a mine. The United States inadvertently supplied such weapons to the enemy. The dud rate for artillery rounds was two percent and five percent for bombs dropped from aircraft, providing the enemy with hundreds of tons of explosives monthly. [154]

On September 11th, at about 0600, L-hour (landing hour—the hour at which a helicopter landing operation is to begin) Operation Rice Straw-Golden Fleece, south of Da Nang, in the Quang Nam Province, began. My squad was the first group to assemble and get into the helos that were waiting for us on the deck of the LPH. It was raining fairly hard at the time, and I was already soaked. I sensed it was not going to be a pleasant day. Our group lifted off the flight deck of the USS Princeton; as we moved away from the aircraft carrier, we could immediately tell we were in deep trouble!

The gunner sitting next to me with his M60 machine gun at the ready, received a distress message from the pilot. He, as quickly as he could, voiced

---

[154] Otto J. Lehrack, *No Shining Armor–The Marines at War in Vietnam,* pp. 53-54, (University Press of Kansas, 1992).

to us, very loudly, we were too heavy and that we had to unload some of our gear. While we did not want to discharge our stuff, we had no choice. We threw out our extra ammunition. Otherwise, we were headed smack dab into the ocean. As a matter of fact, our helicopter was taking in lots of water as we were trying to unload some of the extra weight. Naturally, we were all scared. One of the other Marines in the helo could not swim. He almost panicked. I could tell that he was definitely terrified. Since the aircraft carrier was still close by, we did not know what to do in the event we had to bail from the helicopter. I am telling you, we were all quite tense. If truth be told, we were looking at each other with a real sense of uneasiness. We were all very worried. In my case, my buttocks puckered up like there was no tomorrow. After what seemed like an eternity, but which only took a couple of minutes, the helicopter was able to lift off the ocean surface. Nonetheless, we certainly did not want to go through this anxious and on-edge experience a second time.

We then headed directly for Hill 55 in Quang Nam, another site of heavy fighting.. Notable battles and operations included Operation Chinook 1966–1967, the Battle of Hill 488, Operation Swift, Operation Wheeler/Wallowa, Operation Union I & II, the Hue–Da Nang Campaign, the Ha My massacre and the Phong Nhị and Phong Nhat massacre.) In the meantime, the first wave of amtracs carrying more Marines headed for the area as well. They quickly established a defensive position. Other warriors swooped in from the north.

Just as the helicopter that I rode in on landed on this hill, all hell broke loose. The engine of the helo was revving up with such intensity. The roar of the engine was all around us. It was deafening. The gunner of the UH-34 was extremely nervous. Meanwhile, my butt, once again, was puckered tight indicating the intensity I felt. The pilot, nevertheless, landed the helo in an open area landing zone (LZ) with the nose up and the tail leaning down, as can be seen in picture 5.9. [155] Sniper fire was constant. During this time, Lieutenant Colonel Joseph Eugene Muir, from Meadow Bridge, West Virginia, Commander of the 3rd Battalion, 3rd Marines, 3rd Marine Division (3/3/3), and his group were on another side of the hill. After the command post was established, the Colonel (a Navy Cross recipient from the previous operation—Operation Starlite/Battle of Chu Lai) and his staff, who were heading back to the command post, stepped on a buried booby-trapped and hostile 155-mm artillery shell. As told by Captain David A. Ramsey: "I ran over there to see what had happened and the colonel had been killed. Both of his legs were gone, most of both arms ... actually, he was gone from about the rib cage down. And there was absolutely no possibility of him being alive." [156] Colonel Muir was killed immediately and so was his radio operator, Private First Class

---

[155] Michael Casey, *The Vietnam Experience–Flags Into Battle,* p. 77, (Boston Publishing Company, 1987).

[156] Otto J. Lehrack, *No Shining Armor–The Marines at War in Vietnam,* p. 54, (University Press of Kansas, 1992).

Paul W. Mansir, from Fort Worth, Texas. Company Commander Captain J. A. Doub was badly wounded and lost one of his eyes.

Captain Ramsey then talked about radio operator Mansir: "Another radioman ... I remember him because he was a tall, good-looking guy with a good personality. He had been my radioman at one time or another. And I liked the guy. And now, one leg, part of another leg, his genitals, and part of the arm was gone. He also had a bad laceration across his forehead, which ... was producing a lot of blood, running down into his eyes. But he thought that was his only wound and he was asking the corpsman, "Will it leave a scar?" He was good-looking and he knew it. But he wasn't aware of the way he'd been mutilated." [157]

In the interim, we were trying to set up a base perimeter as other helos would roll in with more Marines. (As a side note, I understand that Morley Safer was embedded with us [again].) Once that was accomplished, we moved forward into other hamlets around the province. The sniper fire did not let up. It was constant. It was also a *hit-and-run* type of attack by the VC, and they were awfully good at it. Corporal Tony Pascal, one of our squad leaders, was in the point position—the first man in front of a column. It is definitely the most frightening and nerve-racking job of a Marine. I was the slack man, or second man in the patrol. As I was heading directly to the nearest hamlet, Corporal Pascal let out a violent scream. He had just stepped on a booby-trapped punji stake. The razor-sharp bamboo picket went right through his boot, and we could tell that he was really in pain. Yet, I asked him to be quiet because we did not know how close the VC was from our position. However, I knew they were close. To make matters worse, we could not evacuate him. The terrain was too thick for a helicopter to land. So we had him lean on a couple of us as we moved away from the site. With the temperature easily exceeding 100 degrees, and humidity at least 95 percent, it was definitely inhospitable weather for a firefight; and, unfortunately, we already had a wounded warrior on our hands.

We moved at a snail's pace, but we finally broke through to an opening. Meanwhile, our radioman, who was expressive as he had to be, smart and well-informed about the nature of the skirmish, called for a dust-off. This is the radio call-sign for a helicopter medical evacuation. For now, a corpsman attended to the corporal's wound. We later put the squad leader in the helo. I never saw this gung-ho and brave warrior again.

So there we were in the thick of things. Our battalion commanding officer and his radioman, carrying his PRC-25, had been killed, and we had little ammunition very few bullets because we had to dump our extra rounds into the Gulf of Tonkin. What the hell were we going to do? Besides, the VC were shooting at us from the tree line less than 100 yards away. It was not a pleasant time. Only one thing was for sure: we were not going to retreat.

---

[157] Ibid, p. 55.

To best explain our state of mind as well as our outlook at that time, and according to Marine Corps lore, *Tell it to the Marines–Retreat Hell. We just got here:*

Fighting spirit and determination against heavy odds is a sound tradition in the Marine Corps and nowhere is there a more graphic illustration than an incident which occurred in World War I. Legendary or true, it personifies the aggressive attitude of Marines.

The occasion was the third great German breakthrough of 1918, when the 4th Marine Brigade and its parent 2nd Infantry Division were thrown in to help stem the tide in Belleau Wood sector. The 2nd battalion, 5th Marines, had arrived at its position when an automobile skidded to a stop and a French officer dashed out and approached the commanding officer. He explained that a general retreat was in progress and that orders were for the Marines to withdraw. The Marine officer exclaimed in amazement, "Retreat Hell! We just got here."

And the Marines proceeded to prove their point. The battalion deployed and took up firing positions. As the Germans approached, they came under rifle fire, which was accurate at ranges beyond their comprehension. Not in vain had the Marine Corps long stressed in its training the sound principles of marksmanship. The deadly fire took the heart out of the German troops and the attack was stopped.

Back at the skirmish, once there were enough Marines around us, we were able to secure the area. Completing that task, we then headed out to look for the VC. Again, we were not about to back away. Our job was to simply to search and destroy the enemy. We did just that over the next four days, taking prisoners along the way, as can be seen in picture 5.10. [158] As can be seen in picture 5.11, [159] Marines from Delta Company, 1st Battalion, 9th Marines, 3rd Marine Division (1/9/3), my old unit, surveyed the corpses of three Viet Cong guerrillas.

Upon securing this area, which took several days, we were immediately sent to the southern part of Da Nang called Marble Mountain (a unique, domelike rock outcropping where the main Marine helicopter squadrons were located). It is a cluster of five marble and limestone hills located in Ngu Hanh Son ward, south of Da Nang that stretches from the coast inland or westward. On the one hand, our job was to provide security for the Vietnamese villagers who were harvesting their rice. On the other hand, the Viet Cong were there, too, taxing and killing the farmers for the same food.

---

[158] Jack Shulimson and Major Charles M. Johnson, USMC, *U.S. Marines in Vietnam– the Landing and the Buildup 1965*, p. 139, (U.S. Government Printing Office, 1978).

[159] Stephen Weiss, *The Vietnam Experience–A War Remembered*, p. 31, (Boston Publishing Company, 1986).

VIETNAM: MY WAR

While on patrol for about one-half a mile at the base of the mountain, we were walking across a rice paddy dike when we saw a Vietnamese woman standing in front of her hooch. The rice field was off to her right. It appeared as if she was smiling, but she was not. With both hands clasped behind her, she was grinning at us with betel-nut juice in her teeth and she was holding a small machine gun. As we crossed her path, some 75 feet away, she opened fire on us. All hell broke loose in the next few minutes. We did all we could to destroy everything in sight, and we did it fast! We were so pissed off that we left nothing standing. I mean, we obliterated everything in our direct view with our rifles and machine guns.

Lucky for us, no one was injured. Chalk up one kill, which I felt was more than appropriate, for the good guys. I guess we, along with other grunts, killed several Viet Cong rice-extortion parties on several occasions around the area. It was becoming the norm.

As we continued to intervene with offensive combat operations, one right after another, and as the war started to enter a new phase, one U.S. soldier acknowledged it so eloquently: "Making do with a bad situation is what it was all about. You get young kids, throw them into general chaos, they make do with it. You get stable right away, or you do not make it at all." [160]

For the month of October, following three major operations, the Viet Cong decided to back off direct attacks on Marine positions. They decided not to meet us head-on in a confrontational manner. However, many units within our battalion, including my company, would continue to mount more than a half-dozen smaller size operations. On a daily basis, we continued through the patrol process to seek out VC enclaves and hiding places. As was expected, our job was to turn over every rock, uncover every hiding place, and crawl in every cave. And that we did albeit very carefully. When we found the VC, we would quickly gather them up, blindfold them, tape their mouths shut, transport them to another location, and interrogate them through ARVN interpreters, as can be seen in pictures 5.12 & 5.13. [161]

Our counterpart, the ARVN soldier, usually was not nearly as considerate as we were. We, too, were not that compassionate toward the Viet Cong. Because we could not speak Vietnamese, the ARVN did take advantage of their ability to communicate with the VC, verbally and non-verbally. It would not be unusual for a Vietnamese soldier to thrust the butt of his weapon hard in the Viet Cong's face, knocking out some of his teeth or breaking his nose along the way. And if the VC did not respond, the South Vietnamese soldier would kick him in the testicles as hard as he could while he was tied up. He would repeat this at least three or four times, maybe more.

---

[160] Harry G. Summers, Jr., *Historical Atlas of the Vietnam War*, p. 98, (Houghton Mifflin Company, 1995).

[161] *Life–The Blunt Reality of War in Vietnam*, November 26, 1965, Volume 59, Number 22, Cover Page, (*Time* Inc., 1965).

If the suspected Viet Cong was a female, sometimes the South Vietnamese soldier would submerge her in the water, one form of waterboarding. They might even cut her face with their knives, as can be seen in pictures 5.14 [162] & 5.15. [163] You see, the ARVNs, like us, hated the VC. They reviled what these people stood for. They considered them social outcasts, the pariahs of their peasant society. A Vietnamese soldier could get away with things we would never do—and we never did. They did not care about the results of their actions. Whenever possible, they tormented and even tortured the Viet Cong, sometimes to death.

What makes this story a little more interesting and close to my heart is that I was in charge of these VC during the evening we captured them. They were hiding in one of the huts in one of the hamlets we patrolled. As usual, it was raining hard the evening we captured three scrawny combatants. That night, I was assigned guard duty of the prisoners for about four hours. For whatever reason, my rear left leg cramped while I was on watch that night. My left calf muscle bubbled like a watermelon. It was as hard as a rock, or it seemed like it. I was really in agony and sweating heavily. My leg was so cramped that I could hardly move. To this day, I cannot remember being that confined. To make matters worse, I really did not know what to do; but I did not want to wake up a fellow Marine. The closest Marine was about twenty feet away. Sleep was a precious commodity. All of us wanted to take advantage of a snooze whenever we could since we slept only for short periods of time, especially when we were out on night patrol. So I pulled out my .45 caliber handgun and waved my hand at one of the apprehended VC. By the way, they were all firmly tied up. Through hand signals, I expressed to one of them to come to me. He did, and I untied him. Then, I placed his hands on the cramped portion of my leg. I could tell that he knew immediately and exactly what was wrong with me. I indicated to him, through hand gestures again, to rub my leg. He did so while I kept my fully-loaded gun pointed directly at his head. Rubbing my leg definitely helped relieve my cramps. Despite the risk involved, which I did not worry about it at the time, I elected to take this action so that my fellow grunts could catch some much needed shuteye for a few hours.

I did what I had to do. It was no big deal. Every time my left leg cramps up, which still happens to this day (probably because of the medication I take), I think about this incident that happened five decades ago. It is strange how vividly I remember this one particular incident.

As a result of our search and destroy actions and snooping out the enemy whenever we could, we honestly thought the Viet Cong would give up. We thought we had overpowered the enemy to the point where they did not have any fighting energy left. Boy, were we so very wrong! The VC, in fact, did

---

[162] Horst Faas and Tim Page, *REQUIEM–By the Photographers Who Died in Vietnam and Indochina*, p. 116, Random House, 1997).

[163] Ibid, p. 117.

not remain idle for long. In late October, they hit both the newly completed Marble Mountain helicopter facility near Da Nang and, once again, the Chu Lai Air Base. All of these mountains had cave entrances and numerous tunnels. And Chu Lai was a place that we secured only two months earlier through Operation Starlite.

Edward F. Murphy, in his book, *Semper Fi Vietnam*, tells us more about what happened at the Chu Lai airfield and Marble Mountain:

> At Chu Lai about twenty VC sappers infiltrated the base. The first hint the Marines had of trouble was when an aircraft blew up. In the fire's light, sentries caught ghostly glimpses of the loincloth-clad sappers running between the planes, spraying them with machine-gun fire and throwing satchel charges. The sentries tracked them down and killed fifteen of the sappers, but not before two jets were destroyed and six more were severely damaged.
>
> The Viet Cong attack at Marble Mountain was bigger, better organized, and more destructive. Some ninety VC attacked the base under a barrage of mortar fire. As at Chu Lai, the attack caught the airfield defenders by surprise. The sappers raced across the tarmac, tossing explosive charges at the neatly parked helicopters. Firing automatic weapons at the sentries, the sappers finally withdrew after a thirty-minute rampage. They left behind seventeen of their own dead and four wounded plus nineteen destroyed helicopters, eleven severely damaged craft, and another twenty that were badly damaged. Three Marines died and ninety-one were wounded in the attack. [164]

As you can tell, the VC assaults on Marine positions proved that they were the ones who chose when, where and how the war intensified. Unfortunately, the brilliant strategy by our opponents would last for *ten more years*.

By the way, during this month, I finally received replacement military utilities. These were quick drying coats and trousers made of tightly woven, rip-stop or twill cotton poplin fabric. They provided good protection against the sun, insects, and other tropical hazards. The loosely fitted garments provided ventilation and moisture dissipation. The coat was worn outside of the trousers and the trousers were bloused into the boots. Jacket sleeves were rolled up or cut off. Under authorization CGFMPac-msg-160300Z, whatever this code meant, I needed these new uniforms. Believe me, I really needed the new shirts. My old ones plumb wore out.

During this same month, the United States Defense Department ordered a military draft call for 45,224 men for the month of December, the largest quota of men drafted, many against their own wishes, since the Korean War

---

[164] Edward F. Murphy, *Semper Fi Vietnam*, pp. 29-30, (Presidio Press, 1997).

in 1950. [165] The Defense Department also reported that casualty losses by the Viet Cong were 25,000 killed in action while 830 U.S. military personnel were killed in combat in South Vietnam from January to October 18, 1965. [166]

---

[165] Leo Daugherty, *The Vietnam War–Day by Day*, p. 58, (Chartwell Books, Inc., 2011).

[166] Ibid, p. 58.

Picture 5.1
Map of Batangan
[via Author]

Picture 5.2
Marine tell Vietnamese to evacuate
[via Author]

Picture 5.3
Vietnamese carrying children
[via Author]

Picture 5.4
VC captured
[via Author]

VIETNAM: MY WAR

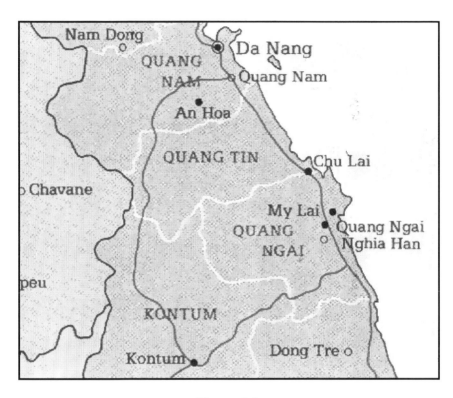

Picture 5.5
Map of My Lai
[via Author]

Picture 5.6
Burning My Lai
[via Author]

Picture 5.7
My Lai massacre
[via Author]

Picture 5.8
LPH *Princeton*
[via Author]

Picture 5.9
Helicopters letting off troops
[via Author]

Picture 5.10
Taking prisoner
[via Author]

Picture 5.11
Golden Fleece capture of VC
[via Author]

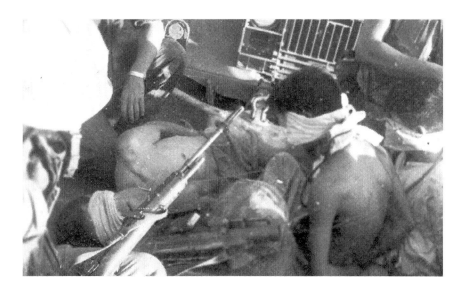

Picture 5.12
Prisoners on a truck
[Author photo]

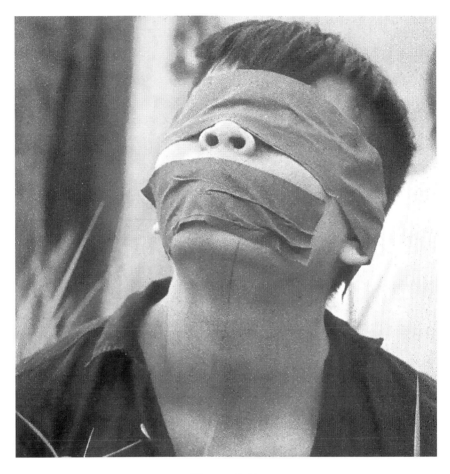

Picture 5.13
Prisoner taped up
[via Author]

Picture 5.14
VC woman in water
[via Author]

Picture 5.15
Interrogation of VC woman
[via Author]

Chapter 6

Vietnam
Que Son Valley

FOR the most part, it appeared to me that one combat operation against the Viet Cong and/or NVA was no different from another. One skirmish was like the next scuffle, and it all looked the same. Battle after battle, we either made an amphibious landing or we were trucked to the outskirts of a village, brought in by amtracs or were flown in by Marine helicopters. Regardless of the transportation method, we would almost always land on the outskirts of a hamlet. Soon after arriving at a so-called VC stronghold, we would establish a baseline perimeter around the village. When we had Vietnamese interpreters with us, which we did numerous times, they instructed the villagers to form a group and move to a centralized or staging location outside of their living quarters. Once the Vietnamese people moved away from their huts and enclave, we would come in with fire teams to search for the enemy. Almost always, VC snipers met us with resistance. [167]

We knew our opponents as raggedy-looking individuals. They were small and always very slim. They were barefooted sometimes, however, they wore Ho Chi Minh sandals, usually poorly armed, but not always. However, they were as determined as us Marines. They were evasive and slippery, sly and untiring, crafty as well as deceitful. Of course, they could and often did kill. Furthermore, I personally felt they enjoyed engaging a small group of warrior units like ours.

The VC fought in small bands and many times they fought alone. When wounded or killed, a VC could expect to be deserted by his cohorts if we were nearby. So much for watching out for their buddies! So much for the concept of *esprit de corps!*

Now we were in the heart of the Quang Tin Province, as can be seen in the map [168] (picture 6.1). The Quang Tin region is directly between Da Nang and Chu Lai. Bordered on the north and south by rugged mountains, the Que Son Valley—in the southern part of South Vietnam's I Corps—was fertile lowlands with lots of agricultural fields or rice paddies, as can be seen in picture 6.2. At times, these paddies were magnificent-looking bright green speckled with the browner green of the palm orchards protecting the villages.

---

[167] Jack Shulimson and Major Charles M. Johnson, USMC, *U.S. Marines in Vietnam–the Landing and the Buildup 1965*, p. 109, (U.S. Government Printing Office, 1978).

[168] Terrence Maitland and Stephen Weis, *The Vietnam Experience–Raising the Stakes*, Into the Long Tunnel, p. 66, (Boston Publishing Company, 1982).

It had been relatively quiet for the past couple of weeks. We did go out on patrol almost every day, but our encounters with the Viet Cong were minimal until a revitalized VC group was headed our way. The Que Son Valley (populous and rice-rich, the valley was viewed as one of the keys to controlling South Vietnam's five northern provinces)—is located along the border of Quang Nam and Quang Tin provinces and was considered strategically important to our Armed Forces in this part of Vietnam.

According to Professor Andrew A. Wiest, founding director of the Center for the Study of War and Society at the University of Southern Mississippi, stated that by late 1965, the United States military mission had broadened considerably, allowing for offensive operations to find, fix and finish the communists by locating and destroying their major troop concentrations (from North to South Vietnam). On the other hand, and in consideration of this, U.S. military planners at MACV decided to turn their attention (away from our area–I Corps) to the Mekong Delta (IV Corps), where the U.S. Army (7th, 9th, and 21st Divisions) and the South Vietnamese Armed Forces were stationed. While some of this area was considered "pacified," others were under nearly complete VC rule. In fact, the Viet Cong enjoyed open control of 24.6% of the delta, enough to choke off the critical flow of rice to the markets of Saigon. [169]

In early December 1965, during the height of the monsoon season, a weather system where heavy rains blown by winds that came off the sea and out of the mountains that few Americans had ever withstood, leaving us unendingly soaked to the bone, Marines were either airlifted by helicopters or brought into the Que Son Valley by amphibious vehicles. My group was in the amphibious group. Incidentally, a monsoon is a wind pattern that reverses direction with the seasons. The term was originally applied to seasonal winds in the Indian Ocean and Arabian Sea. The word is also used more specifically for the season in which this wind blows from the southwest and adjacent areas that is characterized by very heavy rainfall, and especially, for the rainfall associated with this wind.

Once again, we (3rd Marines, along with the 7th Marines), were engaged in another battle. This one was called Harvest Moon; yet another American search-and-clear operation that was specifically intended to find and attack VC units in the Phuoc Ha Valley, a jungle covered with hills and valleys, a communist base area midway between the Chu Lai enclave and Da Nang. The attack on the VC (I believe elements of the 60th and 80th Viet Cong Battalions) was supported by A-4 Skyhawks and F-4 Phantoms, which would drop bombs on the VC and North Vietnamese Army positions. In addition, our unit would provide further support to the South Vietnamese Army who also assisted us with this operation.

---

[169] Andrew Wiest, *The Boys of '67–Charlie Company's War in Vietnam*, p. 26, (Osprey Publishing, 2012).

The North Vietnamese Army, some of who we faced in Operation Starlite four months earlier, and possibly the Battle for the Ia Drang Valley, was dug into the nearby foothills. From the beginning, they had achieved a secure foothold in the area. For a while, they were safe. They were, for the most part, out of harm's way because this was during the monsoon season, thus allowing the enemy freedom of movement without being observed from the air. Unrelenting fighting raged on. With the help of constant close air support and the support of the South Vietnamese soldiers, we were able to take over a small area that was less than a one-square mile region.

Nonetheless, close air support took its toll. During the heat of battle, as the VC pinned us down, one of our radio telephone operators called in for a bomb run. It was called a TACAIR, or tactical air support. I could hear the radioman, with his PRC-25 (the major field radio of the Vietnam War), trying to guide the lead Phantom jet in for a bomb run. The "PRC" meant it was a portable radio, "25" meant it was the twenty-fifth one the military had standardized. It was inevitably referred to as a "Prick Twenty-Five" or "Prick" for short. The PRC-25 was about the size and weight of a case of soda. He gave the navigator of this air strike team our grid coordinates. Grid coordinates are divided into one-kilometer squares (that is, each side of a square is six-tenths of a mile). In other words he gave the go-ahead for bombs to be dropped precisely around and immediately in front of our own positions. This was worse than absurd because bombs were dropped within 75–100 feet or closer of where we were dug in. We did not know what to do. Even so, we were panicked. I could hear the noise of the bomb fragments wiz right by me. It was an unnerving sound. To say the least, it was a menacing time. We were jumpy and very worried. We could not move, and neither could our opponents.

As the jets screamed in for the bomb drop, one of our guys would shoot a *Willie Pete* (white phosphorous, also called smoke rounds) in the direction of the enemy to guide the jets toward enemy lines. Then came the jets. The sound of the aircraft flying close to the ground in excess of 450 miles per hour was deafening. We could also hear whistling sounds as they dropped those 250-pound bombs. We were all shaken up as they hit the ground and exploded all around us. It was like being hit by thunder, one vociferous boom after another. As mentioned, we could hear the whistling sound of the shrapnel from the bombs fly by our heads. Metal fragments were soaring everywhere. I could feel the heat of the shards as they flew by my face. We were terrified to the core. One large piece of shrapnel missed me by inches. We all thought we were goners.

As a result of bombs constantly exploding so close to us, along with so many other piercing and intense sounds to the ears, I was eventually awarded, by the Department of Veterans Affairs, a ten percent service-connected disability rating. It is called tinnitus. Tinnitus can be perceived in one or both ears or in the head. It is usually described as a ringing noise, but in some patients it takes the form of a high pitched whining, buzzing, hissing, humming, or whistling sound. It has also been described as a "whooshing" sound, as of wind or waves. Tinnitus can be sporadic or it can be continuous. In my case, it is intermittent.

As it turned out, only one warrior took a direct hit. We were lucky, but the VC was not. When all was said and done, the bombs took a toll on the enemy. Although I do not know the exact count, many VC lay dead around us.

We were finally able to establish a night defensive perimeter. The next day, two more Marine battalions advanced toward each other, squeezing the Viet Cong between them.

Operation Harvest Moon, which started in early December 1965, geared up to rescue the ARVN 1st Battalion, 5th Regiment from a severe firefight north of Chu Lai, [170] that was overrun by the VC. This operation lasted for almost two weeks. Monsoon rains, unluckily, dogged the battle, and our pace was dismally slow.

Our adversaries did not give up; they kept coming back for more and more. They were tenacious and unmerciful fighters. In one incident, they hit the South Vietnamese Army with a fierce and close counterattack that killed many South Vietnamese soldiers. As soon as we learned of the South Vietnamese troops' situation and demise, we moved in for the kill. Helicopters picked us up and rushed us in for the attack. My squad joined up with one of the South Vietnamese Army groups. As we were all moving forward together as a unit, I could tell how afraid the South Vietnamese regulars were. They were poorly trained and downright scared. Sad to say, they were not much help to us during this skirmish. As soon as we were attacked, the South Vietnamese soldiers did not want to move forward. They wanted to stay right where they were—behind us. That was not our style. Even if we came under attack, our job was to advance and take the enemy out (at any cost). Again, the VC were dug in. We could not overrun them. So we called in for more artillery and air strikes. With enough might, we were able to drive the enemy away. However, this was costly.

The next day, December 19th, all three Marine Battalions completed their movement for all practical purposes the operation was over, Harvest Moon (Lien Ket 18) officially ended on December 20th. The USMC-ARVN Operation accounted for 407 enemies killed and 33 captured, while 45 Marines were killed and 218 wounded. General Lam's ARVN suffered 90 killed, while 91 went missing, and 141 wounded, most occurring during the first two days. Despite poor weather conditions air power played a major role and the Marines learned valuable lessons in air-ground coordination for future operations.

Even though Operation Harvest Moon officially ended on December 20, 1965, and was considered the last major Marine operation for that year, President Johnson and his top aides met to decide the future course of action of the

---

[170] Colonel H. Avery Chenoweth, USMCR (Retired), *Semper Fi–The Definitive Illustrated History of the U.S. Marines,* p. 345, (Fall River Press, 2005).

Vietnam War. This was just after Defense Sectary McNamara, who briefly visited South Vietnam, warned the President that American casualty rates of up to 1,000 dead per month could be expected.

Despite poor weather conditions during this battle, air power played a major role while the Marines learned valuable lessons in air-to-ground coordination for future operations. During this same month and throughout Operation Harvest Moon, the communists greatly increased their infiltration along the Ho Chi Minh Trail. This took place despite the extensive bombing that took place along the Trail. Given this knowledge, our military commanders continued to concentrate airpower upon a small segment of the Trail closest to South Vietnam that was used most extensively by the enemy. As a result, covert Operation "Tiger Hound" was initiated in December 1965, utilizing aircraft from the Air Force, Army, Navy, Marines, the NVAF, and the Royal Laotian Air Force. On December 11th, strategic B-52s were also called in to this tactical operation, with their first use over Laos. [171] The purpose of this operation was to interdict the flow of supplies to the People's Army of Vietnam (PAVN) on the Ho Chi Minh Trail. This was the Truong Son Strategic Supply Route to the North Vietnamese from the Democratic Republic of Vietnam (North Vietnam), through southeastern Laos, and into the northern provinces of the Republic of Vietnam (South Vietnam). The missions were originally controlled by the 2nd Air Division until that headquarters was superseded by the 7th Air Force on April 1, 1966. [172]

In-country for barely two weeks, and immediately involved with Operation Harvest Moon, artillery forward observer First Lieutenant Harvey C. Barnum, Jr. assumed command of Hotel (H) Company, 2nd Battalion, 9th Marines, 3rd Marine Division (2/9/3), still another infantry battalion that was originally formed in World War I, nicknamed *"Hell in a Helmet,"* during a Viet Cong ambush.

As told later by Colonel Barnum, U.S. Marine Corps (retired):

> As 1965 came to a close, the 1st Viet Cong (VC) Regiment, which had suffered a resounding defeat at the hands of the U.S. Marines during Operation Starlite in August, was back in the picture. In late November, the enemy unit attacked the Army of the Republic of Vietnam (ARVN) outpost at Hiep Duc, twenty-five miles west of Tam Ky. (At this same time—November 30th, pacifists demonstrated against the war directly in front of the White House. [173]) By occupying this key position, the communists had a clear road to the Nui Loc Son Basin, also called the Que Son Valley, in I Corps' Quang Tin province. Abundant in farms and heavily populated, the valley was

---

[171] *Laotian Civil War, December 11, 1965,* Wikipedia.

[172] *Operation Tiger Hound,* Wikipedia.

[173] Leo Daugherty, *The Vietnam War–Day by Day,* p. 63, (Chartwell Books, Inc., 2011).

considered an extremely important area, situated as it was between the major South Vietnamese cities of Da Nang and Chu Lai. The monsoon season provided excellent cover to the VC units attempting to occupy that vital region.

Walt was justifiably concerned about the rising Communist threat to Que Son, and the burly Marine commander conferred with ARVN Maj. Gen. Nguyen Chanh Thi about the next course of action. The pair concluded that action must be taken to drive the VC from this rich farming area. As a result, Operation Harvest Moon/ Lien Ket 18 was initiated. Marine and ARVN units immediately went on the offensive to quell the enemy drive into the Que Son Valley. On December 18, Lieutenant Colonel Leon N. Utter's 2nd Battalion, 7th Marines (2/7), ran headlong into the 80th VC Battalion. As the Marines trudged through extremely rugged terrain, consisting of flooded rice paddies and jungle-covered hills, the enemy hit the rear and flanks of the column.

At the rear of the column was Hotel Company, 2nd Battalion, 9th Marines (2/9), which had been attached to Lieutenant Colonel Leon Utter's battalion for the operation. When both the company commander and his radio operator were killed, the artillery forward observer (FO), Lieutenant Harvey Barnum, Jr., on temporary duty in Vietnam from the Marine Barracks at Pearl Harbor, took command. After hours of intense combat, Barnum and his Marines successfully broke contact and joined the remainder of their unit in the village of Ky Phu. For his heroic actions on that day, Barnum was awarded the Medal of Honor, becoming the fourth Marine to receive our nation's highest military decoration during the Vietnam conflict.

According to Jack Shulimson and Major Charles M. Johnson, USMC (who served two tours of duty in Vietnam), Operation Harvest Moon was not without its problems:

> The hastily established provisional headquarters, the fast moving ground situation, poor weather conditions, and the large number of tactical aircraft operating over the Que Son Valley caused coordination and control difficulties. Colonel Leslie E. Brown, who had relieved Colonel John D. Noble as commander of MAG-12, believed that better advance planning prior to the operation could have alleviated some of the problems encountered by his pilots. His group operated throughout Harvest Moon with practically no coordination with support units except that which was accomplished in the air over the target area. [174]

---

[174] Jack Shulimson and Major Charles M. Johnson, USMC, *U.S. Marines in Vietnam– the Landing and the Buildup 1965*, p. 110, (U.S. Government Printing Office, 1978).

As 1965 came to a close, Ho Chi Minh and the North Vietnamese leadership ordered a change in a way the war was to be fought. From then on, the Viet Cong would avoid pitched battles with the Americans unless the odds were clearly in their favor. There would be more hit and run attacks and ambushes. To counter the American build-up, Viet Cong recruitment would be stepped up and more regular North Vietnamese Army troops would be infiltrated into South Vietnam. Also, as American air strikes against North Vietnam began in 1965, and, again, in July 1966, Ho Chi Minh sent a message to the country's people that *"nothing is as dear to the heart of the Vietnamese as independence and liberation."* This became the motto of the North Vietnamese cause.

Meanwhile, Edward F. Murphy, in his report, *Semper Fi Vietnam*, shares with us what Marine Corps policy was like in Vietnam:

> The Marines were becoming experienced combat veterans, adept at fighting the determined foe. Unfortunately, the Marine Corps' policy of rotating its troops out of the war zone after a thirteen-month tour, assuming they had survived death or serious injury, meant that many of the lessons learned in the early days were doomed to be relearned over and over again as the years passed. [175]

Although we may have been so-called experienced combat veterans, with six months of fighting under our belt, some of our replacements were not. Like me six months ago, these guys were now the FNGs. Just before Operation Harvest Moon, our company commander, was a new, young, totally inexperienced officer merely out of his duty station in Quantico, Virginia. His recruit training at Camp Lejeune, North Carolina, made our squad go out on a patrol in the height of the rainy season. That, alone, made no sense to us more seasoned combat veterans. Supposedly a combat officer, he wanted to show us his true colors and that he did. Naturally, he had to tag along with us. After spending about four hours out in the miserable stormy weather, soaked to the bone on his first patrol, I think the lieutenant got the hint. We did not go out on patrol again in monsoon type of weather.

We went around the same village at least twice, but our company commander did not realize it. I went up to the officer and told him that we had walked around the same village a second time. At first, he had a hard time accepting what he did. Keep in mind that he was totally unfamiliar with Vietnam and its conditions, and I do not think he knew what he was getting into. Although not completely experienced, we certainly were a lot worldlier about Vietnam than he was. From that day on he listened more to his front-line men, and he did not try to pull his rank on the troops. He, too, quickly became one of us. With this in mind, Mark A. Lawrence, Associate Professor of History and Senior Fellow at the Robert S. Strauss Center for International

---

[175] Edward F. Murphy, *Semper Fi Vietnam*, p. 34, (Presidio Press, 1997).

Security and Law at The University of Texas at Austin, in his book, *The Vietnam War–A Concise International History*, acknowledged that:

> Combat grunts endured arduous patrolling—humping the boonies, in GI jargon—amid forbidding terrain, soaring temperatures, and torrential rain. Averaging just nineteen years old, *they fought repeatedly over the same ground* and anticipated ambushes from every direction. [176]

Even though my opponents' guns did not wound me, I did suffer from *jungle rot* in my feet. As can be seen in picture 6.3 [177], where two Marines are trying to deal with the problems of their feet, the continual wetness left my feet crinkled and colorless. At times, I felt as if the skin was going to fall right off my feet. Having trudged through the ground that was always water-saturated, I also incurred a disease called cellulitis. Today, as a result of constantly keeping my feet submerged in water in Vietnam, all of my toenails are full of fungus, much like mold (which include all species of microscopic fungi that grow in the form of multicellular filaments), that does not respond to medication. The beating that my waterlogged feet took in the soaked ground for almost a year finally took its toll. Today, my toenails are yellow, very hard and thick, yet quite brittle. The curvatures of my toenails have changed dramatically over the past five decades. Rather than ordinary-looking rounded cuticles, most of my toenails have rotted into jagged, irregular, and uneven shapes. To say the least, they are unsightly and are not easy to maintain. As such, every two months, I go to the VA Sierra Nevada Health Care System and have the doctor of podiatric medicine (David F. Giles) cut my toenails with razor-sharp, professional, toenail cutters which look like heavy-duty sharp-shaped pliers.

From a medical terminology standpoint, this fungus is called onychomycosis (also known as "dermatophytic onychomycosis–ringworm of the nail"). As a result of this service-connected problem, the Department of Veterans Affairs has also granted me a disability rating of 10%.

As I look back at it all, I would like to put things into perspective. From the Internet, I was able to retrieve the following information that you might find interesting: "During the year of 1965, a total of fifty-two Marines from the 3rd Battalion, 3rd Marine Division were killed in action in various places in South Vietnam. (Three of these Marines were from my company.) The first Marine was killed on May 29th, and the last one on December 14th."

Though we organized and carried out three large-scale operations against the VC main- force units in the last five months of 1965, our commanders

---

[176] Mark Atwood Lawrence, *The Vietnam War–A Concise International History*, p. 107, (Oxford University Press, 2008).

[177] Jack Murphy, *History of the US Marines*, p. 189, (World Publications Group, 2002).

were still concerned how well-organized the Viet Cong were in regular and guerrilla-like encounters.

Referring again to Edward F. Murphy's book, *Semper Fi Vietnam*, the following quote ties directly to what we were experiencing on the frontline:

> In General Walt's mind the Marines' main objective was to win the loyalty of the population for the government: eliminate the VC from the hamlets and villages and you would win. As far as Walt was concerned, it made little sense for his troops to sweep through a village, clear it of VC, then move on, leaving the gate wide open for the VC to return. [178]

However, that is what happened only too often during my stay in Vietnam. My company would go into an unsecured area such as a small hamlet, seek out and possibly destroy the enemy, stay there for a short time and leave. Weeks, months, and even years later the Viet Cong would come back and create havoc.

On another note, here is one more story worth telling. It is that of "Hanoi Hannah." Hanoi Hannah, as she called herself, or Trinh Thi Ngo, her real name, was more than cold-hearted. She called herself Thu Houng, *"the fragrance of autumn."* Her job was to chill and frighten, not to charm and seduce. As callous as she was, she thoroughly enjoyed attacking Marines verbally over the radio waves and grunts like me.

Ngo, on the other hand, was an unlikely choice to become Communism's voice. She had grown up as the pampered daughter of a glass-factory owner, taken private English lessons and steeped herself in French-subtitled Hollywood movies. When North Vietnamese President Ho Chi Minh started his drive to reunite the partitioned country in 1955, Ngo eagerly volunteered as the Voice of Vietnam. Little did she realize how useful English skills would be when American troops began pouring in ten years later. "I had to do something for the country," she said.

As Hanoi Hannah, she would broadcast radio messages and propaganda, over the local airways in a soft spoken manner, to convince U.S. troops to go AWOL (absent without leave). This was a psychological warfare scheme set forth by the Communist North Vietnamese. She made up to three broadcasts a day talking to American servicemen. Between Elvis Presley and Herb Alpert records, Hanoi Hannah coolly recited the names of newly killed or captured American servicemen, read articles from U.S. newsweeklies about peace demonstrations back home, and played taped messages from stateside antiwar activists. Moreover, she tried to plead with us that our involvement in Vietnam was unwarranted and immoral. She also suggested, with a tranquil sense of urgency, that we leave straightaway to avoid a dreadful fate. Of course, she played those popular American anti-war songs to incite and in-

---

[178]   Edward F. Murphy, *Semper Fi Vietnam*, pp. 36-37, (Presidio Press, 1997).

flame feelings of nostalgia and homesickness amongst servicemen fighting in the field—guys like me.

When I was at platoon headquarters, which usually had a portable transistor radio available, I was able to hear Hanoi Hannah's voice. Part of her brainwashing included rock n' roll music as a background to her raunchy propagandizing.

According to *The Search for Hanoi Hannah*, here are a few of Hanoi Hannah's radio broadcasts:

> How are you, GI Joe? It seems to me that most of you are poorly informed about the going of the war, to say nothing about a correct explanation of your presence over here. Nothing is more confusing than to be ordered into a war to die or to be maimed for life without the faintest idea of what's going on. [179]

> American GIs, do not fight this unjust, immoral and illegal war of Johnson's. Get out of Vietnam now and alive. This is the voice of Vietnam Broadcasting from Hanoi, capital of the Democratic Republic of Vietnam. Our program for American GIs can be heard at 1630. Now here's Connie Francis singing "I almost lost my mind." [180]

> Now for the war news. Here are the American casualties in Vietnam. Army Corporal Larry J. Samples, Canada, Alabama ... Staff Sergeant Charles R. Miller, Tucson, Arizona ... Sergeant Frank G. Hererra, Coolidge, Arizona ... [181]

Intriguingly enough, about one-and-half years after I fought in the Que Son Valley region in February 1967, more than two regiments of the 2nd North Vietnamese Army (NVA) Division infested, again, the strategically vital Que Son Valley. This populous, rice-rich valley was seen as one of the keys to controlling South Vietnam's five Northern provinces. Thus, coincidental with the 2nd NVA Division's arrival, which had hitherto operated mainly in the coastal areas of southern I Corps, was tasked with permanently bolstering the outnumbered and ineffectual South Vietnamese governmental forces in the valley.

The ultimate objective of bringing U.S. combat units into the Que Son Valley, all over again, was to eject all communist forces from a locale that provided the I Corps region and other areas of South Vietnam with both an abundant rice harvest and a seemingly inexhaustible supply of conscripts. The battles that were shaping up in the Que Son Valley were less a matter of real estate than control of a fertile food-producing region that also happened to be a major population center.

---

[179] *The Search for Hanoi Hannah,* Hanoi Hannah, 16 June 1967.
[180] Ibid, p. 12.
[181] Ibid, p. 15.

One reinforced U.S. Marine company (F [Foxtrot] Company, 2nd Battalion, 1st Marine Regiment) had been permanently assigned in mid-January 1967 to man the outpost atop the southern Que Son Valley's dominant overlook, Nui Loc Son (Loc Son Mountain). The Communist forces operating in the valley did not initially take much notice of the Marine outpost, and the small combatant force confined its activities to observation, close-in patrolling and a number of light-action projects. However, as the two fresh NVA regiments gained political and physical dominance over more and more of the valley and its people, a clash between them and the Marines became inevitable. On April 15, 1967, the Marine company commander advised his regimental commander that communist units appear to be preparing for an all-out assault on Nui Loc Son.

On the morning of April 19, 1967, Colonel Emil J. Radics, the commander of the 1st Marine Regiment, 1st Marine Division, presented Major General Herman Nickerson Jr., a Silver Star recipient of the Korean War, the commanding general of the 1st Marine Division, with the plan for Operation Union, a multi-battalion assault and sweep aimed at clearing NVA units from the vicinity of the mountain. General Nickerson assented to the operation the next day, and the Marine infantry were ordered to jump off the following morning, April 21st.

In a typical U.S. Marine response of that period, Foxtrot Company left its position atop Nui Loc Son and swept toward the nearest NVA-held village, a complex of several hamlets called Binh Son. The NVA began harassing Foxtrot Company around 0700 and at 0930 they attacked the Marine company in force. The NVA managed to pin Foxtrot Company in a tree line near Binh Son, but, in so doing, also fixed themselves to that particular location.

So far, events were unfolding according to the plan for Operation Union. At 1100, Foxtrot Company attacked Binh Son behind a sustained air and artillery bombardment; shortly after, most of the 3rd Battalion, 1st Marines, joined the fight by way of a "hot" helicopter assault. Quickly, the fresh Marine battalion fought through to the bait company. Later in the afternoon—1600—the 3rd Battalion, 5th Marines, landed from helicopters east of the battlefield in order to block the most likely escape route of the embattled NVA force. During the afternoon, U.S. Army 175mm self-propelled artillery and Marine 105mm howitzers moved into separate fire bases near the battlefield, and a third fresh Marine battalion (1st Battalion, 1st Marines) landed atop Nui Loc Son that evening.

On the morning of April 22nd, the NVA forces were driven out of the Binh Son area and forced to withdraw in a northerly direction. From then until May 14, when Operation Union was abruptly terminated, a revolving cast of U.S. Marine infantry battalions, bolstered by the 1st ARVN (Army of the Republic of Vietnam) Ranger Group, hotly pursued the NVA force and fought a series of bitter battles that were extremely costly to both sides.

Although the 2nd NVA Division had sustained hundreds of casualties in Operation Union and had lost ground around Nui Loc Son, it remained in firm control of much of the rest of the Que Son Valley. Indeed, there is evidence to suggest that the NVA division was reinforced during that period. In any case, on May 26th, Colonel Kenneth J. Houghton's 5th U.S. Marine Regiment, which had assumed control of the latter stages of Operation Union, kicked off Operation Union II.

Aimed at sweeping the NVA from the southern rim of the Que Son Valley, Operation Union II developed into a series of long-range sweeps centered on Nui Loc Son. A number of large, bitter and extremely costly battles stretched to early June, with the last one fought on June 2nd, 1967. (One result of that final action of Union II was that Marine Captain James A. Graham was awarded a posthumous Medal of Honor for defending to the last the dead and wounded of his Foxtrot Company, 2nd Battalion, 5th Marines, following an overwhelming NVA ambush.) In the end, the 2nd NVA Division ceded control of the southern Que Son Valley to the 5th Marines.

The Que Son Valley remained quiescent through the summer of 1967 as the 2nd NVA division licked its wounds and built itself up to a force of three NVA regiments and the 1st Viet Cong Regiment, which was a full-time main force unit. Two battalions of the 5th Marines continued to operate in the valley, but contacts were light; the Marines did not patrol aggressively, and the communist forces did not pester them.

Following several major, multi battalion operations around Da Nang, the 1st U.S. Marine Division (commanded by Major General Donn J. Robertson since June 1, 1967) refocused its attention on the Que Son Valley in early August. In the wake of a modest build-up, three Marine battalions launched Operation Cochise on August 11th. This maneuver, synchronized with the 2nd ARVN Divisions operation Lien Ket 112, had four battalions sweep the Hiep Duc region northeast of Que Son for the 21st NVA Regiment and the logistics base for the 2nd NVA Division. The NVA avoided the traps and pitfalls of the Union and Union II operations, and Cochise ended on August 28th with only modest results.

Operation Swift, the fourth and the last series of spring and summer battles in the Que Son Valley, was one of the worst-run and bloodiest Marine Corps operations of the Vietnam War. A direct outgrowth of sweep operations designed to shield the populace from election-day intimidation, Swift began unofficially on September 4, 1967, when Delta Company, 1st Battalion 5th Marines, on foot patrol, was attacked before dawn by a superior NVA force.

In typical reactive mode, the local Marine battalion commander attempted to relieve Delta Company with one other company, a force too small to take on the larger NVA force. After both Marine companies had been pinned in separate enclaves by 0900, two companies from the adjacent 3rd Battalion, 5th Marines, were sent to relieve them. The two fresh companies were attacked and also became pinned in separate enclaves during the early afternoon.

The battle was taking on classic characteristics. If the Marine Corps's high command in Vietnam deserves to be made accountable for only one thing, it is the steady stream of ad hoc operations that grew out of meager responses to situations precisely like the one that shaped up in the Que Son Valley on September 4, 1967. By late afternoon, the four Marine companies were barely hanging on to their respective areas. All four companies were under resolute attack by vastly superior NVA forces that, no doubt, had carefully planned the trap. Only the timely arrival of Marine jet fighter-bombers and the pinpoint accuracy of Marine artillery prevented the Marine infantry companies from being overrun.

Two posthumous Medals of Honor would be awarded for the September 4th fighting. Although wounded in the leg while locating an enemy position, Sergeant Lawrence D. Peters, a squad leader serving with Mike Company, 3rd Battalion, 5th Marines, refused relief so that he could continue to lead his Marines. Peters bled to death during the night. Also in the company's perimeter, Father Vincent R. Capadonno, the 3rd Battalion Chaplain, refused relief when he was wounded. Father Capadonno was hit twice, but he continued to administer medical and spiritual aid to the wounded until he was, regrettably, killed by enemy fire.

Despite a large and growing toll of wounded and dead Marines, the night of September 4 - 5 was used to good advantage in aggressive air and artillery strikes against several NVA positions. A dawn counterattack by yet another fresh Marine company then succeeded in relieving pressure on the two surrounded companies of the 1st Battalion. As a result, the NVA broke contact and withdrew from the area, thus freeing the two trapped companies of the 3rd Battalion. With that, the commander of the 5th Marines, Colonel Stanley Davis, ordered his bloodied 1st and 3rd battalions to pursue, and Operation Swift officially began.

The enemy reappeared in the early afternoon of September 6th, when two battalions of the 1st VC Regiment attacked B (Bravo) company, the lead company of the 1st Battalion, 5th Marines. Bravo was isolated and nearly overrun before artillery-delivered tear gas brought respite. Meanwhile, the nearby 3rd Battalion became heavily engaged a few hours later. When I (India) Company was dispatched to attack a VC-held hill, it was isolated and nearly overrun by the 1st VC Regiment's previously uncommitted 3rd Battalion. K (Kilo) Company was sent to relieve India and, though it fought through, the two company force could not move because it was burdened with many casualties. Two determined VC night assaults were repulsed, and Mike Company eventually fought through against meager opposition. By dawn, the VC had melted away.

And so it went. The enemy withdrew and the Marine battalions attempted to run them down or run them out of the Que Son Valley. Terrible, costly battles ensued and hasty, drastic measures had to be implemented to prevent disasters. Nevertheless on September 15th, the 2nd NVA Division and 1st VC Regiment had largely given up the southern half of the Que Son Valley. As ill-considered as the Marines' successive piecemeal strategy had been in response to the initial attacks, still the crack Communist forces were ultimately defeated. In fact, U.S. intelligence agencies determined that the two enemy regiments that had been most active during Operation Swift were subsequently unfit for combat.

Almost coincidental with the conclusion of Operation Swift was the arrival in southern I Corps of very large U.S. Army units. As a result, the 1st Marine Division was able to base a substantial force in the Que Son Valley on a permanent basis. From then until the Marines turned all of southern I Corps over to the U.S. Army at the beginning of 1968, the reinforced 2nd NVA Division never seriously assaulted the Marines who had bested them. Oddly, for all the tactical mismanagement, the Marines' 1967 spring and summer operations in the Que Son Valley turned out to be among the strategically most successful of the entire U.S. involvement in I Corps.

Remarkably enough, in August 1969, the U.S. Army handed the northern portion of the Que Son Valley back to the Marines as part of their TAOR. The 7th Marine Regiment was back to a familiar area, the regiments 2nd Battalion, had fought there before in Operation Harvest Moon their first battle in the Que Son Valley back in 1965. Moving into the valley the Marines inherited three combat bases from the U.S. Army, LZ Baldy the easternmost of the three combat bases was located at the intersection of Route 1 and 535 about 20 miles south of Da Nang. Baldy became the Regimental Headquarters, Fire Support Base (FSB) Ross, west of Que Son District Town, and the most western of the three FSB Ryder on Hill 579 which covered both the Que Son Valley which lay east and Antenna Valley to the west completed the Marine presence in the Que Son's.

Picture 6.1
Map of Quang Tin Province
[via Author]

Picture 6.2
Fertile valley
[Author photo]

VIETNAM: MY WAR

Picture 6.3
Jungle rot
[via Author]

Chapter 7

Vietnam
An Trach

I N early November 1965, just before Operation Harvest Moon, my company received word that we were going to move out of the Chu Lai region and head back to the Da Nang area, as can be seen in picture 7.1 (that is me in the forefront of the picture). I thought the peninsula of Chu Lai was considered secure, only to hear later that the NLF had moved back into the area after we left. During this same time, the 3rd Marine Division, interestingly enough created a fourteen-day course, also near Da Nang. Some 70 plus snipers were trained, with plans for one scout-sniper platoon in each Marine infantry regiment. They were also trained with Winchester Model 70 target rifles with target scopes. These snipers, as I was later told, could hit their targets—Viet Cong—as far as 800 yards away.

In his work, *No Shining Armor–The Marines at War in Vietnam,* Otto Lehrack provides us with added insight about the Vietnam War:

> The November move was the first of a series of northward migrations that would culminate in the battalion's fighting along the DMZ for nearly three years. During November, the unit also had its first experience with the monsoon, its heavy rainfall, overcast skies, and relative cold. The weather's side effects included a rise in diseases from sanitation problems associated with the dampness and difficulty of maintaining personal hygiene. [182]

Private Paul Tackes, also with Mike Company, 2nd Platoon, had hardly come back from a patrol when he noticed that something was crawling around inside his skivvies. He immediately called for a corpsman. The corpsman told him to drink lots of water, and only water; as much water as he possibly could. The next thing Paul knew, he was airborne and on his way to the hospital ship, "The Angel of the Orient," USS Repose (AH-16). She was originally commissioned on May 26, 1945, and joined the Pacific Fleet on July 14, 1945. The Repose was decommissioned in December 1954. After ten and one-half years with the Reserve Fleet at Suisan Bay, California (the Suisun Bay is a shallow tidal estuary in northern California) docks at the mouth of the Sacramento and San Joaquin Rivers, forming the entrance to the Sacramento–San

---

[182] Otto J. Lehrack, *No Shining Armor–The Marines at War in Vietnam,* p. 61, (University Press of Kansas, 1992).

Joaquin River Delta, an inverted river delta. She was again called to active service in October 1965. On February 14, 1966 she arrived in Chu Lai, and in April 1967 she was joined by her sister ship USS Sanctuary (AH-17).

Once on this floating infirmary—with a bed capacity of 750 and a complement of 564, one of the doctors, along with a nurse, put some kind of medical instrument in Paul's penis. Naturally, Paul was quite concerned, making him wary and fidgety. This unpleasant experience became worse when the doctor retrieved one of his tools from the table, he calmly asked the nurse to grab Paul's penis. To say the least, Paul was embarrassed. The next thing he knew, this long, slippery, ugly creature was coming out of his male sex organ. For all this commotion and excitement, the doc pulled out a good old five-inch Vietnamese leech.

Moving from one sector to another was only too common for my company. As we moved out of the Chu Lai enclave to the Da Nang district, a battalion of the 7th Marines from Da Nang moved into Chu Lai.

Yes, it seemed like we were constantly on the go. Transported in those open M35 two-and-half ton cargo trucks, as can be seen in pictures 7.2 and 7.3 [183], was invariably nerve-wracking. To say the least, it was creepy as well as scary to sit in those open motor vehicles. Ten to fifteen of us would assemble in those trucks. As we drove along the dirt, muddy roads, moving through one village to another, the VC would take potshots at us. After a while, we simply got used to it. The problem was that we could not easily get out of those vehicles. In addition, we could not jump out of the truck for the reason that the driver would not stop even though the enemy was shooting at us. It truly was a surreal and menacing feeling, knowing that we could easily die from just one shot, and we had no chance to fight back. It was next to impossible to hide within those transport trucks because our company commander always wanted to pack us in like sardines.

As I look back at these particular pictures five decades later, I still get goose bumps. It is hard for me to imagine that our commanding officers would pack us in like fish in a glass bowl, knowing that anyone of us could have gotten wounded or killed with one shot. I guess you just do not think of those things at the time. They have become a reality check many years later.

As we gathered our gear, we headed northwest toward the villages of An Trach, as can be seen in maps 7.4 (Da Nang Area–July–December 1965) [184] & 7.5 (map showing the village of An Trach). Our mission was to clear-and-secure as well as clear-and-hold the area. Once again, word spread around the company that there was a lot of VC activity in this sector. We were also told that the Viet Cong were out there, acting as farmers by day, plowing their fields, picking rice, raising domesticated animals, living much as their ances-

---

[183] Gordon Hardy, *The Vietnam Experience–Words of War,* p. 10, (Boston Publishing Company, 1988).

[184] Jack Shulimson and Major Charles M. Johnson, USMC, *U.S. Marines in Vietnam–the Landing and the Buildup 1965*, p. 60, (U.S. Government Printing Office, 1978).

tors had for millennia, being the enemy by night, looking very much like the man in picture 7.6. Does that look like the adversary to you? Of course not and we did not think so, either. The reality was just the opposite. They were lethal professionals focusing in on, if possible, medics, radiomen, and officers. They often fired one round, followed by a rapid burst of automatic fire, before fleeing. Unquestionably, they knew every fold in the land—every tree line and concealed bunker, and every prepared field of fire for a potential deadly ambush. These confrontations and attacks on U.S. and South Vietnamese emplacements were usually quite transitory affairs. Once their perceived tactical advantage was lost, they usually attempted to break contact and flee again, under the cover of darkness. To this point, we certainly tested that theory. We went on patrol routinely—almost every day. We combed the area thoroughly, but never extensively enough. Whether it rained or not, hot or cold, we went on patrol.

It was Christmas time. It was our first Christmas in this country. Even though I cannot remember the specific details, this particular Yuletide was no different from any other day in this war-torn land.

I was told that the battalion managed to obtain and distribute presents for the troops. However, my three-man team, which was stationed in a forward-looking position along the river's edge of La Bong, did not get anything. It was also communicated that our battalion had a Christmas Eve party for the children in the village of An Trach. I guess they handed out candy and toys to the children. We were not fortunate enough to participate in the festivities.

Although a cease-fire was supposedly in effect during this time of the year, it was not apparent to us. In fact, a few Viet Cong fired on our post and a post across the river manned by India Company. We could not tell if any VC were wounded or killed, but I was told that one VC fell and had to be carried off by another.

As a seek-and-destroy unit our job was to kill the enemy. As mentioned before, we went out on patrol at least every other day. Sometimes we went on reconnaissance twice in one day, walking through one covered canopy area to an open rice paddy and back into a covered sugarcane field or to another covering. This was always a test of our nerves, (as can be seen in picture 7.7—we are in a holding position), making sure that it is clear to move forward. We never knew if the enemy was ready to take us on in a firefight. In this particular instance, early January 1966, we were ambushed as soon as we reached the open area. As soon as we arrived in the clearing, the VC opened fire. As usual, we were like sitting ducks in a pond. It was easy for the Viet Cong to take potshots at us. Unfortunately, there was not much we could do about it. Too often, as we made it to an opening, one of our team members would be wounded or possibly killed by enemy fire. We would instantly call for a medic (if we had one). Regardless of the endless supply of mental strain and emotional tension, a corpsman would quickly attend to the injured Marine(s). Once in motion, he would work miracles. With total disregard for his own life, many times putting himself in harm's way, he would attend to and console a fallen warrior. For a moment, it was fantastic and unbelievable to watch this gung-ho sailor, truly a fellow leatherneck, in action. It was astonishing how they would put their life on the line to take care of a wounded Marine. Once we had control of the area, and knew that it was secure and safe to bring in a helicopter, we would then call for a medical evacuation.

When we did encounter the enemy while on patrol, they were usually about 50–100 yards away. For the most part, there were three to five of them hiding out at the edge of the village. We sensed they could always tell when we were coming. No matter what the situation was, whether we were resting behind a muddy rice paddy dike, crossing an open rice paddy, patrolling a river with the use of amtracs or standing guard (as I was in picture 7.8), the Viet Cong knew where we were. How would they know our positions? I am telling you, they knew our every move–every time!

Even so, the job had to be done. We continuously canvassed the area, one village after another, always looking for our foe. As we went out on reconnaissance, surveying the area, for hours at a time, we knew they would most likely open fire on us, take a few potshots and then quickly flee the scene. They would create enough havoc and damage to really piss us off. They would usually be lucky and get one or two of us wounded or killed. It was truly a game of cat and mouse. We would try to catch up to them, laying down enough firepower while advancing forward, but it was difficult to capture or kill them. Those little gaunt-looking fighters were too fast for us. They knew the lay of the land, and they knew it only too well. After firing on us, they would abruptly move to the next village, hide their weapons if needed, and play farmer again. For now, what could we do? Right or wrong, the only recourse we thought we had left was to burn down their village, like we did in Cam Ne.

One time, while we were charting the region about a mile from base camp, patrolling one behind the other, about ten feet apart, walking on the dike of a rice paddy, just one shot rang out from the tree line. This five-foot skinny peasant with half of his teeth missing must have been no more than 100 feet away. I could hear the whistling noise of the bullet from his assault rifle as it passed by me. That it did. It passed directly over my left shoulder and hit my fellow Marine directly behind me in the upper part of his chest. Blood was gushing from his back like a geyser. We could not stop the bleeding, and he could not talk. He went into shock. The rest of us were bewildered and f____g pissed! The corpsman tried to stop the hemorrhaging, but to no avail. He tried to work wonders, but the blood loss was too much to handle. My fellow leatherneck died in about 45 seconds, just a few days after the New Year.

During this same time, on January 7, 1966, U.S. and Australian forces launch Operation Crimp, later renamed Operation Buckskin. Deploying almost 8,000 American and Australian Armed Forces, it was the largest joint operation of the war to date. The goal of the campaign is to capture the Vietcong's headquarters for the Saigon area, which was believed to be located in the district of Chu Chi. Though the area in Chu Chi is razed and repeatedly patrolled, American forces fail to locate any significant Vietcong base. Despite that, they did experience a significant number of sudden engagements and ambushes, indicating that the Vietcong were using tunnels for movement and concealment. On this same day, General Walt ordered the establishment of the 3rd Marine Division Reconnaissance Base at the *Ba To* U.S. Special Forces Camp in the Quang Ngai Province. A few days later, Captain William C. Shaver, the commanding officer of the unit, deployed his first patrols from the company's new headquarters. [185]

Meanwhile, during January 1965, the Student Nonviolent Coordinating Committee (SNCC) took a stand against the Vietnam War saying:

> We believe the United States government has been deceptive in claims of concern for the freedom of the Vietnamese people, just as the government has been deceptive in claiming concern for the freedom of the colored people in such other countries as the Dominican Republic, the Congo, South Africa, Rhodesia (now Zimbabwe), and in the United States itself.

Just think about the above-mentioned statement for a moment. Now, imagine about this assertion from my perspective. Please try to put yourself in my shoes, knowing what the SNCC believed, and knowing, from my standpoint, that they knew nothing about our job of trying to free the South Vietnamese people from their adversaries in the north. How do you think I felt hearing this kind of rhetoric?

This is what life was like, day after day, shot after shot, death after death. You are probably asking, what happened to this bony, half-starved guerrilla fighter? Naturally, we wasted no time in killing him, but it was a painful kill for all of us. It was agonizing not because we killed a VC, and who cared whether we wasted 100 bullets or just one on him–he was the enemy. It was beyond depressing for us because a fellow Marine never had the chance to fight back in the way he knew how. He certainly never had the opportunity to go back to the States and be with his loved ones. Even after killing that Viet Cong, it did not relieve our anger. It was a heart-rending event that will, undoubtedly, trouble me for the rest of my life.

As you read about this one brief encounter with our foe, please try to imagine how thousands of other warriors and soldiers going through similar incidents cannot keep these emotions out of their minds—even five decades later. Even though many of us try to forget about the past, these incidents do not go away. This stuff just keeps haunting many of us–our parents, wives, children, friends, and employers, day after day; even five decades later for this was truly *our war*.

---

[185] Leo Daugherty, *The Vietnam War–Day by Day*, p. 70, (Chartwell Books, Inc., 2011).

Retired Marine, Sergeant Major Richard G. Kidwell, L (Lima) Company, 3rd Battalion, 3rd Marines, 3rd Marine Division, who was in Vietnam the same time I was, describes being obsessed by a similar circumstance:

> It seems like only yesterday that I picked up a young Marine who had his legs and arms blown off. He kept saying to me, "Let me up so I can walk." He died in the helicopter before he reached the hospital ship that was stationed offshore.
>
> It wasn't right to send us to a place that we knew we could not win. More than 58,000 young Americans are gone for nothing. Jamy, please write your book for all of them and pray it will never happen again. [186]

It was a hot day outside of the villages of An Trach. We were out on another reconnaissance mission. For the most part, it was a quiet day. As fate would have it, only one shot was fired. A little later, one Marine was dead. Again, chalk up one for the VC. I guess he felt he deserved the kill. One hundred shots later, and you got a bunch of enraged jarheads–fortunately, one Viet Cong is dead, too. We wasted that son of a bitch! Now, chalk up one for the good guys. Is that what war is all about? Is this how we could win a war? Not according to the very talented military strategist Sun Tzu. Is that what I tell my son about what Vietnam was really like? You tell me!

Let me share another real-life story about day-to-day combat life in the frontline, as expressed to me by Lance Corporal Bill Morton. It probably resembles the patrol scene in picture 7.9. [187]

> The squad leaders had been briefed the night before on the mission for today. The so-called Christmas cease-fire was officially over - or was it? Even if it was New Year's Day, it didn't matter out here. We were on the frontlines and didn't care, but the VC certainly did.
>
> I had been going over the map of the area where we were going to be today. As always, it was one of my least favorite places to be. It was typical delta country, which consisted of large rice paddies with plenty of strands of bamboo. I would be constantly picking off the leeches that had attached themselves to my body. The brush was heavy throughout and, as usual, I felt like a sitting duck.
>
> The whole platoon was moving out this morning, which was a rarity. Usually, a squad would stay behind with the command group. In this reconnaissance mission, we were going to be working with other units on a sweep. I was not looking forward to it. Coordina-

---

[186] Former retired Marine, Sergeant Major Richard G. Kidwell, L (Lima) Company, 3rd Battalion, 3rd Marines, 3rd Marine Division, 1966.

[187] Gordon Hardy, *The Vietnam Experience–Words of War,* p. 32, (Boston Publishing Company, 1988).

tion was always a major hassle, and it would keep things messed up the whole day.

I woke up the other men and continued watching the river as they slowly began to stir. My nerves were bothering me. For some reason I felt queasy and uneasy. I tried to eat ham and chopped eggs from my C-rations. Sorry to say, the food wouldn't stay down. I was getting the runs. I was really working myself into a foul mood that I could not shake off.

Dawn had now lit the sky, and it was getting hotter by the minute, which was normal around here. Last-minute details came from our squad leader. We then saddled up, as the saying goes, and moved out. I was on the point, as usual, as we moved along the river. We were patrolling an area that had become familiar to us over the past few weeks.

We were running late. Our company commander, a lieutenant, was griping at me to pick up the pace. I felt we were moving fast enough. We were getting to an area I was not familiar with, so I started to slow down. The lieutenant and I had been butting heads a lot recently. He was a good officer, but he had spent too much time in base camp and still needed to learn the ropes of jungle tactics.

It was about 0700—we started taking sniper fire from a large stand of bamboo and trees. The rounds were short, but they still made me nervous. We dropped behind the levee of a rice paddy. Word finally came forward for my fire team to cross the paddy and flush out the snipers. My stomach sank to the bottom of my boots. There was at least 800 yards, or about one-half mile, of open rice paddy to the thicket. We would be sitting ducks as we moved into their firing range.

It was now time to tell my team what we already knew: "Keep moving. Save some energy for a final sprint if we have to, and don't waste ammo while we are in the crossing." We moved out and worked our way over to the snipers' area, changing our pace often but never stopping. After what seemed like a lifetime, we made it to the other side. Now the firing had stopped, which, by the way, was normal when we moved through the trees. Then, the radio squawked. It was the lieutenant ordering us to come back because either the 81mm mortars or other artillery were going to shell the area. We packed up and made a quick dash back across the open space. Right on cue, Charlie opened fire on us and chased us all the way back. Luckily, no one was hurt.

No sooner had we caught our breath than the word came down—no artillery support, friendly villages in the area. The skipper wanted us to go back over the same area. I groused about that to the lieutenant, which really ticked him off. It did not matter. We still ended up going there again. This time, though, the firing had increased. This time Charlie was finding his mark.

We ran most of the way, and were really huffing and puffing when we made it to the far side. I told the guys to sit tight. We had to catch our breath. No sooner had I said that when the radio crackled and the operator was yelling to us. He cried, "Didi!," which means *get out*. Air support was coming any minute, so we took off as fast as we could and crossed the rice paddy again.

By now, I was furious. We just couldn't get our shit together. We waited for about ten minutes, but no helos showed. Again, the lieutenant directed me to go back over there. This time, I flat out refused. "I will bring you up on charges," he threatened. "I do not give a damn," I said, and I did not give any ground. By this time, I was ready to take off his head. And the lieutenant was equally as angry at me.

The situation was getting ugly. Fortunately, the company commander saved the day by ordering us to move out and not worry about the snipers. Naturally, the lieutenant was fuming. I was, too. To say the least, things were going poorly, far worse than I had anticipated. The platoon was edgy. Most of the guys were really pissed at the lieutenant.

We reached the point at which we were to turn left, form a line, and start our sweep. We planned to regroup behind a small peninsula that juts out into the river. I told the lieutenant I was going to cross the small inlet and clear the area before our sweep. "No–forget it. We'll try to keep the men dry," he said. I felt that was a huge mistake.

I had been into it with the lieutenant all morning. Again, I voiced my disapproval. He said, "If you are afraid to walk the point, I will replace you." No one walks the point for me. I am a jarhead, *and I know my duty!*

I stomped off along the edge, bringing the platoon behind me, knowing all the time we were making a big mistake. To make matters worse, the lieutenant put three brand-new guys up front with me. These Marines had been in Vietnam for less than five days. They didn't belong up here yet. And I didn't even know their names. Hurriedly, I told them, "If anything happens, hit the deck. Don't do anything. Just stay down."

I hear a noise from the brush ahead so I stopped to listen. It sounded like voices. Was it the unit we were to link up with? It was quiet. I eased forward. I stopped again, looked, and listened. Nothing!

I started to move again when I heard the unique sound of an M1 rifle bolt slamming home. The double click it made was unmistakable. I was now moving at a full sprint, trying to reach the flank of the peninsula. *If I get there, I will have a chance to best assist the rest of the outfit.*

Then I heard a loud boom. *Shit, I am hit!* Next, I am flat on my back. I had my weapon in my right hand, but now it was gone. I could hear the air sucking in my chest, but there was nothing I could do. My arm felt like hot water had been poured on it. I had just taken a round through my right arm at the shoulder. It had deflected off my ribs, gone through the right lung, and exited from my back. It just missed my spine.

Desperately, I tried to feel my rifle with my left hand as heavy automatic fire erupted. All hell was breaking loose. I had fallen into some tall grass, which, to a certain degree, hid my location. The sniper who had wounded me was still taking shots at me, but now he missed.

For one terrible moment, I thought I was going to die. *I felt bad, but not bad enough to die, I told myself.* I braced my rifle against my hip and over my boot. If Charlie came out of the thicket, I had a surprise for him. I concentrated on trying to breathe evenly, but I kept choking on my own blood and gasped for air.

It was 0915. I had just checked my watch only seconds before. Why was nobody coming for me? The firing remained heavy all the time. Finally, two of the guys from my team reached me. They dragged me back into a small depression. The corpsman who came up to me was new. I did not know him. By lowering my head, he was choking me. I could not breathe. I tried to tell him that, but my voice came out garbled. He didn't understand what I was saying. Finally, one of my fellow Marines lifted me up, and I cleared my windpipe.

Helos were over us almost immediately, or so it seemed. However, our group was not able to secure a LZ (landing zone for helicopters–uneven, often sloping, cleared areas of ground in the jungle or elephant grass, whose diameter was only about twice the expected helo's length, to larger, better-constructed zones on hilltops). I could hear the yelling and firing, but it was all just noise. There were three other Marines near me who were also hurt. The corpsman was trying to help them, too. I closed my eyes and concentrated on surviving.

The helicopters finally came in. "Dust off" eventually happened—I finally took off on one of the helicopters. It took about thirty minutes to get me out of this shithole of a hot spot. I was in the hospital in a matter of minutes. At 1000, I was in the operating room. I was freezing. It was so cold. I begged the doctor to not cut off my arm. He assured me he wouldn't. I felt a sharp jab in my neck, and I was out.

I awoke later that night. A corpsman was right there waiting for me to wake. He asked me, "Do you have any pain?" I shook my head, "no," to which he then replied "good," and he gave me another shot.

The next morning, I was loaded on a Jeep. The doctor ran out of the emergency room before I left and slid an envelope under my pillow. He told me it was my pay record! He also handed me something else: a Purple Heart medal. For me, the war was finally over. I had paid the price along with so many other servicemen.

In late January/early February 1966, Marines from the 2nd Battalion, 4th Marines, 3rd Marine Division, as well as units from the U.S. Army, participated in another battle in the Quang Ngai and Quang Tri Provinces. It was called Operation Double Eagle I. This confrontation was designed to initiate a coordinated offensive against the enemy buildup in the region of I and II Corps border. [188] I, on the other hand, did not participate in this skirmish. That said, I became aware that the enemy kill count was set at 312. Regrettably, 120 warriors and soldiers were also killed in action.

Since our job, as always, was to seek out and destroy the enemy, we did get lucky now and then. One day in February 1966, some twelve of us were on reconnaissance again near An Trach, when we ran into a bunch of Viet Cong. We were definitely lured into an ambush, and the VC knew it. So did we! These peasant fighters decided to open fire on us while we were hanging around in the mire and the sludge of the rice paddies. And open fire they did. Once again, all hell broke loose that morning and it did not help that our muscles felt so stiff. We were pinned down, we could not move, and we were miserable.

For the most part, they were no more than 50 yards away from us. Bullets were flying from three frontal directions directly to the front of us and to our flanks.

Two fellow Marines got hit. One grunt ran right into a booby trap with two grenades with a trip wire wired between them. The explosive device literally blew off his legs and groin area. We could hear him cry out in pain, but could not do anything about it. And as always, we did not have enough firepower to take the VC out. To make matters worse, we did not have a corpsman with us on patrol. Crawling on our bellies toward the enemy and laying down some machine gun firepower was all we could do to stay alive. And with fellow Marines hurt, that made matters all that much more difficult.

The squad leader told one of the guys that he had to go back to the village and seek additional help. That in itself was no small feat. Being pinned down, made it next to impossible to move, let alone leave the unit and summon more Marines. But, it had to be done, and it had to be done quickly. So we laid down a burst of fire, trying to create some diversion so that one of the warriors could get help. It worked. He was able to sneak out of there and

---

[188] Leo Daugherty, *The Vietnam War–Day by Day*, p. 71, (Chartwell Books, Inc., 2011).

make it back to base camp. For his successful performance, despite the dreadful conditions he was faced with, we were soon joined by more men, who helped us out. With a barrage of firepower, we were able to take control and medevac the wounded. Of course, we never saw those Marines again.

To this day, I can still vividly remember An Trach as a quaint and charming little village. It had a church, which served as the main supply point for our unit. From what I understood, this was the only way various provisions (e.g. ammunition, food, water, etc.) came to us. This was special because we were not supplied that often.

On February 21, 1966, while at company headquarters in An Trach, I was assigned the task of repairing a USMC Mule (M274), a Jeep-like, four-wheel drive vehicle (refer to picture 7.10—I am the driver in this picture). How, I did not know; but I had just received my government-issued driving license for this vehicle. And why the lieutenant selected me to fix the mule is beyond my understanding. Upon trying to fix the mule, my job was to bring the vehicle back to our area, a quick drive from our company headquarters, because on the mule's flatbed were supplies that we needed for our team during the next few days.

As I crawled under the vehicle to see what was wrong, we were being attacked by the Viet Cong. Somehow, while trying to correct the problem, while taking on lots of incoming enemy fire, I must have touched a gear by mistake. The next thing I knew my right hand, at the pinky and fourth finger, was almost completely severed. In the meantime, bullets were flying all around.

There I was. I had now been in Vietnam for seven months without being wounded. Bullets had flown by me left and right, but God only knows, they missed me—and I was not about to question His ways. Bombs, from our own planes, missed me by inches. All of a sudden I am about to lose two fingers on my right hand, my shooting hand. I immediately called for a corpsman that happened to be nearby. He looked at my fingers and uttered that I had to be evacuated to a hospital. The medic voiced that my hand would require numerous stitches since the fingers were severely lacerated. I expressed to him, "This sucks big time." The corpsman bandaged my hand, gave me a fair amount of morphine to ease the pain, and prepared me for my airborne medevac helicopter trip to the field hospital.

About six hours after the accident, waiting to be evacuated, I arrived, via a 20-minute helicopter ride, at the tent camp hospital in Chu Lai. It was the 91st Field Evacuation Army Hospital (located on a rocky bluff overlooking the South China Sea) that was staffed by numerous medical officers and enlisted personnel. This tent field hospital was capable of treating all types of acute injuries, including brain surgery as well as heart and eye surgery,

> As was true of other hospitals in Vietnam, patients were moved directly from the battlefield either to a clearing station or a nearby hospital ... Most patients arrived at the hospital within ten minutes of

pickup, and some of these were in such critical condition, usually from internal bleeding or respiratory problems, that further evacuation even by helicopter would likely have been fatal.

Patients were moved from the helicopter pad directly into the preoperative and resuscitation station where they were met by the surgical team and the registrar's section to initiate immediate life support measures and medical records. Patients were nearly always admitted in groups of three to ten. Surgical priorities were established after blood administrations and other stabilizing measures had been taken, and X-rays and laboratory results had been obtained.

On arrival, along with other helicopters bringing in the wounded, I walked directly over to the preoperative room. However, the area was busy with wounded Marines who required immediate attention. These guys were actually in very bad shape. Some had their intestines hanging out of their bellies. Others had half their faces missing. Still, others lost their limbs. It was not a pretty scene, and I was just sitting there.

The emergency room surgeon came over to me and stated that he would see me once it calmed down, but not before. "That is fine," I said. Unfortunately, the operating room stayed busy for about six hours before I could be seen. I sat there listening to the moans and groans as well as the whines and whimpers of other warriors, soldiers, and other servicemen who had serious, life-threatening wounds. It was disturbing to hear these men, who were about to lose an arm or a leg. It certainly was annoying and difficult to listen to these gutsy and spirited warriors scream with pain. Most important, it was exasperating, knowing that some of these young brave fighters would soon die because it was too late for the doctors to help them. Some of the head and chest wounds were so serious that the doctors were unable to save the men. Other brave troops died there on a gurney. As you could probably imagine, it was an eerie feeling that day. Chills fluttered up and down my back as I awaited my turn to be operated on.

Once the acute-care surgery slowed down, the doctor on duty called me in. I could tell he was tired and needed sleep. There were blood and organ parts all over his gown—it was truly gross. Before he operated on me, he told me a story that I would like to share with you. It is not a pleasant one, but one that I will remember for the rest of my life. Also, it is not a story for the faint of heart. As such, if you do not want to read this narrative, please skip reading the next paragraph. It is an anecdote, as grossly offensive and vile as it may sound, still worth telling. The narrative, whether true or not, goes something like this:

The doctor stated to me passionately: "Marine, I have an obligation to tell every warrior/soldier that he could be severely disfigured as a result of sexual activities that are happening in the cat houses or brothels of Da Nang and other big cities throughout Vietnam." [189]

After that moving statement, he told me, with a serious and stern face, the following account (see below), which may be perceived as a ghost story—a supernatural fictional tale that has been passed down through the telling of them to friends. Informally, the term also can refer to any kind of scary story.

> *There are North Vietnamese hookers working the streets, trying to lure American soldiers for a quickie. Obviously, some servicemen would take advantage of the opportunity. For ten dollars or less, the doctor articulated, 'You could get an orgasm.' What the troops did not know was that these young Vietcong women would stick razor blades up their own vaginas. As the serviceman would begin to thrust his penis in the woman's vagina, during intercourse, these rotten, good for nothing, sluts would thrust their vaginas at the soldier's penis. As the soldier's penis would enter the vagina, his penis would immediately be cut by the razor blade. Of course, he would scream bloody murder. [190]*

The surgeon finally articulated, in a soft and tender, but exact, voice:

> *When I saw some of the soldiers after their ordeal, their penises were cut so badly that they wanted to kill themselves rather than go back to the United States to their loved ones. [191]*

I was sickened by this (sea) story. Whether true or not, and I suspect it was a widespread myth or cold-blooded propaganda circulated by the Pentagon brass through their sergeant thugs starting in boot camp, in order to dehumanize the Vietnamese people and hype up the U.S. soldiers to get them to commit atrocities as revenge; it was one that really shook me up. It gave me a case of the chills. I suspect that the encounter with the hooker was a complete fabrication. More vital, I thank God that I did not have the guts to have sex with any of these severely underweight women while I was in Vietnam. I had the desire, but I did not have the guts to go through with the act—not on my life. And I was certainly not about to start now. I did have pity, however, for those guys who wanted to commit suicide (as told by this medical doctor) this was probably a total cock-and-bull story to scare us GIs. I might have done the same thing.

After the doctor shared with me this repulsive yet riveting story, he attended to my mangled and lacerated fingers. The operation and stitches took about an hour, and he gave me some penicillin. I thanked him for his time. He then sent me to another room where a nurse put a cast on my hand. For

---

[189]   J. E. Jones, M. D.
[190]   Ibid.
[191]   Ibid.

that service-connected combat-related injury, I was awarded, by the Department of Veterans Affairs, a 20% disability rating in my right hand.

When all was said and done, I then joined the rear echelon staff of my company for the next three days—I was what the guys called a *broke-dick*, where I met up with the First Sergeant (i.e., Trujillo) for the second time. If you recall, he, like me, was transferred out of D Company, 1st Battalion, 9th Marines, 3rd Marine Division, into M Company, 3rd Battalion, 3rd Marines, 3rd Marine Division. Once again, I was now at the battalion headquarters in Chu Lai. Supposedly, these guys—office pogues—were in the so-called rear echelon of where the day-to-day fighting took place.

Unluckily during the second evening of my rest and recuperation at the main command center, while talking to some of the administrative personnel in a large canvas tent, including the First Sergeant, we were suddenly attacked. Unexpectedly, mortars activated by the VC about three-quarters of a mile from camp, were hitting the headquarters area. As can be seen in picture 7.11, this is the kind of mortar setup the VC used. Still, they would not have dug themselves in like we did.

The mortar rounds were landing everywhere. One shell, in fact, came close to our tent. As it landed, the concussion from the blast knocked many things over. Again we could hear the whistling sound as the shells flew through the air. Although most of the guys were trying to run for cover, the First Sergeant screamed to me, in a high-pitched voice, *"Schaap, get a Jeep. Steal one if you have to, but get it now!"* I quickly got my rifle. I slung it over my left arm being that my right one was incapacitated, and headed for the camp motor pool. I could not have shot my weapon, though, because I had a cast on my right hand. When I arrived at the motor pool the incoming rounds had subsided, so I went back to my area to look for the First Sergeant.

What makes this story interesting is that the First Sergeant and I were planning to go and find the Viet Cong with their mortars. I could tell this decorated Marine was upset. He did not like what happened and he was definitely pissed off. I guess it brought back memories of him being in the Korean War. Nevertheless, he wanted me to take a Jeep so that we could go out in the boonies and find where the enemy was hiding. For me, it was no big deal except for the fact that I did not think we would find them in time. Remember what I have revealed before: the VC liked to hit us quickly and then run like the dickens. They were awfully good at this routine. They did just that this time.

Moreover, the type of mortars that the Viet Cong utilized weighed about forty pounds, as can be seen in picture 7.12. It was broken down into three parts: the barrel, bipod, and the base plate. We, too, as mentioned on the previous page, would have a three to five men team who would handle this type of equipment.

The mortar's overall length was almost three feet. It had a muzzle velocity of about 500 feet per second with a maximum range of about one mile. The VC could shoot about 15 rounds per minute.

About a week later, with my cast off but still with a very sore hand, I was flown back, via another helicopter ride, to where my company was located. I was now back with my squad. Our unit was actually stationed on the outskirts of An Trach and it was considered a listening post (LP). Just a little over one-half a mile away from the main village and where the company headquarters was established, at least from what I remember, a group of us were stationed in an even smaller hamlet called La Bong. The platoon leader assigned to my squad was one of the most forward positions around the main camp. We set up our site at the river's edge, as can be seen in picture 7.13. Three of us occupied this forward-looking and well-fortified hellhole of a position. This became our living quarters for the next few weeks.

Positioning us in forefront of our platoon meant that we were the most vulnerable and susceptible to attack—and attacks came frequently.

It was easy for the enemy to take potshots at us. It was about 0800 one clear and sunny day. I had just awakened from about four hours of sleep since I had the 2400 to 0400 duty watch. I was standing directly outside our covered area, and I had made some hot chocolate. The heat provided for my drink was C-4—a plastic explosive. I was drinking it out of my military-issued tin cup, which was part of my mess kit.

All of a sudden, a few VC opened fire on us. The shots came, all at once, from the tree line across the river. As you can tell from picture 7.13, that was not that far away. As that day came alive with gun fire with the Viet Cong shooting at us from all directions, one bullet went right through my tin cup and sprayed the hot chocolate all over me. I was mad as hell, but also grateful. God only knows why the bullet went through the tin cup and not through me. Once again, the Deity was looking over me.

As a result of this near-death experience, the three of us rebuilt our fort— a significantly modified foxhole, as can be seen in picture 7.14. Yes, those are empty beer cans on one side of the position. We collected them from the rest of the guys in our unit. We put those there to see if the VC could knock any of them over when they decided to shoot at us. In looking back, I guess we were pretty gutsy young Marines. May be we were just a little crazy.

As can be seen in picture 7.15, we also decided to dig about a three-foot deep trench around one side of the perimeter of the position so that we could escape out of our manufactured hand-made dwelling if need be. The Viet Cong would use the river not only for target practice on our position, but they would actually swim down at night to seek out other Marines who were positioned further down the river.

When not out on patrol, many of us took the opportunity to write to loved ones and close friends. Although I cannot remember how this particular pen pal correspondence came about, I enjoyed writing to this lovely female college student who was living in Michigan at the time. She was sweet and caring, and it seemed like she really wanted to know what was going on with the war. We wrote each other for about a month. Writing home, even though we did not write that often, was a great emotional release mechanism. It was a way, at least for a short time, to take our minds off the job at hand—seek out and kill the enemy. And, in my case, I always kept my writing paper and pen along with my toilet paper *(for use at a four-holer),* in a small plastic bag. I did this with the hopes of keeping both papers dry.

When not on reconnaissance, we were fortunate enough to take a little time to fish the local river. We enjoyed catching freshwater fish, as can be seen in picture 7.16 (me with fish). Because we were in a remote area or at least in a region away from the main supply lines, we were only provided with C-rations as our meal source. This food was at least twelve years old, dating back to 1952-53. Some of the cans had small pin-like holes in them. In truth, I loathed eating these one-man canned meals that were left over from the Korean War, as can be seen in picture 7.17. [192] In order to overcome my disdain for C-rations, fishing was the next best alternative.

When we knew we were not in imminent danger or possibly being observed by the VC, we would take a grenade and throw it in the river. The concussion would instantly kill the fish. The local kids of the village then would swim and retrieve the fish. That evening if we were not out on patrol, we would be invited to have a home-cooked dinner with some of the local Vietnamese people. Dinner consisted of some type of clear soup with things that looked like beans sprouts, vegetables that I had never seen before, and some kind of meat—possibly dog meat. Naturally, they served us rice with chopsticks.

When not out on patrol, we would try to buy some food from the villagers. For the most part, fruit was a readily obtainable food source in the hamlet. Bananas and green oranges were the most abundant in the area we were stationed. In turn, we would use the little amount of Vietnamese currency that we had in our possession and negotiate for extra edibles.

When not on a seek-and-destroy mission, we would take time out to play a little poker. Believe me, the stakes were high. The bets were big—really big (ha, ha). And the guys were not afraid to "call you." We certainly knew how to put our money where our mouth was–and we did that with our bullets (from our weapons), as can be seen in picture 7.18. Because we had so little money in our possession, this was our way of having a good time without losing any money.

Does this not look like fun? It was a great way to pass time. Besides, it was a means for us to talk about home or anything else that was on our mind. It was a way for us, at least for a short time, to forget our woes and anguish about the war.

Harry G. Summers, Jr., in his book, *The Vietnam War Almanac,* talks about the war of pacification and attrition in the following way:

---

[192] Stephen Weiss, *The Vietnam Experience–A War Remembered,* p. 61, (Boston Publishing Company, 1986).

Clear-and-hold or clear-and-secure is a basic tactic of pacification. Clear-and-hold operations involved driving enemy units out of a populated area so that pacification efforts could proceed. While U.S. Army infantry units were often involved in clearing operations, the long-term effort necessary to hold an area, (i.e., to eliminate local guerrilla units and uproot the enemy's political infrastructure), was normally conducted by South Vietnamese Army or Regional Forces. In I Corps the U.S. Marine Corps used a different approach. While Marine infantry units were also used to clear an area, Marine combined-action platoons were used to hold these areas. [193]

General Walt stressed that the objective of the war was to win the loyalty of the populace to the government, and the only way to obtain this objective was to eradicate the Viet Cong in the villages and hamlets. This was what the Marines sought to do. [194]

In further describing this pacification effort, one former Marine staff officer, Colonel George W. Carrington, Jr., the 3rd Marine Division G-2 in January 1966, later wrote that:

> To reassure the villagers that they were safe, supported and protected, U.S. Marines undertook a most demanding pattern of intensive, multiple, day-and-night, patrols. The incredible number of man-hours devoted to this end and the sincere, compassionate, and dedicated manner in which thousands of Marines did their duty were never understood or appreciated by outsiders. [195]

General Krulak, the Pacific Commander at the time, however, saw things a little differently. He argued:

> It is our conviction that if we can destroy the guerrilla fabric among the people, we will automatically deny the larger units the food and the intelligence and the taxes, and the other support they need. At the same time, if the big units want to sortie out of the mountains and come down where they can be cut up by our supporting arms, the Marines are glad to take them on, but the real war is among the people and not among these mountains. [196]

General Westmoreland, in early 1966, had yet another different viewpoint. He believed that the introduction of North Vietnamese Army units

---

[193] Harry G. Summers, Jr., *The Vietnam War Almanac*, p. 122, (Presidio Press, 1985).
[194] Jack Shulimson, *U.S. Marines in Vietnam –An Expanding War 1966*, p. 11, (U.S. Government Printing Office, 1982).
[195] Ibid.
[196] Ibid, p. 13.

into the south actualized an entirely new direction by the communists. His view was: "Yes, we accept the Marine Corps' concern about pacification, but we want you to do more." He wanted the Marines to experiment with lighter battalions and new tactics. Also in early 1966, Westmoreland began a crucial campaign to decimate the VC and NVA forces through a series of search-and-destroy operations. [197] General Walt's position was, "Yes, I will engage the enemy's main force units, but first I want to have good intelligence." [198]

By 1967 (my last year in the Corps), the enemy was still not running out of fighters. The North Vietnamese fielded some 280,000 men, and their ranks were growing. U.S. and allied forces by this time numbered some 1,173,800 men and women. This was an impressive number, but not against a mysterious and shrewd adversary that fought only when it chose to fight and only where it had nearby shelters preventing the full application of American power. [199] Knowing this, I feel this is exactly how my unit fought in this war—against an enemy that battled with us only when it chose to fight, and on their terms.

In itself and possibly because of the discussions that the Armed Forces commanders had at the time, the New Year (1966) brought about some interesting changes and reorganization to my unit. The whole Da Nang area with its large presence of Marines and Air Force, especially in and around the air base, now became a tempting target for the Viet Cong.

In his paperback, *No Shining Armor–The Marines at War in Vietnam,* Otto Lehrack mentions what life was like for Marines of my unit:

> Viet Cong activity in 3/3/3's new home increased both in number of events and in intensity. Sniper incidents now often meant being on the receiving end of several hundred rounds of small arms fire by a small group rather than a random shot from an individual. However, if there was ever a period in Vietnam when it could be said that the battalion had a relatively easy time, the first nine months of 1966 would probably fit the bill. In spite of this, Marines fought and died, but their operations were generally minor affairs conducted against Viet Cong guerrillas who were organized in small units and armed with outmoded weaponry. From January to August, the battalion was in the relatively civilized area west and south of Da Nang. We had some access to amenities such as showers, tents, recreational opportunities, and prepared food. For a few months in early 1966,

---

[197] Donald L. Gilmore and D. M. Giangreco, *Eyewitness Vietnam–Firsthand Accounts from Operation Rolling Thunder to the Fall of Saigon,* p. 86 (Sterling Publishing Company, 2006).

[198] Jack Shulimson, *U.S. Marines in Vietnam –An Expanding War 1966,* p. 14, (U.S. Government Printing Office, 1982).

[199] Donald L. Gilmore and D. M. Giangreco, *Eyewitness Vietnam–Firsthand Accounts from Operation Rolling Thunder to the Fall of Saigon,* p. 86 (Sterling Publishing Company, 2006).

the battalion even had a limited *liberty* policy in the Da Nang area. During daylight hours, several groups of carefully supervised Marines could go to some of the shopping areas and make purchases. Limited as it was, it was one of the few times that the average Marine ever had any normal contact whatsoever with Vietnamese civilians.

By February 1966, all but a few of the original members of the battalion had departed or were about to. Their thirteen-month tours were over. All of the men of 3/3/3 from this point forward would be replacements who reported to Vietnam in ones and twos and were assigned to a unit upon arrival. No longer would most of the men in the unit spend much of the tour together. When a new man arrived, he found himself surrounded by some Marines who were about to finish their tours, others who had been in the country for only a few days, and the rest who were in between. [200]

As a follow-up to the above statement, many of my fellow Marines and I never really had an easy time during our tour of duty in Vietnam. We never had access to such niceties as showers, recreational opportunities, and prepared (hot) food. In fact, I cannot remember eating a Marine Corps-provided warm meal more than a few times during my entire time in Vietnam. C-rations were a way of life–every day. I did, though, have a two/three-man tent. Most of us were certainly not able to go shopping in Da Nang and make purchases. We were too far away from a large Vietnamese city. For whatever reason, we were never told that this opportunity even existed.

While our unit was not involved in pacification, confrontation, and conflict every day, we would meet the VC regularly, in one skirmish after another. Most of these encounters and possible rendezvous with death are still vividly etched in my mind. Our more significant scuffles, which usually turned into minor battles with the Viet Cong, were frequent and they still haunt me today.

In the meantime, and according to the U.S. Marine Corps–1966:

Marines continued to fight a different kind of war, alongside the South Vietnamese who, for years, had been carrying on the struggle for their very existence as a people and as a nation. From the Marines' first landing at Da Nang in March 1965, marking the initial commitment of U. S. combat forces to South Vietnam, the Free World served notice that it was answering the Republic of Vietnam's call for help.

The challenge was fourfold:

---

[200] Otto J. Lehrack, *No Shining Armor–The Marines at War in Vietnam,* pp. 68-69, (University Press of Kansas, 1992).

1. To defend and provide security to the base areas from which our forces operate;
2. To find, fight, and destroy the Communist main-force units, whether guerrillas or conventional North Vietnamese Army forces;
3. To extend the area under positive government control, root out the Viet Cong infrastructure, and provide a screen of security;
4. Behind this screen of security, to assist the Vietnamese in an organized program of Revolutionary Development (nation-building), the Marine part of which is called "Civic Action."

The Marine air-ground team, operating from bases at Da Nang, Chu Lai, Hue/Phu Bai, and more recently, Dong Ha, expanded their perimeters along the rich and populous coastal area. This coastal plain, made up one-fourth of the total 10,000-square mile I Corps area in which the Marines primarily operated. It was the breadbasket of I Corps, producing salt, fish, and almost 470,000 tons of rice annually. Here, too, lived approximately 1.7 million of the 2.6 million Vietnamese who inhabited the five I Corps provinces.

With the arrival of more Marine units, the number of direct actions against the enemy spiraled. By continuous patrolling, counter-guerrilla actions, and multi-battalion operations, Marines forced the Communist armed forces into the open in an ever-widening area. Combat patrols rose to 400 and ambushes to 150 during each day and night. Large-scale operations against the Viet Cong totaled more than 160 by year's end. [201]

[201] *United States Marine Corps–1966*, p. 5, (U.S. Government Printing Office, 1967).

Picture 7.1
Getting ready for a mission
[Author photo]

Picture 7.2
In trucks
[Author photo]

Picture 7.3
Marine convoy
[via Author]

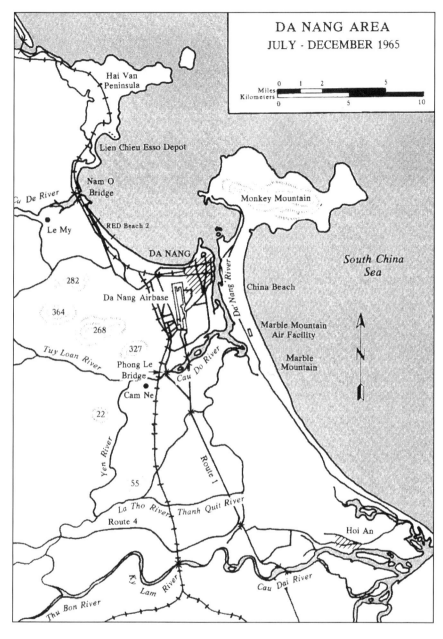

Picture 7.4
Map of Da Nang area 1965
[viaAuthor]

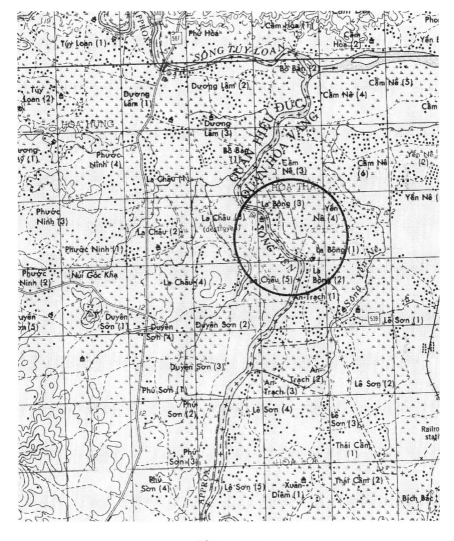

Picture 7.5
Map of An Trach
[via Author]

Picture 7.6
Vietnamese farmer
[Author photo]

Picture 7.7
In a canopy area
[Author photo]

Picture 7.8
Me standing guard
[Author photo]

Picture 7.9
Patrolling through a river as a platoon
[via Author]

Picture 7.10
Me on a Mule
[Author photo]

Picture 7.11
Mortar
[Author photo]

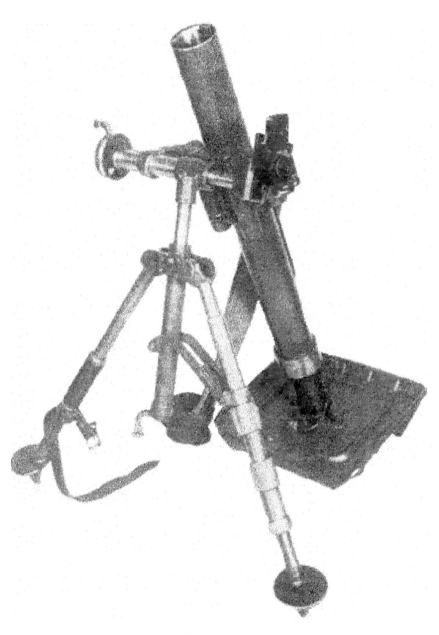

Picture 7.12
Mortar
[via Author]

Picture 7.13
Living quarters
[Author photo]

Picture 7.14
Rebuilt living quarters
[Author photo]

Picture 7.15
Building a trench
[Author photo]

Picture 7.16
Me with fish
[Author photo]

VIETNAM: MY WAR

Picture 7.17
Eating C-rations
[via Author]

Picture 7.18
Paying poker with the guys
[Author photo]

VIETNAM: MY WAR

Chapter 8

Vietnam
It is Time to Go Home, or is It?

L A Bong, a place that you would probably never find on a map, was located near the village of An Trach, some fifteen miles southwest of Da Nang. With its lovely but dangerous river it was something unique. It was not like most of the other villages we frequented, occupied or even destroyed. It was a place that was somewhat surreal. Unfortunately, it was a site that the VC enjoyed attacking. Yet, it was a locale where kids could be kids and have fun, as seen in picture 8.1. As soon as the children heard gunfire, they instantaneously ran for cover. They certainly knew what a hail of bullets sounded like. Unfortunately, they too knew what death looked like. Sometimes, because of their proximity to us, they would hide out in our fortified positions. At least there they felt safe. Other times, they would get caught in the crossfire. Unluckily, an occasional stray bullet would hit and kill one of the locals.

What made this village even more special was that these kids truly trusted us. We were, for once, seen as the good guys. They would say things like, *"GI number one."* In the past, though, the villagers, young and old alike, hated us. I could understand why. When we burned their hooch (their village), we took away their castle. Their chateaus that were made out of thatched material. We ruined what little they possessed. To make matters worse, when our amtracs drove over their rice paddies and vegetable gardens, they were furious. Again, I could understand why. Rice and vegetables were their staple foods and their lifeline for eating survival. They ate it every day. The people around La Bong treated us as their saviors. Interestingly enough, they wanted us here, and they wanted us here in a big way. When times were right and comfortable for them, they would show their closeness and affection. The children would even sit on our laps and let us take pictures of us together, as can be seen in picture 8.2. That is me with a warm Coke in my right hand and a young Vietnamese girl on my lap.

This was the Vietnam that made it more tolerable for us. This was the Vietnam that we really fought for. Peace for these peasants and their loving offspring—who had so little in the way of material possessions was our goal. And this was the Vietnam that brings back a few pleasant memories.

What was significant not just to La Bong but to all of Vietnam, is the Asian water buffalo. It was a large black animal with huge curving horns. The water buffalo was the farmer's lifeline. It was the planter, cultivator, and grower—the tiller of the soil. Farmers used his buffalo for many different tasks. Foremost, he used the water buffalo for plowing his rice or vegetable fields. Essentially, this gentle beast was of the utmost importance to the farmer and his family, as can be seen in picture 8.3. It was a creature they cherished. The water buffalo was precious and dear to them in many different ways. It was a living thing that these people domesticated thousands of years ago. Weighing between 700–1,000 pounds, these tame beasts brought happiness to the entire village. Even the littlest child could lead a buffalo by means of a ring in the animal's nose. They were led by these small boys, from their enclosures to the river wallows, where the farmer would come out to till the fields. This truly was a gentle and peaceful animal and I loved watching them in action.

Unfortunately, the water buffalo sometimes got in our way. When we encountered the Viet Cong in a firefight, at times we also ran into this bovine. Although these beasts of burden had a certain level of intelligence, they would, from time to time, be caught in the crossfire, and, regrettably, be killed. That, sadly enough, caused us a great deal of consternation. As such, the local farmer would charge us with murdering his friend. We were definitely caught between a rock and a hard place when we killed his mainstay. I was told when that happened our company commander would give the farmer one hundred dollars so that he could replace his water buffalo with another animal.

As I mentioned earlier, the villages of An Trach and La Bong were home to many small-unit attacks by the VC. It was an area full of hamlets where the enemy could hide. If we did not go out on foot patrol or if we were not airlifted into another area of operations, we would patrol with amtracs. As can be seen in picture 8.4, these 30-foot long armored assault military vehicles with machine guns mounted on top were frequently used for this special type of reconnaissance.

Early one day, February 10, 1966, at about 0600, while we were at our forward-looking entrenched outpost; a Viet Cong must have swum down the river west of our three-man fortified position. One of my fellow Marines was on duty at the time. His job was to scan the area for any invading VC, but he was asleep on his watch. Two of us were still sleeping underneath the nylon covering. The Viet Cong, who was now at the river's edge, threw a grenade directly at our sandbag-based built fort. It hit the nylon canopy and bounced off toward the river. It then exploded, and shrapnel flew everywhere. Fortunately, it did not hit us. Unfortunately, the grunt who was sleeping on guard duty could not handle the situation. He went ballistic on us. He went, at least from our perspective, temporarily insane and had no thought process whatsoever. He was so confused and bewildered—we call that the *"thousand-yard stare."* I felt he was senseless. I had never seen this before in the seven months I had been in Vietnam. Although the Marine was not physically hurt, he was emotionally impaired (beyond our imagination). Knowing what had materialized, we immediately called for a corpsman. It took three of us to pin him down so that the medic could shoot him full of morphine. What seemed to last for an eternity, lasted only for a few minutes. He was medevaced out of the area, and I never saw him again.

Here was an opportune time for the VC to take three jarheads out. It would have been simple for the Viet Cong to kill us. He almost did it this time. The grenade could have easily landed inside our tent, but we were lucky that day. God only knows why the hand-thrown bomb bounced off the nylon cover and exploded on the dirt. Only the Devine knew why the enemy did not crawl up the embankment and kill all three of us. It could easily have happened.

We do not know what happened to the VC. We think he must have swum further down river and escaped. As I have stated before, we were always sitting ducks and our adversary knew it. Even when we prepared the sides of our perimeter with barbed wire and punji stakes, as can be seen in picture 8.5, in order to keep the Viet Cong away from us, they still came close.

Occurrences like this did take an emotional peal on us. These kinds of skirmishes were psychologically disturbing. It is not easy to overcome incidents like the one I just mentioned. Thus, when there was alcohol available, which was rare, we would waste no time drinking a whole bottle of liquor to relieve our mental anguish. It was easy to get a bad case of the jitters from an event with potentially serious consequences like this. This created undue stress, pressure and strain that definitely took its toll.

Today, I still have the shakes in my hands, and I feel it is the result of what happened in Vietnam. These trembles have affected me in social situations, and to make matters worse, the president of a company that I worked for laughed at me when I congratulated him for the purchase of some land. There was a group of us in the conference room, and we all had some champagne in our glasses to celebrate. As I was about to propose a toast to him, with the drink in my right hand, my whole hand started to quiver—I got the jitters again. I could not stop the shaking. For whatever reason, he made fun of it. I will not forget that event. Some people do not know how to have empathy for others. Once he revealed his insensitive nature, I lost all respect and admiration for him and I realized he did not care about our veterans—warriors like me.

After spending nine months in Vietnam, and longer overseas, we were wondering when we might go home. We knew that we had a thirteen-month tour of overseas duty, but we were getting tired and quite aggravated being constantly attacked. Some of the guys were troubled enough about the war that they were openly questioning the future of this conflict. The hit-and-run maneuvers by the VC were unquestionably wearing us down and it never stopped. The Viet Cong were intense nuisances, and they knew it. They created enough ongoing provocation to keep us restless, day after day, week after week, and month after month. I hate to say this, but we could not win a war this way. As stated by General Sun Tzu, there are five essentials for military victory:

1) He will win who knows when to fight and when not to fight.
2) He will win who knows how to handle both superior and inferior forces.
3) He will win whose army is animated by the same spirit throughout all its ranks.
4) He will win who, prepared himself, waits to take the enemy unprepared.
5) And, he will win who has military capacity and is not interfered with by the sovereign. [202] In addition to this, this magnificent tactician declared: "He wins his battles by making no mistakes." [203]

This last clash, as I mentioned, created lots of anxiety and worry for many of us. Some of the guys were nervous and anxious all the time. A few were afraid of not surviving the next day. In fact, one Marine shed tears and mentioned to us that he wanted to go home now—right now. He could not take it any longer. The patrols and ambushes that he went on so frequently were now too much for him to take. He was becoming profoundly distressed and on the edge of a mental breakdown. In fact, he expressed to us that the next time we managed to get into a close-up fire fight; he was going to throw a grenade in front of himself and let the shrapnel hit his (raised) arm so that he could be evacuated.

The next firefight for this Marine happened only too soon. Although it was not a major showdown with the enemy, it still was another skirmish with the VC. That grunt did throw the grenade close to his body, and he immediately put his arm up in the air. As the small bomb exploded, some of the shrapnel tore up his limb. I guess he was willing to do just enough damage to himself so that he could get out of the war. I was overly stressed too, but I was not about to go home this way. I did not care if I was worn-out, (which I was all the time), nor did I care how badly underfed I was but I was sick and tired of eating those crappy old C-rations, and I did not care about my weight loss. I was not about to let the Marine Corps down—no way! I had to keep up my morale, and I did just that. Believe me, it was not easy.

Some Marines were becoming so nervous and jumpy, that when we were involved in an ambush, a couple of guys almost shot themselves in the foot. How could this have happened? When our rifles were slung over our shoulders, the barrel of the weapon, in most cases, faced the ground and at our feet. When the Viet Cong shot at us, we would, at times, stand there and fire right back. In order to do that, of course, we had to raise our weapons so that we could shoot in the enemy's direction. Out of trepidation these warriors would pull the trigger before their weapon was aimed properly at the enemy. They would accidentally jerk the trigger too hastily, while the rifle was pointed at

---

[202] Sun Tzu, *The Art of War,* p. 21, (Dodder and Stoughton Ltd., 1981).
[203] Ibid, p. 24.

their feet. It is easy to understand, as heartrending as it may sound, how someone could shoot himself in the foot.

Finally, in March 1966, I got word that I was going home in a month, and I, at last, received my papers for a transfer back to the United States to Camp Pendleton. It had been a year since I left the port of San Diego, a key location of the U.S. Navy's Pacific Fleet. I had one month more to go, but I was fixated on returning home right now—on making it out of Vietnam alive to reclaim my life. And after nine months in combat, covering a lot of areas from Da Nang to Chu Lai, I was exhausted and totally burned out. To say the least, I was psychologically spent. I was constantly fighting in the front (imaginary) lines. But it was not over for me however. Our unit heard that more Viet Cong were headed our way. About five miles from our base camp, the VC attacked us. There must have been quite a few of them close by. They were so near that we had to call for an air strike with F-4 Phantom jets dropping Napalm. As can be seen in picture 8.6, you can see the fire burning from the drop of a Napalm bomb, and a VC running from it. The fire was intense, and one certainly did not want to be caught in it. As soon as he ran away from his hiding place and reached the clearing, we shot him. Right or wrong, that was simply our job—seek out and destroy our foe.

Napalm was first engineered by a group of chemists led by Professor Louis F. Fieser at Harvard University. It is a mixture of gasoline and a thickening agent that rapidly deoxygenates the available air as well as creating large amounts of carbon monoxide causing suffocation.

Napalm is an acronym derived from naphthenic and palmitic acids, whose salts are applied in its manufacture. It is a thick and very hot jelly that flows under pressure and sticks to any target as it burns. For example, water boils at approximately 212 degrees Fahrenheit. Napalm, on the other hand, generates temperatures of 1,470 to 2,190 degrees Fahrenheit. Being doused with Napalm is the most terrible pain you could imagine.

Interestingly enough, our government decided to contract the manufacturing of Napalm with Dow Chemicals. They, in turn, produced the sticky goo in mass quantities for military use. It was truly a product of mass destruction and devastation. Napalm was primarily exploited to burn down the jungle. Once it starts to burn, because of its intense heat, it is difficult to put out.

This skirmish continued for two days. Out there in the front lines, wherever that was, I was assigned a new piece of armament. It was a throwaway M72 Light Antitank Assault Weapon, or LAAW, as can be seen in picture 8.7.

According to a source that I pulled from the Internet:

> The LAAW was the Army's primary shoulder-fired, man-portable, one-shot 66mm light anti-tank rocket. It was a revolutionary idea: a pre-packaged rocket, which could be fired and the launcher then thrown away. It was manufactured by Talley Industries in the U.S. under license from Norway. The LAAW was later produced in Czechoslovakia and Russia. It had an effective range of about 500–

600 feet. It also had a muzzle velocity of about 475 feet per second, meaning that it could hit its effective range target in a little over a second. The LAAW weighed five pounds and when fully extended it was almost three feet in length. In the closed position, it was about twenty-five inches long. It carried one high-explosive anti-tank warhead.

Good, bad, or indifferent, I did not have the chance to train with the M72. Nonetheless, I took advantage of this anti-tank assault weapon during our offensive on the VC over the next two days. Because it was new to me, I tested it by firing it in the vicinity of a hooched area. It certainly was not the best piece of military armament for combat situations I encountered. It was also impractical for the reason that I was not firing against tanks or solid metal objects. I never did. I was constantly shooting at skinny and gaunt little people wearing coolie hats with black pajama-like clothes, also wearing those thinly made Ho Chi Minh flip-flops who were always hiding behind thatched shelters and the like.

That scuffle with the Viet Cong and the Napalm drop netted us a few prisoners. Once captured, they were brought in for questioning, as can be seen in pictures 8.8, 8.9, and 8.10. We also sustained two casualties over a two-day period of fighting. We were lucky that it was not worse since it seemed like we were always caught in an ambush.

Having encountered the wrath of Napalm, the VC quickly told us where more of their comrades were hiding. As always, we went after them, and it was just a matter of time before we caught up with their comrades.

Just about this same time, March 4–8, U.S. Marines and ARVN regulars participated in a joint ground war operation. The battle was called Operation Utah/Lien Kiet 26, in the vicinity of Quang Ngai City, against the North Vietnamese Army and Viet Cong main forces. Fortuitously, about one-third of the NVA's 36th Regiment's original strength had been decimated. Marine and ARVN forces confirmed 632 enemy casualties in this operation.[204] Unfortunately, 83 Marines and 32 ARVN soldiers were killed in action.[205]

As we were trying new equipment (e.g., the M72) in the field, U.S. commanders, mistakenly believed that the vast technological advantages of the American forces would change the ground rules of guerrilla warfare. (I never thought this to be the case.) Traditional military theorists had concluded that a government needed an advantage of about ten to one over guerrilla forces.[206] From my own first-hand experiences, I feel that advantage needed to be at

---

[204] Leo Daugherty, *The Vietnam War–Day by Day*, pp. 76-77, (Chartwell Books, Inc., 2011).

[205] *List of allied military operations of the Vietnam War (1966)*, Wikipedia.

[206] Alan Axelrod, *The Real History of the Vietnam War–A New Look at the Past*, p. 192, (Sterling, 2013).

least thirty to one, if not more. As you know, those types of odds are unrealistic in conventional warfare—and certainly would not be acceptable by the American public.

Early in 1966, as I was getting ready to leave Vietnam, my battalion began a new type of operation called *County Fair*.

Described by the Marines as the "seeds of population control," these were cordon and search tactics designed to separate the guerrillas from their population bases. As officially described, County Fairs were to convince the people that the GVN (i.e., Government of Vietnam) was an effective government that was interested in the welfare of the people and that a GVN victory against the VC was inevitable. County Fair was also a combination of military, civic and psychological warfare actions to reestablish the Vietnamese government control over the populace of a given area. It was designed to flush the Viet Cong from the community in which they were a parasite, while at the same time insuring that the populace was not alienated towards the government. Military actions were accompanied by a vigorous civic action program which attempted to convince the population that the government was interested in the welfare of the people and that a government's victory over the Viet Cong was inevitable. On the surface, this sounded good, but I do not think it did much good in the long run!

Typically lasting for a day or two, the operations began by sealing off one or more hamlets with our troops. The people would then be herded through a tent where identification cards were checked against the census of those who lived in the village. Those who could not properly identify themselves were moved off to one side for questioning. To minimize the potential for resentment, the verified population was then examined by the battalion doctors and corpsmen for illnesses and, when necessary, received treatment on the spot. In fact, by late spring, 3/3/3s medical people were treating more than 6,000 Vietnamese civilians around Da Nang each month for hookworm, diarrhea, and more serious diseases. General Westmoreland grew to like the County Fairs and in his memoir stated that he pressed for countrywide adoption of the program. [207]

I do remember taking part, in a small way, in the inception of this program. I also noticed that our corpsmen were constantly treating the Vietnamese peasants. On the surface, I felt it was a good humanitarian gesture; however, I believe the program did not really work. If it did, we would not have had to spend ten years fighting this war.

My departure was drawing near. I could feel the days ticking away. Regardless, it was a tough time for me. I was emotionally drained from the constant hit-and-run attacks from the Viet Cong. Essentially, I was starting to rationalize every movement I made. Each time that I went out on patrol it was that much more nerve-wracking—menacing, from a mental standpoint.

---

[207] Otto J. Lehrack, *No Shining Armor–The Marines at War in Vietnam*, pp. 72-73, (University Press of Kansas, 1992).

Here, summarized, were the scenarios as I saw them: One of our fellow Marines went insane on me. Others, as corny as it may sound, wanted to find stupid ways to earn a trip back home, such as self-inflicting shrapnel injuries of a grenade. Even my so-called girlfriend stopped writing me. That, in itself, was a real bummer. Of course, my parents were extremely worried about me. And, I was asking myself whether it was now my time to be hit—because others were.

I had to shake this stuff off since my job was not yet done. I was *not* about to mentally break down. And I was *not* about to lay down my rifle and quit. At times, it was close. I tried my best to put these psychological upsetting feelings behind me. I had to be strong and resilient. I had to be brave. I had to have the audacity to persevere. I had to convince myself that I could make it. More important, I had to have the mettle and discipline to continue. It was all about survival mentality—something I trained for, and something I knew I had. And most importantly, I had to show my fellow Marines that I was resolute. I had to be a grunt, a Leatherneck with dignity and poise, just like them.

Seven days before my departure from An Trach, never having been to a PX, or any type of club for enlisted men in Vietnam, I was back on reconnaissance. Once again, we ran into more VC. This time, two more warriors from my company were killed in action during a night ambush. On top of that, two other Marines were wounded earlier in action. March 29 and 30, 1966, were not good days for the men of our unit.

During this last skirmish we used our M79s. These are grenade launchers or "Bloopers," as they were called, looked like a fat shotgun. They are break-open type of weapons that fire a high-explosive grenade-type of cartridge. The M79 also had an effective range of 350 yards.

Another source on the Internet describes the infamous M79: This weapon first appeared during the Vietnam War and closely resembled a large bore, single-barrel, sawn-off shotgun. The M79 was also designed as a close support weapon for the infantry, and was intended to bridge the gap between the maximum throwing distance of a hand grenade, and the shortest range of supporting mortar fire, an area of between 50 and 300 meters.

The M79 was a single shot, shoulder fired, break-barrel loading weapon, which fired a spherical 40mm diameter grenade. The M456 HE grenades fired from the M79 traveled at a muzzle velocity of 75 meters per second, and contained enough explosive within a steel casing that upon impact with the target would produce over 300 fragments at 1,524 meters per second with a lethal radius of up to five meters. [208]

A wounded Marine, Private Stephenson, was evacuated via helicopter to the USS Repose (nicknamed *Angel of the Orient*, a 520-foot hospital ship, capable of handling about 800 patients), that was stationed in the Gulf of Tonkin. He was later transferred to the Oakland Naval Hospital. In 1968, he was

---

[208] *M79 grenade launcher,* Wikipedia.

medically discharged with a 100% disability rating. Another Marine wounded and later killed in action in Vietnam in 1968 was Stephenson's close friend too.

Our unit participated in many combat operations and skirmishes over our tour of duty in Vietnam. The probability of getting wounded or even killed was only too high during that time. Dealing with that reality was simply part of our job.

Taking care of our wounded combatants, warriors who would experience insurmountable pain and agony, as well as the dead was the job of a corpsman. We usually called them *Doc.* These special and gifted comrades, as mentioned before, were our real heroes. They had to deal with physically and emotionally overwhelming situations. I do not know how these guys dealt with our men who were bleeding to death, but they did it with compassion, humility, and, most of all, bravery. They were our heroes!

Bob Hingston and Carl King, former Marines and Vietnam Veterans, have provided a wonderful tribute to Navy Corpsmen that is worth sharing. While drawn out, their affectionate, tender, and lengthy story goes like this:

> The corpsman is a Navy enlisted man who has medical training and is skilled enough to get you and whatever pieces that are left of you back to a hospital. Although he is a Navy man, he has the respect of the Marines and is thought of as one of them and is known to everyone as "Doc." He is the one that responds to the call, "Corpsman up!" He is the one who will run to you when you have taken one in the chest, or elsewhere, and the wind is knocked out of you. He is the one that will run to you when Charlie is pumping more rounds into you. He is there when there is complete chaos: automatic rifle fire, hand grenades exploding, M79 rounds being lobbed into the brush a few meters in front of you, and more noise than anyone ever hoped to make on the Fourth of July.
>
> When it seems like you have been laying in the dirt forever, the corpsman is the one that has exposed him to enemy fire. He is the one that runs up to you and screams in your ear, "Where are you hit?" You are, sorry to say, gasping for air because it is leaking out of your lung like a tire with a hole in it. You are trying not to go into shock, but you feel like your whole body is on fire. You are wrenching with pain. The bullets, for the time being, are flying all around your head and body because they, the VC, are trying to kill you and now the Doc.
>
> For some strange reason, God knows where the courage comes from; the corpsman seems immune to or oblivious of all that is going on around you. His only focus (which may only last for a few minutes, because he has to attend to others) is on you. You are the Marine that has been hit in the chest. In the movies, nevertheless, a guy gets hit once and that is about it. In Vietnam, there was not any

limit to the number of times in one firefight you could be hit. Hell, you could get hit a dozen or more times if someone had little else to do but try to nail your young butt.

It should be easy to realize how panic and fear can work on a guy who has been wounded and is basically helpless as the enemy keeps shooting at him. It is not fair. It is fear, knowing that every round that just misses you means the next one will not. And while one is laying there powerless, disabled, and unable to move or breathe can cause a terror that does its damnedest to conquer your soul and leave you pissing all over yourself in sheer anxiety.

The corpsman yells for a medevac. One is soon called by a radioman while someone else is calling in a fire mission. This may take twenty minutes before the first friendly round comes in. A lot can happen in those twenty minutes; your whole outfit could be wiped out. If the ambush is big enough and you are caught in crossfire, it could take a lot less than twenty minutes. The action is hot, bullets burn your skin. They get close enough to feel without actually hitting you. The dirt and sand are red hot as the bullets kick it in your face. You think, for a split second, "God, that was close." You think again. "Please God; get me out of this one. I promise to be good from now on!" Suddenly, someone is dragging you by your collar or some other piece of clothing. You are not sure what is going on, but you do know that the pain is bringing you close to unconsciousness. Your whole body is shaking uncontrollably. Your chest has a hissing sound coming from where you think your lung is. It is spouting air and filling up with this warm substance that makes it harder to breathe. You are sure that blood is now filling your lung up to the point of collapsing. Fear and panic is now gone. It has been replaced with sheer terror and shock. Yet this Navy guy, "Doc," keeps miraculously dragging your body toward safety, while half the enemy forces are trying to nail him. "Mother up!" you hear through the fog. "Mother up" was used frequently for the reason that the Viet Cong knew when you shouted "Corpsmen up" that a doc was coming to help a wounded Marine. You know another one of your fellow Marines has just taken a hit and could possibly be worse than you are. "Coming," screams the Doc. He tells someone to keep pressure on the rag covering your chest and not to take his hand off it. He turns and heads in the direction of the last caller, while the enemy continues to do their best to nail him before he can reach his next casualty.

Maybe this is why we considered the corpsmen to be one of us. Although they never went through boot camp at Parris Island or San Diego, they were Marines at heart, and damn good ones. Only a fool or a hero would leave a place of safety to throw his body in harm's way for someone he may not even know. I never met a corpsman that I thought was a fool. To me, a hero does things that his logical mind is telling him not to do. His logical mind says to stay put, get further down. Above all, do not get up and go where someone else just got shot. The hero ignores what his mind is telling him and goes forward in the face of the enemy fire. His only thought is to get to the Marine that has called for help. He will get to him! He may get shot himself but he will not let that warrior die by himself. Sometimes they are not alive when he gets there, but he is there and exposed to the same fire that killed the Marine he came to rescue. He goes from wounded to wounded doing the best that he can do to save their lives, and give them a little more time. After that, he will help get them back to an aid station where they may be saved.

Let me be a point man any day over being a corpsman in a Marine infantry unit. At least, I can take cover and return fire. (Having been a point man numerous times, I wholeheartedly agree.)

The corpsman is uniquely special. And while the Navy offers a lot of other programs that are a hell of a lot less dangerous, the corpsman knows that going on a mission they will be placed in harm's way. They knew that they would be assigned to the heaviest fighting areas in Vietnam, yet they volunteered anyway. They care about human suffering and wanted to do all in their power to aid. They were willing to put their lives on the line.

Check out the Wall. In Washington, D. C., you will find a lot of corpsmen's names on the Wall. They gave their all. Many of us, who were fortunate enough to return home, did so because of their unselfish acts of heroism. In many cases, they did so without any medals or rewards except the personal feeling of having done their job, and did it well. Because of them, thousands of Marines today can greet each other and say welcome home.

When you go to see the Wall, a tribute dedicated to the Vietnam Servicemen who paid the ultimate price for their country, you will see a statue dedicated to the grunts. You will also see an area dedicated to the nurses who served their country. What you will not see, though, is a tribute to the corpsmen. A compliment and mark of respect should be made to the men who risked their lives by exposing themselves to tremendous enemy fire, by running, crawling, and by inching their way into the thickest of the thick of fighting, all to answer the call for "help." They sacrificed their safety to save others' lives.

I wonder why there are no special honors awarded to these brave individuals? These were the men who prevented so many of us here today from having our names placed on the Wall.

There is a place where a statue could and should be placed. It is an image of a single individual, loaded down with his medical gear. It should be a statue representing those that were always ready and willing to give their lives in the hopes that they might save a life. Corpsmen are a special and distinct breed of men who stand out proud and strong. Their everyday acts of bravery and heroism deserve to be recognized by their brothers in arms. They gallantly served, and were more than willing to give their all. Because of them, many of us were given the opportunity to make a difference in the world.

There may never be a work of art, a bronze figure in honor of the corpsmen who served our country so well, and who were so important to the Marines in the battle field. Statue or not, I would like to personally salute you and to say to you: Semper Fidelis Marine—as the title is well earned, and the honor is long overdue. Thank you for your willingness of service, and self-sacrifice, so that many like me today are able to say, welcome home, Doc, a job well done.

To add to Hingston's and King's narrative, here is some addition information. Contributions of hospital corpsmen in Vietnam were noteworthy. They cared for over 700,000 Navy and Marine Corps combat casualties and countless military and civilian sick call patients. Their valor was great. Three earned the Medal of Honor for heroism. Furthermore, 30 hospital corpsmen received the Navy Cross, 127 received the Silver Star Medal, and 290 Bronze Star Medals. Regrettably, 638 hospital corpsmen were killed in action, more than any other war except World War II. Another 4,563 would earn the Purple Heart.

Sadly, the overwhelming majority of enlisted Navy casualties in Vietnam were members of the Hospital Corps (they serve as battlefield corpsmen with the Marine Corps, rendering emergency medical treatment to include initial treatment in a combat environment). If they were discharged as the result of injury due to combat, they were not eligible for the Good Conduct Medal regardless if their conduct and performance ratings were exceptional. The Navy, in May of 1974, changed its policy and now conforms to the other services. But, those who served in Vietnam and possibly other conflicts were not eligible.

By far, the Hospital Corps' largest contribution in Vietnam was with the Marine Corps units. Starting with the 50 who landed with the Marines at Da Nang in 1965 (with my battalion), the enlisted medical component would grow to 2,700 hospital corpsmen assigned to the 1st and 3rd Marine Divisions.

From March 20 - 28, 1966, two weeks before me leaving Vietnam, Operation Kings went into effect. Two units from my regiment (3rd Marines & 9th Marines) and the 3rd Tank Battalion advanced to a VC stronghold close to where we were currently located. Even though my unit did not participate in this skirmish, both companies from my regiment met with stiff enemy resistance from the well-entrenched Viet Cong. Thank goodness, air support destroyed the dug-in enemy, allowing my fellow warriors to carry on with their mission to kill 58 Viet Cong. Unfortunately, eight Marines were killed and 60 more were wounded in action. More importantly, the Viet Cong were, by and large, cleared from an area they previously dominated for a long period of time. [209]

On April 4th, Major General Wood B. Kyle, commanding general of my unit, 3rd Marine Division issued an operations order extending the civic action program known as Golden Fleece II to all new harvesting areas in the 3rd Marine Division's TAOR. [210]

On April 5th, 1966, it was with powerfully mixed emotions what I was going to leave behind in Vietnam, which proved later to be disastrous. Having heard *Good Vibrations* on the radio, sung by The Beach Boys, I departed my Company almost 13 months after having left the port of San Diego for Okinawa, and jumped into a helicopter from our company headquarters in An Trach. That day, I left the brave men of Mike Company. Most were fearless, 3rd Battalion, 3rd Marines, 3rd Marine Division (3/3/3). Later that day, I arrived at battalion headquarters in Da Nang as my 13-month rotation was coming to an end. There, I grabbed my sea bag. I spent one night in Da Nang before I would catch a second helicopter ride to the Da Nang Air Base. From there, and on April 6, 1966, I boarded a government air Fairchild C-123 Provider, also known as a military transport plane, and headed straight for Okinawa. (Interestingly enough, this same type of aircraft was utilized to spray Agent Orange throughout Vietnam). I left Vietnam, still as a teenager, only 19 years of age, with youthful and strong shoulders that bore a transformed troubled head. As I flew away from death's hold, I could see the rice paddies and the green pleated mountains where I had lost so many friends—fellow Marines. This is where I, unequivocally, lost my youth. My boyish personality was gone forever. Yes, in such a short period of time, my formative years were so far behind me.

For your edification, the C-123 Provider served in Vietnam as transports for cargo and/or personnel. With a crew of three, it carried both servicemen, who were heading home, as I was, and litter military patients who needed to be airlifted for major medical treatment. It could hold up to 60 passengers. Besides carrying cargo and/or personnel, this aircraft, to my surprise, was specifically used as part of the United States' defoliation operation. It gained notoriety for its use in "Operation Ranch Hand." [211]

Operation Ranch Hand was a U.S. military operation during the Vietnam War, lasting from 1962 until 1971. Largely inspired by the British use of 2,4,5-T and 2,4-D (Agent Orange) during the Malayan Emergency in the 1950s, it was part of the overall herbicidal warfare program during the war called "Operation Trail Dust". Operation Ranch Hand involved spraying an estimated 20 million U.S. gallons (76,000 m³) of defoliants and herbicides over rural areas of South Vietnam in an attempt to deprive the Viet Cong of food and vege-

---

[209] Leo Daugherty, *The Vietnam War–Day by Day,* pp. 82-83, (Chartwell Books, Inc., 2011).

[210] Ibid, p. 84.

[211] *Fairchild C-123 Provider,* Wikipedia.

tation cover. The Vietnamese government reckons that 400,000 people were killed or maimed and 500,000 children born with birth defects as a result of this spraying of what were called by Americans 'rainbow herbicides'. [212] (Note: I personally saw these type of planes spray Agent Orange. However, and at the time, I did not know that they were scattering this deadly herbicide on the jungle foliage. From what I later read about, they spewed large amounts of Agent Orange in at least two different locations where I was stationed during my tour of duty in Vietnam.) Once full-scale military operations began in South Vietnam, it became clear to commanders that the jungle overgrowth (where I fought most of the time) posed a major obstacle to uprooting the Viet Cong from their lairs. Some form of defoliant or plant suppressant was needed to clear guerrilla-infested areas, strip away their cover, so that successful operations could be effected. [213]

I was quarantined at Camp Smedley D. Butler, a U.S. Marine Corps base, located in the Japanese prefecture of Okinawa. Camp Butler is physically separated throughout the island into a number of different camps. It was named for legendary Marine Major General Smedley D. Butler (July 30, 1881–June 21, 1940) who was awarded with two Medals of Honor, the highest rank authorized at that time. At the time of his death he was the most decorated Marine in U.S. history. [214] While there, I had several physical examinations. On April 7th, I was given a thorough examination and found physically qualified to rotate back to the United States. However, I do not believe I was mentally qualified to return home. I was told by the medical officer at this transit facility, in accordance with BUMED Instruction 1590.2B, that I would have to receive a chest x-ray at my next permanent duty station.

On April 11th, after three days of rest, recuperation, and constant medical checkups, I walked over and stood in line at the edge of the runway, sweating profusely through my starched khaki uniform, as a harried-looking young private first class, I boarded a government air, combat-loaded Boeing 707 jet from Kadena Air Force Base, located in the towns of Kadena and Chatan, Okinawa. This method was called, at the time, military out-processing. This base was the hub of U.S. airpower in the Pacific, and home to the USAF's 18th Wing and a variety of associate units. Travelling at a speed of nearly 500mph and high above the earth (presumably around 35,000–40,000 feet above sea level) I landed that same day at Marine Corps Air Station (MCAS), in El Toro, California, located near the City of Irvine. During the 1960s, many U.S. Marines left for and returned from Vietnam at El Toro MCAS. MCAS also served as the primary base for Marine Corps west coast fighter squadrons during the Vietnam War.

---

[212] *Operation Ranch Hand*, Wikipedia.

[213] Donald L. Gilmore and D. M. Giangreco, *Eyewitness Vietnam–Firsthand Accounts from Operation Rolling Thunder to the Fall of Saigon*, p. 88 (Sterling Publishing Company, 2006).

[214] *Smedley Butler*, Wikipedia.

I landed, about twelve hours later, with no fanfare or welcome of any kind. I landed back in the states feeling so isolated and solitary. My time in Vietnam was over so abruptly. It was surreal that I had been in the jungles on operations and facing death only days before. It was especially lonely and I felt deserted. I had very little time to decompress. My spine tingled as I stepped off the plane and on to American soil. Even though returning home was not confrontational, it was nonetheless unnerving. I returned to a country riven by our presence in Vietnam. There was no parade greeting for returning Vietnam veterans, because it was a nation that was clearly divided and torn, and few people felt like celebrating. Still, we returned home to endure ... We had persevered and that was our only victory. Because we landed at a military base, we were fortunately not greeted by antiwar protesters. Demonstrators really did not know why we were there, but would blame us for America's involvement in the war. Luckily, we did not have to hear the antiwar protesters yelling, "baby killer," "rapist," and worse. Strictly from my point of view, I believe they blamed us for the very same reason that the activists were, themselves (more than) morally confused. Even though the pacifists thought they understood the war in Vietnam, I honestly feel that they really did not comprehend our involvement in this country that was being taken over by the communists.

One group that opposed the Vietnam conflict and American intervention throughout the globe was the Black Panther Party (BPP). Having met and chatted with a few members of the BPP, I too believed this organization was confused and misguided. They were heavily into the drug culture at the time. They were also deeply involved with the widespread antiwar sentiment. As such, Marines like me thought their toughest opponent was not the NVA but rather these social vicissitudes that seemed to attack the very fundamentals of the Corps.

The BPP was founded on October 15, 1966 by Huey P. Newton and Robert George "Bobby" Seale. And in their initial ten-point program, they demanded that Black men be exempt from the draft:

> We want all Black men to be exempt from military. We believe that Black people should not be forced to fight in the military service to defend a racist government that does not protect us. We will not fight and kill other people of color in the world who, like Black people, are being victimized by the white racist government of America. We will protect ourselves from the force and violence of the racist police and the racist military, by whatever means necessary. [215]

During the first three months of 1966 that I fought in Vietnam, "A total of nine grunts from my unit were killed in action in various places in Vi-

---

[215] Joe Allen, *Vietnam: the (last) war the U.S. lost,* p. 95, (Haymarket Books, 2008).

etnam. Four of those Marines were from my company (M Company). The first Marine was killed on January 7th. The last one was killed on March 30th."

As I was leaving Vietnam, puzzled and disoriented, I felt there was a fair amount of unrest with our Vietnamese allies. Having fought alongside them in both major battles and minor skirmishes, some of these soldiers were starting to become wary of our presence. When we were involved in a direct conflict with the enemy, I could tell, at times, that these men did not want to participate in the war.

As stated by Otto Lehrack, in his book, *No Shining Armor:* "Buddhist leaders dissatisfied with the Saigon government organized heated anti-government demonstrations that revealed a country on the brink of civil war. They were particularly militant in Da Nang after Premier Nguyen Cao Ky dismissed General Nguyen Can Thi, a Buddhist favorite and the Vietnamese commander of the military region that composed I Corps. Although the Marines attempted to stay clear of the dispute, they were drawn into it by a series of incidents. Numerous ARVN units sided with the dissidents, and on May 18th, after I left Vietnam the most dramatic of the confrontations took place. The rebel 'Struggle Forces' seized the Da Nang River bridge and rigged it with demolitions. Without this bridge, III MAF (Marine Amphibious Force—two or more Marine divisions plus necessary Marine air support) headquarters and the Marine helicopter facility at Marble Mountain would be cut off from the rest of Da Nang. Lieutenant General Lewis Walt, the senior Marine in Vietnam, went to the scene personally to take charge." [216]

By now, the war was taking a psychological toll on our administration. George Ball, a longtime critic, finally resigned as Undersecretary of State. McGeorge Bundy, the national Security Adviser, decided troop buildup had assumed ridiculous proportions. He left the White House in 1966. President Johnson replaced him with Walt Rostow, who preached military victory over North Vietnam and the modernization of South Vietnam. Westmoreland reported victory after victory to Johnson in a continuous string of battles. To say the least, President Johnson was frustrated and confused. He had a sinking feeling that he was losing control of the war. One night, in June 1966, he could not sleep. Pacing the floor and cursing, he woke up Lady Bird Johnson and complained that victory does not really mean victory. I cannot get out. I cannot finish it with what I have got. So what the hell do I do? [217]

As you can tell, President Johnson's attitude toward the Vietnam War was a real mystery and challenge. His memoirs record events and policies but not his private thoughts. In fact, the President wrote only a few notes for the record and kept no diary as far as we know; his telephone calls are unreliable because this democratic president used the phone to convince, cajole, and oth-

---

[216] Otto J. Lehrack, *No Shining Armor–The Marines at War in Vietnam*, p. 85, (University Press of Kansas, 1992).

[217] James S. Olson and Randy Roberts, *Where the Domino Fell–America and Vietnam 1945–1990*, p. 152, (Diane Publishing Company, 1991).

erwise manipulate—as an instrument of politics and diplomacy. Army officer H. R. McMaster, who holds Master of Arts and Ph.D. degrees in American History from the University of North Carolina at Chapel Hill, cites telephone conversations to prove that the president wanted no war, but not those in which he talked of *"touching up"* the men in Hanoi. LBJ did, indeed, say he had never seen such a mess and had no idea what America could get from its commitment. [218]

For you history and trivia buffs, here are some of the other major events that happened in 1966:

> January 16, protest singer Joan Baez is put in jail for ten days. She was among 124 anti-Vietnam War demonstrators arrested for blocking the entrance to a U.S. Army induction center at Oakland, California.
>
> January 24–March 6, in the largest search-and-destroy mission up to that point in the war, Operation Masher, 2,389 Vietcong casualties were reported.
>
> January 31, the U.S. bombing over North Vietnam is renewed.
>
> February 14, General Maxwell Taylor becomes U.S. Ambassador to South Vietnam.
>
> March, Australia sends over 4,000 troops to fight in Vietnam.
>
> March 2, the U.S. announces that its forces in Vietnam now number 215,000 with another 20,000 en route.
>
> March 4–8, Operation Utah conducted by U.S. Marines/ARVN units in the vicinity of Quang Ngai city, I Corps, against NVA and VC main force units; 632 known enemy casualties. [219] Interestingly enough, I participated in Operation Starlite, twenty-five miles to the north of Quang Ngai City, seven months earlier. At that time we thought we secured the area. I guess not!
>
> March 9, Communist forces capture a U.S. Special Forces camp in the A Shau Valley, gaining control over a vital access route into South Vietnam. U.S. Marine helicopters manage to rescue twelve of the seventeen Green Berets and 172 of the 400 South Vietnamese.
>
> April 12, U.S. B-52 bombers commence bombing over North Vietnam.
>
> June 29, U.S. planes attack fuel storage facilities around Hanoi and Haiphong, North Vietnam, marking the first time that facilities around Hanoi are hit.
>
> August, Nguyen Cao Ky becomes Prime Minister of South Vietnam.

---

[218] John Prados, *Vietnam: The History of an Unwinnable War, 1945-1975*, p. 105, (University Press of Kansas, 2009).

[219] Harry G. Summers, Jr., *The Vietnam War Almanac*, p. 37, (Presidio Press, 1985).

August 14, President Johnson, after conferring with General West-moreland, says, "A Communist military takeover in South Vietnam is no longer improbable ... it is impossible."

October 26, President Johnson visits U.S. troops in Vietnam. [220] I, because of my role at the time—a rifleman, never had the opportunity to see him in person.

December 2 (Black Friday), fuel dumps and truck parks are hit around Hanoi. A record eight U.S. planes are downed, bringing U.S. aircraft losses over North Vietnam to a total of 435 planes.

December 31, U.S. Military forces are now at 385,300, 6,644 U.S. military personnel killed in action to date, 52,500 allied military personnel in Vietnam. 79,000 air sorties have been flown against North Vietnam compared with 25,000 in 1965. You would think by now that we are winning the war?

Total Marine casualties, during 1966, from my unit alone (3/3/3): "enlisted–forty-three; officers–two."

Besides knowing a little more of what happened in Vietnam, from an abbreviated perspective, during 1966, I feel it is also important for you to be more familiar with Agent Orange and the effect it had on Vietnam, its people, and our troops. This information is shared by Harry G. Summers, Jr., in his manuscript, *The Vietnam War Almanac:*

One of the terrible legacies of the Vietnam War is what veterans believe to be their contamination with Agent Orange. (As mentioned earlier in this chapter), it was used as a herbicide and applied by the U.S. Air Force from C-123 aircraft in a defoliation operation called Ranch Hand from 1962 to 1971, this chemical contained minute amounts, approximately 2.0 parts per million, of a poisonous substance called 2, 3, 7, 8-tetrachloridibenzo-para-dioxin (TCDD), a type of dioxin, which has been claimed to result in various, serious health problems.

According to a Veterans' Administration study, the major herbicides sprayed in Vietnam were assigned code names corresponding to the color of identification bands painted on the herbicide storage drums. During the initial stages of light herbicide use in Vietnam, from 1962 through 1964, the most commonly used herbicide was purple and pink.

During this period of Operation Ranch Hand, approximately 140,000 gallons of purple and 123,000 gallons of pink were sprayed in South Vietnam. After 1964, the most widely used herbicides were orange, white, and blue, which rapidly replaced purple and pink.

---

[220] Ibid.

Heavily sprayed areas included inland forests near the DMZ; inland forests at the junction of the borders of Cambodia, Laos, and South Vietnam; inland forests north and northwest of Saigon; mangrove forests on the southernmost peninsula of Vietnam; and mangrove forests along major inland shipping channels southeast of Saigon. Crop-destruction missions were concentrated in northern and eastern central areas of South Vietnam.

Most of the herbicides used in Vietnam were sprayed by fixed-wing aircraft; although a substantial number were also carried out by helicopter, particularly after mid-1970. Only small amounts of herbicides were sprayed by ground sources such as river boats, trucks, and personnel wearing backpack sprayers.

Since the late 1970s, the Veterans Administration has provided free medical tests to veterans citing health problems that they believe may be related to Agent Orange. [221]

I personally have received this medical test. As such, I have also been diagnosed by the DVA, as a possible result of Agent Orange spraying, with ischemic heart disease; also called ischemia with a disability rating of 10%.

---

[221] Ibid.

Picture 8.1
Kids by river
[Author photo]

Picture 8.2
The Author with a small Vietnamese girl
[Author photo]

Picture 8.3
Water buffalo
[Author photo]

Picture 8.4
Us on an amtrac
[Author photo]

Picture 8.5
Wire and punji stakes
[Author photo]

Picture 8.6
Napalm attack
[Author photo]

Picture 8.7
Author with a LAAW
[Author photo]

VIETNAM: MY WAR

Picture 8.8
Prisoner 1
[Author photo]

Picture 8.9
Prisoner 2
[Author photo]

Picture 8.10
Prisoner 3
[Author photo]

Chapter 9

Camp Pendleton
The Later Years

ON my return to the United States, now as a Vietnam veteran and truly in need of some rest and relaxation, I was assigned the job of a general warehouseman with Headquarters Company, Service Battalion, Headquarters Regiment, Marine Corps Base, Camp Pendleton. My MOS now changed to 3051. I was a *box-kicker*. I felt like an outcast. More important, I felt completely rejected, as if I were an outsider looking in and an untouchable. I truly hated this duty because it was like being in exile. On top of this, the world, as I knew it before, did not understand me. As a result, I immediately requested, using the appropriate chain of command, a transfer, which was quickly granted. I had nothing against the job or the work, it had to be done, but it was definitely not for me. I was not meant to be a warehouseman. Even though this was certainly an honorable job, it entailed handling food products for the Marines and Navy personnel on the base.

Having just come back from the front lines of Vietnam, I was unquestionably not ready for this type of drudgery. This work was a grind for me. For whatever reason, I basically could not handle the mundane and monotonous duties this assignment required. I was starting to go crazy. Post-Traumatic Stress Disorder (PTSD) was already setting in. Characterized by an inability to concentrate, a tendency to tire easily, chronic nightmares, and a phobia of loud noises, especially cars backfiring. Because I felt so slighted and insulted, I requested that I be reassigned to a job that required more action; one that hopefully would include carrying a weapon.

As luck would have it, I was transferred out of this unit and joined the men of Military Police Company, Service Battalion, Headquarters Regiment at the same base. Boy was I a happy camper! I now was a military policeman (MP) with a new MOS of 8151. I was also assigned a revolver which felt so good when it was my turn to go on duty. The job of an MP was varied, and, at times, potentially precarious. The key job functions were to: support the base commander by enforcing the law and providing for appropriate security requirements, maintain good order and discipline, prevent and suppress crime, investigate offenses, apprehend offenders, protect property and personnel, control traffic and investigate traffic accidents, guard military prisoners and absentees/deserters who were being returned to military control, and supervise brig operations/correctional custody units.

Unfortunately, I was under the direction of Second Lieutenant John T. Stone (not his real name), who came off as an arrogant and egotistical Marine.

It seems that each branch of the Armed Forces has their fair share of pompous types. On March 13, 1967, only three months before my enlistment would conclude with the Corps, Lieutenant Stone issued me Violation Article 92 of the UCMJ (Uniform Code of Military Justice). An Article 92 is a failure to obey an order or regulation. Any person subject to this chapter who (1) violates or fails to obey any lawful general order or regulation, (2) having knowledge of any other lawful order issued by any member of the armed forces, which it is his duty to obey, fails to obey the order, or (3) is derelict in the performance of his duties, shall be punished as a court-martial may direct. He did it because he stated I was derelict in the performance of my duties. Bullshit! Stone blabbered, "I failed to get a haircut for guard mount," which was on March 10, 1967. As a result, I had to forfeit $25.00. I guess this young and condescending officer had nothing better to do than issue Article 92s, especially to Vietnam veterans like me. There were so few of us at the time. I hope he enjoyed the process. In the meantime, I have not forgotten about the incident. While he may not be conceited today, he certainly was, at least in my opinion, a big-headed imbecile back then.

As soon as I settled into military police work, I attended a four-week general military subject's course at the regimental training school in Camp Pendleton. I enjoyed this instruction and the accompanying workshops. Equally as important, I enjoyed the fieldwork and its related activities. Once again I was able to practice firing various weapons. Whether it was with a .45-caliber pistol (M1911), shotgun, or the M14, I felt comfortable and at ease. As strange as it may sound, it was like being *at home in Vietnam*. I was active again. I requalified with these arms in July 1966, and was issued a governmental motor vehicle permit, which allowed me to drive up to three-quarter-ton military police emergency vehicles on and off the base.

Even though I was stateside, stationed at Camp Pendleton again, I was still thinking about the guys that I fought with in Vietnam—Delta Company, 1st Battalion, 9th Marines, 3rd Marine Division and Mike Company, 3rd Battalion, 3rd Marines, 3rd Marine Division. I thought of what they had to go through. From July 4–October 27, 1966, Operation Macon began in the Quang Nam Province. [222] Operation Macon commenced when two VC companies ambushed one Marine company on a routine search and clear mission northeast of An Hoa, which is located in the Quang Nam Province. An Hoa was to be the site of an industrial complex and was politically important to the South Vietnamese government, and hence the military. By the end of the day, III MAF developed the operation that normally consisted of a single battalion-size force but for a few days had five battalions. There were three phases to the operation which finally concluded on October 27th. The operation claimed 380 enemy KIAs versus twenty-four U.S. KIAs and 172 WIAs.

---

[222] Leo Daugherty, *The Vietnam War–Day by Day,* p. 89, (Chartwell Books, Inc., 2011).

Almost coinciding with the above mentioned clash, starting on August 3, 1966 and lasting to January 31, 1967, five Marine battalions began and participated in Operation Prairie. One of those battalions was my unit (3rd Battalion, 3rd Marines, 3rd Marine Division). This encounter started off as a search and destroy operation against the 324th Battalion, NVA Division in the hills at Con Thien/Gio Linh, areas just south of the DMZ at Mutter's Ridge, the Razorback, Hill 400, Hill 484, and The Rockpile (i.e., in the northern part of South Vietnam). [223] It was reported that 1,397 enemy were killed. Sadly, 200 Marines also died in this conflict. [224] More so, 1,000+ warriors were wounded in action. [225]

On August 29th, I was sent to the main Camp Pendleton Dispensary for another thorough examination. Even though my toenails were bothering me to no end from the fungus I accumulated while I was in the jungles of Vietnam, I was found physically qualified for yet another transfer, which I did not know was forthcoming. Still, I feel I was starting to develop some early but significant symptoms of PTSD. Nonetheless, I was scheduled, via a set of new military orders, to go back to Vietnam, again as a combat infantryman, for a second tour of duty. I am sure that Lieutenant Stone had something to do with my mandate to go back to this Hell-hole. I was to go back to Vietnam within three months and do it all over again. Fortunately, with God looking over my shoulders, it never happened.

In mid-summer 1966, I knew that I wanted to go to college. I also knew I wanted to leave the Corps. With the necessary permission, I drove off base and attended evening classes at Palomar College in San Marcos, California. This community college offered, at the time, numerous associate's degrees and certificate programs. They also presented programs for students, like me, wishing to transfer to many different four-year universities, including institutions in the University of California and California State University systems. There, I initially took a basic class in English. For my efforts, I received a B, a grade for which I was certainly proud of achieving. Surprisingly, the commander of the Military Police was also attending college. His name was Colonel Kelly. He asked me what I was doing there. I told him that I was going to leave the Marine Corps, come next June and go to college full-time. He said, "great." I asked him why he was there. He alluded that he, too, was going to leave the Marine Corps after 20 plus years of service. He was attending classes in the evening so he could attain his real estate license.

In the meantime, demonstrations grew in 1966, spurred by a change in the Selective Service System's draft policy that exposed students in the bottom of half of their classes to the possibility that their deferments would be revoked and they would be drafted. Teach-ins changed to sit-ins as student takeovers of administration offices. A three-day event at the University of Chica-

---

[223] *List of allied military operations of the Vietnam War (1966),* Wikipedia.

[224] *Operation Prairie (August 3–October 27, 1966),* Wikipedia.

[225] *List of allied military operations of the Vietnam War (1966),* Wikipedia.

go got national attention in May 1966, and University of Wisconsin students also staged their own occupation of an administration building that month. The Madison draft protest, which, in part, was against Dow Chemical Company, drew several thousand students to one rally but was peacefully resolved by a promise that the faculty would review the school's draft policy. In spite of this, tensions rose at campuses like Cornell University in Ithaca, New York, where students tried to organize a national burn-your-draft-card movement; and Harvard University in Cambridge, Massachusetts, where protesters trapped Secretary of Defense Robert McNamara in a police car and assailed him with questions about the war.

As mentioned, during my last nine months in the service, I got word that I was going back to Vietnam. I had received military orders that I was being transferred back to the frontline villages and hamlets of South Vietnam. I was sure I was going to re-join the men of the 3rd Battalion, 3rd Marine Division. With only nine months remaining in my enlistment, I could not understand, let alone comprehend, why they wanted me back in Vietnam. After an in-person meeting with Colonel Kelly, who knew that I would not reenlist, my orders to go back to Vietnam were cancelled. God bless you Colonel! I say that I was most likely going to re-join the men of the 3rd Marine Division because on February 1, 1967, Operation Prairie II commenced. Marines (one from my unit–3rd Battalion, 3rd Marines, 3rd Marine Division), in conjunction with ARVN forces, once again set out to seek out and destroy all enemy forces in Quang Tri and Thua Thien Provinces (the DMZ area, around Con Thien, and Gio Linh) and to defend the area against further attack. Backed up by three infantry battalions, two reconnaissance companies, and supporting units, my fellow leathernecks conducted extensive patrols and sweeps by units of various sizes, including large-scale operations with infantry battalions. This confrontation lasted until March 18th. [226] It was stated that 693 enemy soldiers were killed, while 129 Marines were also killed in action. [227]

Going back to school was great. This was the first time I had the chance to mingle and socialize with civilians, especially women. It had been two years since I communicated regularly with the outside world. As a military policeman, I had the opportunity to go off base for a couple of days at a time. Essentially, this was called "liberty." When possible, I took advantage of these one and two-day mini-vacations. Whenever I could I drove home to Santa Monica, about 96 miles north of the base, to see my friends and parents.

Trying to fit in again with my friends was not easy. I now spoke a different language. Over the past two years I became used to the Marine Corps jargon. I forgot words like "bitchin," "boss," and "gnarly." My vocabulary now consisted of words like "yes sir/no sir," "at ease," "dinks/gooks/VC/Victor Charlie," "didi," "lock and load," "incoming," "dig in," "get down," "I'm hit,"

[226] Leo Daugherty, *The Vietnam War–Day by Day,* p. 102, (Chartwell Books, Inc., 2011).

[227] *List of allied military operations of the Vietnam War (1967),* Wikipedia.

and "corpsman up." Meeting women was also not easy. In fact, it was very hard. I had been away from them for so long that conversing with the young ladies in a normal way was a difficult adjustment. Modifying my jargon to civilian words was also not easy. All I could talk about was Vietnam and more about Vietnam which had been my life for the past year. All I could discuss were the battlefront encounters and skirmishes that I so frequently experienced. I felt I had nothing else to offer—zero! After all, I had lived the life of a combat infantry Marine, a grunt, in the various villages of Vietnam. I was a warrior and proud of it. I did not know the outside civilian world, or at least it seemed that way.

At a party I attended in Santa Monica, I met a beautiful young woman. Her name was Daryl. She was sensitive and sympathetic to my situation. It seemed that she understood my past involvement in Vietnam. If she did not understand it, I think she tried to be accommodating to my needs and tolerant of my experiences. She lived around the corner from my parent's place in Santa Monica. She lived with her grandmother on 20th Street, between Arizona Avenue and Wilshire Blvd. It was great. I was in love with her. When I had the chance, I drove home just to be with her. We did many things together. I felt as if we were truly boyfriend and girlfriend, a real couple. I was starting to feel like a normal person again.

I was in love with Daryl through and through. "It was really puppy love." She, though, was not in love with me. She eventually met another young man and had a one-night stand with this horny dude. As a result of her sexual interlude with this guy, she got pregnant.

I did not know about this romantic episode for about two months. When I came home one weekend, she told me that she was with child. More significant, she stated to her parents that I was the one who had knocked her up. I knew that was not true. I conveyed to her that she had to go back and tell her parents what she said was a lie. Daryl refused. I told her that if she could not tell her parents the truth, I would. To make a long story brief, I did tell her mother and father that I was not the one who got her pregnant. They believed me. I never saw her again.

I thoroughly enjoyed my existence as a military policeman. Besides standing guard at the various points of entry at Camp Pendleton (as can be seen in picture 9.1), such as San Luis Rey or rear gate (Fallbrook) in the northwest end of the compound, I constantly confiscated alcohol from Marines and Navy personnel who were coming back to the base with contraband. I had too! It was part of my duties as an MP. Liquor was not allowed on base. I also had an opportunity to patrol the entire base. At times, I issued tickets to those drivers who were recklessly speeding. One time, a civilian taxicab driver was in a rush to get off the base and was driving at least 90 to 95 miles per hour. However, the road system in Camp Pendleton was designed to handle traffic only moving 55 miles per hour. He was endangering himself and certainly those who might have been in his way. For that reason, I followed protocol. I pulled him over and asked him to get out of his car. After some discussion, I escorted him off base in my military police vehicle, to the main office where the other taxicab drivers hung out. To say the least, he was not pleasant to be with. Oh well, I had a job to do, and I wanted to make sure that I did it to the best of my ability. Just because he was a civilian creating havoc, did not give him the right to do what he did. He broke the law. I had no other choice but to remove him from the base.

Late one night while on duty, I noticed a car parked at one of the live firing ranges (as can be seen in picture 9.2) at San Mateo Firing Range (within Camp San Mateo—62 Area [USMC School of Infantry—at the time]). At first, I thought the vehicle was abandoned, so I did not call for backup. When I got close to the car, I noticed that there were two people in the backseat. I suspected they were engaged in sexual activity, and they did not know I was nearby. I pulled out my revolver along with my flashlight. In fact, I had left my vehicle about 100 yards down the road. I walked quietly up to the car, and I shined my flashlight into the vehicle. The woman, who was on top of the man jumped out of the car stark-naked. She almost went into total hysterics. The Marine laughed his head off, so much so that I think he peed in his car. After things settled down and they put on their clothes, I informed them, in a stern way, that they could not park at a live firing range. They got the hint and I let them drive off back to civilization.

One of my close friends from high school, Ron Oehlkers, who was supposed to join the Corps when I did, finally decided to enlist in the Marines. He, along with a couple of our friends, Dave Marshall and Jerry Koploff, determined it was time to serve their country. I am so proud of them for stepping up to the batter's box and serving in the Armed Forces–more important–the Marines.

On November 18, 1966, I drove down from Camp Pendleton to the Marine Recruit Training Depot in San Diego (MCRD). MCRD San Diego's main mission is the initial training, a.k.a. boot camp, of enlisted male recruits living west of the Mississippi River. This is where it all started for me on June 28, 1964. This is where I would eventually become a Hollywood Marine. This is where over 21,000 recruits were trained each year. (Note: Recruit training for those enlisted in the U.S. Marine Corps, includes a 13 week process during which the recruit becomes cut off from the civilian world and must adapt to a Marine Corps lifestyle. During training, drill instructors train recruits in a wide variety of subjects including weapons training, Marine Corps Martial Arts Program, personal hygiene and cleanliness, close order drill, and Marine Corps history. The training emphasizes physical fitness, and recruits must attain a minimum standard of fitness to graduate by passing a physical fitness test. Recruits must also meet minimum combat-oriented swimming qualifications, qualify in rifle marksmanship with the M16A4 service rifle [it was the M14 when I was in boot camp], and pass a 54 hour simulated combat exercise known as "The Crucible".) [228]

---

[228] *Marine Corps Recruit Depot, San Diego,* Wikipedia.

I went to MCRD, about a 50 mile trip from Camp Pendleton, to visit my good friends, from Santa Monica where we all grew up, as can be seen in picture 9.3. The people in the picture are as follows: Far left - Ron's girlfriend Julie Sigman (later to be his wife). Second from the left - Ron Oehlkers. Third from the left is me, the handsome guy smiling. Fourth from the left - Dave Marshall. Far right - Jerry Koploff. And second from the right - I believe this is one of Jerry Koploff's sisters.

We chatted for a while. It was nice to see the guys graduate together from Marine Corps boot camp. They seemed to be happy. They were now ready to move on to advanced infantry training at Camp Pendleton. For me, it was déjà vu all over again. They did not know if they were going to Vietnam. Jerry did, in fact, fight in the war, and was later wounded in action.

During Ron's advanced infantry training in Camp Pendleton, I paid him a second visit. However, he was not expecting it. As a MP, I commanded respect, even among officers and staff non-commissioned officers. Officers and NCOs alike did not question my presence, regardless where I was. I was free, without restriction, to travel anywhere on the base. As such, I told Ron's commanding officer that I had to see him. I divulged to him that it was of the utmost importance. Ron, then again, did not know it was me, and he did not know what to expect. Since he did not recognize me, I really surprised him. Naturally, we laughed about this escapade.

In November 1966, while enjoying myself with Ron Oehlkers and friends at MCRD's boot camp graduation ceremony, five members died in action and another 23 were wounded from my past battalion—3/3/3. In December, this climbed to 26 and 90 wounded. Mike Company (my former company) was bombed accidentally by U.S. aircraft, resulting in 17 of the KIAs that month.

Even though I enjoyed being a military policeman (with a weapon positioned on my side), times were not always fun. There was the case of a supply sergeant who was taking food off the base for his personal use. When he had finished work for the day, he would go over to one of the mess halls and load up large pieces of beef. Although this did not happen daily, it did occur frequently. The problem was that I knew what was going on. I saw him load up food supplies and put them in the trunk of his vehicle. I later saw him take the stuff home. It was an unpleasant ordeal. Because he had numerous inside connections, with other Marines in power, he could easily take advantage of his role in the company. Nevertheless, I had to tell someone about this. As always, thefts of this type got ugly.

On another occasion, one of our own military policemen was addicted to cocaine.

I do not know how this happened, but it did. Unfortunately, he was sent to the brig for his wrongful actions.

For the most part, crimes on the base were minimal. They were petty or misdemeanor incidences. Infrequently, we were called to the women's section of the base. Occasionally, males would go over to the female barracks and harass the women. We called them *BAMs*. Most of the women did not mind as long as it was in good taste. They did not care as long as the male Marines were having good, clean fun. However, when it got out of hand, we were called over to resolve the situation.

I especially enjoyed patrolling the beaches of Camp Pendleton. Once again, déjà vu set in. I really liked watching the surfers catch those beautiful breakers, standing either goofy or regular stance. It brought back so many good memories of my own youth. As a 13-year-old, I grew up riding the waves off the various beaches, on my 8'6" Yater, up and down the Southern California coastline. (Reynolds [Renny] Yater—a surfboard builder—founded and opened Santa Barbara Surf Shop in 1959, trademarking Yater Surfboards at the same time.) At one of the northern points of the base, I sat down with a bunch of Marines who were relaxing at one of the enlisted men's pubs. They were having some beers at the beer garden. I was on duty so I did not take a swig even though I was offered a taste. When I came back to headquarters later that day, I was threatened with a court martial. I was wrongfully accused of drinking beer while on duty, when, in fact, I drank nothing with the guys. I guess someone was out to get me in to trouble. I suspect it was the Lieutenant who was in charge. In any case, I was never formally charged with a crime.

With only 90 days left to serve in the Corps, ending March 1967, I was feeling that I was becoming a short-timer. My behavior started to change. I was not feeling the gung-ho attitude that I had when I first joined the Marines. I was ready to move on with my life. Even now, I could not keep my mind off my past involvements in Vietnam and the guys that I had served with in combat. In fact, March 19–April 19, 1967, Operation Prairie III began. Warriors from the 3rd Battalion, 3rd Marines, 1st Battalion, 4th Marines, 3rd Battalion, 4th Marines, 1st Battalion, 9th Marines, 3rd Battalion, 9th Marines and 2nd Battalion, 26th Marines, initiated a search and destroy maneuver against the NVA 324th Battalion and 341st Division, in and around the DMZ. [229] Records indicated that Operation Prairie III cost the enemy 252 killed, four captured, and 128 weapons seized. Marine losses were set at 56 killed and 530 wounded. I also could not keep my mind off what other warriors, from my same unit, were going through in Vietnam. From March 20–April 3, 1967, Operation Beacon Hill was in force by key elements of combat units from the 3rd Marine Division. This effort featured the amphibious landing of a Marine battalion and the participation of Navy destroyers, as a coordinated effort with Operation Prairie III, on a "gun line" to furnish fire support near Gio Linh, Camp Carroll, and Dong Ha in northern I Corps (Quang Tri Province - South Vietnamese coast just below the DMZ). During the first two days the Marines, pinned down by North Vietnamese fire, found their adversary had many positions with connecting tunnels, and decided to stand back while naval guns and air strikes bombarded these spots for the next two days. When all was said

---

[229] *List of allied military operations of the Vietnam War (1967),* Wikipedia.

VIETNAM: MY WAR

and done, Marine losses were recorded at 16 killed. VC and NVA fighters suffered 334 KIAs.

Three years had passed since I first stepped on that bus at the Marine Corps Recruit Depot in Los Angeles. Over three years had gone by since I first met Marine recruiter extraordinaire, Sergeant Robert C. Dambeck, in Santa Monica. A full year had gone by since I patrolled the many villages and hamlets of South Vietnam. Over a year had passed since I trained so feverishly in the island of Okinawa. And over three months had passed since my numb-skull company commander issued me that uncalled-for Article 92. Well, it was my turn to pack my bags for good. It was my turn to give that last salute. And it was my last turn to say, "Yes, sir!"

On Friday, June 30, 1967, when my three-year enlistment expired, having just turned 21 years of age, and escaping the chance of dying an early death in Vietnam, I packed my gear, sea bag, and my medals from Military Police Company, Service Battalion, Headquarters Regiment, Marine Corps Base, Camp Pendleton. I turned in my sidearm and the rest of my military police gear. I emptied my wall locker for the last time, as I was ready to be *"back on the block."* I was no longer an active Marine. It was an eerie feeling. I say this, because I already began growing melancholy for the war. I was feeling nostalgic even at a time when the Vietnam War was becoming quite intense. On that same day, I was finally assigned to standby reserve duty. And that afternoon I stepped into my fast-traveling four taillights1961, 283 cubic inch (4.6 L), small-block, V8 Corvette, as can be seen in picture 9.4, and drove off into the sunset and back to Santa Monica, California, never to return to Camp Pendleton nor the Marines. Still, I was almost completely ill-informed about the things of everyday life like dating, renting an apartment, and building some type of a career. I had no idea what I wanted to do in the business world. I only had a high school diploma, albeit from a great institute, but with no civilian skills. The only thing I really attained and had some know-how in was the *"art of killing."* I knew how to face mortality and how to produce it, with everything on the evolutionary scale of my small hand-held revolver to my very large shoulder-mounted 3.5-inch rocket launcher. More so, the easiest repairs on a vehicle engine were, outside my skill level, but I was more than able to field-strip and put together my M14 blindfolded, and in under a minute.

Even though I had been away from combat operations for over a year and specifically away from the Da Nang region for about 15 months, the ground war was not letting up at all. As July 1967 began, the 1st and 7th Marines, both from the 1st Marine Division, commanded by Major General Donn J. Robertson, operated in the densely populated area around Da Nang, a place that we (3rd Marine Division) thought we had secured a year earlier. Two battalions of the 5th Marines continued operations against elements of the 2nd NVA Division in the Que Son Basin. Another battalion of the 5th Marines, the 2nd, provided security for an industrial area near An Hoa and the Nong Song coalmine, located southwest of Da Nang. At the same time, Operation Buffalo began on July 2nd, with elements of the 1st Battalion, 9th Marines (the unit I first served with in Vietnam), in and around the fire base at Con Thien. The campaign was designed to clear the area of enemy activity, though the U.S. Marine patrols were encountering less and less activity as the enemy regrouped for a major attack somewhere else along the DMZ. [230] Out of nearly 400 Marines, the two companies suffered 84 killed, 190 wounded and nine missing, making this the worst one-day loss for the Marines in the Vietnam War. Only 27 Marines from Bravo Company, about 90 from Alpha Company, were fit for duty after the first day of fighting. [231]

So much for these battles, the day-to-day skirmishes as well as all of the other clashes that we encountered in 1965, 1966 and the first half of 1967 are mentioned in my tome. The Vietnam War still had a long way to go for so many grunts like me. In the intervening time, more than a million tons of supplies were going each month into Vietnam to nourish the U.S. Armed Forces. This is an average of a hundred pounds a day for every American serviceman in-country. In addition, this same year saw a huge build-up of the United States military presence in Vietnam (and an even more massive build-up of objection in opposition to that military). In fact, President's Johnson's 1967 *go-it-alone policy* ultimately led to the commitment of about a half-million U.S. troops in South Vietnam. The President and the Secretary of Defense (Robert McNamara), whose team of corporate "whiz kids" from the Ford Motor Company who had no combat experience, decided to micromanage the war from the basement War Room of the White House. [232] This was supported by, at least in part, as stated in the publication, *Profile 68, U. S. Marine Corps:*

> As 1967 ended, 78,000 Marines–more than one-fourth of the approximately 300,000-man Corps–were in combat in Vietnam with the Third Marine Amphibious Force (III MAF). Operating primarily in I Corps (the five northern-most provinces of South Vietnam), the Marine Air-Ground Team repelled several invasions across the DMZ by units of the North Vietnamese Army.
>
> The mission of the Marines in Vietnam was to assist the South Vietnamese in defeating the enemy trying to seize their country; and help the people build their nation. The goals were accomplished by defending the main base areas; destroying the organized combat forces of the North Vietnamese Army and the Viet Cong; eradicating the

---

[230] Leo Daugherty, *The Vietnam War–Day by Day*, p. 112, (Chartwell Books, Inc., 2011).

[231] *Operation Buffalo (1967)*, Wikipedia.

[232] Colonel H. Avery Chenoweth, USMCR (Retired), *Semper FI–The Definitive Illustrated History of the U.S. Marines*, p. 336, (Fall River Press, 2005).

Communist guerrilla infrastructure (as can be seen in picture 9.5 [233]); and participating in nation-building programs. [234]

While the Vietnam War was gaining in momentum with more combat-ready troops arriving in South Vietnam, a famous African-American defied the United States government's war policy. Heavyweight boxing champion Muhammad Ali, a member of the Nation of Islam, and conscientious objector, refused, on April 28, 1967, induction into the Army on religious grounds. However, Ali's draft board found that his pious views were disingenuous and denied his request for a deferment. Ali responded:

> It would be no trouble for me to accept on the basis that I will go into the armed services boxing exhibitions in Vietnam, or traveling the country at the expense of the government, if it wasn't against my conscience to do it. I would not give up the millions that I gave up and my image with the American public ... If I was not sincere. [235]

Ali was convicted of draft evasion in June 1967, stripped of his heavyweight title by the World Boxing Association and sentenced to five years in prison. He did stay out of jail on bond until the Supreme Court overturned his conviction on a technicality. He became one of the most contentious celebrities of the Vietnam War era, respected by opponents of the war and denigrated by its proponents.

In the later part of 1967, one of the most prominent anti-war demonstrations took place, as some 100,000 protesters gathered at the Lincoln Memorial; around 30,000 of them continued in a march on the Pentagon later that night. After a brutal confrontation with the soldiers and U.S. Marshals protecting the building, hundreds of demonstrators were arrested. One of them was the author Norman K. Mailer, an American novelist, journalist, essayist, playwright, film-maker, actor and political activist—who chronicled the events in his book *"The Armies of the Night,"* and published the following year to widespread acclaim. Also in 1967, the anti-war movement got a big boost when the civil rights leader Martin Luther King Jr. went public with his opposition to the war on moral grounds, condemning the war's diversion of federal funds from domestic programs as well as the disproportionate number of African-American casualties in relation to the total number of soldiers killed in the war. Furthermore, in 1967, the anti-war movement became a foremost element in American political and social life. Demonstrations involving first tens of thousands and later hundreds of thousands of protesters exploded across the country. Yet, because of deep internal divisions, the op-

---

[233] *Profile 68–U.S. Marine Corps,* p. 2, (U.S. Government Printing Office, 1968).
[234] Ibid, p. 3.
[235] George Donelson Moss, *Vietnam–An American Ordeal,* p. 257, (Prentice-Hall, 1990).

position to the war was less successful in ending it than it might have been. Adversaries of the war differed among themselves over reasons for opposing the war and the best methods to stop it. [236]

In accordance with MMD (Material Management Department), Article 16.14, on August 8, 1967, at 13137 Dispensary, Marine Corps Base, Camp Pendleton, California, my health record was finally closed by reason of release to inactive duty.

On March 2, 1970, about three years after my active duty time expired, I was released from inactive status and completely discharged from the Marine Corps. On that day, Lieutenant Colonel J. A. Polidori, U.S. Marine Corps Reserve Officer in Charge, Class III Reserve, presented me with an Honorable Discharge from the Armed forces of the United States of America.

It was still 1967, and James S. Olson and Randy Roberts, authors of *Where the Domino Fell*, described the troops' mood at this time:

> On April 28, 1967, his starched uniform tattooed with medals and ribbons from other wars, General Westmoreland stood ramrod straight and begged for time and support from the President. The greatest problem American boys faced in Vietnam were not enemy troops, he argued, but the will to continue at home: These men believe in what they are doing ... Backed at home by resolve, confidence, patience, determination, and continued support, we will prevail in Vietnam over the Communist aggressor. [237]

And seven months later, in November of that same year, General Westmoreland so candidly remarked: "It lies within our grasp–the enemy's hopes are bankrupt. With your support we will give you a success that will impact not only on South Vietnam, but on every emerging nation in the world." [238] Further to this point, it is significant that the enemy has not won a major battle in more than a year. In general, he can fight his large forces only at the edges of his sanctuaries ... His guerrilla force is declining at a steady rate. [239] (I beg to differ with you, General. I do not think so!)

During 1967, the Reverend Martin Luther King, Jr. (an antiwar activist and prominent leader in the African-American Civil Rights Movement), made the following observation:

> What do the peasants think as we ally ourselves with the landlords and as we refuse to put any action into our many words con-

---

[236] Robert D. Schulzinger, *A Time for War–The United States and Vietnam, 1941-1975*, p. 229, (Oxford University Press, 1997).

[237] James S. Olson and Randy Roberts, *Where the Domino Fell–America and Vietnam 1945–1990*, p. 153, (Diane Publishing Company, 1991).

[238] *General William Westmoreland,* National Press Club, November 21, 1967.

[239] Ibid.

cerning land reform? What do they think as we test our latest weapons on them, just as the Germans tested out new medicine and new tortures in the concentration camps in Europe? Where are the roots of the independent Vietnam we claim to be building? ... We must find new ways to speak of peace in Vietnam and justice throughout the developing world. ... If we do not act we shall surely be dragged down the long, dark and shameful corridors of time reserved for those who possess power without compassion, might without morality, and strength without sight. [240]

Also during this same time frame, the Spring Mobilization Committee to End the War in Vietnam, which became the National Mobilization Committee to End the War in Vietnam, was a coalition of antiwar activists formed in 1967 to organize large demonstrations, as a mass movement, in opposition to the Vietnam War. The organizations were informally known as "the Mobe". What's more, on April 15, 1967, the Spring Mobilization's massive march against the Vietnam War from New York's Central Park to the United Nations attracted 300,000+ people, including Dr. Martin Luther King, Jr., Harry Belafonte, James Bevel, and Dr. Benjamin Spock, who marched and spoke at the event. During the event many draft cards were burned, according to the *New York Times*. A simultaneous march in San Francisco was attended by Coretta Scott King. The Mobe then planned and organized a large demonstration for Washington D.C. on October 21, 1967. This demonstration was a rally at West Potomac Park near the Lincoln Memorial and a march to the Pentagon, where another rally would be held in a parking lot, followed by civil disobedience on the steps of the Pentagon itself. The action was known as the "March on the Pentagon." [241]

As mentioned, I was now a Vietnam Veteran and full of pride to have served in what I believe was the finest branch of the Armed Forces. I was also content with having served my country with dignity and honor. Nonetheless, it was time for me to move on, and continue my pursuit for a college degree. In late August of 1967, I enrolled at Santa Monica College, a two-year public community college, Santa Monica, California, which was first opened in 1929. [242] As a veteran, along with the help of other comrades, we formed the Veterans Club (see picture 9.6–I am in the second row, and third from the right), now called the Student Veterans Association (SVA). As a founder and pioneer of this fabulous fraternal organization, it was a wonderful way to communicate with others that understood what I had been through in Vietnam. Non-veterans and anti-war protestors, on the other hand, did not or

[240] Martin Luther King, Jr. *"Declaration of Independence from the War in Vietnam,"* April 4, 1967.

[241] *National Mobilization Committee to End the War in Vietnam,* Wikipedia.

[242] *Santa Monica College,* Wikipedia.

could not comprehend or appreciate what we went through in this God for-saken part of the world.

As a veteran among other troupers of this brethren club, we all began growing evocative for the war. Oddly enough, we felt a weird affection and connection to Vietnam and, even more out of the ordinary, some of us experienced a longing to return (and fight again). Many of us enjoyed the captivating appeal of combat. It was an uncharacteristic gratification because it was mixed with a corresponding amount of pain and sorrow, knowing that death could be just around the corner. More so, we felt different from the rest of the students and everyone who had not shared with us the miseries of the rainy season, the daily grind of fatiguing patrols, and the fear of a full combat assault on our positions by the Viet Cong. At the very least, we had very little in common with these other classmates, especially those who were against the war. Even though we were private citizens again, the civilian world seemed foreign. We did not fit in as much as we did in our club where we had fought and our fellow servicemen had died.

Of course, the war was still being fought really hard in 1967, especially by the Marines. In fact, on February 13, 1967, following the failure of diplomatic peace efforts, President Johnson announced the U.S. will resume full-scale bombing in North Vietnam. Three weeks later, Congress authorized $4.5 billion for the war. On April 6th, Quang Tri City is attacked by 2,500 Viet Cong and NVA. On April 24–May 11, hill fights rage at Khe Sanh between U.S. 3rd Marines (my unit) and the North Vietnamese Army. While an estimated 940 NVA were slain, 155 Americans were killed and 425 wounded. In July, General Westmoreland request an additional 200,000 reinforcements on top of the 475,000 soldiers already scheduled to be sent to Vietnam. As more troops headed to Vietnam, North Vietnamese Prime Minister Pham Van Dong publicly stated that Hanoi will *"continue to fight."* During September through October, U.S. Marines were, once again, besieged by NVA at Con Thien located two miles south of the DMZ. NVA losses were calculated at over 2,000. [243] In the meantime, on September 4–15, the Marines were back in the Que Son Valley (as mentioned in Chapter 5). (Note: I fought there in late 1965 as part of a search-and-destroy operation.) Now, the 1st Marine Division carried out another search-and-destroy mission under the code name of Operation Swift (as also mentioned in Chapter 5). The ensuing battle, regrettably, killed 114 Americans while an estimated 376 North Vietnamese were killed. And, November 3–December 1, the Battle of Dak To occured in the mountainous terrain along the border of Cambodia and Laos as the U.S. 4th Infantry Division heared off a planned NVA attack against the Special Forces camp located there. NVA losses are put at 1,644. U.S. troops suffered 289 killed.

After a two-year stint with an award-winning faculty at Santa Monica College, I continued my undergraduate studies at the University of California Los Angeles (UCLA) and California State University, Northridge, California

---

[243] *1967 in the Vietnam War,* Wikipedia article

(CSUN), where I earned a Bachelor of Science in Business Administration degree. At this school, I majored in finance and minored in accounting. Soon after, I went on to earn a Master's degree in Business Administration degree from Pepperdine University, Malibu, California (where I actually started my teaching career by instructing a graduate-level economics class in August 1978). Shortly after the completion of my graduate studies, I was awarded a California Community College Life Time Instructor Credential. And at the age of 59, thinking that I might be perceived as a so-called Renaissance Man (a person who is skilled in multiple fields or multiple disciplines and who has a broad base of knowledge), I earned a second Master's degree as well as a Doctoral degree in Philosophy (Ph.D.), all degrees achieved were at the expense of the Department of Veterans Affairs, under the superb guidance of Miguel Guilarte, Ph.D., from Fielding Graduate University, Santa Barbara, California. While attending this institution, I majored in human development with an emphasis in strategic management and organizational leadership.

Picture 9.1
Standing guard at San Luis Rey gate
[Author photo]

Picture 9.2
Live firing range
[Author photo]

Picture 9.3
Ron, Dave and Jerry
[Author photo]

Picture 9.4
My Corvette
[Author photo]

Picture 9.5
Marine Profile 68
[via Author]

Picture 9.6
Santa Monica College Veterans Club
[Author photo]

Chapter 10

Five Decades Later
So, What Does It All Mean?

C URIOUSLY enough, there still exists a widespread and exaggerated public image of the Vietnam veteran. Everyone knows the stereotypes. These are the veterans who joined Vietnam veterans against the war, the veteran loner (me), the veteran ready to go off any minute, the homeless veteran, etc.

So, what does it all mean to me ... five decades later? To say the least, it is complex. In time, but maybe not yet, the skirmishes and major battles that I partook in will most likely be forgotten, my and my fellow warriors' sacrifices discounted, and my sanity will also be reduced to nothing more than a slight memory of my youth gone by. Then again, I will never forget when I went to all the different Armed Forces recruiting branches in early 1964. I will never overlook the words that I heard from Marine Corps Sergeant Dambeck, "pride of belonging," "courage," and "self-discipline." I will never forget that he, the recruiter, talked at great length about the Marines as a great fighting elite force. I will never ignore what this steadfast warrior held to be correct: *"You would truly be part of the privileged few. When you become a warrior, you become someone special."* I will never forget the heartfelt speech that this man made about military tradition in the Marine Corps:

> For more than 175 years, we have helped build America's history. We were there during the Revolutionary War, Mexican War, Spanish-American War, World War I and II, and, most recently, the Korean War. We were there at the Halls of Montezuma, Shores of Tripoli, Guadalcanal, Guam, Tarawa, Iowa Jima, and Okinawa. We are Leathernecks to the end. And we have only one motto–Semper Fidelis–meaning Always Faithful, which lives on. That is our belief. That is our tradition. And that is life in the Marine Corps.

And I will never disregard what Sergeant Dambeck believed in so proudly: *"The Corps is an elite fraternity, a spiritual brotherhood. Becoming a Marine is the challenge of a lifetime. The change is forever."*

I am so proud and honored to have served our country as a Marine! In retrospect, I believe my peers (but I can only speak for myself) and I were possibly conditioned for war during our most vulnerable years. In fact, my earliest childhood recollections are all related to World War II.

Again, thank you, Sergeant Dambeck, for your words of wisdom. I feel it made a huge and positive difference in my life. I will never, ever forget. The change, of June 28, 1964, the day that I arrived at MCRD, has been without end, and I am sure it will be permanent. I will also never forget the full-on, rifles at the ready, the beachhead landing that I made at the Da Nang harbor on July 7, 1965 and the change of that day that is also everlasting—even five decades later.

So, what does the Marine Corps and all this military stuff mean to me today? As an 80% service-connected disabled veteran, with both the physical and mental scars to prove it, a college graduate with an academic doctoral degree in human development, a husband of 39 years to my lovely and beautiful wife, a father of a wonderful 34-year-old son, who is also a college graduate (and a fantastic hockey player; see picture 10.1), a 70-year-old adjunct professor with over 38 years of university teaching under his belt, I have read (according to a survey released on Veterans Day 1999 by the Vietnam Veterans Memorial Fund) that our high school and college students of today are taught less about the Vietnam War than the Revolutionary War and World War II. That is why I wrote this hybrid memoir. I composed this manuscript especially for the high school and college ROTC student in mind.

I wrote this work for the reason that I believe our young people, especially those who are involved in ROTC (The Reserve Officers' Training Corps) programs. High school seniors and college freshmen do not know what many great and unwavering combat Marines and other Army soldiers, like me, experienced firsthand in Vietnam. This is, in my humble opinion, a crying shame. Even now, I wrote this manuscript so that our future military leaders (noncommissioned and commissioned officers alike) can possibly learn from my experiences (as a frontline ground-pounding warrior).

Why don't our present-day educators want to tell our children about a military conflict, one perhaps in which their parents participated, a war that was lost, in mind and spirit only, by this great country? Is it that much of an embarrassment? Is it that humiliating to talk about Vietnam? Most important, is it that disgraceful?

Even though the antiwar and antimilitary attitude in the United States was pervasive in newspapers, on television, among writers (especially the journalists like Morley Safer, etc.), in movies, and certainly in colleges, the students targeted anyone in the military as fair game for their antiwar stance. Still, many of our countrymen came to hate the war we fought. On top of this, many veterans never admitted they were in the service for years after Vietnam. Angry at the antiwar faction, some guys, me included, wanted to set the record straight by proving that the servicemen I served with had fought and died with honor. [244]

---

[244] Frederick Downs, *The Killing Zone–My Life in the Vietnam War*, p. 266, (W.W. Norton & Company, 2007).

We, as Marines, have been told, whether true or not, that we have won every 'major' battle in Vietnam, battles such as Operation Starlite, Piranha, Rice Straw, Golden Fleece, etc. These are conflicts that my fellow Marines and I participated in only too often. Some feel that we did not win all the major battles in Vietnam. Okay, maybe we did not. That does not matter at this time—not at all. These are a few battles in which some paid the ultimate price—their lives. Yet, I believe the United States sustained the greatest military downfall in its short history. What kind of a paradox or contradiction is that? I feel that our military and political leaders, during the early 1960s (and especially now), should have read Sun Tzu's great work, the *Art of War* (before the Vietnam War really got started). If so, I believe we would have never been faced with such a military disgrace and, for some, so much dishonor. This, of course, is just my opinion. As stated by Michael Lind, a well-known writer and a guest lecturer at Harvard Law School, Johns Hopkins University, and at Virginia Polytechnic Institute and State University, "it was a mistake to intrude in Indochina at all, but once the United Stated had intervened, it should have used unlimited forces to quickly win an unqualified victory." [245] I wholeheartedly agree with Mr. Lind's statement. He too must have read Sun Tzu's famous treatise.

Knowing this, thinking and writing about the type of combat fighting that I confronted was not an easy undertaking. Frequently, I found myself, having discussed the Vietnam War, at length, with my father, who suffered, more than most could ever imagine, through the drudgeries of World War II, wishing that I had been a veteran of a more orthodox type of war (like World War II). In fact, my dad lost his entire family, including his brother, while living in Amsterdam, Holland as the result of Adolf Hitler's henchmen carrying out mass annihilations of Jews throughout Europe. The Holocaust (a program of systematic state-sponsored murder by Nazi Germany, led by Adolf Hitler and the Nazi Party, throughout the German Reich and German-occupied territories) was a deliberate and systematic extermination of European Jews during World War II. Frequently too, as part of my own PTSD, having served as a frontline combatant, this gave me an unusual amount of pleasure that was also mixed with even a more proportionate amount of anguish.

Under fire (in various locations throughout Vietnam), I believe my powers of life was certainly heightened in proportion to the proximity of death. I certainly felt an elation as extreme as dread. My senses more than accelerated, especially while being attacked in Vietnam. The adrenal rush, when we were engaged in a fire fight, was nothing less than intense. I attained, at times, a sharpness of awareness that was enjoyable and at the same time unbearable. During those heightened levels of combat mindfulness, my mind was elevated to an extreme level of consciousness. At the same time, it was a sensitivity that would have been impossible if the Vietnam War had been significantly less brutal. That said, the battlefields of South Vietnam were a crucible in which a

---

[245] Michael Lind, *Vietnam–The Necessary War,* p. xv, (Simon & Schuster, 1999).

generation of American soldiers and warriors, guys just like me, were fused together by a common confrontation with death and a sharing of hardships, dangers, and fears. The very ugliness of the war, the sordidness of our daily lives, and the degradation of having to take part in body counts made us draw still closer to one another. It was as if in comradeship we found an affirmation of life and the means to preserve at least a vestige of our own humanity. [246]

This conflict was, at least for me, mostly a matter of long days and nights of anxiously awaiting and, at arbitrary interludes, of performing harrowing manhunts through the villages (and huts within those hamlets), jungles, and rivers where a few snipers harassed us regularly. This type of combat exertion was intermittently relieved by larger scale search-and-destroy missions. This resulted in us warriors shouting vulgarities about the detonations of grenades, bombs, and the rapid, undulating eruptions of automatic rifle fire. Most of all, we learned about death at such a young age when it was normal to think of oneself as enduring. I certainly thought of myself as immortal. I was a teenager with everything to look forward to in life. In spite of this, everyone loses that fantasy sooner or later, but in noncombatant situations it vanishes in life chapters, over the years, as one gets a lot older. Most of us combat warriors were under the age of 25, and, in a period of a week (or less), passed from youth to an early middle-aged man. What is more interesting, beyond adding a few more corpses to the regular body count, none of these encounters, as I look back five decades later, achieved anything; none will ever appear in military history books or be studied by ROTC students unless you tell your high school instructor or college professor that my manuscript, as well as others, are truly worth reading. I hope you will tell these instructors and professors alike that my work is worthy of a book review and a read in their classrooms.

In the meantime, and as mentioned before, it is truly a dishonor to those who served in Vietnam that our youth, our offspring, will learn more about the Revolutionary War and World War II than the Vietnam War. What is more alarming; many students do not even know where Vietnam is located. However, maybe there is a glimmer of hope.

According to Gloria Emerson—author, journalist, and New York Times war correspondent—in her volume, *Winners & Losers–Battles, Retreats, Gains, Losses, and Ruins from the Vietnam War*: "We have always been people who dropped the past and then could not remember where it had been put." [247]

In October 1999, according to the Vietnam Veterans Memorial Fund: "Every American high school received the Echoes From the Wall curriculum package, featuring a 156-page teachers' guide with source material; posters about the Vietnam War era and The Wall; compilations of essays about the

---

[246] Philip Caputo, *A Rumor of War*, pp. xvii-xviii, (Henry Holt and Company, 1977).

[247] Gloria Emerson, *Winners and Losers: Battles, Retreats, Gains, Losses, and Ruins from the Vietnam War*, (W. W. Norton & Company, 1976).

war and the Memorial; a Veterans of Foreign Wars combat chronology and the Vietnam episode of CNN's Cold War series."

Special thanks go to the men and women of the Vietnam Veterans Memorial Fund. An extra-special thank you goes to these same people who are trying to preserve the legacy of the Vietnam War on American society.

Now, according to some additional statistics about the Vietnam War, here are a few other thought-provoking and notable details for you to consider:

1. Isolated atrocities committed by American soldiers produced torrents of outrage from antiwar critics and the news media while Communist atrocities were so common that they received hardly any attention at all.
2. Americans who deliberately killed civilians received prison sentences while communists who did so received commendations.
3. From 1957 to 1973, the National Liberation Front assassinated 37,725 South Vietnamese and abducted another 58,499. The death squads focused on leaders at the village level and on anyone who improved the lives of the peasants such as medical personnel, social workers, and schoolteachers.
4. Vietnam Veterans are less likely to be in prison–only one-half of one percent of Vietnam Veterans have been jailed for crimes.
5. Vietnam Veterans' personal income exceeds that of our non-veteran age group by more than 18 percent.
6. Average age of the 58,220 killed in Vietnam was almost 23 years. Although 58,220 names are in the November 1993 database, only 58,148 have both an event date and a birth date. Five men killed in Vietnam were only 16 years old. The oldest man killed was 62 years old. 11,465 killed in action were less than 20 years old.
7. Medevac helicopters flew nearly 500,000 missions. Over 900,000 patients were airlifted, nearly half American. The average time lapse between wounding to hospitalization was less than one hour. As a result, less than one percent of all Americans wounded who survived the first 24 hours died. [248]

Even though there were over 58,000 U.S. Forces killed in action and almost 304,000 U.S. Forces wounded in action during the Vietnam War—me included, "estimates, however, indicate that the North Vietnamese lost between 1 million and 2 million soldiers and civilians and the South Vietnamese suffered at least 1 million casualties. Similarly, no numbers are available for

---

[248] Ronald B. Frankum, Jr. and Stephen F. Maxner, *The Vietnam War for Dummies*, p. 9, (Wiley Publishing, Inc., 2003).

Laos or Cambodia, but each of those countries underwent periods of destruction that continue to plague them today." [249]

For my hard work in the Vietnam War and military service in general, I received the Combat Action Ribbon (CAR). I obtained this award from the Office of the Chief of Naval Operations. This honor is granted and presented to Navy and Marine Corps veterans who served in combat during or after World War II. Furthermore, and by the order of the President of the United States, members of my company and I were awarded the Presidential Unit Citation (refer to Appendix 4):

This ribbon was bestowed by President Johnson for extraordinary heroism and outstanding performance of duty in action against the North Vietnamese Army and Viet Cong forces in the Republic of Vietnam. Because of my direct involvement with Operation Starlite (Battle of Chu Lai, August 18 to 23, 1965), my unit ("M" Company, 3rd Battalion, 3rd Marines, 3rd Marine Division), I was bestowed the Navy Unit Commendation, which is granted by the Department of the Navy to Navy and Marine Corps units for heroism in action against an armed enemy or for extremely meritorious conduct in support of military operations. And just as important, I was presented with the Good Conduct Medal upon my completion of military service, having *honorably* served active duty over three years in the Marines. Likewise, I was granted the National Defense Service Medal, which was first authorized during the Korean War and was later awarded to all members of the U.S. Armed Forces who honorably served during the Vietnam era January 1, 1961, through August 14, 1974. Additionally, I was conferred with the Vietnam Service Medal with two bronze stars. This decoration was authorized by Presidential Executive Order 11231. This medal is awarded to all members of the Armed Forces of the United States serving in Vietnam after July 3, 1965, through March 28, 1973. The two bronze stars indicate that I participated in two of seventeen major campaigns - Vietnam Defense 1965 and Vietnam Counteroffensive 1965–1966. Also, I was given the Republic of Vietnam Meritorious Unit Citation (Gallantry Cross Color with palm and frame). This ribbon is awarded to members of the Armed Forces of the United States for valorous achievement in combat during the Vietnam conflict, March 1, 1961, through March 28, 1973. Besides this, all members of the U.S. Armed Forces who served in Vietnam for six months or longer were awarded the Republic of Vietnam Campaign Medal by the South Vietnamese government.

All in all, I received a total of eight ribbons including five medals. In addition, I earned a sharpshooter rifle badge along with a marksman pistol badge, both of which I am proud to have earned. During my short-lived career with the Marine Corps, I can honestly say that I was just another warrior trying to do his best, like so many other leathernecks.

---

[249] Harry G. Summers, Jr., *The Vietnam War Almanac*, pp. 87-88, (Presidio Press, 1985).

So as I sit here in a bedroom of our house completing this manuscript, I wonder what the Vietnam War meant. As can be seen in picture 10.2, I am standing in an M113 Armored Personnel Carrier or APC, Vietnam reminded me of what World War II must have been like for our warriors and soldiers who were transported from one battlefield to another. (Note: The APC was widely used by U.S. and allied forces in Vietnam. With the addition of gun shield, hatch armor, and heavy and medium machine guns, the standard APCs were primarily utilized as assault vehicles by the Marine Corps.) Despite initial command concerns over their ability to traverse tropical terrain, the APCs proved a valuable addition to allied mobility and shock power on the battlefield.

As we prepared ourselves for one fight after another with the enemy, we, too, had to catch a ride with these two-tracked armed utility vehicles with an M2 .50 caliber machine gun (or fifty-cal) mounted on the top. These carriers, though, had some drawbacks. For one thing, they could easily blow up from driving over a landmine. In fact, one did explode during one of our operations. It hit a large landmine, and, unfortunately, some of the Marines who were in the vehicle were hurt.

The inside of the carrier was like a furnace. We could hardly breathe. Since it was so hot inside, numerous times we would ride on the top of the vehicle. However, this presented an immediate danger because we were only targets for the Viet Cong to shoot at us. To reduce that threat, we would put a layer of sandbags on the top to give us a little added protection.

Just look at picture 10.3. In this situation, I was actually firing into a hooch some 100 feet away. I was part of a lead fire team. We were on a sweep when we spotted the VC.

This scenario was so repetitive during my combat tour of duty in Vietnam. Even though it made no sense, we often headed out on reconnaissance for the boonies in the morning, mid-day, or evening. Remember that our job was to seek and capture or destroy the Viet Cong. The mission was always the same: days of mundane patrolling and then we would be hit, by the VC, unexpectedly by the explosion of land mines or an ambush. We knew it only too well. So did the enemy. The VC, in turn, would make contact with us. They would fire at us. When that happened, we were so enraged that we would lay down firepower at an overwhelming amount for the mission at hand. When that did not happen while on patrol, we would take a breather, a well-needed rest, even with ripped utilities at the knees, as can be seen in picture 10.4.

Many nights I would wake up from a bad dream sweating profusely, about combat in the jungle, sweating profusely—I still do. Sometimes I would literally jump out of bed because of similar nightmares. Today, five decades later, it is still vivid and lifelike in my mind. My memories of Vietnam have not always been of doom and gloom. They have not always been about death. My recollections also included me rebuilding my life (as a civilian), my profession, my marriage, raising a child as well as waiting patiently for America to come to its senses. As somewhat of an extrovert by nature, and as mentioned,

I enjoyed making friends with the local kids and their families who lived in the hamlets, where we controlled and occupied, even though they were Vietnamese and possibly the Viet Cong. I prayed that they were not the enemy. Although they were assuredly hard to trust, at least the ones I came into contact with seemed to like our military presence. After a while, some of them even invited us into their thatched huts for dinner, as can be seen in picture 10.5.

On a rare occasion, we would receive a one-can ration of warm beer per Marine from headquarters. In return for a hot and tasty meal from a peasant Vietnamese family, we would share our beer with them. Occasionally, like the beer we received, we would also acquire a few soft drinks.

We had to be careful around Vietnamese families and even their kids. Word had spread around that the VC had put fine, crushed slivers of glass in our soda bottles. Thank God none of us encountered this. We were careful to check the caps of the bottles before we started drinking the soda—almost always Coca-Cola. But, that was a rare occurrence. The beer (sometimes Vietnamese beer—BA Mui BA "33") and soft drinks were all stored at the main Post Exchanges (PX). A PX is a department or grocery store located on a military post such as the Da Nang Air Base.

As can be seen in pictures 10.6 & 10.7, we captured another Vietcong, blindfolded and tied him to a pole, and then took him to our headquarters for further interrogation. I can still recall that single event today.

How ironic it is that I can remember this incident as well as so many other skirmishes/clashes about the Vietnam War, but I cannot remember my wedding anniversary. I have been married since August 27th, 1977. Why can I not remember this all-important date? As sad as it is, I have forgotten our anniversary. Does that tell you something about me? I do not know, but maybe it does.

As I remember Vietnam, it always seemed muddy. Water was everywhere. We could not get away from it. A Marine either hoofed it, as I did, or eventually acquired immersion foot disease and cellulitis (a skin disease similar to trench foot), or was transported to another location by some type of military vehicle.

What about the Vietnam War? I am sure that the Vietnamese people called it the "American War." It is one part of a sad history of many wars and constant occupations. Was it really an American War, or was it a war over American politics? You tell me!

For more than 1,000 years, Vietnam was kept under China's thumb. For about 100 years, 1854–1954, it was considered a French colony and part of French Indochina. From 1965–1975, the United States intervened with troops supporting the anti-Communist government in Saigon. I suspect it is a painful memory for most of us who were there. General Vo Nguyen Giap, the great North Vietnamese military strategist, who conquered the French and later the Americans, alleged on May 1, 2000: "Winning the war in 1975 was the happiest moment in my life because it meant the end of more than 30 years of fighting." [250] It is most significant that for the MIAs who still may be there. As of 2013, 1,649 Americans remained unaccounted for, of which 850 were listed as killed in action (body not recovered and 749 are listed as a presumptive finding of death), [251] the painstaking hunt for our MIAs goes on with the hope of ending families' mourning and suspicion.

According to a fellow warrior by the name of Lieutenant Philip J. Caputo, who served in Vietnam as a rifle platoon leader in 1965–1966 (the same time I was there, who, unlike me, later became an antiwar protester) has also written a heart-warming, touching, and eloquent memoir about his personal toils of the Vietnam War (*A Rumor of War*), here is what still matters:

> By the second century A.D., the Roman Empire extended from Britain in the north to the Nile Valley in the south, and from the Atlantic Ocean to the Tigris and Euphrates. There was a current of opinion among some Roman leaders, at that time, to expand the Empire beyond the Persian Gulf and fulfill Alexander the Great's dream to bring Persia and India permanently under the rule of Western civilization. The emperor Hadrian, who built Hadrian's Wall across northern England, was skeptical about these expansionist dreams. He seemed to sense that enlarging the empire to such an extent would lead it to fall of its own weight, and he declared the Terminus, the Roman god off limits, had set the empire's eastern boundary at the Tigris and Euphrates for time. If Lyndon Johnson, Robert McNamara, and all the best and brightest, who led us into the catastrophe of Vietnam had read their Roman history, perhaps then they would have realized that there are limits to the power even of the greatest nations and would have kept the troops home. [252]

America's best-known prisoner, U.S. Senator and one-time presidential candidate from Arizona, John S. McCain III, a Navy A4 Skyhawk flier, was shot down over Hanoi in October 1967. He spent five-and-half years in North Vietnamese prison camps, namely Hoa Lo Prison, nicknamed the Hanoi Hilton. The French originally built this dungeon to house Vietnamese prisoners. Senator McCain was beaten numerous times. He was also kept in solitary confinement for two years. He now says he has made his own peace with Vietnam and with the Vietnamese.

Many disabled veterans around the world, like me, are still suffering from the after-effects of our military service. We are the victims and sufferers of a

---

[250] *People: A Lion in Winter*, p. 59, May 1, 2000.

[251] *List of United States service members and civilians missing in action during the Vietnam War (1961–1965)*, Wikipedia.

[252] Jan Craig Scruggs, *Why Vietnam Still Matters*, p. 13, (Vietnam Veterans Memorial Fund, 1996).

stress and anxiety reaction called Post-traumatic Stress Disorder. Not only does the veteran suffer, but so do the spouse, children, families, close friends, and employers.

According to information adapted from material provided by the Point Man International Ministries (PMIM is a service organization with an evangelical purpose):

> The professional secular community has generally pronounced PTSD as an incredible misfortune that veterans will be plagued with for the rest of their lives. Many have found this to be true, many have not. Delayed war stress or Post-traumatic stress is caused by traumatic events that are outside the range of usual human experiences, such as bereavement, chronic illness, business losses, and marital conflict. Further, according to Point Man International Ministries:
>
> The most common trauma involves either a serious threat to life, threat of harm to family members, sudden destruction of ones' home or community, or seeing other people killed and/or maimed as a result of an accident or physical violence. Many refer to the event as Critical Incident Stress or CIS.
>
> PTSD occurs primarily because the issues of CIS do not get identified and resolved. The PTSD victim persistently re-experiences the distressing event(s). An event causing PTSD may be experienced alone, such as rape, or in the company of groups of people, such as military combat, airplane crashes, natural disasters, and vehicle crashes. The disorder appears to be evidently more severe and longer lasting when the event is caused by human means and design: bombings, shootings, combat, etc.

I can only speak for myself. I have experienced lots of flashbacks from Vietnam. For example, the sound of helicopters and jets, gun and rocket fire, automobile backfires, etc., trigger many flashbacks. I have encountered anger with masked rage toward my family. For the most part, I feel isolated. I have only a few close friends. Sometimes I appear to be cold, aloof, uncaring, and detached. It is not unusual for me to feel an emotional numbing. Cans popping or the backfire of a car always startle me. Alienation, memory impairment, and irritability have all been part of my adult life. Other symptoms of this condition include: emotional constriction, depression, alcohol and substance abuse, and the desire to commit suicide—suicidal ideation. Many of the regular symptoms and characteristics are there and prevalent. In fact, on May 1, 2001, Jerry A. Howle, M.D., Ph.D., a psychiatrist, wrote the following brief memorandum about me to the Department of Veterans Administration: "James Schaap suffers from Post-Traumatic Stress Disorder. This disorder has its origin in his combat experiences in Vietnam. This condition has been untreated; as a result, he is now also experiencing symptoms of Generalized Anxiety Disorder and Dysthymia."

On August 3, 2001, three months later, Patricia M. Chatham, Ph.D., a United States Department of Veterans Affairs Clinical Psychologist, specifically stated in the last paragraph of her report to the Department of Veterans Affairs the following statement: "The veteran (James Schaap) appears to have posttraumatic stress symptoms related to combat stressors in Vietnam." For this, the Department of Veterans Affairs gave me a service-connected PTSD disability rating of 70 percent (just for this one type of disability). I was given this disability rating because I was/have been unable to adequately heal from my own experiences of combat. The Vietnam War has always been a major presence in my life. It no longer dominates my existence. But make no mistake, the events of yesteryear are still with me.

As so brilliantly written by Bryan A. Floyd, here is what the war was all about some 45 years later: "We would find a VC village, and if we could not capture it or clear it of Cong, we called for jets. The jets would come in, low, and terrible, sweeping down, and screaming, in their first pass over the village. Then they would return, dropping their first bombs that flattened the huts to rubble and debris. And then the jets would sweep back again and drop more bombs that blew the rubble and debris to dust and ashes. And then the jets would come back once again, in a last pass, this time to drop Napalm that burned the dust and ashes to almost nothing. Then the village that was not a village any more was our village." [253]

According to Le Luu, a Vietnamese Veteran, states what the war is all about: "Many of us have some of the war still inside us. This creates difficulties in our lives." [254]

For me, and I am sure for many others, Vietnam does not seem to go away and I doubt if it ever will. However, I have accepted it. Or have I? To this point, I read *Pointman*, written by William R. Kimball and Roger L. Helle. It is a true story of a young Marine's brutal ordeal in Vietnam. In the book, the authors talk about their emotions. I, too, feel these emotions some five decades later:

> The galling images of long-haired freaks, protesting by the thousands and burning their draft cards, angered him. A rage began to well within him at the sight of activists spitting on the flag and waving the North Vietnamese flag in defiance. *"Is that what I was fighting for?" "Is that what my friends died fighting for?"* America had turned her back on her young men who had gone to Vietnam in good faith, but Roger (Roger L. Helle,) couldn't. The sense of national rejection was galling enough, but the self-righteous criticism that his friends died in vain was a slap in the face he couldn't bear.

---

[253] W.D. Ehrhart, editor, *Carrying the Darkness: American Indochina - The Poetry of the Vietnam War*, (Texas Tech University Press, 1985).

[254] Le Luu, Vietnamese Veteran and Novelist.

When the My Lai atrocities hit the front pages, the news media seemed to revel in its chastisement of Lieutenant Calley and, with him, every other Vietnam vet. It seemed like they were condemning them all. It didn't matter that Roger had seen both sides. He had seen the Communist atrocities and the brutalizing of innocents, but the news seemed conveniently to ignore that. It didn't seem to matter to the media that many men were serving out of the heartfelt conviction they were doing something honorable to help the Vietnamese. They seemed only to want to characterize those who served as a pack of sociopathic adolescents who got their kicks burning down innocent villages in "Zippo raids," raping helpless virgins, and butchering babies.

It was one thing to come home to the loneliness of an empty terminal or bus station, with no welcome home banners or shouts of "we're proud of you!" So what if he didn't get any brass bands or ticker-taped parades, or yellow ribbons. Yeah, it hurt, but what hurt even more was the knowledge that good men were still dying in good conscience for what they believed was right. They were still giving themselves in service to their country. So what if a thankless nation called them on the one hand and held them in contempt with the other. The nation might be able to ignore their sacrifices, but Roger couldn't. [255]

Every day, I am trying to do a little better because of my post-traumatic stress disorder. It is a slow and often difficult process. Like Senator McCain, I, too, am trying to be calm and unruffled with my Vietnam experiences, but, at times, this is not easy—not easy at all. I am trying to be at peace with myself, but this too is not easy. As previously mentioned, they are there in my daily memories and are as vivid today as they were over five decades ago.

If you are interested in reading some of the firsthand reports produced by our government about Vietnam, I encourage you to log onto the website for the United States Department of State. This information comes from the State Department, Foreign Relations of the United States.

Conversely, if you are not interested in the government-produced documents about Vietnam, try this next quote out for size. It is presented to you by James S. Olson and Randy Roberts, *Where the Domino Fell*, and goes like this:

For the generation after the fall of Saigon in 1975, the American people wondered how it had happened, how the Vietnam War had gone out of control, how the richest country in the world could sacrifice hundreds of billions of dollars and tens of thousands of young men in a military effort that seemed, in the end, to have so little sig-

---

[255] William R. Kimaball and Roger L. Helle, *Pointman*, pp. 205-206 (U.S.A., 1991).

nificance. Vietnam, Laos, and Cambodia fell to Communism, but the rest of Asia survived. Only three dominoes went down. During the 1970s and 1980s the victorious Socialist Republic of Vietnam slipped into stupefying poverty, while the United States recovered from its malaise and enjoyed a period of unprecedented growth and prosperity. Around the world there were nearly 60,000 graves covering the bodies of Americans who lost their lives, but few people in the United States knew whether their sacrifice meant anything at all. Communism had taken over Indochina in the end, and the United States was just fine anyway. [256]

Today, as strange or as peculiar as it may seem, I still think that I am a Marine—a leatherneck through and through—and all that it implies. Perhaps it has best been defined by U.S. Senator Paul H. Douglas (1892–1976), from the great State of Illinois, in his introduction to *The United States Marines: A Pictorial History:* "Those of us who have had the privilege of serving in the Marine Corps value our experiences as among the most precious of our lives. The fellowship of shared hardships and dangers in a worthy cause creates a close bond of comradeship. It is the basic reason for the cohesiveness of Marines and for the pride we have in our Corps and our loyalty to each other."

Before I close my book, I would like you to write down a man's name. Please do it for me. His name is Bill McCloud. He, too, is a Vietnam Veteran, and has written a wonderful paperback called, *What Should We Tell Our Children About Vietnam?* It was published by the University of Oklahoma Press: Norman and London, 1989, ISBN: 0-8061-2229-3. It is truly worth exploring in many ways. Here is a synopsis: "What should we tell our children about Vietnam?" This was the question facing junior high school teacher and Vietnam Veteran Bill McCloud as he prepared to teach his students about the war. To find his answer, McCloud went straight to the people who directed, fought, protested, and reported the war: politicians, military officers, protestors, soldiers, returned POWs, nurses, refugees, scholars, writers, and parents of soldiers who died in the war. He sent them all a handwritten letter: "I am a Vietnam Veteran and junior high school teacher ... If you could find the time, please send me your response to the following question: What do you think are the most important things for today's junior high school students to understand about the Vietnam War? Even a brief reply would be most helpful. Thank you. Sincerely, Bill McCloud."

From all over the country and from all walks of life, responses poured in. "It was," McCloud said, "as if they were waiting to be asked the question." Some responses were embittered, some were rueful, some almost elegiac; but every one of them took the question seriously. Collectively these 128 letters

---

[256] James S. Olson and Randy Roberts, *Where the Domino Fell–America and Vietnam 1945–1990*, p. 281(Diane Publishing Company, 1991).

form a remarkable historical record, and they confirm that the learning of lessons is as much the statesman's duty as it is the student's.

Although there is much material in print concerning the Vietnam War, there is little that deals specifically with the lessons of the war. The answers to McCloud's provocative question represent a unique and heartening outpouring of national conscience, hindsight, reflection, sorrow, and wisdom. As the country has moved completely out of the national amnesia about the bitter Vietnam years, these letters can, in this writer's opinion, still serve as beacons for students, educators, statesmen, scholars, and everyone else interested in learning the lessons of one the most wrenching eras in our national history.

Here is one citation from Bill McCloud's work, written by M. Chuck Bowman, a two-tour Vietnam Veteran, Marines, 1964–1966:

> I think our youth should be taught the lesson of Vietnam in a comparative context, as it relates to our own American Revolution and its success. That revolution probably would have been doomed to the might of England had not the French and others, for self-serving reasons, assisted the colonies.
>
> The struggle by the South Vietnamese to resist Communism was doomed when the politicians of this country couldn't find the moral courage, or even selfish reasons, to support them.
>
> When our cowardly, self-serving, reelection-at-any-cost Congress capitulated to the equally cowardly, self-serving antiwar protest, Vietnam, Cambodia, and Laos became the sacrificial lambs on the altar of political expediency.
>
> The lesson of Vietnam—it should have been learned from the Nazis and every other terrorist government that has ever existed. Stated simply and eloquently, by someone whose name escapes me, it can be paraphrased this way:
>
> 'When they came for my neighbor, I only stood and watched. When they came for my other neighbor, I turned away. When they came for me, there was none left to help me.'
>
> I can only wonder how many generations will pass before there is no one to assist when Communism comes for the United States, as it surely will if we continue to turn away. I can be grateful that it probably won't happen in my lifetime, but sad for the probability that it will happen.
>
> Since history has been and will be written by the victors, it is unlikely that my view will be the one that survives in the future.
>
> Peace at any price is a poor God to worship, and, coming from a nation that has sacrificed so much for freedom, one that galls me to no end.
>
> Our forebears cannot but be ashamed at what we are becoming. I am.

Even though M. Chuck Bowman shares an interesting point about Jane Fonda and Tom Hayden in McCloud's book, Professor Emeritus Henry Mark Holzer, Brooklyn Law School, NY, also has a poignant and insightful comment to make about Ms. Fonda:

> During the Vietnam War, Jane Fonda journeyed to Hanoi. She met with senior Communist civilian and military officials, held press conferences, toured sites of alleged bombing, 'interviewed' American prisoners of war and, most important, made a series of propaganda broadcasts (tapes of which were incessantly played to our POWs).
>
> By examining Fonda's childhood motivations, her radicalization, her POW 'audience,' her activities in North Vietnam, and through a detailed analysis of the American law of treason, *Aid and Comfort* makes the case that more than sufficient evidence existed to indict and convict Jane Fonda for the crime of treason. The appendix to *Aid and Comfort*: Jane Fonda in North Vietnam contains the text of Fonda's broadcasts from North Vietnam.

While I can possibly forgive Ms. Fonda for her cowardly and anti–U.S. propaganda activities, I still feel she should have been convicted, for her crimes of disloyalty to the United States. In fact, during her two-week visit to the Hanoi area, Fonda taped as many as ten propaganda messages; some broadcast live, for her North Vietnamese hosts. She also told seven American POWs that "Americans are fighting for Esso, Shell, and Coca-Cola" during a photo op staged mainly for the Communist press. However, the photo op at the three-gun anti-aircraft battery was well attended by the Western media, and dozens of photos exist of Fonda smiling, clapping, and laughing. She later expressed regret at having her picture taken and that her actions caused pain to many vets (like me), but clarified that *"I did not, have not, and will not say that going to North Vietnam was a mistake.*

As mentioned, I feel Ms. Fonda was unfaithful and traitorous to our government. She was, during this tumultuous time, the enemy from within! She made broadcasts made in Hanoi that were reprehensible as well as despicable. They were wicked and immoral comments about servicemen, people like me, doing a job, and serving their country, to the best of their ability. Ms. Fonda also helped in the organization of a production group, here in the United States, called the F.T.A. (F _ _ k The Army). This group helped to set up coffee houses near military bases where they would perform anti-war derogatory sketches for the visiting soldiers. Having said all this, I feel that Ms. Fonda, today, is all but a sad faint shadow (of her exercise videos) and can no longer hurt any of us. In reality, she never did (physically) harm any of us.

I know that this type of Communist threat is over. And, although Vietnam presented a grim appearance in the 1960s, 1970s, and even in the 1980s, it was not atypical of what transpires after a/any civil war. And it can be said that the Vietnam War is not as horrible as what happened in Cambodia. In the meantime, the Vietnam War has been over for 40 years. Since then, a reunited Vietnam is not doing so badly in 2015 even though there is still corruption and abuse, a lack of transparency and a lack of media freedom. The Socialist Republic of Vietnam is a Communist dictatorship characterized by political repression and has a lack of respect for basic human rights.

As I begin to close on this chapter, there is one last story I would like to share with you. It was passed on to me by J. Dave Steel, Company Radio Operator for Mike Company, 3rd Battalion, 3rd Marines, 3rd Marine Division (3/3/3). He, too, was a Vietnam Veteran, 1965–1966, from my unit. His lesson, dedicated to all of us, goes like this:

> Please take out a one-dollar bill and look at it.
>
> The one-dollar bill you are looking at, in its present design, first came off the press in 1957. This so-called paper money is in fact a cotton and linen blend, with red and blue silk fibers running through it. It is actually material. We've all washed it without its falling apart. A special blend of ink is used, the contents we will never know.
>
> It is overprinted with symbols and then it is starched to make it water-resistant and pressed to give it that nice crisp look. If you look on the front of the bill, you will see the United States Treasury Seal.
>
> On the top you will see the scales for the balance a balanced budget. In the center you have a carpenter's T-square, a tool used for an even cut. Underneath is the key to the United States Treasury. That's all pretty easy to figure out, but what is on the back of that dollar bill is something we should all know. If you turn the bill over, you will see two circles. Both circles, together, comprise the Great Seal of the United States. The First Continental Congress requested that Benjamin Franklin and a group of men come up with a Seal. It took them four years to accomplish this task and another two years to get it approved. If you look at the left-hand circle, you will see a pyramid. Notice the face is lighted and the western side is dark. This country was just beginning. We had not begun to explore the West or decided what we could do for Western Civilization. The pyramid is uncapped, again signifying that we were not even close to being finished. Inside the capstone you have the all-seeing eye, an ancient symbol for divinity. It was Franklin's belief that one man couldn't do it alone, but a group of men, with the help of God, could do anything.
>
> IN GOD WE TRUST is on this currency. The Latin above the pyramid, ANNUIT COEPTIS, means "God has favored our undertaking." The Latin below the pyramid, NOVUS ORDO SECLORUM, means "a new order has begun." At the base of the pyramid is the Roman numeral for 1776.
>
> If you look at the right-hand circle, and check it carefully, you learn that it is on every National Cemetery in United States. It is also

on the Parade of Flags Walkway at the Bushnell Florida National Cemetery and is the centerpiece of most hero's monuments. Slightly modified, it is the seal of the President of the United States and it is always visible whenever he speaks, yet no one knows what the symbols mean. The Bald Eagle was selected as a symbol for victory for two reasons: first, he is not afraid of a storm; he is strong and he is smart enough to soar above it. Secondly, he wears no material crown.

We had just broken from the King of England. Also, notice that the shield is unsupported. This country can now stand on its own. At the top of that shield you have a white bar signifying congress, a unifying factor. We were coming together as one nation.

In the Eagle's beak you will read, E PLURIBUS UNUM, meaning "from many, one." Above the eagle you have thirteen stars representing the thirteen original colonies, and any clouds of misunderstanding rolling away. Again, we were coming together as one. Notice what the Eagle holds in his talons: olive branch and arrows. This country wants peace, but we will never be afraid to fight to preserve peace. The Eagle always wants to face the olive branch, but in time of war, his gaze turns toward the arrows.

They say that the number 13 is an unlucky number. This is almost a worldwide belief. You will usually never see a room numbered 13, or any hotels or motels with a 13th floor. But, think about this: 13 original colonies, 13 signers of the Declaration of Independence, 13 stripes on our flag, 13 steps on the pyramid, 13 letters in the Latin above the pyramid - ANNUIT COEPTIS, 13 letters in E PLURIBUS UNUM, 13 stars above the Eagle, 13 plumes of feathers on each span of the Eagle's wing, 13 bars on that shield, 13 leaves on the olive branch, 13 fruits, and if you look closely, 13 arrows. And for minorities; the 13th Amendment. Why don't we know this?

Your children don't know this as they don't know anything about Vietnam, and unfortunately their history teachers don't know it either. Too many veterans have given up too much to ever let the meaning fade. Many veterans remember coming home to an America that didn't care. Too many veterans, unfortunately, never came home at all.

Tell everyone what is on the back of the one-dollar bill and what it stands for, since nobody else will. *Semper Fidelis.*

If you do not mind, I ask that you tell your friends, especially the ROTC youth in high school and college students, about my hybrid memoir/biography, *Vietnam: My War–Five Decades Later.*

I hope to return, someday, to the forts, rice paddies, huts, villages, cemeteries, pagodas, and battlefields of Vietnam to make peace with my life and ghosts of the past. I hope to do this someday with my son. I will probably have to return to Da Nang and the French fortress, where the war began for me on July 7, 1965. I will no doubt have to come back to Cam Ne, where many huts were burned to the ground. I will certainly have to return to Chu Lai and its beautiful beaches, where one of the greatest battles the Marines ever fought during the Vietnam War–Operation Starlite took place. I will, in all likelihood, need to return to the area of An Trach and the small hamlet of La Bong, where we were ambushed almost daily, and other surrounding villages of this peasant country. I will presumably have to come back to all of these places that are still so clear in my mind. It is as if I were there yesterday. I am certain that I will need to make reconciliation with my fellow Marines who also survived, and with my former enemies whom I will not find. I know they are adversaries no longer. Meanwhile, I have tried to make peace, every day, with my beloved and deceased parents. Without their courage to overcome monumental obstacles, I would not be here today to tell you about my sojourn with the people who were supposedly my enemies. I love you, Mom and Dad. You are not forgotten, and you never will be. May God be with you! Although I say many prayers for you, I will cite a special prayer for the both of you every Fourth of July–your birthdays, as can be seen in picture 10.8.

I also hope to take my son to the Vietnam Veterans Memorial in Washington, D.C., located in the Constitution Gardens near the Lincoln Monument. "The Wall," as it is called is about 246 feet long and ten feet high at its vertex. It, too, has 140 separate panels, each for a particular time in the history of the war. And while the Marines made up only a small portion (i.e., about one-tenth) of all the United States Armed Forces during the Vietnam War, *one in every four names* on the Vietnam Memorial is that of a United States Marine.

Dedicated on November 13, 1982, the black granite slabs arranged as a wall, with its 58,307 names of the dead and missing from the war (as of Memorial Day, 2015), has been the object of some debate. It includes two sculptures depicting three servicemen and women in uniforms. The monument, paid for with private donations from the public, was intended to separate the U.S. policy during the war from the issue of those who served as an act of national reconciliation. Unfortunately, many veterans feel that its stark contemporary design by a 21–year-old architectural student at Yale by the name of Maya Yan Lin, failed to properly pay homage, and failed to respect the sacrifice of the men and women who fought and died in Vietnam. Many of these same Vietnam Veterans today have overcome their concern with this unmistakable plain and contemporary design, and they make it a point to visit this memorial when they can. As well, I will need to take my son to the Marine Corps War Memorial, sometimes called the Iwo Jima Memorial. Rising from hallowed ground, the Marine Corps War Memorial, along with the names of its five Marines and their corpsman are forever immortalized, overlooks the beauty of the Potomac River in Arlington, Virginia. Standing next to the Arlington National Cemetery, it is the largest bronze monument in the world. It may even be argued by fellow Marines like me that it is also the most famous monument in the world.

"The Marine Corps War Memorial honors the *supreme sacrifice* of all Marines who have fallen in battle in the service of their country. Here, they will never grow old. Here, they live eternally. Here, they live on *hallowed ground.* Never forget." [257]

In closing, the Marine Corps, beyond any shadow of a doubt, gave me something special—something very unique, which, at times, is hard to put into words. It gave me lots of confidence in myself. It made me feel like I was somebody. More important, it made me feel like I was someone special. And while I do not have many friends, I have never felt such an attraction and an affinity as I have felt to the Corps—Semper Fi!

I knew what Vietnam was like. I knew how we looked, acted, talked, and smelled. No one in America, at the time, did. Of course, I am exaggerating a little. More so, in all the Vietnam movies that were produced by Hollywood, they too got it all wrong—every damned time, always rousing twisted political knives on the bones of our dead servicemen. [258]

I hope my book, *Vietnam: My War–Five Decades Later,* has opened your eyes, even in a small way, to some of the trials and tribulations of war and Marine Corps life, at least by one warrior, during the mid-1960s. As one who lives with PTSD every day, I also hope you have felt the sadness of loss and bloodshed that I felt while fighting such a political war; as well as the love of my fellow Marines who live and died for you and me. Would I do it again? Without equivocation, and in a heartbeat! I am ready to go. Just call my name, and I will pack my sea bag. On the other hand, I do hope our political and military leaders choose our future battles more carefully. I hope our political leaders will let the military powers (i.e., generals and admirals) to take control of the battlefield. If it is run by politicians, as it was in Vietnam, I doubt if we will win another war.

If my manuscript is not enough to whet your appetite, and you would like to read more about the Marines of yesterday, a sentimental journey of the past, I suggest you purchase, possibly through eBay, George P. Hunt's volume, *The Story of the U.S. Marines,* 1951, published by Random House. Mr. Hunt was a former managing editor of Life magazine.

In the meantime, here are some more gripping data about the Vietnam War. The figures have been retrieved from the Internet that will tell you a little more, directly and indirectly, about this all-important conflict (refer to Appendix 1). (Note: All numbers shown are approximations only. Actual figures may vary.)

---

[257] Marion F. Sturkey, *Warrior Culture of the U.S. Marines,* p. 91, (Heritage Press International, 2002).

[258] Lieutenant General Harold G. Moore (Retired) and Joseph L. Galloway, *We Were Soldiers Once ... and Young,* p. xvi, (Random House, 1992).

1. American, South Vietnamese, and Allied Troop Count Levels (i.e., before and during the Vietnam War)
2. American Troop Count Levels by Branch of Service
3. American Military Deaths by Branch of Service
4. American Military Deaths and Wounds by Cause of Death and Wound
5. American Military Deaths by Country Location
6. American Military Deaths by Ethnicity
7. American Military Deaths by Ethnicity and Rank
8. American Military Deaths by Type of Casualty
9. American Military Deaths by Pay Grade and Service
10. American Military Deaths by Religion
11. American Military Deaths by Component Code
12. American Military Deaths by Marital Status
13. American Military Deaths by Home State
14. Non-American Deaths by Country
15. Wounded in Action, but not Mortally, requiring Hospitalization
16. Status of Unaccounted-for Americans (MIA) lost in the Vietnam War
17. Status of Unaccounted-for Americans (MIA) lost in the Vietnam War, by Branch of Service
18. Prisoners of War in the Vietnam War but Returned Alive (1961–1973)
19. Miscellaneous Facts about the Vietnam Conflict
20. Medal of Honor Recipients (1965–1973)

Postscript: Should a fellow warrior from any of my units, during my enlistment in the Corps, June 1964 through June 1967, and especially in Vietnam, July 1965 through April 1966, D Company, 1st Battalion, 9th Marines, 3rd Marine Division (1/9/3) or M Company, 1st Platoon, 3rd Battalion, 3rd Marines, 3rd Marine Division (3/3/3), read this tome and remember who I am, it would truly be a privilege and an honor to hear from you. I can be contacted, via my website. I hope that you will contact me to say hello.

For now, if you are interested in learning more about the 3rd Marine Division, you can contact the Third Marine Division Association through the Internet. The 3rd Marine Division Association is a fraternal group that was founded in 1949. It holds annual reunions, raises funds for division causes, and publishes a directory and newsletter. It is open to all warriors, like me, and corpsmen, who served with the division. If, however, you want to contact or know more about former Marines and Corpsmen of the Third Marine Division that were in Vietnam from 1965 through 1969, pleaser go to their website.

Postscript 2: On the lighter side, although I am 70 years young, sometimes I feel I am 70 years old. According to Jeffrey Fink, a former U.S. Marine Corps Sergeant and Vietnam Veteran, 1965 - 1966, from my same unit, Mike

Company, 3rd Battalion, 3rd Marines, 3rd Marine Division (3/3/3), "old" is when:

- You can't remember if you've sent this out already!
- Your sweetie says, "let's go upstairs and make love," and you answer, "Honey, I can't do both!"
- Your friends compliment you on your new alligator shoes and you're barefoot!
- A sexy babe catches your fancy and your pacemaker opens the garage door.
- Going bra-less pulls all the wrinkles out of your face.
- You don't care where your spouse goes, just as long as you don't have to go along.
- You're cautioned to slow down by the doctor instead of by the police.
- "Getting a little action" means I don't need to take any fiber today.
- "Getting lucky" means you find your car in the parking lot.
- "An all-nighter" means not getting up to pee!

And specifically for you (former) Magnificent Grunts, Gyrenes, Jarheads, Devil Dogs, and Leathernecks, here are some happy hour decrees of combat:

- In combat, any Marine who does not openly consider himself the best in the game is in the *wrong* game.
- If you can avoid it, never get into a fair fight.
- If you can avoid it, never get into a fight without at least three times as much ammo as the other guy.
- Speak softly, but *forget* the big stick. Carry a belt fed weapon.
- War doesn't determine who is right. War determines who is left.
- Do unto the enemy, and do it *first*.
- If at first your well-planned attack does not succeed, don't be a fool about it. Don't try *again*. Try something *different*.
- Cover your fellow Marines, so they will be around to cover you.
- To triumph in war, like in love, you must initiate contact.
- And lastly, medals are OK. Having all your Marine brothers alive is better. [259]

AGAIN, SEMPER FIDELIS!

---

[259] Ibid, pp. 152-153.

Picture 10.1
My son
[Author photo]

VIETNAM: MY WAR

Picture 10.2
Author standing in APC
[Author photo]

Picture 10.3
Author prone with a rifle
[Author photo]

Picture 10.4
Author resting
[Author photo]

Picture 10.5
Eating with Vietnamese people
[Author photo]

Picture 10.6
Taking a prisoner (1)
[Author photo]

Picture 10.7
Taking a prisoner (2)
[Author photo]

VIETNAM: MY WAR

Picture 10.8
My parent's grave
[Author photo]

Chapter 11

Epilogue

FROM the perspective of the early 21st century, the Vietnam War seems so long ago. As such, I do not believe many people really understand or appreciate the Vietnam War (any more), especially our youth and young adults of today. More so, they do not comprehend the vicious realisms of war and combat. For me, July 1965–April 1966, was a moment in time when I fought in Vietnam (for the most part, brutal, small-unit fighting that typified the Vietnam War during those early days). The war was in a phase that I thought we could clear up because I also thought it was the right decision for America to aid and defend the people of South Vietnam. It remains one of the most significant years of my life—nothing else mattered at the time. In fact, and as a tangential side note, I have always felt a peculiar connection to Vietnam, even weirder, a longing to return to this peasant country. Why? Simply stated, there were no frontlines. The enemy was everywhere, for the most part, as a low-level guerrilla insurgency (at least at the time that I served in-country). He/she dressed as farmers by day and as the enemy by night—or so I thought! On the other hand, for our youth and young adults of today, it was before their birth. In fact, many people do not really care about the Vietnam War, even though militarily we were successful in South Vietnam, because it was so political in nature, yet for many, politically wrong. It was, indubitably, "America's War." It was America's War since we, as Vietnam veterans, later cried out for justice and support, but got little notice. It was, as mentioned before, not a war that the United States lost. It was a conflict that our nation's leaders abandoned—*those people that work in the halls of Congress and in the White House, and in the lack of concern as well as apathy of thousands of Americans who did not give a damn!* Knowing this, it has been described, by some, as a tragedy. It also has been labeled as a war that was challenging to understand. This difficulty ran from the top to the bottom. As such, it was a war that truly tore apart this country. Americans have a tolerance for loss, it is only to a point. It is only to a point because the misfortune of this conflict is that parents had to bury their children; young wives quickly became widows, younger siblings lost their idols, and children lost their fathers. It was a struggle, according to Otto Lehrack, "once the number of grieving families passed the 10,000 mark, and then the 15,000 mark, public protest against the war began in earnest and steadily increased. By the time the *blood debt* hit 30,000 lives, popular opposition widened and support for the war began to melt away. The American crossover point had been reached, a goal the communists long kept in mind. In our case, it was not a question of losing men faster than we could replace them but a question of losing men faster than we were willing to replace them. [260] More so, it was a war that also felled a presidency. Most imperative, it was a conflict with one fire fight after another that most likely achieved nothing and is almost lost from memory. Still, I believe it was a noble war fought with M14s, M16s, helicopters, and jets to stop Communism from further spreading in Southeast Asia. Even if it was a principled war, just envision how tough it must have been for the Vietnamese people, who died in massive numbers, suffered unbearably, and were the targets of mayhems committed by both sides. Many, on the other hand, found it to be a meaningless conflict, and here is why they thought this way: There was the North Vietnamese victory over South Vietnam. There was a withdrawal of American forces from Indochina. There was the dissolution of the Republic of Vietnam. In addition, the Communist government took over power in South Vietnam. And, South Vietnam was annexed by North Vietnam. Notwithstanding, I believe the task of being there was necessary. [261]

What happened in Vietnam during the late 1960s and early 1970s was part of this process, hard though it may have been to identify it thus at the time. In 1975, the Communist conquest in Vietnam was not a misfortune in the milieu of the Cold War, nor was it part of the downfall of Asia to Communism. In 1965 (when I first arrived in Vietnam), it would have seemed both of these things. Another way of looking at Vietnam was in terms of the way the U.S. military viewed the world. Vietnam showed that everlasting military verities cannot be gainsaid: that a clear, realizable aim is at the heart of any strategy. It is to be hoped that such coherent methods to the colossal difficulties of formulating military strategy continue to inform the commanders of the world's greatest war machine. [262]

As so eloquently stated by Edward F. Murray, founder and president of the Medal of Honor Historical Society, "America's military involvement in South Vietnam polarized this country as have few other events in our history." [263] Not many people want to know about the Vietnam War because it started over 50 years ago. The only ones who do really comprehend what we went through are my contemporaries–the men and women—the best of the best—that I met at this ethereal event, our reunion. It was easy to talk with these Marines about our past. It was easy to talk about the Vietnam War because these former combat warriors, like me, had been there in the midst of fighting this terrifying war. We understood each other; we all spoke the same language. Additionally, these colleagues and heroes fought their own personal war as well. Knowing this, I am sure they too have PTSD as I do.

---

[260] Otto J. Lehrack, *The First Battle–Operation Starlite and the Beginning of the Blood Debt*

[261] *List of wars involving the United States,* Wikipedia.

[262] Leo Daugherty, *The Vietnam War–Day by Day,* p. 190, (Chartwell Books, Inc., 2011).

[263] Edward F. Murray, *Vietnam Medal of Honor Heroes,* p. xi, (Ballantine Books, 2005).

I feel it is appropriate to provide you, especially you Vietnam Veterans, with another quote. This meaningful address, presented by retired U.S. Army Lieutenant General James M. Link, after 33 years of distinguished service as an ordnance officer and logistician, was provided to me by Thomas Carl Crouson. He was the number three son in the Crouson family and the number two Marine, serving in the Corps for six years. He, too, later entered the Army Reserves, retiring as a Command Sergeant Major.

I feel this excerpt is worth reading and reflecting upon. Further to this point, I believe you will appreciate this speech. It provides a perspective often overlooked by the media in characterizing the conflict in South East Asia.

General Link, the former Commander of the Redstone Arsenal, delivered this address at the breakfast commemorating the arrival in Huntsville, Alabama, of the traveling Vietnam Veterans Memorial Wall. (Note: The Arsenal is a garrison [a U.S. Army post and a census-designated place adjacent to Huntsville in Madison County, Alabama, United States and is part of the Huntsville-Decatur Combined Statistical Area] for a number of tenants including the U.S. Army Materiel Command, Army's Aviation and Missile Command, the Missile Defense Agency of the Department of Defense, and NASA's Marshall Space Flight Center.) [264]

Thank you, ladies and gentlemen, distinguished guests, fellow veterans, and especially fellow veterans of the war in Vietnam. It is indeed a tremendous honor for me to stand before you this morning as we come together to remember fallen comrades, MIAs/POWs and a very important time in our lives.

It was a time of war, a time of conflict not only in Southeast Asia, but throughout our nation. Indeed a time that has shaped our national consciousness, and for us veterans, a time which forged a sense of self that in many ways defines us still today.

Lest we forget, how then do we remember? How do we honor those who did not come home, or came home broken and bent in both body and spirit?

I remember when the architectural design of the Vietnam War Memorial Wall was first proposed. Many of us recoiled at the thought of a ditch on the Mall, listing nothing more than the names of those who paid the ultimate sacrifice. Surely, this was yet one more insult hurled at those who had answered the call to serve their nation rather than serve themselves.

That Wall has transcended all things political and overcome controversy, as it reaches out to us who served, and even those who did not serve, while deeply touching all of us who lost comrades, friends, neighbors and loved ones during that troubled time.

---

[264] *Redstone Arsenal*, Wikipedia.

The mystery of the Wall is found in its majestic simplicity. Panels of black stone that hold not only the names of those killed, but in its mirror-like finish, the faces of all of us who come to witness its solemn statement. In that reflection, we are made one with the monument, we join its essence, and are consumed by images behind the names. Images of young men, their lives cut short, their personal sacrifices often unrecorded, their selfless service, unflinching courage, and the unique love and caring that is shared by comrades in arms. It is the wound on our National Mall that never heals, but it does serve to soothe the deep scars on those of us who carry heavy memories, and for some perhaps a little guilt for having been the ones fortunate enough to return to the world.

As this Memorial travels around the country it invariably brings with it a lot of discussion and perhaps even rekindled old arguments about the Vietnam War. The arrival of the Vietnam Memorial Wall in whatever city it arrives provides an opportunity for us to reflect on this important period in our individual lives and our nation's history. Of course, there are those who might say we veterans are still too close to the heat of battle, too burdened by personal experiences to make objective judgments about the Vietnam War. To that, I say Bull! I have grown very weary of those in the media, even some in academia—of which I have belonged to for almost 40 years, and certainly the entertainment industry, like Jane Fonda, who would purport to speak for us, or to try to define us a bunch of hair-trigger psychopaths on the verge of insanity or some unspeakable violence. We who were actually there know what we saw, and we know what we did. Each of us is just one of the millions who proudly served our country, having done our duty with honor. In addition, I see little of what I experienced reflected in Oliver Stone's movies. I personally think Oliver donated a few too many of his brain cells to his drug use. (Nonetheless, he is a veteran of the Vietnam War. Stone served with the U.S. Army from April 1967 to November 1968. He specifically requested combat duty and was assigned to the 25th Infantry Division and the 1st Cavalry Division, and was wounded twice in action. His personal awards include the Bronze Star with "V" for valor for "extraordinary acts of courage under fire", and the Purple Heart with one Oak Leaf Cluster. He is, unequivocally, to be congratulated for his heroism and dedication to serve his country–he too is my hero.) Also, and in my view, movies like "Apocalypse Now", directed by and produced by Francis Ford Coppola and starring Marlon Brando, Robert Duvall, and Martin Sheen, were nothing more than a collection of psychotic experiences made up in Hollywood bearing scant resemblance to the reality we experienced. This film, interestingly enough, follows the central character, U.S. Army special operations officer Captain Benjamin L. Willard (Martin Sheen), of MACV-SOG, on a mission to kill the renegade and presumed insane U.S.

Army Special Forces Colonel Walter E. Kurtz (Marlon Brando).[265] Having said this, I am sure that you and I can certainly recognize the difference between a remarkable artistic license and a lie; can't we?

America's direct involvement in Vietnam lasted for over 13 years, from 1960 to 1973. Of course, the result was not victory at all. Not even a cease-fire or a demilitarized strip of land between North and South as happened in Korea, who negotiated terms allowing the United States of America to *"withdraw with honor."* In fact, and as already mentioned, the Paris Peace Accords of 1973 intended to establish reconciliation in Vietnam and an end to the Vietnam War which ended direct U.S. military involvement, and temporarily stopped the fighting between North and South Vietnam. The governments of the Democratic Republic of Vietnam (North Vietnam), the Republic of Vietnam (South Vietnam), and the United States, as well as the Provisional Revolutionary Government (PRG) that represented indigenous South Vietnamese revolutionaries, signed the Agreement on Ending the War and Restoring Peace in Vietnam on January 27, 1973. The agreement, though, was not ratified by the United States Senate.[266]

So we did not return home to victory parades or hugs and kisses in Times Square. Most of us were merely another passenger aboard a chartered airliner (mine was a Braniff Airlines Boeing 707 painted a heinous green color). Others came home in Air Force cargo planes to be dumped at some military base usually in the middle of the night.

Remember, we (especially the "combat" kind of Marine) came home to antipathy and in many cases antagonism. Some had a real hatred for what we did. As such, we were told to quickly get out of our uniforms, a military outfit that I was proud to have worn, in order to avoid confrontations on city streets. These streets were filled with apathies and aggressions toward servicemen, like me, for we returned home to a populace that seemed not to care about us.

No wonder it has taken so long for many of us to even want to talk about the war. Talk we must for we are living witnesses—even though we are starting to die at high rates, and if we are silent others will continue to spin a version of their own truth that best suits their personal agenda.

We must also dispel the myths that have settled in around this war, and there are so many. Those of us who served must debunk these fables at every opportunity, and now is one of those. I say this, because even today, opinions about this war: its unfairness, its aptness, its outright inevitability, its utter pointlessness are closely held and hotly argued.

The first myth is that the Armed Forces of the United States suffered a major military defeat in Vietnam. I believe our forces were *never* defeated in terrible (major) battles where our soldiers and Marines suffered awful casualties, like Dak To and Hamburger Hill. Our airmen suffered too. Many were

---

[265] *Apocalypse Now*, Wikipedia.
[266] *Paris Peace Accords*, Wikipedia.

killed and captured in the air campaign, but the war was not lost as a result of these battles. In truth, where we found the enemy we defeated him, and in large numbers. Some, however, will certainly disagree with this statement. After the Tet Offensive in 1968 (a military campaign during Vietnam War that began on January 31, 1968 where regular and irregular forces of the People's Army of Vietnam fought against the forces of the Republic of South Vietnam), the Vietcong and the North Vietnamese operating in the south were so soundly defeated that they could not launch another major offensive until 1972. Nonetheless, that did not deter Ho Chi Minh and the North Vietnamese, since they were definitely willing to lose the war on the battlefield; they were clearly after victory. To this point, Ho Chi Minh, founder of the Communist Party of Vietnam who devoted his later years to seeking reunification of the North with the South, under his Communist rule, stated the following all-important quote: *"You will kill ten of our men, and we will kill one of yours, and in the end it will be you who tire of it."* This same ruler went on to state that: *"Although our fight will be long and hard, our people are resolved to fight till final victory."*

All along, the North Vietnamese leaders predicted that the U.S. public would tire of the war more quickly than would the Vietnamese. This view proved visionary. American warriors and soldiers fought for twelve months in the far-off jungles of Vietnam before returning home. When their North Vietnamese counterparts went south they were told, "The trip has no deadline for return. When your mission is accomplished you will come back." Ho Chi Minh personally declared, *"Your mission is to fight for five years or even ten or twenty years."* They did, and their perseverance carried the day. [267]

It is also important to note that Ho Chi Minh was able to expertly manipulate the nationalism of his people in an attempt to unite all members of his ethnic group into a single extended state under communist-nationalist rule. The dictator's administration, ignoring a proviso by the United States and its allies, stuck it out by sponsoring a low-intensity war against the inhabitants of its neighboring territory, South Vietnam, in order to bring them under his control. [268]

Perhaps we could have won a military victory, it would have taken many more than the 500,000+ troops we had in Vietnam at the height of the war. Meanwhile, Secretary of Defense Robert McNamara, in a confidential letter to President Johnson, May 1967 (one month before I left the Marine Corps), stated:

> Who is the enemy? How can you distinguish between the civilians and the non-civilians? The same people who come and work in the bases at daytime, they just want to shoot and kill you at

[267] Robert D. Schulzinger, *A Time for War–The United States and Vietnam, 1941-1975*, p. 183, (Oxford University Press, 1997).
[268] Michael Lind, *Vietnam–The Necessary War*, p. ix, (Simon & Schuster, 1999).

nighttime. So how can you distinguish between the two—the good or the bad? All of them look the same.

Besides, by 1969, public opinion in the United States clearly wanted us out of Vietnam. The role of the media in deciding this issue has been the subject of many books and articles, so I will not go into that here. I will say I do not believe the media caused us to lose the war, although some in the press were trying their best to make it so, i.e. Morley Safer (just my own personal opinion).

At an AUSA (Association of the United States Army) Conference in Washington, D.C., General C. Frederick Weyand (pronounced Wy-und), commander of American forces in Vietnam in the final year of the war, a duty he carried out despite having become convinced as early as 1967 that the war was a hopeless venture, had an interesting interview with Walter L. Cronkite Jr. (an American broadcast journalist, best known as anchorman for the *CBS Evening News* for 19 years [1962–1981]). In fact, at a cocktail party in Saigon in 1967, General Weyand, speaking of Westmoreland, had articulated to Murray Fromson, a CBS news correspondent: "Westy just doesn't get it. The war is unwinnable. We've reached a stalemate, and we should find a dignified way out." [269] On top of this, and in earlier discussions with President Kennedy, I believe in 1961—which I believe most people do not know, General Douglas MacArthur's statement to him was that: "It would be a mistake to fight in Southeast Asia. [270]

Following Tet 1968, General Weyand was questioned by Cronkite in the Mekong Delta following the resounding defeat of enemy forces there by the U.S. military, including U.S. Navy Riverine Forces.

Cronkite acknowledged the victory, but told General Weyand he preferred to report on the thousands of Vietnamese he had seen being put in mass graves in Hue after Tet. In reporting this rather than any American victory, he stated he hoped to bring a quicker end to the war.

It did not seem to bother Cronkite that the bodies were those of South Vietnamese brutally killed by the North Vietnamese during Tet. Nor did it seem to bother him that he had compromised his own objectivity and integrity in reporting the war. Of course, we who have dedicated our lives to defending the Constitution against all enemies (foreign and domestic) certainly support all its provisions to include the First Amendment. I only hope what we saw in the press in Vietnam and still see today is not as good as it gets. Our nation deserves much better!

As far as social representation, studies have shown that blacks and Hispanics were actually slightly underrepresented compared to their percentage

---

[269] William Grimes, *New York Times*, February 13, 2010. *Frederick C. Weyand, Vietnam Commander, Dies at 93.*

[270] Arthur Schlesinger Jr., New York Times, March 29, 1992. *What Would He Have Done?*

of the total population. For instance, Blacks comprised thirteen and one-tenth percent of the age group subject to the military; they comprised twelve and six-tenth percent of the armed forces, and represented twelve and four-tenth percent of the casualties. In 1992, a study looked at the 58,220 Americans killed in Vietnam and found that 30 percent came from families in the lowest third of the income range while 26 percent came from the highest. Not much of a disparity when you look at the facts.

Some feel the draft evasion was rampant during the Vietnam era and higher than in World War II. Not so! During the Vietnam War about half a million men were draft dodgers. I bet you know some of their names! Only about 9,000 cases were actually prosecuted, and very few ever served prison time. In World War II, on the other hand, 350,000 were prosecuted for draft evasion and many went to prison. It is interesting to note that during the Vietnam War, 10,000 Americans went to Canada, but up to 30,000 Canadians joined the U.S. Armed Forces, and of those Canadians 10,000 served in Vietnam. We all know cowardice in the face of the draft is not a new phenomenon, but during Vietnam it became an art form. More important, draft dodgers made themselves out to be ethical and moral, while those of us who served were made out to be morally inferior, stupid, or unlucky. The radical left—the so-called *"draft dodgers"*—at our college campuses had a clear goal of transforming the shame of the self-serving and the fearful into the guilt of the courageous. Thank God they did not succeed!

Some think that the casualties in Vietnam were disproportionately higher for enlisted men than for officers. Actually, while officers killed in action accounted for 13.5 percent of those who died in Vietnam, they comprised only 12 percent of the troop strength. Proportionally, more officers were killed in Vietnam than in World War II. In Vietnam, unfortunately, we lost twice as many company commanders as we did platoon leaders, confirming in the Vietnam War that leaders led from the front.

Another interesting fact you can use to debunk a popular myth is that volunteers, not draftees, accounted for the majority (i.e., 77 percent) of combat deaths in Vietnam. How many of those do you think were 18-year-olds? Just 101, or less than one tenth of one percent of all those killed.

So much for myths versus facts about the Vietnam War. I now would like to remind you of the humor that accompanied American soldiers and warriors in this war, as it has all the others.

I suspect you may have heard of the time honored Murphy's Laws of combat. Murphy's Law is an adage or epigram that is typically stated as: anything that can go wrong will go wrong:

1. If the enemy is in range, so are you.
2. Incoming fire has the right of way.
3. Don't look conspicuous, it draws fire.
4. There is always a way, and it usually doesn't work.

5. The problem with the easy way out is that it has already been mined.
6. Try to look unimportant, they may be low on ammo.
7. Professionals are predictable, it's the amateurs that are dangerous.
8. The enemy invariably attacks on two occasions:
   a. when you are ready for them.
   b. when you are not ready for them.
9. Teamwork is essential; it gives them someone else to shoot at.
10. If you cannot remember, then the claymore is pointed at you.
11. The enemy diversion you have been ignoring will be the main attack.
12. A "sucking chest wound" is nature's way of telling you to slow down.
13. If your attack is going well, then it's an ambush.
14. Never draw fire, it irritates everyone around you.
15. Anything you do can get you shot, including nothing.
16. If you build yourself a bunker that's tough for the enemy to get into quickly, then you won't be able to get out of it quickly either.
17. Never share a foxhole with anyone braver than yourself.
18. If you are short of everything but the enemy, you're in a combat zone.
19. When you have secured the area, don't forget to tell the enemy.
20. Never forget that your weapon is made by the lowest bidder.
21. Friendly fire isn't.
22. If the sergeant can see you, so can the enemy.
23. Never stand when you can sit, never sit when you can lie down, never stay awake when you can sleep.
24. The most dangerous thing in the world is a second lieutenant with a map and a compass.
25. There is no such thing as an atheist in a foxhole.
26. A grenade with a seven second fuse will always burn down in four seconds.
27. Remember, a retreating enemy is probably just falling back and regrouping.
28. If at first you do not succeed call in an air-strike.
29. Exceptions prove the rule, and destroy the battle plan.
30. Everything always works in your HQ, everything always fails in the colonel's HQ.
31. The enemy never watches until you make a mistake.
32. One enemy soldier is never enough, but two is entirely too many.
33. A clean (and dry) set of BDU's (Battle Dress Uniform) is a magnet for mud and rain.

34. Whenever you have plenty of ammo, you never miss. Whenever you are low on ammo, you can't hit the broad side of a barn.
35. The more a weapon costs, the farther you will have to send it away to be repaired.
36. Field experience is something you don't get until just after you need it.
37. Interchangeable parts aren't.
38. No matter which way you have to march, it is always uphill.
39. If enough data is collected, a board of inquiry can prove ANYTHING.
40. For every action, there is an equal and opposite criticism (i.e., in boot camp).
41. The one item you need is always in short supply.
42. The worse the weather, the more you are required to be out in it.
43. The complexity of a weapon is inversely proportional to the IQ of the weapon's operator.
44. Airstrikes always overshoot the target, artillery always falls short.
45. When reviewing the radio frequencies that you wrote down, the most important ones are always illegible.
46. Those who hesitate under fire usually do not end up KIA or WIA.
47. The tough part about being an officer is that the troops don't know what they want, but they know for certain what they DO NOT want.
48. To steal information from a person is called plagiarism. To steal information from the enemy is called gathering intelligence.
49. The weapon that usually jams when you need it the most is the M60.
50. The perfect officer for the job will transfer in the day after that billet is filled by someone else.
51. When you have sufficient supplies and ammo, the enemy takes two weeks to attack. When you are low on supplies and ammo the enemy decides to attack that night.
52. The newest and least experienced soldier will usually win the Medal of Honor.
53. A Purple Heart just goes to prove that were you smart enough to think of a plan, stupid enough to try it, and lucky enough to survive.
54. Murphy was a grunt.

Should anyone think the war was conducted in an incompetent manner? They should look at the numbers: Hanoi admits to 1.4 million of its regulars were killed on the battlefield compared to our 58,220, and about 250,000

South Vietnamese. From 1954 to 1976, it was the capital of North Vietnam. The city is located on the right bank of the Red River. And if someone tries to convince you that Vietnam was "a dirty little war," where Air Force and Navy bombs did all the work, you might remind them that this was the most costly war for the grunts of the U.S. Marines Corps. Five times as many were killed as in World War I, three times as many died in Korea, and more total killed and wounded than in World War II.

To the Vietnam veterans here today (especially you Marines) and to all those whose names appear on the Wall, I say "you are all heroes." Brave men and women who faced the issues of this war, including your own possible death, and after weighing those concerns against your obligation to your country, you decided to serve with honor.

In the words of a timeless phrase found on the Confederate Memorial in Arlington Cemetery, *"Not for fame or reward, not for place or for rank, but in simple obedience to duty, as they understood it."*

I ask each of you to treat each other with the dignity and respect that you have earned. Reach out and welcome a fellow Vietnam veteran home.

God bless each of you, and may God continue to bless this America we love and serve.

I hope that you felt this quotation was worth reading and reflecting upon. In the meantime, here is another excerpt about the roots of tragedy, one that is truly a misunderstanding about the Vietnam War:

> One of the great tragedies of the Vietnam War is that although American Armed Forces defeated the North Vietnamese and Viet Cong in every major battle, the United States still suffered the greatest defeat in its history. A clue to how this could happen was provided by Sun Tzu, the famous Chinese strategist, over 2,500 years ago. "If you know ... not the enemy," he wrote, "for every victory gained, you will suffer a defeat."
>
> The sad truth is that before the U.S. involvement began, American knew almost nothing about Vietnam. Although it had been discovered earlier, East Asia, including Southeast Asia, only fully entered Western consciousness in the 19th century as colonial empires began to blossom there. As a result, when the United States began to become concerned with Vietnamese affairs in the closing days of World War II, its maps did not even show the existence of a country called Vietnam. It was hidden under the label "French Indochina." The name Indochina itself was confusing, since it suggested that the area was simply an appendage of China. This misperception held at the very highest reaches. For example, at the Yalta Conference (sometimes called the Crimea Conference) in early 1945, when the Allied powers were deciding the makeup of the postwar world, President Franklin D. Roosevelt asked General Chiang Kai-shek, China's leader, "Do you want Indo-China?" With full knowledge of Viet-

namese history and tradition, Chiang replied: "We don't want it. They are not Chinese. They would not assimilate into the Chinese people." The United States took 30 years and a bitter and divisive war to discover what Chiang Kai-shek then knew only too well. [271]

On a much lighter, humorous note is the following, which refers to an effort to ensure proper training and readiness among the military services, and the approval by Congress of the following changes to basic principles of recruit training. It was provided to me again by Terry Crouson and was forwarded to him by Roy Mefford:

Haircuts
Marines: Heads will be shaved.
Army: Stylish flat-tops for all recruits.
Navy: No haircut standard.
Air Force: Complete makeovers as seen on the Jenny Jones show.

Training Hours
Marines: Reveille at 0500, train until 2000.
Army: Reveille at 0600, train until 1900.
Navy: Get out of bed at 0900, train until 1100, lunch until 1300, train until 1600.
Air Force: Awaken at 1000, breakfast in bed, train from 1100 to 1200, lunch at 1200, train from 1300 to 1400, nap at 1400, awaken from nap at 1500, and training ceases at 1500.

Meals
Marines: Meals, Ready-to-Eat three times a day.
Army: One hot meal, two MREs.
Navy: three hot meals.
Air Force: Catered meals prepared by the Galloping Gourmet, Julia Child, Wolfgang Puck, and Emeril Lagasse. All you can eat.

Leave and Liberty
Marines: None.
Army: four hours a week.
Navy: two days a week.
Air Force: For every four hours of training, recruits will receive eight hours of leave and liberty.

Protocol
Marines: Will address all officers as "Sir," and refer to the rank of all enlisted members when speaking to them (e.g., Sergeant Smith).

---

[271] Harry G. Summers, Jr., *The Vietnam War Almanac*, p. 1, (Presido Press, 1985).

Army: Will address all officers as "Sir," unless they are friends, and will call all enlisted personnel "Sarge."

Navy: Will address all officers as "Skipper," and all enlisted personnel as "Chief."

Air Force: All Air Force personnel shall be on a first-name basis with each other.

Decorations/Awards

Marines: Medals and badges are awarded for acts of gallantry and bravery only.

Army: Medals and badges are awarded for every bullet fired, hand grenade thrown, fitness test passed, and bed made.

Navy: Will have ships' engineers make medals for them as desired.

Air Force: Will be issued all medals and badges as they will most likely be awarded them at some point early in their careers anyway.

Camouflage Uniforms

Marines: Work uniform, to be worn only during training and in field situations.

Army: Will wear it anytime, anywhere.

Navy: Will not wear camouflage uniforms; they do not camouflage you on a ship. (Ship captains will make every effort to attempt to explain this to sailors.)

Air Force: Will defeat the purpose of camouflage uniforms by putting blue and silver chevrons and colorful squadron patches all over them.

Career Fields

Marines: All Marines shall be considered riflemen first and foremost.

Army: It doesn't matter; all career fields promote to E-8 in first enlistment anyway.

Navy: Nobody knows. The Navy is still trying figure out what sailors in the ABH, SMC, BNC and BSN rates do.

Air Force: Every recruit will be trained in a manner that will allow them to leave the service early to go on to higher paying civilian jobs.

Although the American war in Vietnam ended in early 1973, with the signing of the Paris Peace Accords (as mentioned earlier), here are a few events that have occurred since that time:

In the summer of 1992, a Senate Select Committee chaired by Massachusetts Senator John F. Kerry, a Vietnam Veteran, held extensive hearings into the POW/MIA matter. In sensational testimony before the committee, former Secretary of Defense James R. Schlesinger acknowledged that at the time of the return of the POWs, there may have been some unaccounted-for POWs who were left behind in Laos.

By 1993, the Clinton administration cautiously moved toward Normalization. Vietnam had clearly met the U.S. standards for Recognition.

Clinton finally lifted the embargo in February 1994. Thirty U.S. corporations opened branch offices in Vietnam the day after the boycott ended. Thus began, in historian George Herring's words, "the battle for Vietnamese hearts and wallets."

In January 1995, as a symbolic gesture, the Vietnamese returned the embassy compound in Ho Chi Minh City to the United States.

On May 9, 1997, Douglas Brian "Pete" Peterson, a former U.S. Air Force pilot shot down over North Vietnam in 1966, who spent six and one-half years as a prisoner-of-war in Hanoi, arrived at the city's Noi Bai Airport on the way to assuming his duties as the new ambassador to Vietnam. [272]

In his paperback, *Vietnam–The necessary War - A Reinterpretation of America's Most Disastrous Military Conflict,* Michael Lind made a statement that really caught my eye. He affirmed:

> Let there be no doubt: There will be "Vietnams" in America's future, defined either as wars in which the goal of the United States is to prove its military credibility to enemies and allies, rather than to defend U.S. territory, or as wars in which the enemy refuses to use tactics that permit the U.S. military to benefit from its advantage in high-tech conventional warfare. Preparing for the credibility wars and the unconventional wars of the twenty-first century will require both leaders and publics in the United States and allied countries to understand what the United States did wrong in Vietnam—and, no less important, to acknowledge what the United States did right. [273]

In closing, was it meaningful for the United States to be involved in Vietnam, knowing that we lost 58,220 dedicated servicemen/women—serving our country with distinction, dedication, desire, and, most important, honor? Furthermore, was it imperative for America to get involved in South Vietnam by stopping communism from further spreading to Southeast Asia? May be, may be not; but please consider the following as a possible *yes.* "The West has won the Cold War, of which the Vietnam War was an important part. In the 1960s more than 60 percent of the world's population lived under govern-

---

[272] George Donelson Moss, *Vietnam–An American Ordeal,* pp. 445-443, (Prentice-Hall, 1990).

[273] Michael Lind, *Vietnam–The Necessary War,* p. xviii, (Simon & Schuster, 1999).

ments that were, or claimed to be, communist. By the year 2000, except for Cuba, North Korea, Vietnam and China, dissolved communist government rule. Vietnam and China seem to be moving haltingly toward market economies, which can only flourish in liberal political surroundings. Cuba's government will arguably change, or so we think, after the passing of Fidel Castro (Fidel Alejandro Castro Ruz, commonly known as Fidel Castro, was a Cuban politician and revolutionary who served as Prime Minister of the Republic of Cuba from 1959 to 1976 and then President from 1976 to 2008) [274]. North Korea, with its current president (who is also the supreme leader of the country), Kim Jong-un (who is rarely seen in public), remains a wild card, as do several totalitarian but non-communist regimes, such as Syria, Libya, Iran, especially under the rein of its past president, Mahmoud Ahmadinejad, and Belarus. Certainly, it is beyond the scope of this work to determine the effect that economic loss to the Soviet Union in support of their client state, Vietnam, had on its own downfall. Suffice to say that the Evil Empire is dead." [275] What is also meaningful, at least for me, is that you, the reader, take from my manuscript whatever you find worthwhile. Whether you find my work overly/slightly impartial, prejudiced, or insufficiently discerning, it is, all the same, a frank account of a penetratingly tender and enormously revelatory ribbon of American military history through which I, like others who share my time and place, lived. As such, I ask of you what I gave to my subject: understanding. The Vietnam War that I participated in was, in fact, very hard to write about.

---

[274] *Fidel Castro,* Wikipedia.
[275] Otto J. Lehrack, *The First Battle–Operation Starlite and the Beginning of the Blood Debt in Vietnam,* p. 187, (Ballantine Books, 2004).

Glossary

BELOW is a list of many popular acronyms, expressions, euphemisms, jargon, military slang, and sayings in common or formerly common use in the U.S. Marine Corps. Many of the words or phrases have varying levels of approval among different units or communities, and some also have varying levels of appropriateness (usually dependent on how senior the user is in rank). Many terms also have equivalents among other service branches that are not acceptable among Marines, but are similar in meaning. Many abbreviations and phrases have come into common use from voice procedure use over communication channels, translated into the phonetic alphabet, or both. Many are or derive from nautical terms and other naval terminology.

A-4	The workhorse of the Vietnam War, which was also called the (Douglas) A-4 Skyhawk. This small, nimble, single-seat, and dependable, light attack aircraft was the perfect surgical weapon for the day war over Vietnam. It had a top speed of about 600 miles per hour. It flew more strike missions than any other Navy aircraft and its losses in combat amounted to thirty-seven percent of all Navy combat losses.
AC-47	The AC-47 "Puff, the Magic Dragon" gunship, made by the Douglas Aircraft Company, was a military version of the DC-3 that had been modified by mounting three 7.62 mm General Electric mini-guns to fire through two rear window openings and the side cargo door, all on the left (pilot's) side of the aircraft. This modified craft's primary function was close air support for ground troops.
AK-47	Soviet-manufactured Avtomat Kalashnikova Assault Rifle - 1947. It was a semi- or fully-automatic combat weapon and the firearm of choice used by the Vietcong and North Vietnamese soldiers. Known as the Type 56 to the Chinese, it was characterized by an explosive popping sound.
Amtrac	Portmanteau *for amphibian tractor* (i.e., or amtrac). It is a lightly armored vehicle that is designed to carry troops and/or cargo from ship to the beach as well as inland. It was usually armed with a .30-caliber machine gun.
Annamite Cordillera Range	A mountain range of eastern Indochina, which extends approximately 680 miles through Laos, Vietnam, and a small area in northeast Cambodia.
An Trach	A small hamlet that is about fifteen miles southwest of Da Nang.
AO	An *Area of Operations* is a section assigned in which a military

	unit operates. It is often an area around a major emplacement or an area assigned for a specific military operation or sweep).
Ao Dai	The Vietnamese national costume worn by women. It skillfully combines practicality with sensuality. It also consists of loose trousers worn under a knee-length tunic that is split up the sides, so that the body is completely covered but with a figure-hugging design.
APA	An *amphibious attack* transport ship. A troop ship that carries Marines to an objective area.
A-Ration	A-ration is a term used in the United States Armed Forces for a meal provided to troops which is prepared using fresh, refrigerated, or frozen foods. The use of fresh, refrigerated or frozen foods distinguish 'A' rations from 'B' rations, which use canned or preserved ingredients to enable them to be served without adequate refrigeration or freezer facilities. 'A' ration meals may be served in dining facilities, prepared in the field by the use of field kitchens, or prepared at a fixed facility and transported to field locations in containers.
Article 92	Article 92 (which stands for dereliction of duty) of the UCMJ— Uniform Code of Military Justice—is a specific offense under United States Code Title 10892. Article 92 applies to all branches of the United States military. A service member who is derelict has willfully refused to perform his duties (or follow a given order) or has incapacitated himself in such a way that he/she cannot perform his duties.
ARVN	The *Army of the Republic of Viet Nam*, also known as the South Vietnamese Army, were the ground forces of the Republic of Vietnam Military Forces, the Armed Forces of South Vietnam, which existed from 1955 until the Fall of Saigon in 1975.
AWOL	*Absent Without Official Leave* is a term used in the United States Military to describe a warrior or other military member who has left his or her post without permission (usually in disagreement with a particular order). AWOL can refer to either desertion or a temporary absence.
B-52	The Boeing B-52 Stratofortress is a long-range, subsonic, jet-powered strategic bomber. The B-52 was designed and built by Boeing, which has continued to provide support and upgrades. It has been operated by the U.S. Air Force since the 1950s. The bomber is capable of carrying up to 70,000 pounds of weapons.
Back on the Block	Ready to behave like a civilian (again).
BAM	*Broad Ass Marine;* derogatory name for woman Marine.
Bamboo Whip	They are constructed of a length of green bamboo with spikes (normally bamboo) attached to one end. The bamboo whip is set off by a trip wire. It is a shoot of bamboo under tension, and set with poisoned spikes at chest-high. As it whips the warrior, it leaves severe wounds in the chest area.
Ba Mui Ba (33)	A Vietnamese beer.
Batangan Peninsula	The Ba Lang An Peninsula (Vietnamese: mui Ba Lang An, literally "land nose of Three Villages called An") is a peninsula in South Vietnam. The name was often mispronounced as "Ba

Tang An" and known as Batangan during the Vietnam War. Since 1963, the Vietcong converted the Peninsula into a fortified stronghold. Following the conclusion of Operation Starlite, on August 24, 1965, Marine intelligence concluded that the 1st VC Regiment had withdrawn into the Peninsula.

Battalion
A military unit composed of a headquarters and two or more companies, batteries, or similar units. A battalion is also a military unit with 800 to 1,000 warriors that usually consists of two to seven companies, including and H & S (headquarters and service) company and is commanded by either a lieutenant colonel or a colonel, if in the U.S. Army or the U.S. Marine Corps. Several battalions form a regiment or brigade.

Battery
An artillery unit equivalent to a company. Six 105mm or 155mm howitzers or two 8-inch or 175mm self-propelled howitzers.

Beachhead
A designated area on a hostile shore that, when seized and held, ensures the continuous landing of troops and material.

Beer Garden
A social area permitting the consumption of alcohol—may contain barbecue or picnic facilities.

Binh Trams
Equivalent of a regimental headquarters and was responsible for securing a particular section of the network of the Ho Chi Minh Trail.

Black Panther Party
The Black Panther Party or BPP (originally the Black Panther Party for Self-Defense) was a black revolutionary socialist organization active in the United States from 1966 until 1982. The Black Panther Party achieved national and international notoriety through its involvement in the Black Power movement and U.S. politics of the 1960s and 1970s.

Blood Debt
In Vietnamese (i.e., *han tu*) means revenge or hatred, debt of honor, or blood owed for blood spilled.

Blooper
Another name for M79 Grenade launcher: from the distinctive noise made when one is fired.

Blown Away
Another term for *to be killed.*

BLT
Also known as a *battalion landing team.*

Booby Trap
A device or setup that is intended to kill, harm or surprise a person, unknowingly triggered by the presence or actions of the victim. Booby traps were used extensively by the VC. The most common types, in Vietnam, included grenades fixed to a monofilament line that hung slack in the water or on the ground. When a passing warrior's leg caught the line, the pin would be pulled from the grenade.

Boo-Coo
Another word for many or much—in French it was called *beaucoup.*

Bouncing Betty
An anti-personnel mine designed to be used in open areas. It is a mine with two charges. When tripped, a small propelling charge launches the body of the mine three to four feet into the air, where the main charge detonates and sprays fragmentation at roughly waist height.

Box-kicker
Pejorative for a Marine who works in supply—0351 (basic warehouseman).

Braniff Airlines	It was an American airline that operated from 1930 until 1982. It flew primarily in the midwestern and southwestern United States, Mexico, Central America, South America, and in the late 1970s, Asia and Europe.
Brass	Another name for a Marine officer.
Broke-dick	A Marine on limited or no duty status—for medical reasons.
Bronze Star	The Bronze Star Medal, unofficially the Bronze Star, is a United States decoration awarded to members of the United States Armed Forces for either heroic achievement, heroic service, meritorious achievement, or meritorious service in a combat zone. Whenever the medal is awarded by the Army and Air Force for acts of valor in combat, the "V" Device is authorized for wear on the medal and whenever the medal is awarded by the Navy, Marine Corps, and Coast Guard for acts of valor or meritorious service in combat, the Combat "V" is authorized for wear on the medal.
C-4	A *plastic explosive* commonly carried in Vietnam that was impervious to shock and had to be set off using a detonator. When set alight, it burned hot and slowly and was often used to heat C-Rations.
C-130	The Lockheed AC-130 Hercules gunship is a heavily armed ground-attack aircraft transport plane. The basic airframe is manufactured by Lockheed, while Boeing is responsible for the conversion into a gunship and for aircraft support. The C-130 Hercules was used to improve mission endurance and increase capacity to carry munitions during the Vietnam War. It was also used as a cargo aircraft.
Cam Ne	A village made up of several interconnecting smaller hamlets, connected by a commonly farmed rice field. It is about seven miles southwest of the Da Nang Air Base. U.S. Marines, in early August 1965, set fire to the homes of villagers, purportedly because the village was a Viet Cong stronghold. It was one of the first news reports to present the U.S. military in a negative light, and had a reverberating impact on America's attitudes toward the Vietnam War.
Camp Hansen	A U.S. Marine Corps base located in Okinawa, Japan. The camp is situated in the town of Kin, near the northern shore of Kin Bay, and is the second-northernmost major installation on Okinawa, with Camp Schwab to the north.
Camp Lejeune	Marine Corps Base Camp Lejeune is a 246-square-mile United States military training facility in Jacksonville, North Carolina. The base's 14 miles of beaches make it a major area for amphibious assault training, and its location between two deep-water ports (Wilmington and Morehead City) allows for fast deployments. In April 1941, construction was approved on an 11,000-acre track. On May 1 of that year, Lieutenant Colonel William P. T. Hill began construction on Marine Barracks. The first base headquarters was in a summer cottage on Montford Point, and then moved to Hadnot Point in 1942. Later that year it was renamed in honor of the 13th Commandant of the Marine

	Corps, John A. Lejeune.
Camp Pendleton	Marine Corps Base Camp Pendleton is the major West Coast base of the U.S. Marine Corps. It is located on the Southern California coast, in San Diego County, and bordered by Oceanside (also called ocean slime) to the south, San Clemente, Cleveland National Forest, Orange and Riverside counties to the north, and Fallbrook to the east. The base is split into North and South and was established in 1942 to train U.S. Marines for service in World War II. By October 1944, Camp Pendleton was declared a "permanent installation" and by 1946, it became the home of the 1st Marine Division. It was named after Major General Joseph Henry Pendleton (1860–1942), who had long advocated setting up a training base for the Marine Corps on the west coast. Today it is the home to myriad Operating Force units including the I Marine Expeditionary Force and various training commands.
Camp Smedley Butler	Marine Corps Base Camp Smedley D. Butler (or Butler Marine Base to natives) is a U.S. Marine Corps base located in the Japanese prefecture of Okinawa. It was named for legendary Marine Smedley D. Butler.
Cam Ranh Bay	A deep-water bay in Vietnam in the province of Khanh Hoa. It is located at an inlet of the South China Sea situated on the southeastern coast of Vietnam, between Phan Rang and Nha Trang, approximately 180 miles northeast of Ho Chi Minh City (formerly Saigon).
Cannon Cockers	Marine Artillerymen.
CAS	*Close Air Support*—aircraft fire on ground troops in support of nearby friendly troops.
CBS	The corporate name of CBS Broadcasting, Inc. It is an American commercial broadcast television network, which started as a radio network. The name was derived from the initials of the network's former name, *Columbia Broadcasting System*.
Chams	The Cham people are an ethnic group in Southeast Asia. They are concentrated between the Kampong Cham Province in Cambodia and central Vietnam's Phan Rang-Thap Cham, Phan Thiet, Ho Chi Minh City and An Giang areas.
Cham Towers	Po Nagar is a Cham temple tower founded sometime before 781 and located in the medieval principality of Kauthara, near modern Nha Trang in Vietnam.
Chow	A slang word for food.
Chu Lai	A sea port, urban and industrial area in Nui Thanh, Quang Nam Province of South Vietnam. It was a U.S. Marine Corps base from 1965 -1971 during the Vietnam War. It is roughly fifty-six miles southeast of Dan Nang. The base had an air field to supplement the major base at Da Nang.
Chu Lai Air Base	Chu Lai Base Area (also known as Chu Lai Combat Base) is a former U.S. Marine Corps, U.S. Army and Army of the Republic of Vietnam (ARVN) base in Chu Lai in central Vietnam. On May 6, 1965, units from the ARVN 2nd Division and 3rd Battalion, 9th Marines secured the Chu Lai area. On May 7th,

the 3rd Marine Expeditionary Brigade (United States) (3rd MEB), composed of the 4th Marine Regiment, 3rd Reconnaissance Battalion, elements of Marine Aircraft Group 12 (MAG-12) and Naval Mobile Construction Battalion 10 landed at Chu Lai to establish a jet-capable airfield and base area.

CIC
Combat Information Center is a space containing radar equipment, plotting devices and communications (internal and external) equipment manned by specifically trained personnel and charged with keeping the commanding officer and higher commands embarked informed of the location, identity, and movement of friendly and/or enemy aircraft and surface ships within the area.

Civic Action
A *civic action* program also known as civic action project is a type of operation designed to assist an area by using the capabilities and resources of a military force or civilian organization to conduct long-term programs or short-term projects. This type of operations include: dental civic action program (DENTCAP), engineering civic action program (ENCAP), medical civic action program (MEDCAP), and veterinarian civic action program (VETCAP).

Clergy and Laity Concerned about Vietnam
In October 1965, about 100 clergy members met in New York to discuss what they could do to challenge U.S. policy on Vietnam. Believing that a multi-faith organization could lend credible support to an anti-war movement often labeled as Communist, they created the Clergy Concerned about Vietnam.

Close Air Support
Close Air Action (CAS) against hostile targets that are in close proximity to friendly forces and that require detailed integration of each air mission with the fire and movement of those forces.

CO
Commanding Officer. The CO is the officer in command of a military unit. Typically, the commanding officer has ultimate authority over the unit, and is usually given wide latitude to run the unit as he or she sees fit, within the bounds of military law. In this respect, commanding officers have significant responsibilities (for example, the use of force, finances, equipment, the Geneva Conventions), duties (to higher authority, mission effectiveness, duty of care to personnel), and powers (for example, discipline and punishment of personnel within certain limits of military law).

Committee for a Sane Nuclear Policy
Peace Action is a peace organization formed through the merger of The Committee for a SANE Nuclear Policy and the Nuclear Weapons Freeze Campaign (also known as "The Freeze"). The organization's focus is on preventing the deployment of nuclear weapons in space, thwarting weapons sales to countries with human rights violations, and promoting a new United States foreign policy based on common security and peaceful resolution to international conflicts.

Company
A military unit, typically consisting of 80–250 warriors and usually commanded by a captain or a major. Most companies

are formed of three to six platoons although the exact number may vary by country, unit type, and structure. Several companies are grouped to form a battalion or regiment, the latter of which is sometimes formed by several battalions.

Conventional Warfare
Conventional warfare is a form of warfare conducted by using conventional weapons and battlefield tactics between two or more states in open confrontation. The forces on each side are well-defined, and fight using weapons that primarily target the opponent's military. It is normally fought using conventional weapons, and not with chemical, biological, or nuclear weapons. The general purpose of conventional warfare is to weaken or destroy the opponent's military, thereby negating its ability to engage in conventional warfare. In forcing capitulation, however, one or both sides may eventually resort to unconventional warfare tactics.

Corpsman
A hospital corpsman is an enlisted medical specialist of the U.S. Navy who serves with the Navy and Marines. They are the only enlisted corps in the U.S. Navy.

County Fair
A keystone of the United States to attempt to pacify the population of South Vietnam. The technique consisted of Marines rapidly forming a wide cordon around a village/hamlet. This was to prevent any VC from escaping. Subsequently, RVN Forces personnel would enter the village to check the identity of the villagers and to interrogate them. Searches were conducted for arms, VC, food caches, tunnels, etc.

CP
Command Post. The field headquarters used by the commander of a military unit.

C-Rations
Combat rations were issued to American servicemen/women—often called C-rats. In many cases, they were leftovers from the Korean War. Each ration consisted of a can of some basic course, a can of fruit, a packet of some type of desert, a packet of powdered cocoa, a small pack of cigarettes, and two pieces of chewing gum.

Da Nang
A major commercial port and later became one of the key command centers for the Armed Forces during the war. It is the biggest city on the South Central Coast of Vietnam. Da Nang was the headquarters for South Vietnamese Army's I Corps and its Third Division. It was also the site of several major U.S. installations during the Vietnam War. A major jet-capable airfield was constructed there. It served at one time or another as the headquarters for the U.S. III Marine Amphibious Force, the U.S. First and Third Marine Divisions and later the U.S. Army's XXIV Corps.

DC-3
Also called the "gooney bird" in World War II. This aircraft incurred limited application in the Vietnam War.

Deploy
To relocate forces to desired areas of operations.

Devil Dog
Nickname for Marines, from the German word *Teufelhunden,* supposedly given by German troops during the Battle of Belleau Wood.

Didi
Slang from the Vietnamese word *di,* meaning "to leave" or "to

Dishonorable Discharge	The discharge of a person from military service for an offense more serious than one for which a bad-conduct discharge is given (e.g., sabotage, espionage, cowardice, or murder).
DMZ	The Vietnamese *Demilitarized Zone* was established in 1954 at the Geneva Convention as a dividing line between North and South Vietnam as a result of the First Indochina War. The Vietnamese Demilitarized Zone ran from east-west near the center of present-day Vietnam (spanning more than sixty miles) and was almost two miles wide. It ran along the Ben Hai River for much of its length, and an island nearby was controlled by North Vietnamese forces during the Vietnam War. Although it was nominally described as being at "the 17th parallel," almost all of the zone lies to the south of the parallel, with only a small portion of the zone near the eastern end actually including the parallel.
DOC	Another word for corpsman or medic. Medical officers, who are physicians, on the other hand, are always called *doctors*.
Dog Patch	A small village or hamlet just on the outside of Da Nang to the north almost at the foot of Hill-327. Of course, it was off limits to all Marines and all other American personnel.
Dog Tag	The informal name given to the identification tags worn by military personnel, because of their resemblance to actual dog tags. The tag is primarily used for the identification of dead and wounded and essential basic medical information, such as blood type.
Dust-Off	A casualty evacuation, also known as CASEVAC or by the call sign Dust-off or colloquially Dust-Off, is a military term for the emergency patient evacuation of casualties from a combat zone. Dust-Off can be done by both ground and air. "DUST-OFF" is the call sign specific to U.S. Army Air Ambulance units. DUST-OFF is an acronym meaning Dedicated Unhesitating Service to our Fighting Forces.
Embark	To load aboard (e.g., a ship).
Esprit de Corps	Feelings of loyalty, enthusiasm, and devotion to a group among people who are members of the group.
F-4	The McDonnell Douglas F-4 Phantom is a tandem two-seat, twin-engine, all-weather, long-range supersonic jet interceptor attack fighter/fighter-bomber originally developed for the U.S. Navy by McDonnell Aircraft. It first entered service in 1960 with the U.S. Navy. Proving highly adaptable, it was also adopted by the U.S. Marine Corps and the U.S. Air Force, and by the mid-1960s had become a major part/workhorse of their respective air wings, especially in the Vietnam War. It had a top speed of Mach 2.2 (or about 1,540 MPH). It could carry over 18,000 pounds of weapons on nine external hard-points, including air-to-air missiles, air-to-ground missiles, and various bombs.
F-102	The Convair F-102 Delta dagger jet (the world's first supersonic all-weather jet interceptor and the USAF's first operational

delta-wing aircraft) was an American interceptor aircraft that was built as part of the backbone of the U.S. Air Force's air defenses in the late 1950s. Entering service in 1956, its main purpose was to intercept invading Soviet bomber fleets during the Cold War. Later, the F-102 served in Vietnam, flying fighter patrols and serving as bomber escorts.

Fairchild C-123 An American military transport aircraft designed by Chase Aircraft and subsequently built by Fairchild Aircraft for the U.S. Air Force. In addition to its USAF service, which included later service with the Air Force Reserve and Air National Guard, it also went on to serve most notably with the U.S. Coast Guard and various air forces in South East Asia. During the Vietnam War, the aircraft was used to spray Agent Orange.

Fat-body An overweight service-member.

Fellowship of Reconciliation The largest, oldest Interfaith Peace organization in the United States and is dedicated to the promotion of nonviolent conflict resolution.

Field of Fire An area which a weapon or group of weapons may cover effectively with fire from a given position.

Fighting Mad The radio call sign for the 3rd Battalion, 3rd Marines for much of the Vietnam War.

Fire Mission A specific assignment given to a fire unit—a call for fire.

Flak Jacket An armored vest or body armor, made by Rachman Manufacturing Company, and issued to American servicemen/women. It was a form of protective clothing designed to provide protection from shrapnel and other indirect low velocity projectiles, made of ballistic nylon and weighing about eight pounds that usually stopped shrapnel but not rifle bullets.

Flare An illumination projectile. It was hand-fired or shot from artillery, mortars, or air.

Flower Hmong An Asian ethnic group from the mountainous regions of China, Vietnam, Laos, and Thailand. Hmong are also one of the sub-groups of the Miao ethnicity in southern China. Hmong groups began a gradual southward migration in the 18th century due to political unrest and to find more arable land. Hmong people are known to be fiercely independent and rich in their culture, art, religion, family life and martial history, and are distinguished by costume/dress (fabric patterns represent fruit, vegetables, farming, chickens, eggs, etc.).

FMF *Fleet Marine Force*—a balanced force of combined arms comprising land, air, and service elements of the U.S. Marine Corps. Also referred to as the operational forces of the Corps.

FNG *Fucking new guy*—someone who is new to a unit or new to an area. FNG, more appropriately, was called BNG—brand new guy.

Forward Observer An observer operating with the front line troops and trained to adjust ground or naval gunfire and air bombardment and pass battlefield information to the rear.

Four-Holer A field toilet facility.

Frag Fragmentation grenade; verb form of "fragging". Fragging refers to the act of murdering members of the military, particularly commanders of a fighting squad. Additionally, the term can be applied to manipulating the chain of command in order to have an individual, or unit, deliberately killed by placing the personnel in harm's way, with the intended result being death.

Friendly Fire
Accidental attacks on U.S. or allied soldiers by other U.S. or allied warriors.

FSB
Fire support base. It was a temporary military encampment widely used during the Vietnam War to provide artillery fire support to infantry operating in areas beyond the normal range of fire support from their own base camps. FSBs followed a number of plans, their shape and construction varying based on the terrain they occupied and the projected garrison.

Gear
Also called equipment.

Geedunk
Junk food—candy and other sweets. Also called pogey or pogey bait.

General Orders
A series of permanent guard orders that govern the duties of a sentry on post. They are also concerned with matters of policy or administration.

Geneva Agreements
The Geneva Agreements of 1954 (also called the "Geneva Accords") arranged a settlement which brought about an end to the First Indochina War. The agreement was reached at the end of the Geneva Conference. A ceasefire was signed and France agreed to withdraw its troops from the region. French Indochina was split into three countries: Laos, Cambodia, and Vietnam. Vietnam was to be temporarily divided along the 17th Parallel until elections could be held to unite the country. These elections were never held; following repeated refusals to hold nationwide elections by Ngo Dinh Diem and his declaration of leadership of a new state, South Vietnam, the Vietminh established a communist state in the North led by Ho Chi Minh. The U.S. gave Diem considerable support in the form of financial aid; due to the corruption evident in his regime, and the question of the depth of support for him in Vietnam, there was a certain amount of reluctance in doing so.

Geneva Convention Card
Adopted in 1949, basically for the protection of prisoners of war. It is a special identity card bearing a distinctive emblem. This card shall be water resistant and of such size that it can be carried in the pocket. It shall be worded in the national languages, shall mention at least the surname and first names, the date of birth, the rank and the service number of the bearer, and shall state in what capacity he is entitled to the protection of the present Convention. The card shall bear the photograph of the owner and also either his signature or his fingerprints or both. It shall be embossed with the stamp of the military authority. The identity card shall be uniform throughout the same Armed Forces and, as far as possible, of a similar type in the Armed Forces of the High Contracting Parties.

Greased
Another term for killing the enemy.

Great Society
A set of domestic programs in the United States first an-

nounced by President Lyndon B. Johnson, and subsequently promoted by him and fellow Democrats in Congress in the 1960s. Two main goals of the Great Society social reforms were the elimination of poverty and racial injustice.

Grunt	Also called a ground pounder. A combat infantryman. Originally slang for a Marine fighting in Vietnam but later applied to any warrior fighting there.
Guerrilla Warfare	Military and paramilitary operations conducted in enemy-held or hostile territory by irregular, predominantly indigenous forces.
Gulf of Tonkin	A body of water located off the coast of northern Vietnam and southern China. It is a northern arm of the South China Sea. The Gulf is defined in the west by the northern coastline of Vietnam, in the north by China's Guangxi province, and to the east by China's Leizhou Peninsula and Hainan Island.
Gunny	Nickname for a Marine Gunnery Sergeant.
GVN	The *Government of Vietnam* is the executive arm of the Vietnamese state, and the members of the Government are elected by the National Assembly of Vietnam.
Gyrene	Nickname for a Marine. Some consider it to be a grievous insult; combination of the words "GI" and "Marine."
Hai Duong	A province in the Red River Delta of northern Vietnam. Its name derives from Sino-Vietnamese, meaning "ocean", though in fact, the province is landlocked. Nowadays, Hai Duong is among the most industrialized and developed provinces in Vietnam.
Haiphong	The third largest city of Vietnam and northern Vietnam's most important seaport with its deep-water anchorage and large maritime facilities. The city's name means "coastal defense". Haiphong is also nicknamed *"The City of the red flame trees"* because of the many Delonix regia planted throughout the city.
Ham and Mothers	Another (detested C-ration) name for ham and lima beans.
Hamlet	A small rural village. In Vietnam, (strategic) hamlets would consist of villages consolidated and reshaped to create a defensible perimeter.
Hanoi	From 1954 to 1976, it was the capital of North Vietnam, and it became the capital of a reunified Vietnam in 1976, after the North's victory in the Vietnam War.
Hanoi Hannah	Trịnh Thị Ngo (born in 1931), also known as Hanoi Hannah, is a Vietnamese radio personality best known for her work during the Vietnam War, when she made English-language broadcasts for North Vietnam directed at U.S. troops. During the Vietnam War in the 1960s and 1970s she became famous among U.S. warriors for her propaganda broadcasts on Radio Hanoi (in fact, there were several "Hanoi Hannahs", but she was the senior and most frequently heard one). At that time, she made three broadcasts a day, reading the list of the newly killed or imprisoned Americans, attempting to persuade U.S. GIs that the U.S. involvement in the Vietnam War was unjust and immoral and played popular U.S. anti-war songs in an at-

	tempt to incite feelings of nostalgia and homesickness amongst U.S. troops.
Hanoi Hilton	The Hoa Lo Prison was a prison used by the French colonists in Vietnam for political prisoners, and later by North Vietnam for prisoners of war during the Vietnam War when it was sarcastically known to American prisoners of war as the "Hanoi Hilton". The prison was demolished during the 1990s, though the gatehouse remains as a museum.
Heliborne	A heliborne air assault is the movement of ground-based military forces by vertical take-off and landing aircraft—such as the helicopter—to seize and hold key terrain which has not been fully secured, and to directly engage enemy forces.
Helo	Another name for helicopter. Chopper is an Army term.
H-Hour	In connection with planned operations, it is the specific hour the combat operation begins.
Highway One	National Route 1A, Hamrong to Hanor, is the trans-Vietnam highway. The route begins at km 0 at Huu Nghi Quan Border Gate near the China-Vietnam border. It was constructed by the French colonists in early 20th century.
Ho Chi Minh	Born Nguyen Sinh Con or Nguyen Sinh Cung, he was a Vietnamese communist revolutionary leader who was prime minister (1945–1955) and president (1945–1969) of North Vietnam. He was a key figure in the foundation of North Vietnam in 1945, as well as the People's Army of Vietnam and the Viet Cong during the Vietnam War. He led the Viet Minh independence movement from 1941 onward, establishing the communist-ruled Democratic Republic of Vietnam in 1945 and defeating the French Union in 1954 at the battle of Dien Bien Phu. He officially stepped down from power in 1965 due to health problems, but remained a highly visible figurehead and inspiration for those Vietnamese fighting for his cause—a united, communist Vietnam—until his death. After the war, Saigon, the former capital of the Republic of Vietnam, was renamed Ho Chi Minh City, however, the name Saigon is still very widely used.
Ho Chi Minh Sandals	Footwear worn by the enemy—made from discarded tires and inner tubes.
Ho Chi Minh Trail	Also known in Vietnam as the "Truong Son Trail", named by the Americans, was a logistical system that ran from the Democratic Republic of Vietnam (North Vietnam) to the Republic of Vietnam (South Vietnam) through the neighboring kingdoms of Laos and Cambodia. It was 6,000-mile network of trails, dirt roads, and river crossings stretching at least thirty miles wide. The system provided support, in the form of manpower and material, to the National Front for the Liberation of South Vietnam (called the Vietcong or "VC" by its opponents) and the People's Army of Vietnam, or North Vietnamese Army, during the Vietnam War. It is estimated, since 1964 that over a half-million North Vietnamese troops have crossed the Ho Chi Minh Trail in Laos to invade South Vietnam.

Hollywood Marine	Marine who has graduated from Marine Corps Recruit Depot San Diego, stemming from rivalry between the two recruit depots (the other being Marine Recruit Depot Parris Island).
Hooch	The term used by many Americans in Vietnam that referred to a hut or simple thatched dwelling. Also a Vietnam War-era military slang for a thatched hut that were made by the Vietnamese peasants that dotted the countryside.
Hot-Shit	Sarcastic reference to an overly arrogant/conceited Marine.
Howitzer	A short cannon used to fire shells at medium velocity and with relatively high trajectories. The M102 105mm howitzer is used in air mobile (helicopter) and light infantry operations. The weapon carriage is lightweight welded aluminum, mounted on a variable recoil mechanism. The weapon is manually loaded and positioned, and can be towed by a two-ton truck or High Mobility Multipurpose Wheeled Vehicle (HMMWV), can be transported by helicopters, or can be dropped by parachute with airborne units.
Huey	Generic term for what the U.S. Army called the Bell HU-1E Iroquois and the Marines called the UH-1E helicopter. A light-attack and passenger helicopter.
Hump	To march—to climb or walk under burden for long distances.
Ia Drang Valley Battle	Was the first major battle between regulars of the U.S. Army and regulars of the People's Army of Vietnam of North Vietnam during the Vietnam War. But it was not the first major of the Vietnam War—Operation Starlite was (August 18–23, 1965). The two-part battle took place between November 14 and November 18, 1965, at two landing zones northwest of Plei Me in the Central Highlands of South Vietnam (approximately thirty-five miles south-west of Pleiku) as part of the U.S. air-mobile offensive codenamed Operation Silver Bayonet.
I Corps	Pronounced "eye," is the northernmost military region in South Vietnam. The I Corps Tactical Zone was a corps of the Army of the Republic of Vietnam (ARVN), the army of the nation state of South Vietnam that existed from 1955 to 1975.
Incoming	Hostile fire being received.
In-country	Phrase referring to someone being within a war zone (Vietnam).
Infantry Assaultman	The infantry assaultman, with an MOS of 0351, employs rockets, the Anti-Personnel Obstacle Breaching System (APOBS), and demolitions. Assaultmen provide rocket fire against fortified positions in support of the rifle squads, platoons, and companies within the infantry battalion. Additionally, assaultmen employ APOBS, demolitions, and breaching/infiltration techniques to facilitate infantry maneuver in the offense, and demolitions and expedient counter mobility measures in the defense. Assaultmen are found in the assault sections of weapons platoons of the infantry rifle companies. Noncommissioned officers are assigned as gunners, team, squad, and section leaders.
In Support Of	Assisting or protecting another formation, unit or organization while remaining under original control.

International Socialist Review	The ISR is dedicated to advancing socialist theory and practice in the U.S. and internationally committed to building a "left" alternative to a world of war. They are committed to "socialism from below," the self-emancipation of workers and the oppressed, the struggle against imperialism and for national liberation, and the building of a socialist current rooted in all of those struggles.
Iron Triangle	120 square miles area in the Bình Dương Province of Vietnam, so named due to it being a stronghold of Viet Minh activity during the war. The region was under control of the Viet Minh throughout the French war in Vietnam and continued to be so throughout the phase of American involvement in the Vietnam War, despite concerted efforts on the part of U.S. and South Vietnamese forces to destabilize the region as a power base for their enemy, the communist North Vietnamese–sponsored and –directed South Vietnamese insurgent movement, the National Liberation Front or Viet Cong.
ITR	*Infantry Training Regiment.* The School of Infantry (SOI) is the second stage of initial military training for enlisted U.S. Marines after Recruit Training. Since the initial training pipeline is divided between coasts, Marines from areas east of the Mississippi River usually graduate from MCRD Parris Island and move on to SOI at SOI East (located at Camp Geiger, a satellite facility of Camp Lejeune in North Carolina), while those from the western half of the nation attend MCRD San Diego and move on to SOI West at the Camp San Onofre area of Camp Pendleton in California. Further, the School of Infantry's training mission ensures "Every Marine is, first and foremost, a Rifleman". At SOI, Marines with the Military Occupational Specialty of infantry (0300 occupational field) are trained at the Infantry Training Battalion—guys like me, while all non-infantry Marines are trained in basic infantry and combat skills at the Marine Combat Training Battalion. SOI marks a transition in the professional training of entry-level students from basically trained Marines to combat-ready Marines.
Jarhead	Pejorative term for a Marine. Jarhead has several supposed origins: one refers to the regulation *"high and tight"* (standard Marine) haircut resembling a mason jar—shaved sides and short on the top.
Jungle Bunny	A Vietnam War-era phrase for infantry.
Jungle Rot	A medical condition caused by prolonged exposure of the feet to damp, unsanitary, and cold conditions. It is one of many immersion foot syndromes. The use of the word trench in the name of this condition is a reference to trench warfare.
Kep	An air field located about forty miles north of Hanoi, North Viet Nam. It served as one of the principal air bases for the North Vietnamese Soviet-built MiGs.
KGB	Komitet Gosudarstvennoy Bezopasnosti is translated in English as Committee for State Security. It was the main security agency for the Soviet Union from 1954 until its collapse in 1991.

Khe Sanh	A U.S. Marine Corps outpost in South Vietnam. The airstrip was built in September 1962. Fighting began there in late April 1967 with the hill fights, which later expanded into the 1968 Battle of Khe Sanh.
Khmer Krom	Indigenous Khmer people in southern Vietnam. In the Khmer language, Krom means "lower" or "below", as it was known as the Southern Kampuchea during the French Colonization.
KIA	*Killed in action.*
Kilometer	1,000 meters or 0.62 miles. Slang for kilometer is *klick.*
Landing Zone	Designated area for the landing of helicopters and the off-loading of men and cargo. It was also a place for wounded warriors to be picked up and sent to a field hospital.
Leatherneck	Nickname for Marine, so named for legends stating that stiff leather collars were once worn to protect the throat from sword-blows. The dress blue uniform, only worn by Marines, still bears a high stock collar today.
Leech	Segmented worms that belong to the phylum Annelida and comprise the subclass Hirudinea. Leeches do not have bristles and the external segmentation of their bodies does not correspond with the internal segmentation of their organs. Their bodies are much more solid as the spaces in their coelom are dense with connective tissues. They also have two suckers, one at each end. The majority of leeches live in freshwater environments, while some species can be found in marine environments, as well. Most leeches are hematophagous, as they are predominantly blood suckers that feed on blood from vertebrate—humans—and invertebrate animals. The leeches in Vietnam were huge, reddish-black, slimy, and blood-sucking. Leeches would find exposed skin. They got under shirts and into our pants.
Liberty	Authorized absence of less than 24 hours.
Lifer	A career enlisted Marine (i.e., for at least twenty years) as opposed to one who serves for a single enlistment.
Little People	This term also refers to the enemy—VC.
Lit Up	Fired upon; shot and killed or wounded—another term for killing the enemy.
Lollygag	To dawdle or fool about—having fun.
LP	Another term for *listening post.* A small group of men are stationed outside the lines or along trails/rivers at night who listen for and are warned of the enemy approaching.
LSD	*Landing Ship Dock.* Amphibious ship that transports amtracs to the objective area.
LST	*Landing Ship Tank* is the military designation for naval vessels initially created during World War II, and later for the Vietnam War. They, these flat-bottomed naval troop landing ships, were used to support amphibious operations by carrying significant quantities of vehicles, cargo, and landing troops directly onto an unimproved shore.
LZ	Usually a small clearing secured temporarily for the landing of resupply helicopters—*landing zone.* Some become more perma-

nent and eventually become base camps.

M1
The M1 helmet, adopted in 1941, is a combat helmet that was used by the United States military from World War II until 1985. The M1 is two "one-size-fits-all" helmets—an outer metal shell, sometimes called the "steel pot", and a hard hat-type liner that is nestled inside the shell and contains the suspension system that would be adjusted to fit the wearer's head.

M1 Carbine
The M1 carbine (formally the United States Carbine, Caliber .30, M1), also called the War Baby, was a lightweight, easy-to-use semi-automatic carbine that became a standard firearm for the U.S. military during World War II, the Korean War and the Vietnam War. It was widely used by U.S. and foreign military, paramilitary and police forces, and has also been a popular civilian firearm.

M2
The M2 Machine Gun or Browning .50 Caliber Machine Gun is a heavy machine gun designed towards the end of World War I by John Browning. The Browning .50 caliber machine gun has been used extensively as a vehicle weapon and for aircraft armament by the United States from the 1930s to the present. It was heavily used during World War II, the Korean War, and the Vietnam War.

M14
The M14 was the weapon of choice while I was in Vietnam (i.e., 1965–1967). It is an American selective fire semi-automatic or automatic rifle that fires ammunition. It is also a combat assault rifle, magazine-fed, gas operated, with one bullet in the chamber and nineteen rounds in the clip, capable of traveling 2,850 feet per second, or 54% of a mile, and a maximum effective range of 1,509 feet or 28.4% of a mile. It was replaced by the M16 in 1967.

M16
The M16 became the standard issue rifle starting in 1967 that fires 5.56mm bullets. It is a fully automatic assault rifle that was used by the South Vietnamese and United States Armed Forces. It weighed only 8.79 pounds loaded. It used ball and tracer ammo. The magazine, like the M14, carried twenty rounds. It was gas-operated and air-cooled. It also had a selector switch that had three positions for firing (e.g., safe, semi-auto, and automatic). The maximum range for this weapon was about 300 yards with a highly effective range of fifty yards or about 150 feet. The rate of fire was 650–700 rounds per minute on full automatic, and 150–200 rounds per minute when reloading 20-round magazines.

M20
The M20 is a 3.5-inch anti-tank rocket launcher—also called a "piss tube," or super bazooka, is a two-piece smooth-bore weapon of the open tube type and is fired by an electrical firing mechanism, which contains a magneto that provides the current and is located in the trigger grip. It was only used by Marines during the early stages of the Vietnam War—it was eventually phased out in favor of the LAAW. It could penetrate up to about one foot of armor, and had an extended range of about 150 meters. It weighed about 8.5 lbs.

M26	The M26 is a fragmentation grenade developed by the United States military. It entered service around 1952 and was used in combat during the Korean and Vietnam Wars. The M26 is also referred to as a "Mike twenty-six," or a "frag". It has a spherical steel body that contains 6.5 ounces of Composition B explosive (a mixture of mostly TNT and cyclonite or hexogen). This grenade weighs approximately twenty-one ounces, and has a safety clip to prevent the grenade from detonating accidentally.
M35	The M35 is a two-and-half ton cargo truck. It was one of many vehicles in U.S. military service to have been referred to as the "deuce-and-a-half." While the basic M35 cargo truck is rated to carry 5,000 pounds off road or 10,000 pounds on roads, they have been known to haul twice as much as rated.
M48	Designed in 1951, the M48 was a battle tank. It was the third tank to be officially named after General George S. Patton, commander of the U.S. Third Army during World War II and one of the earliest American advocates for the use of tanks in battle. The M48 served as the U.S. Army and Marine Corps's primary battle tank during the Vietnam War.
M60	Was officially the United States Machine Gun, Caliber 7.62 mm, M60, is a family of American general-purpose machine guns firing 7.62×51mm NATO cartridges from a disintegrating belt of M13 links. There are several types of live ammunition approved for use in the M60, including ball, tracer, and armor-piercing rounds. It was introduced in the 1950s. It has served with every branch of the U.S. military and still serves with other armed forces. It weighs over twenty-three pounds, and can fire over 500 rounds per minute with an effective range of about 1,200 yards.
M72	The M72 is a Light Anti-Tank Assault Weapon, also referred to as the Light Anti-Armor Weapon or LAAW as well as LAWS Light Anti-Armor Weapons System, is a portable one-shot 66 mm unguided anti-tank weapon. In early 1963, the M72 LAAW was adopted by the U.S. Army and U.S. Marine Corps as their primary individual infantry anti-tank weapon, replacing the M31 HEAT rifle grenade and the M20A1 "Super Bazooka" in the U.S. Army.
M79	The M79 40mm grenade launcher is a single-shot, shoulder-fired, break-action weapon that fires a 40 x 46mm grenade. Because of its distinctive features, it has earned the nicknames of "Thumper", "Thump-Gun," "Bloop Tube," and "Blooper." The M79 can fire a wide variety of 40 mm rounds, including explosive, anti-personnel, smoke, buckshot, and illumination.
M113	The M113 is a fully tracked armored personnel carrier manufactured by BAE Systems. The vehicle was first fielded by U.S. Army's mechanized infantry units in Vietnam in April 1962. The M113 was the most widely used armored vehicle of the U.S. Army in the Vietnam War, earning the nickname 'Green Dragon' by the Viet Cong as it was used to break through heavy thickets in the midst of the jungle to attack and overrun

	enemy positions, but largely known as an APC or ACAV (armored cavalry assault vehicle) by the allied forces.
M1910	The M1910 is a stainless steel/aluminum canteen that was issued to Marines during the Vietnam War.
M1911	The M1911 is a single-action, semi-automatic, magazine-fed, recoil-operated pistol chambered for the .45 ACP cartridge. It served as the standard-issue sidearm for the United States Armed Forces from 1911 to 1985. It was also used in World War I & II, the Korean War, and the Vietnam War.
MAAG	*Military Assistance Advisory Group* is a designation for American military advisers sent to other countries to assist in the training of conventional armed forces and facilitate military aid. Although numerous MAAG's operated around the world throughout the 1940s–1970s, the most famous MAAG's were those active in Southeast Asia before and during the Vietnam War. Typically, the personnel of MAAG's were considered to be technical staff attached to, and enjoying the privileges of, the US diplomatic mission in a country.
MACV	*Military Assistance Command, Vietnam* was a joint-service Command of the United States Department of Defense. MACV was created on 8 February 1962, in response to the increase in United States military assistance to South Vietnam. MACV was first implemented to assist the Military Assistance Advisory Group, controlling every advisory and assistance effort in Vietnam, but was reorganized on May 15, 1964 and absorbed MAAG Vietnam to its command when combat unit deployment became too large for advisory group control.
MAF	*Marine Amphibious Force.* It is a formation of the Marine Air-Ground Task Force of the U.S. Marine Corps. It is forward-deployed and able to deploy rapidly conduct operations across the spectrum from humanitarian assistance and disaster relief to amphibious assault and high-intensity combat.
Maneuver	The operation of a ship, aircraft, vehicle or unit to cause it to perform desired movements.
Marble Mountain	A domelike rock outcropping where the main Marine helicopter squadrons were located—Marble Mountains, as it is actually called, is a cluster of five marble and limestone hills located in the Ngu Hanh Son ward, south of Da Nang that stretches from the coast inland or westward. Marble Mountain Air Facility, at Marble Mountain, was an aviation facility used primarily by the U.S. Marine Corps during the Vietnam War. It was a helicopter facility that was constructed in August 1965 and served as home to Marine Aircraft Group 16, the 5th Special Forces Group and an assortment of other squadrons until May 1971.
Marine Corps Air Station	MCAS was located in El Toro, California. It was a U.S. Marine Corps Air Station located near Irvine, California. Before it was decommissioned in 1999, it was the 4,682 acres home of Marine Corps aviation on the West Coast. Designated as a Master jet station, its four runways (two of 8,000 feet and two of 10,000 feet could handle the largest aircraft in the U.S. military inven-

	tory). During the 1960s, many U.S. Marines left for and returned from Vietnam at El Toro MCAS.
Marine Raiders	Marine Raiders were elite units established by the U.S. Marine Corps during World War II to conduct special amphibious light infantry warfare, particularly in landing in rubber boats and operating behind the lines.
Mayaguez	The *Mayaguez* incident took place between the Kingdom of Cambodia and the United States. It was from May 12–15, 1975, less than a month after the Khmer Rouge took control of the capital Phnom Penh ousting the U.S. backed Khmer Republic. It was the last official battle of the Vietnam War. The names of the Americans killed, as well as those of three U.S. Marines who were left behind on the island of Koh Tang after the battle and were subsequently executed by the Khmer Rouge, are the last names on the Vietnam Veterans Memorial. The merchant ship's crew, whose seizure at sea had prompted the U.S. attack, had been released in good health, unknown to the U.S. Marines or the U.S. command of the operation before they attacked. Nevertheless, the Marines boarded and recaptured the ship anchored offshore a Cambodian island, finding it empty. It was the only known engagement between U.S. ground forces and the Khmer Rouge.
MCRD	*Marine Corps Recruit Depot* is a U.S. Marine Corps military installation in San Diego, California. It lies between San Diego Bay and Interstate 5, adjacent to San Diego International Airport and the former Naval Training Center San Diego. MCRD San Diego's main mission is the initial training of enlisted male recruits living west of the Mississippi River.
MEB	*Marine Expeditionary Brigade* is a formation of the U.S. Marine Corps, a Marine Air-Ground Task Force of approximately 14,500 Marines and Sailors constructed around a reinforced infantry regiment, a composite Marine aircraft group, a logistics group and a command element. The MEB, commanded by a general officer (usually a Major General or sometimes a Brigadier General), is task-organized to meet the requirements of a specific situation. It can function as part of a joint task force, as the lead echelon of the Marine Expeditionary Force (MEF), or alone. It varies in size and composition, and is larger than a Marine Expeditionary Unit but smaller than a MEF. The MEB is capable of conducting missions across the full range of military operations.
MEF	*Marine Expeditionary Force*–A Marine air-ground task force built around a Marine division and a Marine aircraft wing. This unit normally employs the full combat resources of one Marine division/wing team and Marine Logistics Group.
Medal of Honor	The United States of America's highest military honor, awarded for personal acts of valor above and beyond the call of duty. The medal is awarded by the President of the United States in the name of Congress to United States military personnel only. It is often mistakenly called the Congressional Medal of Honor.

Medevac	*Medical evacuation* by a helicopter or other type of military transport. The U.S. Military, specifically in Vietnam, worked tirelessly to ensure that dedicated MEDEVAC platforms with trained medical personnel were available in the event of a casualty. This has, in part, led to a 90.6% casualty survival rate, compared to 80.9% in World War II.
Mekong Delta	The Mekong Delta is the region in southwestern Vietnam where the Mekong River approaches and empties into the sea through a network of distributaries. The area is south of Saigon, dominated by the nine channels of the Mekong River. It is comprised of 15,500 square miles of wetlands and traversed by over 3,500 miles of waterways.
MIA	*Missing in action* is a casualty classification assigned to armed services personnel who are reported missing during active service. They may have been killed, wounded, become a prisoner of war, or deserted. If deceased, neither their remains nor grave has been positively identified. Becoming MIA has been an occupational risk for service personnel for as long as there has been warfare.
MLR	*Main line of resistance.* MLR is a military term describing the most important defensive position of a military unit facing an opposing force over an extended front. It does not consist of one trench or line of pillboxes, but rather a system, of varying degrees of complexity, of fighting positions and obstacles to enemy advance.
Monsoon	Traditionally defined as a seasonal reversing wind accompanied by corresponding changes in precipitation. Monsoons are also large-scale sea breezes which occur when the temperature on land is significantly warmer or cooler than the temperature of the ocean. These temperature imbalances happen because oceans and land absorb heat in different ways.
Montagnards	The Degar, also known as the Montagnards, are the indigenous peoples of the Central Highlands of Vietnam. The term Montagnard means "mountain people" in French and is a carryover from the French colonial period in Vietnam.
Mortar	A muzzle-loading, high-trajectory small artillery cannon with a short tube in relation to its caliber that throws projectiles with low muzzle velocity at high angles.
MOS	A United States military occupation code, or a *Military Occupational Specialty* code, is a nine character code used in the U.S. Army and U.S. Marine Corps to identify a specific job.
Mount Out	To pack up and leave.
MP	*Military Police* personnel provide essential support to their commanding officers with all facets of law enforcement. MPs begin this MOS either on-base, providing security and law enforcement, or on deployment, supervising maneuver and mobility operations and internment operations, as well as providing area security and law enforcement.
Mule	The U.S. Military M274 truck, platform, utility, half-ton, "carrier, light weapons, infantry, aka "mule," "military mule," or

	"mechanical mule" was a four-wheel drive, gasoline-powered truck/tractor type vehicle that can carry up to a half-ton ton off-road. It was introduced in 1956 and used until the 1980s.
Muzzle Velocity	The velocity of a projectile at the instant the projectile leaves the muzzle of a weapon.
Mutter's Ridge	Mutter's Ridge was the name given by U.S. Marines to the Nui Cay Tre Ridge, in the Quang Trị Province. The ridge was formed by Hills 461, 484 and 400 and overlooked the southern edge of the DMZ to the north and Route 9 to the south.
My Lai	The My Lai massacre, which was later called "the most shocking episode of the Vietnam War," took place in two hamlets of Son My village in Son Tịnh District of Quang Ngai Province on the South Central Coast of the South China Sea, 100 miles south of Da Nang and several miles north of Quang Ngai city east of Highway 1. These hamlets were marked on the U.S. Army topographic maps as My Lai and My Khe.
Naha	A port facility, formerly the Naha Military Port, is a United States Forces Japan facility located in Naha, Okinawa, Japan, at the mouth of Kokuba River, which flows into the East China Sea. The Naha Military Port was constructed by the U.S. troops after their landing on Okinawa Island in 1945. It served as a logistic base during the Vietnam War.
Napalm	Napalm is a mixture of a thickening/gelling agent and petroleum or a similar fuel for use in an incendiary device. It was initially used against buildings, and later was used primarily as an anti-personnel weapon that sticks to skin and causes severe burns when on fire. Napalm was developed in 1942, in a secret laboratory at Harvard University in Massachusetts. This mixture creates a jelly-like substance that, when ignited, sticks to practically anything and burns up to ten minutes. The effects of napalm on the human body are unbearably painful and almost always cause death among its victims. U.S. troops used napalm from about 1965 to 1972 in the Vietnam War.
NASA	The *National Aeronautics and Space Administration* is a United States government agency that is responsible for the nation's civilian space program and for aeronautics and aerospace research.
Navy Cross	The United States Navy Cross is the second-highest military decoration for valor the nation awards, second only to the Medal of Honor. The Navy Cross is primarily awarded to a member of the U.S. Navy, U.S. Marine Corps, or U.S. Coast Guard (when operating under the Department of the Navy) for extraordinary heroism in combat.
NCC	The *National Coordinating Committee* to End the War in Vietnam was a group that became an umbrella anti-Vietnam war group. Members of this group convinced Senator Eugene McCarthy to run in the primaries against Lyndon B. Johnson as an anti-war primary candidate.
NCO	A *noncommissioned officer* is a person with the rank of E-4 (Corporal—Marines) or higher. This person is a military officer

who has not been given a commission.

NLF
The *National Liberation Front* is a communist organization, in South Vietnam, that led the fight against the Saigon government and their American allies.

NMC
The (Spring) Mobilization Committee to End the War in Vietnam, which later became the *National Mobilization Committee* to End the War in Vietnam, was a coalition of antiwar activists formed in 1967 to organize large demonstrations in opposition to the Vietnam War.

North Vietnamese Politburo
A ruling council, also known as the Communist Party of Vietnam. It is also known as the Vietnamese Communist Party. It is the founding and ruling political party of the Socialist Republic of Vietnam.

NTA
Known as the *Northern Training Area*—Camp Gonsalves is a U.S. Marines jungle warfare training area, established 1958, located in Northern Okinawa, across the villages of Kunigami and Higashi. It is the largest U.S. jungle warfare training facility in Okinawa.

Number One
The Vietnamese people, at times, would call Marines "Number One"—"The best"

Number Ten
Just the opposite of Number One — the worst. Slang for poor in quality or last.

NVA
On March 8, 1949, after the Élysée Accords, the State of Vietnam was recognized by France as an independent country ruled by the Vietnamese Emperor Bao Dại, and the *Vietnamese National Army* was soon created. In the context of the Vietnam War (1959–1975), the Army was referred to as the North Vietnamese Army.

OD
Olive drab; a camouflage-like color.

Offed
This is still another term used for killing the enemy.

Office Pogue
A desk-bound Marine, usually in the rear echelon of an infantry unit.

Old Man
An informal nickname for the commanding officer (CO). It is considered an inappropriate term of endearment for use by a junior, thus used in reference only but never in address.

Ontos
Greek for "the thing," this was a lightly-armored, tracked-vehicle that sported six 106mm recoilless rifles.

Operation Crimp
Operation Crimp, January 8–14, 1966, later renamed Operation Buckskin, also known as the Battle of the Ho Bo Woods, was a joint U.S.-Australian military operation during the Vietnam War, which took place 12 miles north of Cu Chi in Binh Duong Province, South Vietnam. The operation targeted a key Viet Cong headquarters that was believed to be concealed underground, and involved two brigades under the command of the U.S. 1st Infantry Division, including the 1st Battalion, Royal Australian Regiment which was attached to the U.S. 173rd Airborne Brigade. The operation was the largest allied military action mounted during the war in South Vietnam to that point, and the first fought at the division level. Despite some success, the allied force was only able to partially clear the area and it

	remained a key communist transit and supply base throughout the war.
Operation Harvest Moon	December 8–20, 1965, was the second major battle that involved the U.S. Marine Corps. OHM was a complex battle and is complicated to report and to describe. There were three Marine battalions usually operating apart from each other but working toward the same objective - to trap the enemy.
Operation Oregon	April 1967, was a search and destroy mission that was conducted by Army infantry troops from the 196th Brigade. They landed at the Chu Lai Airstrip and immediately began search operations around the base camp.
Operation Piranha	September 6–8, 1965, was a search and destroy follow-up to operation Starlite aimed at the remnants of the 1st VC Regiment. Its secondary purpose was to shut down reported places of entry for a VC network of seaborne infiltration.
Operation Rice Straw-Golden Fleece	September 10–14, 1965, was designed to protect the rice harvest near Da Nang. It was so named because of the nature of the mission. Working in conjunction with local Vietnamese units and district officials, Marine units conducted search and destroy operations in the vicinity of areas where rice was to be harvested and also provided security for the villagers. This type of operation was successful both militarily and politically and was instrumental in establishing Marine-Vietnamese rapport throughout the regimental zone of action.
Operation Starlite	Also known in Vietnam as Battle of Van Tuong, also known as the Battle of Chu Lai, also known as the battle of the Batangan Peninsula, August 18–24, 1965, was the first major offensive regimental size action conducted by a purely U.S. military unit during the Vietnam War. The operation was launched based on intelligence provided by Major General Nguyen Chanh Thi, the commander of the South Vietnamese forces in northern I Corps area. Lieutenant General Lewis Walt formulated a plan to launch a pre-emptive strike against the Viet Cong regiment to nullify the threat on the vital Chu Lai base and ensure its powerful communication tower remained intact. The operation was conducted as a combined arms assault involving ground, air and naval units. U.S. Marines were deployed by helicopter insertion into the designated landing zone while an amphibious landing was used to deploy other Marines.
Outpost	A stationary body of troops placed at some distance from the main body, while at the halt or in a defensive position, to protect the main body from surprise—an enemy attack.
P-38	The P-38 was first developed in 1942. It is a small can opener with a small folding blade that was issued in the canned field rations of the United States Armed Forces from World War II to the 1980s. P-38s are no longer used for individual rations by the United States Armed Forces, as canned C-rations were replaced by MRE rations in the 1980s, packed in plastic pouches.
Pagoda	It is a tiered tower built in the traditions originating in historic East Asia or with respect to those traditions, with multiple

eaves common in Vietnam and other parts of Asia. Some pagodas are used as Taoist houses of worship. Most pagodas were built to have a religious function, most commonly Buddhist, and were often located in or near viharas. This term may refer to other religious structures in some countries. In Vietnam and Cambodia, due to French translation, the English term pagoda is a more generic term referring to a place of worship, although pagoda is not an accurate word to describe a Buddhist vihara.

Paris Peace Accords	1973 intended to establish peace in Vietnam and an end to the Vietnam War, ended direct U.S. military involvement, and temporarily stopped the fighting between North and South Vietnam. The governments of the Democratic Republic of Vietnam (North Vietnam), the Republic of Vietnam (South Vietnam), and the United States, as well as the Provisional Revolutionary Government that represented indigenous South Vietnamese revolutionaries, signed the Agreement on Ending the War and Restoring Peace in Vietnam on January 27, 1973. The agreement was not ratified by the United States Senate.
Patrol	A detachment of ground, sea or air forces sent by a unit (i.e., large to small) for the purpose of gathering information or carrying out a destructive, harassing, mopping-up or security mission.
PAVN	The *People's Army of Vietnam;* they were fighting for the North Vietnamese during the Vietnam War. PAVN was also known as the NVA (North Vietnamese Army) and the Vietnam People's Army (VPA).
Peasant	A Vietnamese peasant is a poor farmer of low social status who owns or rents a small piece of land for cultivation.
Pentagon Papers	The *Pentagon Papers*, officially titled *United States–Vietnam Relations, 1945–1967: A Study Prepared by the Department of Defense*, is a United States Department of Defense history of the United States' political-military involvement in Vietnam from 1945 to 1967. The papers were discovered and released by Daniel Ellsberg, and first brought to the attention of the public on the front page of *The New York Times* in 1971. A 1996 article in *The New York Times* said that the Pentagon Papers had demonstrated, among other things, that the Johnson Administration "*systematically lied, not only to the public but also to Congress.*" More specifically, the papers revealed that the U.S. had secretly enlarged the scale of the Vietnam War with the bombings of nearby Cambodia and Laos, coastal raids on North Vietnam, and Marine Corps attacks, none of which were reported in the mainstream media
Perimeter	The outer limits of a military position. The area beyond the perimeter belongs to the enemy.
Phuoc Ha Valley	A communist base area southwest of Da Nang. Located in the Quang Nam province, I Corps, this area, which paralleled the Que Son Valley, was also a major NVA staging area. Beginning in 1965, the 3rd Battalion 3rd Marines conducted operations in the valley. On December 12th, a massive B-52 strike targeted the

valley and the Marines assaulted hills 100 and 180.

PLAF
People's Liberation Armed Forces, commonly known as the Viet Cong, the PLAF was the military arm of the National Liberation Front.

Platoon
A subdivision of a company-sized military unit, normally consisting of two or more squads or sections. A platoon is typically the smallest/lowest echelon military unit led by a commissioned officer—the platoon leader or platoon commander, usually a lieutenant (O-1 or O-2). However, the rank of the officer may range from warrant officer (W-1) to captain (O-3), or even major (O-4), in rare cases. He (during the Vietnam War) was usually assisted by a senior non-commissioned officer—the platoon sergeant. In some instances, especially whenever the platoon commander ranks above lieutenant, there was a second officer of lower rank assigned as assistant platoon commander.

Point or Point Man
The forward or lead man on a combat patrol.

POW
Prisoner of war. A POW is someone who is taken prisoner and held captive while engaged in an action against an enemy of the United States.

PRC-25
Portable Radio Communications. It was the major field radio of the Vietnam War. Model 25 meant it was the 25th one the military had standardized. It was inevitably referred to as a "Prick Twenty-Five" by GIs, or "Prick" for short. It is a back-packed FM receiver-transmitter used for short-distance communications (i.e., usually no more than three to six miles).

Presidential Unit Citation
The Presidential Unit Citation (PUC), originally called the Distinguished Unit Citation, is awarded to units of the United States Armed Forces, and those of allied countries, for extraordinary heroism in action against an armed enemy on or after December 7, 1941 (the date of the attack on Pearl Harbor and the start of American involvement in World War II). The unit must display such gallantry, determination, and *esprit de corps* in accomplishing its mission under extremely difficult and hazardous conditions so as to set it apart from and above other units participating in the same campaign.

PTSD
Posttraumatic stress disorder is an anxiety disorder that may develop after a person is exposed to one or more traumatic events, such as sexual assault, serious injury, or the threat of death. The diagnosis may be given when a group of symptoms such as disturbing recurring flashbacks, avoidance or numbing of memories of the event, and hyperarousal (high levels of anxiety) continue for more than a month after the traumatic event.

Pucker Factor
A high level of anxiety experienced by those (e.g., Marines) in tight situations.

Purple Heart
A United States military decoration awarded in the name of the President to those wounded or killed, while serving, on or after April 5, 1917, with the U.S. military. With its forerunner, the Badge of Military Merit, which took the form of a heart made of purple cloth, the Purple Heart is the oldest military award

	still given to U.S. military members.
Punji Stake	Also called Punji stick, Punji trap, or Punji pit. It is a type of foot snare. It is a simple spike, made out of wood or bamboo, generally placed upright in the ground. Punji sticks are usually deployed in substantial numbers. In the Vietnam War, the Viet Cong would also use this method to force the wounded warrior to be transported by helicopter to a medical hospital for treatment, which was viewed as being more damaging to the enemy's cause than death.
PX	*Post Exchange.* It is a department or grocery store that operates on military bases/posts where military personal (and their families) can purchase a wide variety of personal-use items at a lower cost than available in civilian stores.
Quang Ngai	A city in central Vietnam. It is the township of Quang Ngai Province. Quang Ngai City borders Tu Nghia District on the south, west and east and borders Son Tịnh District on the north.
Quantico	Marine Corps training base located in Quantico, Virginia. Quantico is also home to Officer Candidate School, The Basic School, and many other specialty schools. Many people train on Quantico that are military allies.
Que Son Valley	Located along the border of Quang Nam and Quang Tin provinces. During the Vietnam War it lay in the southern part of South Vietnam's I Corps Military Region. Populous and rice-rich, the valley was viewed as one of the keys to controlling South Vietnam's five northern provinces by the communists, and by early 1967 at least two regiments of the 2nd Division of the People's Army of Vietnam had been infiltrated into the area. The Que Son Valley was also recognized as strategically important by the U.S. Military Assistance Command, Vietnam.
R & R	*Rest and recreation* or relaxation. A three- to seven-day vacation from the fighting for a warrior. During the Vietnam War, it was the only getaway from the war offered the field troops. It lasted for five days.
Raid	An operation, usually small in nature, involving swift penetration of hostile territory to secure information, confuse the enemy or destroy installations.
Rand Corporation	A nonprofit global policy think tank formed to offer research and analysis to the United States Armed Forces by Douglas Aircraft Company. This organization did research on insurgency and counterinsurgency measures in Vietnam, Laos, and Thailand during the Vietnam War.
Rate of Fire	The number of rounds (i.e., bullets) fired from a weapon in a minute.
Red Beach	Historically, Red Beach is known as the site where American Marines first landed in Da Nang during the Vietnam War. Called Red Beach because of the rich colors reflected over the water during dawn and sunset.
Reconnaissance	Going out into the jungle to observe for the purpose of identifying enemy activity.

Red Dao	Pronounced Zao—are the 9th largest ethnic group in Vietnam with a population of under 500,000. They belong to the Hmong Dao language group and are believed to have started migrating from China in the 13th century.
Regional Forces	Militia units organized with each district in South Vietnam to engage in offensive operations against local Viet Cong forces.
Re-up	To re-enlist/ship over or volunteer for an additional period of time in the service.
Rockpile	The Rockpile (also known as Elliot Combat Base) and known in Vietnamese as Thon Khe Tri, is a solitary karst rock outcropping north of Route 9 and south of the former Vietnamese Demilitarized Zone (DMZ). It rises to an elevation of 790 feet, about 690 feet above the surrounding terrain. Its relatively inaccessible location, reached only by helicopter, made it an important U.S. Army and Marine Corps observation post and artillery base from 1966 to 1969.
ROK	A soldier/warrior from the *Republic of Korea*. It is also known as the ROK Marine Corps, or the ROK Marines, which is the Marine Corps of South Korea.
Rotate/Rotation	Return home, to a (new) duty station at the end of an overseas deployment.
ROTC	The *Reserve Officers' Training Corps* is a college-based program for training commissioned officers of the United States Armed Forces. ROTC officers serve in all branches of the U.S. armed forces (although the U.S. Marine Corps and the U.S. Coast Guard do not have their own respective ROTC programs, graduates of ROTC programs do currently serve as Marine Corps and Coast Guard officers).
Round	A bullet or artillery or mortar shell.
Saigon	Ho Chi Minh City, formerly named Saigon, is the largest city in Vietnam. On April 30, 1975, Saigon fell and the war ended with a so-called Communist victory. On July 2, 1976, Saigon merged with the surrounding Gia Định Province and was officially renamed Ho Chi Minh City after Ho Chi Minh.
SAM	A *Surface-to-air missile* is a missile designed to be launched from the ground to destroy aircraft or other missiles. It is one type of antiaircraft system.
SANE	This was called the Committee for a SANE Nuclear Policy and the Nuclear Weapons Freeze Campaign. The organization's focus is on preventing the deployment of nuclear weapons in space, thwarting weapons sales to countries with human rights violations, and promoting a new United States foreign policy based on common security and peaceful resolution to international conflicts. As the war in Vietnam escalated, SANE became more active in the anti-war movement.
Salty Dog	Experienced or well-worn Marine—someone who has been in the Corps for a long period of time. This person is also called an old-timer.
Sapper(s)	Enemy engineer troops who are trained and armed to penetrate a fortification.

SDS	*Students for a Democratic Society* was a student activist movement in the United States that was one of the main representations of the New Left. The organization developed and expanded rapidly in the mid-1960s, especially during the Vietnam, before dissolving at its last convention in 1969.
Sea Bag/Seabag	A large canvas bag where Marines manually carry personal items to new or temporary living quarters. A "duffel bag" is an Army term not used by Marines.
Seabees	A Seabee is a member of the United States Navy Construction Battalion. The word "Seabee" comes from initials "CB". The Seabees have a history of building bases, bulldozing and paving thousands of miles of roadway and airstrips, and accomplishing a myriad of other construction projects in a wide variety of military theaters dating back to World War II. Seabees were deployed to Vietnam throughout the conflict beginning in small numbers in June 1954 and extending to November 1972. By 1962, they began building camps for the U.S. Special Forces.
Search and Destroy	Also called seek and destroy, or even simply S & D, refers to a military strategy that became a large component of the Vietnam War. The idea was to insert ground forces into hostile territory, search out the enemy, destroy them, and withdraw immediately afterward.
Sea Story	Story or tale calculated to impress others; often contains exaggeration or even outright lies.
Secure	To gain possession of a position or terrain feature with or without force, and to make such disposition as well prevent its destruction or loss by enemy action.
Selective Training and Service Act of 1940	The Selective Training and Service Act of 1940, also known as the *Burke-Wadsworth Act*, Pub.L. 76–783, 54 Stat. 885, enacted September 16, 1940, was the first peacetime conscription in United States history. This Selective Service Act required that men between the ages of 21 and 35 register with local draft boards. Later, when the U.S. entered World War II, all men aged 18 to 45 were made subject to military service, and all men aged 18 to 65 were required to register.
Semper Fidelis	A Latin phrase meaning *"Always Faithful"* or "Always Loyal." Well known in the United States as the motto of the U.S. Marine Corps (and often shortened to Semper Fi in Marine contexts).
Short/Short-timer	A Marine nearing the end of his tour in Vietnam or completing his/her enlistment in the Corps.
Shrapnel	They are pieces of different types of metal sent flying by an explosion.
Sidearm	The weapon (usually a pistol) carried by a sentry or military policeman/woman.
Silver Star	The Silver Star, officially the Silver Star Medal, is the third-highest military decoration for valor awarded to members of the United States Armed Forces. Any uniformed service member may receive the medal, which is awarded for gallantry in action against an enemy of the United States.

Skipper	An informal term of respect for a Marine captain/commanding officer who is in command of an infantry company.
Skivvies	Another term for underwear.
Slack Man	The second man back on a patrol, directly behind the point person.
Slant	A derogatory term for a Vietnamese person. They were also called slopes.
Small Arms	All arms including automatic weapons, up to and including .60 caliber and shotguns.
Small Wars Manual	The Small Wars Manual is a practitioner's manual written by the Marines who successfully fought America's small wars for the future practitioners of America's small wars.
SNCC	The *Student Nonviolent Coordinating Committee* was founded in early 1960. Its goal was to dissent with United States foreign policy on any issue when it sees fit—opposition to the United States' involvement in Vietnam.
Soldier	A soldier or trooper is considered a grievous insult to refer to as a Marine.
Squad	A small military unit usually consisting of twelve or less men. In Vietnam, mostly corporals, were responsible for the accomplishment of their mission as well as the lives and well-being of the squad while conducting combat operations.
SRV	Vietnam, officially the *Socialist Republic of Vietnam*, is the easternmost country on the Indochina Peninsula in Southeast Asia. With an estimated 90.5 million inhabitants as of 2014, it is the world's 13th-most-populous country, and the eighth-most-populous Asian country. The name Vietnam translates as "Southern Viet" (synonymous with the much older term Nam Viet); it was first officially adopted in 1802 by Emperor Gia Long, and was adopted again in 1945 with the founding of the Democratic Republic of Vietnam under Ho Chi Minh. The country is bordered by China to the north, Laos to the northwest, Cambodia to the southwest, and Malaysia across the South China Sea to the southeast. Its capital city has been Hanoi since the reunification of North and South Vietnam in 1976.
Stingray Patrols	One of the most influential strategies of the Vietnam War, the Stingray Patrol comprised seven to ten Marines in small teams, inserted by chopper deep in enemy territory. Surrounded on all sides by North Vietnamese Army troops and Viet Cong guerrillas, these small, highly-effective teams brought death and destruction to the enemy without ever going head-to-head in a gunfight with them.
TACAIR	*Tactical air support* was established to provide a balance between strategic, air defense, and tactical forces of the post–World War II Air Force.
TAOR	*Tactical Area of Responsibility.* This program was said to have originated as a solution to one Marine infantry battalion's problem of an expanding TAOR. The concept of combining a squad of Marines with local Vietnamese personnel and assign-

	ing them a village to protect proved to be a force multiplier.
Teach-In	A teach-in is similar to a general educational forum on any complicated issue, usually an issue involving current political affairs. The main difference between a teach-in and a seminar is the refusal to limit the discussion to a specific frame of time or a strict academic scope. Teach-ins are meant to be practical, participatory, and oriented toward action. While they include experts lecturing on the area of their expertise, discussion and questions from the audience are welcome. "Teach-ins" were popularized during the U.S. government's involvement in Vietnam. The first teach-in, which was held overnight at the University of Michigan in March 1965, began with a discussion of the Vietnam War draft and ended in the early morning with a speech by philosopher Arnold Kaufman.
Tet	A January holiday, Buddhist lunar New Year. Buddha's birthday.
Tet Offensive	One of the largest military campaigns of the Vietnam War, launched on January 30, 1968 by forces of the Viet Cong and North Vietnamese Army against the forces of South Vietnam, the United States, and their allies. It was a campaign of surprise attacks against military and civilian commands and control centers throughout South Vietnam.
The Rock	Another name for the island of Okinawa.
Thousand-Yard Stare	Unfocussed gaze of a battle-weary Marine.
Tonkin Gulf Resolution	The Gulf of Tonkin Resolution or the Southeast Asia Resolution was enacted August 10, 1964, was a joint resolution that the United States Congress passed on August 7, 1964, in response to the Gulf of Tonkin Incident. It is of historical significance because it gave U.S. President Lyndon B. Johnson authorization, without a formal declaration of war by Congress, for the use of "conventional" military force in Southeast Asia. Tonkin is the northernmost of the three historical regions of Vietnam.
Top	Another term for a Marine Corps First Sergeant. This person is also called "First Shirt."
Topside	The ship's upper deck.
Tracer	A round of ammunition chemically treated to glow or give off smoke so that its flight can be followed.
Treason	It is: 1) the offense of acting to overthrow one's government or to harm or kill its sovereign, 2) a violation of allegiance to one's sovereign or to one's state, 3) the betrayal of a trust or confidence; breach of faith; treachery.
Tunnel Rat	The tunnel rats were American, Australian and New Zealand soldiers and warriors who performed underground search and destroy mission during the Vietnam War. Whenever troops would uncover a tunnel, tunnel rats were sent in to kill any hiding enemy soldiers and to plant explosives to destroy the tunnels. A tunnel rat was equipped with only a standard issue .45 caliber pistol, a bayonet and a flashlight, although most

	tunnel rats were allowed to choose another pistol with which to arm themselves. The tunnels were very dangerous, with numerous booby traps and enemies lying in wait.
UCMJ	*Uniform Code of Military Justice.* It is the foundation of military law in the United States. It was established by the United States Congress in accordance with the authority given by the United States Constitution in Article I, Section 8, which provides that "The Congress shall have Power ...To make Rules for the Government and Regulation of the land and naval forces."
Ugly American	Ugly American is a pejorative term used to refer to perceptions of loud, arrogant, demeaning, thoughtless, ignorant, and ethnocentric behavior of American citizens mainly abroad, but also at home.
UH-34D	The Sikorsky UH-34D is a piston-engine military helicopter that was originally designed by American aircraft manufacturer Sikorsky for the United States Navy for service in the anti-submarine warfare role. It was also known as a Sea Horse or Choctaw. The USMC UH-34Ds were also among the first gunship helicopters trialed in the Vietnam War. They were fitted with the Temporary Kit-1, comprising two M60C machine guns and two nineteen-shot 2.75 inch rocket pods. The operations were met with mixed enthusiasm, and the armed UH-34Ds were quickly phased out.
U.S. Agency for International Development	President John F. Kennedy created the U.S. Agency for International Development (USAID) in 1961 by executive order to implement development assistance programs in the areas authorized by the Congress in the Foreign Assistance Act. The USAID is the United States federal government agency primarily responsible for administering civilian foreign aid.
U.S. Marine	Also called Leatherneck, Jarhead, Devil Dog, Gyrene, or Warrior.
USS	A *United States ship.*
USS Bayfield	APA-33 was a class of 16,000-ton attack troop transport ships, which was built in San Francisco, California, and during the June 1944 Normandy Operation she was the flagship for the "Utah" Beach landings. The USS Bayfield was also used August 17, 1965 as a Marine Corps attack troop transport ship for the first major battle of the Vietnam War—Operation Starlite.
USS Cabildo	LSD-16 was a Casa Grande-class dock landing ship of the U.S. Navy. She participated in numerous campaigns during the Vietnam War—especially during Operation Starlite.
USS Galveston	CL-93/CLG-3 was a Cleveland class light cruiser of the U.S. Navy that was later converted to a Galveston class guided missile cruiser. During 1965, she ranged the Southeast Asian waters from the Gulf of Thailand to the Gulf of Tonkin while supporting the American effort to repel Communist aggression in South Vietnam. She provided gunfire support during search-and-clear operations at Chu Lai and at the Vung Tuong Peninsula. In addition, she provided air defense for 7th Fleet carriers in the South China Sea and conducted search and rescue opera-

USS Orleck DD-886 was a Gearing-class destroyer in service with the U.S. Navy from 1945 to 1982. During the Vietnam War, the Orleck served as plane guard for aircraft carriers on "Yankee Station" in the Gulf of Tonkin, participated in "Operation Sea Dragon", patrolled on search and rescue duties, and carried out naval gunfire support missions.

USS Paul FF-1080 was named in honor of Medal of Honor winner Marine Lance Corporal Joe C. Paul, who was killed in Vietnam. The USS Paul was a Knox class frigate built for the U.S. Navy. It was a 438 foot anti-submarine medium-sized frigate, equipped with long-range multi-mode active sonar, and short-range variable depth active sonar.

USS Prichett DD-561 was a Fletcher-class destroyer, was also a ship of the U.S. Navy. Most of her deployed time was spent off Vietnam. In the combat zone, she served as plane guard for carriers in the South China Sea and provided support fire for R.V.N., U.S., and R.O.K. forces operating along the 1000-mile coastline from the Gulf of Siam to the north of Hue.

USS Princeton LPH-5—LPH stands for Landing Platform Helicopter or Commando Carrier—originally named the Valley Forge, a converted and modified 888-foot aircraft carrier (reclassified in 1959 as an amphibious assault ship)—designed to transport Marine Corps troops and their thirty helicopter transports.

USS Repose AH-16, "The Angel of the Orient," was a Haven-class hospital ship in service with the U.S. Navy, was originally commissioned on May 26, 1945, and joined the Pacific Fleet on July 14, 1945. The Repose was decommissioned in December 1954, but after ten and one-half years with the Reserve Fleet at Suisan Bay, California, she was again called to active service in October 1965. On February 14, 1966 she arrived in Chu Lai.

USS Sanctuary AH-17 was also a Haven-class hospital ship that served in the U.S. Navy in World War II and the Vietnam War.

USS Vernon Country LST-1161 was a U.S. Navy, Terrebonne Parish-class tank landing ship in commission from 1953 to 1973. She participated in numerous campaigns during the Vietnam War—especially during Operation Starlite.

Utilities Marines' combat clothing—the field uniform. The Army calls the same uniform fatigues.

VC The *Viet Cong* was the common name for the National Liberation Front. The term means "Vietnamese Communist." The VC were also called Charlie, Victor Charlie, Slope, Slant, Gook, or Dink—all highly offensive and racial slurs. The Viet Cong was also the name given by Western sources during the Vietnam War (1959–1975). The National Liberation Front was a political organization with its own army - People's Liberation Armed Forces of South Vietnam (PLAF) - in South Vietnam and Cambodia, that fought the United States and South Vietnamese governments, eventually emerging on the winning side. It had both guerrilla and regular army units, as well as a net-

	work of cadres who organized peasants in the territory it controlled.
VDC	The *Vietnam Day Committee* was a coalition of left-wing political groups, student groups, labor organizations, and pacifist religions in the United States of America that opposed the Vietnam War during the counterculture era. It was formed in Berkeley, California in the spring of 1965 by activist Jerry Rubin, and was active through the majority of the Vietnam War, organizing several rallies and marches in California as well as coordinating and sponsoring nationwide protests.
Viet Minh	A communist national independence coalition formed at Pac Bo on May 19, 1941. The Viet Minh initially formed to seek independence for Vietnam from the French Empire. When the Japanese occupation began, the Viet Minh opposed Japan with support from the United States and the Republic of China. After World War II, the Viet Minh opposed the re-occupation of Vietnam by France and later opposed South Vietnam and the United States in the Vietnam War.
Vietnam Day Committee	The VDC was a coalition of left-wing political groups, student groups, labor organizations, and pacifist religions in the United States of America that opposed the Vietnam War during the counterculture era. It was formed in Berkeley, California in the spring of 1965 by activist Jerry Rubin, and was active through the majority of the Vietnam War, organizing several rallies and marches in California as well as coordinating and sponsoring nationwide protests.
Vietnam Veterans Memorial	A national memorial in Washington, D.C. It honors U.S. service members of the U.S. Armed Forces who fought in the Vietnam War, service members who died in service in Vietnam/South East Asia, and those service members who were unaccounted for (i.e., missing in action) during the Vietnam War.
War Resisters League	This League has been resisting war at home and war abroad since 1923. They are committed not only to eliminating war, but the causes of war.
Warrior	Considered a Marine—someone who is engaged or experienced in warfare. A soldier is someone with the Army—one engaged in military service (and combat as well).
Waste/Wasted	To *kill the enemy;* also known as "pop," and "get some."
Water Buffalo	Or domestic Asian water buffalo is a large bovine found in Vietnam. Water buffaloes are especially suitable for tilling rice fields, and their milk is richer in fat and protein than that of the dairy cow.
White Phosphorus	A very hot type of incendiary explosive round from artillery, mortars, or rockets. The (WP) rounds explode with a huge puff of white smoke from the hotly burning phosphorus.
WIA	Someone who is *wounded in action.*
Winchester Model 70	A bolt action sporting rifle. It has an iconic place in American sporting culture and has been held in high regard by shooters since it was introduced in 1936, earning the moniker "The Ri-

fleman's Rifle". In 1965, the war in Vietnam started to really heat up. The need for snipers and sniper rifles was remembered after casualties from enemy snipers reminded the U.S. military how effective the sniper can be. Very early in the war, it become apparent the M14 rifle was in no way useful as a true sniper rifle in its current form.

Women's Strike for Peace	WSP also known as Women for Peace, is a United States women's peace activist group. In 1961, at the height of the Cold War, about 50,000 women brought together by Women Strike for Peace marched in sixty cities in the United States to demonstrate against nuclear weapons. WSP was among the first groups to demonstrate against the U.S. involvement in the Vietnam War.
WRL	The *War Resisters League* is the oldest secular pacifist organization in the United States. Founded in 1923 by men and women who had opposed World War I, it is a section of the London-based War Resisters' International. It continues to be one of the leading radical voices in the anti-war movement. In the 1960s, WRL was the first pacifist organization to call for an end to the Vietnam War. WRL also organized the first demonstration against the war with a September 21, 1963 vigil at the U.S. Mission to the UN, followed by an October 9, 1963 picket of Madame Ngo Dinh Nhu speaking at the Waldorf-Astoria in New York City. WRL was among the primary groups (along with Committee for Nonviolent Action, the Fellowship of Reconciliation, the Socialist Party, and the Student Peace Union) to organize coordinated nationwide protests against the Vietnam War on December 19, 1964.
XO	*Executive officer.* Second-in-command of a military tactical unit.
Zapped	An alternative word for killing of the enemy.
Zippo Raids	Military operations which involved burning down Vietnamese villages. Often Zippo cigarette lighters were used to ignite the hooches/huts.

Notes:
[1]   Most of the definitions from these terms came from the Internet—specifically Wikipedia.
[2]   Some of these meanings also came from the Internet - Glossary of Military Terms & Slang from the Vietnam War
[3]   Other designations came from *Guidebook for Marines,* Nineteenth Edition, pp. A-14–A-22, (Marine Corps Association, 2009).

Appendix 1

HERE are some more compelling statistics about the Vietnam War. This data, shown in Tables I–XX, has been retrieved from various sources off the Internet that will tell you a little more, directly and indirectly, about this long-lasting conflict. Note: All numbers shown are assessments only. Actual figures may vary.

Table I
American, South Vietnamese, and Allied Troop Count Levels
(1959–1973)

Year	American	South Vietnamese	Australia	Korea	New Zealand	Philippines	Thailand
1959	760	243,000	--	--	--	--	--
1960	900	243,000	--	--	--	--	--
1961	3,205	243,000	--	--	--	--	--
1962	11,300	243,000	--	--	--	--	--
1963	16,300	243,000	--	--	--	--	--
1964	23,300	514,000	198	200	30	20	--
1965*	184,300	642,500	1,560	20,620	120	70	20
1966*	385,300	735,900	4,530	25,570	160	2,060	240
1967	485,600	798,700	6,820	47,830	530	2,020	2,200
1968	536,100	820,000	7,660	50,000	520	1,580	6,000
1969	475,200	897,000	7,670	48,870	550	190	11,570
1970	334,600	968,000	6,800	48,450	440	70	11,570
1971	156,800	1,046,250	2,000	45,700	100	50	6,000
1972	24,200	1,048,000	130	36,790	50	50	40
1973	50	N/A	N/A	N/A	N/A	N/A	N/A
Total	2,637,915	8,685,350	37,368	324,030	2,500	6,110	37,640

*Note: Denotes the years that I was stationed in Vietnam.

Table II
American Troop Count Levels by Branch of Service

Branch of Service	Troop Count Level	Troop Count Level in %
Army	1,765,390	66.9
Marines	397,619	15.1
Air Force	297,960	11.3
Navy	176,946	6.7
Total	2,637,915	100.0

Table III
American Military Deaths by Branch of Service

Branch	Deaths	Deaths in %	Male	Female
Army	38,224	65.7		
Marines*	14,844	25.5		
Air Force	2,586	4.4		
Navy	2,559	4.4		
Coast Guard	7	0.0		
Total	58,220	100.0	58,212	8

*Note: Of the 14,844 Marines that were killed in action during the Vietnam War, 747 Marines (and Corpsmen), from 1/9/3, the first unit that I served with in Vietnam (July–August 1965), were killed in action. Unfortunately, this battalion endured the longest sustained combat and suffered the highest killed in action rate in Marine Corps history. Another 545 Marines (and Corpsmen) from 3/3/3, the other unit that I served with (August 1965–April 1966), also made the ultimate sacrifice for their nation in Vietnam. The figure of 58,220 deaths was considered as of April 29, 2008.

Table IV
American Military Deaths and Wounds by Cause of Death and Wound

Type of Death or Wound	Cause of Death in %	Cause of Wound in %
Small Arms	51	16
Fragments from artillery	36	65
Booby traps, mines	11	15
Punji stakes	0	2
Others	2	2
Total	100	100

Source: Ray Bonds–Editor, *The Vietnam War–The illustrated history of the conflict in Southeast Asia*, p. 34, (Salamander Books, 1999).

Note: The proportion of deaths from small arms in Southeast Asia showed a marked increase over World War II (32%) and Korea (33%) and was mainly due to the advent of the lightweight, high-velocity rounds fired by the Soviet AK-47 and captured M16s. These bullets caused large entry and exit wounds, left severe tissue damage, and affected blood vessels out of the direct path of the missile. These weapons' rapid-fire capability increased the proportion of multiple wounds. Wounds caused by mines and booby-traps were often very large and dirty, because the victim was usually close to the device when it exploded. The figures here are averaged over the years 1965–1970; actual proportions varied year to year.

Table V
American Military Deaths by Country Location

Country of Casualty	Deaths
South Vietnam	55,661
North Vietnam	1,120
Laos	728
Cambodia	523
Thailand	178
China	10
Total	58,220

Table VI
American Military Deaths by Ethnicity

Ethnicity	Deaths
White	49,830
Black	7,243
Hispanic	349
Native Hawaiian or other Pacific Islander	229
American Indian	226
Non-Hispanic—more than one race	204
Asian	139
Total	58,220

Note: Overall, Blacks suffered twelve and four-tenths percent of the deaths in Vietnam at a time when the percent of Blacks of military age was thirteen and a half percent of the total population.

Table VII
American Military Deaths by Ethnicity and Rank

Rank Officer/Enlisted	White	Black	Asian	American Indian	Other (including Hispanic)	Total
Major General/ Rear Admiral	5	0	0	0	0	5
Brigadier General/ Rear Admiral/ Commodore	7	0	0	0	0	7
Colonel/Captain	233	5	0	0	0	238
Lieutenant Colonel/ Commander	410	9	0	0	7	426
Major/Lieutenant Commander	863	9	1	0	25	898
Captain/Lieutenant	1,948	44	1	3	49	2,045
1st Lieutenant/ Lieutenant (JG)	2,088	48	11	2	26	2,175
2nd Lieutenant/ Ensign	789	16	0	0	1	806
Warrant Officer—4	12	0	0	0	0	12
Warrant Officer—3	59	1	1	0	0	61
Warrant Officer—2	281	6	1	1	1	290
Warrant Officer—1	900	9	3	1	2	915
E-9	104	10	0	0	1	115
E-8	237	29	2	1	1	270
E-7	1,040	163	6	1	24	1,234
E-6	2,311	458	13	9	64	2,855
E-5	5,590	728	10	19	64	6,411
E-4	16,685	1,824	28	66	112	18,715
E-3	15,050	2,763	32	82	68	17,995
E-2	5,122	1,002	6	35	21	6,186
E-1	378	140	0	6	1	525
Undetermined Rank	-4,282	-21	24	0	315	742
Total	49,830	7,243	139	226	782	58,220

Note: This information does not exactly correspond to Table VI.

Table VIII
American Military Deaths by Type of Casualty

Type of Casualty	Deaths
Gun, Small Arms Fire	18,518
Multiple Fragmentary Wounds	8,456
Air Loss, Crash on Land	7,992
Other Explosive Device	7,450
Artillery, Rocket or Mortar	4,914
Other Accident	1,371
Misadventure	1,326
Drowned, Suffocated	1,207
Vehicle Loss, Crash	1,187
Accidental Homicide	944
Accidental—Self Destruction	842
Other Causes	754
Air Loss, Crash in Sea	577
Burns	530
Illness, Disease	482
Suicide	382
Heart Attack	273
Intentional Homicide	234
Malaria	118
Bomb Explosion	52
Stroke	42
Hepatitis	22
Unknown, Not Reported (520 + 27 [don't know])	547
Total	58,220

Note: Draftees accounted for thirty and four-tenths percent of all combat deaths in Vietnam.

Table IX
American Military Deaths by Pay Grade and Service

Rank Officer/Enlisted	Army	Marines	Air Force	Navy	Coast Guard	Total
Major General/ Rear Admiral	2	1	2	0	0	5
Brigadier General/ Rear Admiral/ Commodore	5	0	1	1	0	7
Colonel/Captain	19	7	186	26	0	238
Lieutenant Colonel/ Commander	117	30	186	93	0	426
Major/Lieutenant Commander	254	79	400	165	0	898
Captain/Lieutenant	1,018	211	651	164	1	2,045
1st Lieutenant/ Lieutenant (JG)	1,473	308	238	154	2	2,175
2nd Lieutenant/ Ensign	496	284	8	18	0	806
Warrant Officer—4	6	2	4	0	0	12
Warrant Officer—3	59	2	0	0	0	61
Warrant Officer—2	283	7	0	0	0	290
Warrant Officer—1	905	6	0	4	0	915
E-9	52	18	41	4	0	115
E-8	190	33	34	13	0	270
E-7	987	115	64	67	1	1,234
E-6	2,233	299	136	186	1	2,855
E-5	5,133	723	228	326	1	6,411
E-4	11,528	2,322	247	618	0	14,715
E-3	12,822	4,379	148	645	1	17,995
E-2	476	5,633	9	68	0	6,186
E-1	143	379	0	3	0	525
Undetermined Rank	28	7	3	4	0	42
Total	38,224	14,844	2,586	2,559	7	58,220

Table X
American Military Deaths by Religion

By Religion	Deaths
Roman Catholic	16,817
Protestant (no denominational preference)	16,647
Baptist	9,480
Methodist	4,077
No Religious Preference	3,106
Lutheran	2,253
Presbyterian	1,303
Episcopal	825
Mormon	589
Protestant (other churches)	558
Church of Christ	528
Unclassified Religions	487
Jewish	270
Church of God	238
Pentecostal	182
Church of the Nazarene	132
Southern Baptist	121
Assemblies of God	117
Seventh Day Adventist	116
First Church of Christ (Christian Science)	63
Brethren	63
Buddhism	53
Unitarian Universalist	45
Reformed Church in America	45
Christian Church	34
Jehovah's Witnesses	26
Quaker	12
Islam	12
United Church of Christ	11
American Baptist Churches in the U.S.A.	4
Catholic (excludes Roman Catholic)	1
Christian (no denominational)	1
Congregational Churches	1
Total	58,220

Table XI
American Military Deaths by Component Code

Service Component	Deaths
Regular	34,508
Selected Service	17,671
Reserve	5,762
Not Reported	182
National Guard	97
Total	58,220

Table XII
American Military Deaths by Marital Status

Marital Status	Deaths	Deaths in %
Married Men*	17,539	30.1
Single Men (Total—Married Men)**	40,681	69.9
Total***	58,220	100.0

Note: Sixty-one percent of the men killed were twenty-one or younger. Average age of the men killed was almost twenty-three years.**

Table XIII
American Military Deaths by Home State

Home State	Deaths
Alabama	1,208
Alaska	57
American Samoa	4
Arizona	619
Arkansas	592
California	5,575
Canal Zone	2
Colorado	623
Connecticut	612
Delaware	122
District of Columbia	242
Florida	1,954
Foreign	4
Georgia	1,581
Guam	70
Hawaii	276
Idaho	217
Illinois	2,936
Indiana	1,534
Iowa	851
Kansas	627
Kentucky	1,056
Louisiana	885
Maine	341
Maryland	1,014
Massachusetts	1,331
Michigan	2,657
Minnesota	1,077
Mississippi	636
Missouri	1,418
Montana	267
Nebraska	396
Nevada	149
New Hampshire	226
New Jersey	1,487
New Mexico	395

Home State	Deaths
New York	4,119
North Carolina	1,613
North Dakota	199
Ohio	3,094
Oklahoma	987
Oregon	710
Pennsylvania	3,147
Puerto Rico	345
Rhode Island	209
South Carolina	895
South Dakota	192
Tennessee	1,295
Texas	3,415
Utah	361
Vermont	100
Virgin Islands	15
Virginia	1,305
Washington	1,047
West Virginia	733
Wisconsin	1,161
Wyoming	119
Total	**58,220**

Table XIV
Non-American Deaths by Country

Country	Deaths
South Vietnam—servicemen	300,000
South Vietnam—civilians	3,000,000
North Vietnam—servicemen	1,100,000
North Vietnam—civilians	2,000,000
Cambodia—civilians	200,000
Laos	30,000
South Korea	5,099
People's Republic of China	1,446
Thailand	1,351
Australia	521
New Zealand	37
Soviet Union	16

Note: I fought alongside with the South Korean Armed Forces a couple of times.

Table XV
Wounded in Action, but not Mortally, Requiring Hospitalization

Branch of Service	Data
Army	96,802
Navy	4,178
Marines	51,392
Air Force	931
Total	153,303

Note: This total figure does not match that of Table XIX.

Table XVI
Status of Unaccounted-for Americans (MIA) Lost in the Vietnam War

Status	Vietnam	Laos	Cambodia	China	Total
Original Missing	1,973	573	90	10	2,646
Repatriated and Identified	705	271	41	3	1,020
Remaining Missing	1,268	302	49	7	1,626

Table XVII
Status of Unaccounted-for Americans (MIA) Lost in the Vietnam War by Branch of Service

Service	North Vietnam	South Vietnam	Laos	Cambodia	China	Total
Army	10	412	73	23	0	518
Navy	254	82	17	0	7	360
Marines	22	163	17	4	0	206
Air Force	180	125	189	17	0	511
Coast Guard	0	0	0	0	0	0
Civilians	1	19	6	5	0	31
Total	467	801	302	49	7	1,626

Table XVIII
Prisoners of War in the Vietnam War but returned alive–1961–1973

Branch	Number
Army	125
Navy	147
Marines	29
Air Force	331
Coast Guard	0
Civilians	54
Total	686

Note: 686 POWs returned alive; some of them were held hostage for ninety-two months in prison camps. In addition, 114 more POWs died in captivity, for a total of 800 POWs.

Table XIX
Miscellaneous Facts about the Vietnam War

Miscellaneous Facts	Data
Total American women served.	7,484
Of the 7,484 American women that served, female nurses that served.	6,250
Total Medal of Honor Recipients.*	690
(Note: Fifty-seven were bestowed to Marines (refer to Table XX).	
Total wounded	303,704
(50.5% required hospitalization—153,329; another 150,375 required no hospital care).**	
Severely disabled (31.0% became 100% disabled).**	75,000
(Note: Amputation or crippling wounds to the lower extremities were 300% higher than in World War II and 70% higher than Korea. Multiple amputations occurred at the rate of 18.4% compared to 5.7% in World War II).	
Total POWs	800
(114 died in captivity).**	
Total Americans that served in Vietnam.	2,709,918
Helicopters that saw action in Vietnam (all branches).***	12,000
Aircraft losses	<10,000
Thousands of U.S. aircraft were lost to antiaircraft artillery (AAA), surface-to-air missiles (SAMs), and fighter interceptors (MiGs). The great majority of U.S. combat losses in all areas of Southeast Asia were to AAA. Among fixed-wing aircraft, more F-4 Phantoms were lost than any other type in service with any nation. In total, the U.S. lost in Vietnam almost 10,000 aircraft and helicopters.****	
Agent Orange	900,000
The use of Agent Orange during the Vietnam War resulted in 400,000 people being killed or maimed, and 500,000 birth defects.*****	
Draft Dodgers	125,000
An estimated 125,000 Americans fled to Canada to avoid the military draft. Around half returned to the U.S. when President Carter, in his first day in office, granted them amnesty.*****	
Number of disabled veterans	75,000
(23,214 are 100% disabled, 5,283 lost limbs. 1,081 sustained multiple amputations).******	
Number of parents who lost two sons in the conflict*******	31
Average number of days an infantryman, like me, served in combat per year*******	240
(Note: This compared to an average of 40 days during World War II over a four-year period of time.)	

Table XX
Marine Corps Medal of Honor Recipients

Rank & Name	Year	Unit
1st LT Harvey C. Barnum, Jr.	1965	9th Marines
CPL Robert E. O'Malley	1965	3rd Marines
LCPL Joe C. Paul*	1965	4th Marines
1st LT Frank S. Reasoner*	1965	3rd Marines
SSGT Peter S. Connor*	1966	3rd Marines
SSGT Jimmie E. Howard	1966	1st Marines
CAPT Howard V. Lee	1966	4th Marines
SSGT John J. McGinty III	1966	4th Marines
CAPT Robert J. Modrzejewski	1966	4th Marines
LCPL Richard A. Pittman	1966	5th Marines
PFC James Anderson, Jr.*	1967	3rd Marines
LCPL Jedh C. Barker*	1967	4th Marines
2nd LT John P. Bobo*	1967	9th Marines
COL Donald G. Cook (POW)*	1967	3rd Marines
SGT Rodney M. Davis*	1967	5th Marines
PFC Douglas E. Dickey*	1967	4th Marines
SGT Paul H. Foster*	1967	4th Marines
CAPT James A. Graham*	1967	5th Marines
PFC Gary W. Martini*	1967	1st Marines
PFC Melvin E. Newlin*	1967	5th Marines
CPL William T. Perkins, Jr.*	1967	3rd Marines
SGT Lawrence D. Peters*	1967	5th Marines
CAPT Stephen W. Pless	1967	VMO-6
SGT Walter K. Singleton*	1967	9th Marines
CPL Larry E. Smedley*	1967	7th Marines
LCPL Roy M. Wheat*	1967	7th Marines
PFC Robert C. Burke*	1968	27th Marines
SGT Alfredo Gonzalez*	1968	1st Marines
2nd LT Terrance C. Graves*	1968	3rd Marines
PFC Ralph. H. Johnson*	1968	1st Marines
CAPT James E. Livingston	1968	4th Marines
CPL Larry L. Maxam*	1968	4th Marines
SSGT Karl G. Taylor, Sr.*	1968	26th Marines
CAPT M. Sando Vargas, Jr.*	1968	4th Marines
LCPL Lester W. Weber*	1968	7th Marines
PFC Dewayne. F. Williams*	1968	1st Marines
LCPL Kenneth L. Worley*	1968	7th Marines
LCPL Richard A. Anderson*	1969	3rd Reconnaissance Battalion
PFC Oscar P. Austin*	1969	7th Marines
PFC Daniel D. Bruce*	1969	5th Marines
PFC Bruce W. Carter*	1969	3rd Marines
PFC Ronald L. Coker*	1969	3rd Marines
LCPL Thomas E. Creek*	1969	9th Marines
PFC Ralph E. Dias*	1969	7th Marines

1st LT Wesley L. Fox	1969	9th Marines
PFC Robert H. Jenkins, Jr.*	1969	3rd Marines
LCPL Jose F. Jimenez*	1969	7th Marines
CPL William D. Morgan*	1969	9th Marines
LCPL Thomas P. Noonan, Jr.*	1969	9th Marines
PFC Jimmy W. Phipps*	1969	1st Marines
LPL William R. Prom*	1969	3rd Marines
PFC Alfred M. Wilson*	1969	9th Marines
PFC Raymond M. Clausen	1970	HMM-263
LCPL Emilio A. De La Garza, Jr.*	1970	1st Marines
LCPL James D. Howe*	1970	7th Marines
LCPL Miguel Keith*	1970	Combined Action Platoon 1-2-3
SSGT Allan J. Kellogg, Jr.	1970	5th Marines

Note: *Denotes posthumously.

The Medal of Honor, the Nation's highest award for military valor, is given only to those who have acted with supreme courage, with total disregard for their own safety in the face of the most hazardous conditions. It is an award that only a comparative handful of men in the world are entitled to wear. It is bestowed by an Act of Congress and reflects Democracy's gratitude to those who, in moments of uncommon risk, offered everything they had in its defense, including life itself. The medal itself is but a humble token, a gesture of recognition for sacrifices which cannot be repaid in worldly goods.

Those who live to wear it do so proudly and yet with the spirit of humility befitting true heroes. They share the highest glory of which it is a symbol, yet hold it in solemn trust for comrades less fortunate. Whether they live or whether they died, our Nation is richer for their actions. [276]

While all fifty-seven Medal of Honor recipients are real heroes in my eyes, from my perspective, one Marine really stands out among these courageous idols, and that is Staff Sergeant Jimmie E. Howard.

After completing advanced infantry training in February 1952, Howard was ordered to Korea where he was assigned duty as a forward observer with the 4.2" Mortar Company, 1st Marines, 1st Marine Division. For his service in Korea, he was awarded the Silver Star, the Purple Heart with Gold Star in lieu of a second Purple Heart, and the Navy Unit Commendation. He was promoted to Corporal in March 1952. Fourteen years later, on the evening of June 13, 1966, now Staff Sergeant Howard along with his platoon of fifteen Marines and two Navy corpsmen were dropped behind enemy lines atop Hill 488. The mission of this recon unit was to observe enemy troop movements in the valley and call in air and artillery strikes. Within days, the enemy descended on them in force; on the night of June 15, 1966, a full battalion of Viet Cong (over 300 men) were engaging the squad of eighteen. After receiving severe wounds from an enemy grenade, Howard distributed ammunition to his men and directed air strikes on the enemy. By dawn, his beleaguered platoon still held their position. During the twelve hours of attack, 200 enemy troops were killed with the loss of six American lives. In addition to receiving the Medal of Honor for his actions

---

[276] Sgt. Karl C. Lippard, *The Warriors–United States Marines*, p. 234, (Taylor Publishing Company, 1983).

on Hill 488, for wounds received on June 16, 1966, Howard received a gold star in lieu of a third Purple Heart. [277]

---

[277] *Jimmie E. Howard*, Wikipedia.

Appendix 2

Below are some more thought-provoking myths and facts about the Vietnam War:

Myth 1–Most American soldiers and warriors were addicted to drugs, guilt-ridden about their role in the war, and deliberately used cruel and inhumane tactics.

Facts–Ninety-one percent of Vietnam veterans say they were glad they served. Seventy-four percent said they would serve again even knowing the outcome. There is no difference in drug usage between Vietnam veterans and non-veterans of the same age group. Ninety-seven percent of servicemen/women were discharged in honorable conditions; the same percentage of honorable discharges as ten years prior to the Vietnam War. And eighty-five percent of Vietnam veterans have made a successful transition to civilian life. And Vietnam veterans have a lower unemployment rate than our non-vet age group. Lastly, eighty-seven percent of the American people hold Vietnam veterans in high esteem.

Myth 2–Most Vietnam veterans were drafted.

Facts–Two-thirds of the men who served in Vietnam were volunteers (i.e., like me). Two-thirds of the men who served in World War II were drafted. Approximately seventy percent of those killed were volunteers.

Myth 3–The media have reported that suicides among Vietnam veterans range from 50,000 to 100,000–six to eleven times the non-Vietnam veteran population.

Facts–Mortality studies show that 9,000 is a better estimate. "The CDC Vietnam Experience Study Mortality Assessment showed that during the first five years after discharge, deaths from suicide were one and seven-tenths times more likely among Vietnam veterans than non-Vietnam veterans. After that initial post-service period, Vietnam veterans were no more likely to die from suicide than non-Vietnam veterans. In fact, after the five-year post-service period, the rate of suicides is less in the Vietnam veterans' group."

Myth 4–The war was fought largely by the poor and uneducated.

Facts–Servicemen who went to Vietnam from well-to-do areas had a slightly elevated risk of dying because they were more likely to be pilots or infantry officers. In addition, Vietnam veterans were the best educated forces our nation had ever sent into combat. Seventy-nine percent had a high school education or better. I was one of them.

Myth 5–*The domino theory was proved false.*

Facts–The domino theory was accurate. The Association of Southeast Asian Nations (ASEAN–Philippines, Indonesia, Malaysia, Singapore, and Thailand) stayed free of Communism because of the U.S. commitment to Vietnam. Without that commitment, Communism would have swept all the way to the Malacca Straits that is south of Singapore and of great strategic importance to the free world. Further, if you ask people who live in these countries that won the war in Vietnam, they have a different opinion from the American news media. The Vietnam War was the turning point for Communism.

Myth 6–*The fighting in Vietnam was not as intense as in World War II.*

Facts–The average infantryman in the South Pacific, during World War II, saw about forty days of combat in four years. The average infantryman in Vietnam, guys like me, saw about 240 days of combat in one year thanks to the mobility of the helicopter. Also, amputations or crippling wounds were 300 percent higher than in World War II.

Myth 7–*Air America, the airline operated by the CIA in Southeast Asia, and its pilots were involved in drug trafficking.*

Facts–The 1990 box office bomb of a movie "Air America" helped to establish the myth of a connection between Air America, the CIA, and the Laotian drug trade. The movie and a book the movie was based on contend that the CIA condoned a drug trade conducted by a Laotian client; both agree that *Air America* provided the essential transportation for the trade; and both view the pilots with sympathetic understanding. American-owned airlines never knowingly transported opium in or out of Laos, nor did their American pilots ever profit from its transport. Yet, undoubtedly every plane in Laos carried opium at some time, unknown to the pilot and his superiors.

Myth 8–*The United States lost the war in Vietnam.*

Facts–The American military was not defeated in Vietnam. The American military did not lose a (major) battle of any consequence. From a military standpoint, it was almost an unprecedented performance. Also, the South Vietnamese did lose the war in Vietnam after the U.S. Congress cut off their funding. The South Vietnamese ran out of fuel, ammunition, and other supplies because of a lack of support from Congress while the North Vietnamese were very well supplied by China and the Soviet Union.

Appendix 3

Here are some additional facts about the Vietnam War:

SOME POSSIBLE CAUSES OF THE VIETNAM WAR

1883–1945: Cochin-China, southern Vietnam, and Annam and Tonkin, central and northern Vietnam, along with Cambodia and Laos make up colonial empire of French Indochina.

1946: Communists in the north begin fighting France for control of the country. Note: When I first arrived in Da Nang—July 1965, South Vietnam, my first duty station was to be a sentry at a fort that was built by the French.

1949: France established the State of Vietnam in the southern half of the country.

1951: Ho Chi Minh became the leader of Dang Lao Dong, Vietnam, the Vietnam Worker's Party, in the north. North Vietnam was Communist. South Vietnam was not. North Vietnamese communists and South Vietnamese Communist rebels, (known as the Viet Cong) wanted to overthrow the South Vietnamese government and re-unite the country.

A FEW OTHER FACTS ABOUT THE VIETNAM WAR

1954: North Vietnamese began helping South Vietnamese rebels fight South Vietnamese troops, thus began the Vietnam Conflict.

June 8, 1956: Technical Sergeant Richard B. Fitzgibbon, Jr. became the first American serviceman officially classified as killed in action in Vietnam. Richard B. Fitzgibbon III, father of Richard B. Fitzgibbon, Jr., joined the U.S. Marine Corps and also served in Vietnam, where he too was killed in September 1965. The Fitzgibbon deaths are one of only three amongst U.S. casualties in which both father and son were killed in the Vietnam War.

May 19, 1959: The NVA creates Group 559, responsible for infiltrating troops and supplies from North Vietnam into South Vietnam via the Ho Chi Minh Trail, which the group developed in neighboring Cambodia. Persuasiveness

1961–1970: Agent Orange was a powerful mixture of chemical defoliants used by U.S. military forces during the Vietnam War to eliminate forest cover for North Vietnamese and Viet Cong troops, as well as crops that might be used to feed them. The U.S. program of defoliation, codenamed *Operation Ranch Hand,* sprayed more than nineteen million gallons of herbicides over 4.5 million acres of land in Vietnam. Agent Orange, which contained the chemical dioxin, was the most commonly used of the herbicide mixtures, and the most effective. It was later revealed to cause serious health issues–including tumors, birth defects, rashes, psychological symptoms and cancer–among returning U.S. servicemen and their families as well as among the Vietnamese population. The most commonly used, and most effective, mixture of herbicides used was Agent Orange, named for the orange stripe painted on the fifty-five-gallon drums in which the mixture was stored. It was one of several "Rainbow Herbicides" used, along with Agents White, Purple, Pink, Green and Blue.

U.S. planes sprayed some eleven million to thirteen million gallons just of Agent Orange in Vietnam between January 1965 and April 1970. According to the U.S. Department of Veterans Affairs (VA), Agent Orange contained "minute traces" of 2,3,7,8-tetrachlorodibenzo-p-dioxin (TCDD), more commonly known as dioxin. Through studies done on laboratory animals, dioxin has been shown to be highly toxic even in minute doses; human exposure to the chemical could be associated with serious health issues such as muscular dysfunction, inflammation, birth defects, nervous system disorders and even the development of various cancers. (Note: I personally saw the U.S. military spray Agent Orange in a few places that I was stationed during 1965 - 1966.)

August 10, 1961: Aerial spraying of herbicides (Agent Orange, etc.) is first tested in Vietnam.

January 12, 1962: In Operation Chopper, the U.S. Army helicopter pilots fly Army of the Republic of Vietnam (ARVN) troops into combat near Saigon. This is the first U.S. combat mission of the Vietnam War.

January 2, 1963: In the Battle of Ap Bac, the Viet Cong (VC) defeat an ARVN unit and kill three U.S. Army advisers.

November 1, 1964: The VC shell the USAF Bien Hoa Ar Base, inflicting four U.S. deaths, wounding seventy-six, and destroying or damaging several USAF aircraft.

December 28, 1964: The VC overrun Binh Gia, South Vietnam, killing some 200 ARVN troops and five U.S. advisers.

February 10, 1965: A VC bomb explodes in a Qui Nhon hotel frequented by GIs, killing twenty-three U.S. soldiers.

Source (May 19, 1959–February 10, 1965): Alan Axelrod, *The Real History of the Vietnam War,* pp. 352-353, (Sterling, 2013).

1965-1967: The North Vietnamese maintained a steady flow of troops to replace casualties in the south. In this way, General Westmoreland's attrition strategy never reached the all-important "cross-over point"—the moment when North Vietnamese losses exceeded their ability to put new forces in the field.

Source: Mark Atwood Lawrence, *The Vietnam War–A Concise International History,* p. 103, (Oxford University Press, 2008).

January–April 1967: As the new year began, the bulk of 3/3's (my old unit) efforts for the entire year were directed at trying to keep this vital land (South Vietnam) open—in and around the DMZ. From January to April, most units fought in the vicinity of the Rockpile while others operated along Highway 561, a loose-surfaced spur of Route 9 that connect Cam Lo with Con Thien.

Source: Otto J. Lehrack, *No Shining Armor–The Marines at War in Vietnam,* p. 112, (University Press of Kansas, 1992).

January 27, 1973: The Paris Peace Accords of 1973 intended to establish peace in Vietnam and an end to the Vietnam War, ended direct U.S. military involvement, and temporarily stopped the fighting between North and South Vietnam. As a result of this agreement, North Vietnam released all 591 U.S. servicemen it held as prisoners of war. The POWs, who had endured as much as eight years of sometimes brutal captivity, returned to patriotic fanfare in the United States.

Source: Mark Atwood Lawrence, *The Vietnam War–A Concise International History,* p. 162, (Oxford University Press, 2008).

March 29, 1973: The last U.S. ground combat troops leave South Vietnam, ending America's direct military involvement in the Vietnam War.

April 30, 1975: South Vietnam surrenders to North Vietnam as North Vietnamese troops enter Saigon, ending the Vietnam conflict. North Vietnamese guerilla forces used the Ho Chi Minh Trial, a network of jungle paths and mountain trails, to send supplies and troops into South Vietnam. The bombing of North Vietnam surpassed the total tonnage of bombs dropped on Germany, Italy, and Japan in World War II. Today, as a result of the Vietnam War, Vietnam is a Communist state.

ABBREVIATED GENERAL TIMELINE
AROUND AND ABOUT THE VIETNAM WAR
(especially during the time that I was stationed in Vietnam, 1965–1966)

September 2, 1945: Vietnam declares independence from France. Neither France nor the U.S. recognizes this claim. President Harry S. Truman aids France with military equipment to fight the rebels known as Viet Minh.

May 1954: The Battle of Dien Bien Phu results in a serious defeat for the French and peace talks in Geneva. The Geneva Accords end the French Indochina War.

July 21, 1954: Vietnam signed the Geneva Accords and divides into two areas at the 17th parallel, the Communist-led north and U.S.-supported south.

1957–1969: By 1964, the Viet Cong, the Communist guerilla force, has 35,000 troops in South Vietnam. As a result, the U.S. sends more and more troops to fight the Viet Cong and North Vietnamese, with the number of U.S. troops in Vietnam peaking at over 475,000 in 1969. Anti-war sentiment in the U.S. grows stronger as the troop numbers increase.

August 2, 1964: Gulf of Tonkin–The North Vietnamese fire on a U.S. destroyer anchored in the area. After President Johnson falsely claims that there had been a second attack on the destroyer, Congress passes the Gulf of Tonkin resolution, which authorizes full-scale U.S. intervention in the Vietnam War. Johnson also orders the bombing of North Vietnam in retaliation for the Tonkin attack.

August 5, 1964: President Johnson now asks Congress for the power to go to war against the North Vietnamese and the Communists for violating the Geneva Accords against South Vietnam and Laos. The request is granted August 7, 1964 in a Congressional joint resolution.

January 27, 1965**: Johnson aides, National Security Advisor McGeorge Bundy and Defense Secretary Robert McNamara, send a memo to the President stating that America's limited military involvement in Vietnam is not succeeding, and that the U.S. has reached a 'fork in the road' in Vietnam and must either soon escalate or withdraw.

February 6–8, 1965**: Viet Cong guerrillas attack the U.S. military compound at Pleiku in the Central Highlands, killing eight Americans, wounding 126, and destroying ten aircraft. I have had enough of this, "President Johnson tells his National Security advisors. He then approves Operation Flaming Dart, the bombing of a North Vietnamese army camp near Dong Hoi by U.S. Navy jets from the super aircraft carrier USS Ranger.

February 22, 1965**: General Westmoreland requests two battalions of U.S. Marines to protect the American air base at Da Nang from 6,000 Viet Cong massed in the vicinity. The President approves his request, despite the "grave reservations" of Ambassador Taylor in Vietnam who warns that America may be about to repeat the same mistakes made by the French in sending ever-increasing numbers of soldiers into the Asian forests and jungles of a "hostile foreign country" where friend and foe are indistinguishable.

March 2, 1965**: Operation rolling thunder begins as over 100 American fighter-bombers attack targets in North Vietnam. Scheduled to last only eight weeks, Rolling Thunder will instead go on for three years.

March 8–9, 1965**: The first U.S. combat troops arrive in Vietnam as 3,500 Marines land at China Beach to defend the American air base at Dang Nang. (Note: I arrived with this same unit in Da Nang on July 7, 1965—performing a full beachhead landing to protect this same base.) They join 23,000 American military advisors already in Vietnam.

March 29, 1965**: Viet Cong terrorists bomb the U.S. embassy in Saigon.

April 1, 1965**: President Johnson authorizes sending two more Marine battalions and up to 20,000 logistical personnel to Vietnam. The President also authorizes American combat troops to conduct patrols to root out Viet Cong in the countryside. (Note: I started patrolling the countryside, with my unit, in early August 1965.) His decision to allow offensive operations is kept secret from the American press and public for two months.

April 15–17, 1965**: A thousand tons of bombs are dropped on Viet Cong positions by U.S. and South Vietnamese fighter-bombers. At the same time, in Washington, D.C., 15,000 students gather to protest the U.S. bombing campaign.

April 20, 1965**: In Honolulu, Hawaii, the President's top aids meet and agree to recommend to the President sending another 40,000 combat soldiers to Vietnam.

May 13, 1965**: The first bombing pause is announced by the U.S. in the hope that Hanoi will negotiate.

May 19, 1965**: U.S. bombing of North Vietnam resumes.

July 1, 1965**: The Viet Cong stage a mortar attack against Da Nang air base and destroy three aircraft. (Note: Members from my unit had already been stationed at this base.)

July 28, 1965**: President Johnson announces he will send forty-four combat battalions to Vietnam increasing the U.S. military presence to 125,000 men.

August 1965**: Combined Action Platoons (CAPS) are formed by U.S. Marines utilizing South Vietnamese militia units to protect villages and conduct patrols to root out Viet Cong guerrillas. (Note: My unit was part of this process.)

August 3, 1965**: The destruction of suspected Viet Cong villages near Da Nang by a U.S. Marine rifle company is shown on CBS television and generates controversy in America. (Note: I was there with my unit, at Cam Ne, when this happened.) Earlier, seven Marines had been killed nearby while searching for Viet Cong following a mortar attack against the air base at Da Nang.

August 5, 1965**: Viet Cong destroy two million gallons of fuel in storage tanks near Da Nang.

August 18–24, 1965**: Operation Starlite begins the first major U.S. ground operation in Vietnam as U.S. Marines wage a preemptive strike against 1,500 Viet Cong planning to assault the American airfield at Chu Lai. (Note: My unit participated in this operation.) The Marines arrive by helicopter and by sea following heavy artillery and air bombardment of Viet Cong positions.

October 16, 1965**: Anti-war rallies occur in forty American cities.

October 19, 1965**: North Vietnamese Army troops attack the U.S. Special Forces camp at Plei Me in a prelude to the Battle of the Ia Drang Valley in South Vietnam's Central Highlands.

November 14–16, 1965**: The Battle of Ia Drang Valley (also named Operation Silver Bayonet) marks the first major battle between U.S. (Army) troops and North Vietnamese Army regulars (NVA) inside South Vietnam. (Note: I do not necessarily believe this statement to be true—we too incurred NVA soldiers in a previous battle (Operation Starlite).

November 27, 1965**: Washington, D.C., 35,000 anti-war protesters circle the White House then march on to the Washington Monument for a rally.

December 7, 1965**: Defense Secretary McNamara tells the President that the North Vietnamese apparently "believe that the war will be a long one, that time is their ally, and that their staying power is superior to ours." (Note: Based on my experiences in Vietnam, I believe this statement to be spot-on.)

January 28–March 6, 1966**: Operation Masher marks the beginning of large-scale search-and-destroy operations against Viet Cong and NVA troop encampments. (Note: I participated with my unit in some of these search-and destroy missions.)

February 3, 1966**: Influential newspaper columnist Walter Lippmann (i.e., an American writer, reporter, and political commentator famous for being among the first to introduce the concept of the Cold War, coining the term "stereotype" in the modern psychological meaning, and critiquing media and democracy in his newspaper column and several books,) lambastes President Johnson's strategy in Vietnam, stating, "Gestures, propaganda, public relations and bombing and more bombing will not work." Lippmann predicts Vietnam will divide America as combat causalities mount.

March 26, 1966**: Anti-war protests are held in New York, Washington, Chicago, Philadelphia, Boston, and San Francisco.

May 2, 1966**: Defense Secretary McNamara privately reports the North Vietnamese are infiltrating 4,500 men per month into the South.

June 4, 1966**: A three-page anti-war advertisement appears in the *New York Times* signed by 6,400 teachers and professors.

July 15, 1966**: Operation Hastings is launched by U.S. Marines and South Vietnamese troops against 10,000 NVA in the Quang Tri Province. This is the largest military operation to date in the war.

September 14–24, 1966**: Operation Attleboro occurs involving 20,000 U.S. and South Vietnamese soldiers in a successful search-and-destroy mission fifty miles north of Saigon near the Cambodian border. North Vietnamese losses are estimated at 1,106 soldiers.

December 27, 1966**: The U.S. mounts a large-scale air assault against suspected Viet Cong positions in the Mekong Delta, South Vietnam, using Napalm and hundreds of tons of bombs.

December 1966***: North Vietnamese leader Ho Chi Minh, states: "I knew that America would never invest the necessary funds or energies in rehabilitation of its poor so long as Vietnam continued to draw me and skills and money like some demonic, destructive suction tube. So, I was increasingly compelled to see the war as an enemy of the poor and to attack it as such."

January 8–26, 1967**: Operation Cedar Falls occurs. It is the largest combined offensive to date and involves 16,000 American and 14,000 South Vietnamese soldiers clearing out Viet Cong from the 'Iron Triangle' area twenty-five miles northwest of Saigon. The Viet Cong choose not to fight and instead melt away into the jungle. Americans then uncover an extensive network of tunnels and for the first time use 'tunnel rats,' the nickname given to special-ly-trained volunteers who explore the maze of tunnels. After the American and South Vietnamese troops leave the area, Viet Cong return and rebuild their sanctuary. This pattern is repeated throughout the war as Americans utilize 'in-and-out' tactics in which troops arrive by helicopters, secure an area, then depart by helicopters.

February 22–May 14, 1967**: The largest U.S. military offensive of the war occurs. Operation Junction City involves twenty-two U.S. and four South Vietnamese battalions attempting to destroy the NVA's Central Office head-quarters in South Vietnam. The offensive includes the only parachute assault by U.S. troops during the entire war. During the fighting at Ap Gu, U.S. 1st Battalion, 26th Infantry is commanded by Lieutenant General Alexander M. Haig who will later become an influential White House aide. Junction City ends with 2,728 Viet Cong killed and thirty-four captured. American losses are 282 killed and 1,576 wounded. NVA relocate their Central Office head-quarters inside Cambodia, thus avoiding capture.

April 24–May 11, 1967**: Hill fights rage at Khe Sanh between U.S. 3rd Ma-rines and the North Vietnamese Army resulting in 940 NVA killed. American losses were 155 killed and 425 wounded. The isolated air base is located in mountainous terrain less than ten miles from North Vietnam near the border of Laos.

1967 to 1971*: Stingray patrols usually consisting of five or six highly trained, lightly armed Marines from force reconnaissance companies or division re-connaissance battalions, equipped with a radio, inserted themselves directly into enemy territory by helicopter. More than 8,000 patrols were run. Only one was lost and not one was captured. The 8,317 patrols had 15,680 sightings of 138,252 enemies. They called in 6,463 artillery-fire missions and 1,328 air strikes, resulting in 9,566 confirmed kills, eighty-five captured, and more than 300 weapons secured.

January 30, 1968: Tet Offensive–The North Vietnamese launch a massive surprise attack during the festival of the Vietnamese New Year. The attack hits thirty-six major cities and towns in South Vietnam. Both sides suffer heavy casualties, but the offensive demonstrates that the war will not end soon or easily. American public opinion against the war increases and the U.S. begins to reduce the number of troops in Vietnam.

July 21–September 25, 1969****: This was the last major combat involve-ment for my former unit (i.e., 3/3/3). It was called Operation Idaho Canyon. It was fought in an area near Mutter's Ridge (i.e., west of Tam Ky, Quang Tin

Province). It is estimated that 565 VC/NVA troops were KIA. Allied forces were registered at 159 KIA.

April 1970: Invasion of Cambodia–President Nixon orders U.S. and South Vietnamese troops to invade border areas in Cambodia and destroy supply centers set up by the North Vietnamese. The invasion sparks even more anti-war protests, and on June 3, 1970, Nixon announces the completion of troop withdrawal.

May 4, 1970: National Guard units fire into a group of demonstrators at Kent State University in Ohio. The shots kill four students and wound nine others. Anti-war demonstrations and riots occur on hundreds of other campuses throughout May—they happened at California State University, Northridge, California, where I was going to school at the time.

February 8, 1971: Invasion of Laos–under orders from President Nixon, U.S. and South Vietnamese ground troops, with the support of B-52 bombers; invade southern Laos in an effort to stop the North Vietnamese supply routes through Laos into South Vietnam. This action is done without consent of Congress and causes even more anti-war protests in the United States.

January 27, 1973: A cease-fire is arranged after peace talks.

March 29, 1973: The last American ground troops leave Vietnam. Fighting begins between North and South Vietnam, but the U.S. does not return.

April 30, 1975: South Vietnam surrenders to North Vietnam as North Vietnamese troops enter Saigon, now called Ho Chi Minh City.

* Colonel H. Avery Chenoweth, USMCR (Retired), *Semper Fi–The Definitive Illustrated History of the U.S. Marines,* p. 352, (Fall River Press, 2005).

Appendix 4

AND lastly, and by the order of the President of the United States, members of my unit (M Company, 3/3/3) and I, were awarded the Presidential Unit Citation:

The President of the United States takes pleasure in presenting the PRESIDENTIAL UNIT CITATION to the THIRD MARINE DIVISION (REINFORCED) for service as set forth in the following CITATION:

For extraordinary heroism and outstanding performance of duty in action against the North Vietnamese Army and Viet Cong forces in the Republic of Vietnam from 8 March 1965 to 15 September 1967. Throughout this period, the Third Marine Division (Reinforced), operating in the five northernmost provinces of the Republic of Vietnam, successfully executed its three-fold mission of occupying and defending key terrain, seeking out and destroying the enemy, and conducting an intensive pacification program. Operating in an area bordered by over 200 miles of South China Sea coastline, the mountainous Laotian border and the Demilitarized Zone, the Third Marine Division (Reinforced) successfully executed eighty major combat operations, carrying the battle to the enemy, destroying many of his forces, and capturing thousands of tons of weapons and materiel. In addition to these major operations, more than 125,000 offensive counter-guerrilla actions, ranging from squad patrols and ambushes to company-sized search and destroy operations, were conducted in both the coastal rice lands and the mountainous jungle inland. These bitterly contested actions routed the enemy from his well-entrenched positions, denied him access to his source of food, restricted his freedom of movement, and removed his influence from the heavily populated areas. In numerous operations, the Third Marine Division (Reinforced) demonstrated the great efficacy of combined operations with units of the Army of the Republic of Vietnam. In July 1966, The Third Marine Division (Reinforced) moved to the north to counter major elements of the North Vietnamese Army moving across the Demilitarized Zone. Imbued with an unrelenting combat spirit and initiative and undeterred by heavy hostile artillery and mortar fire, extremely difficult terrain, incessant heat and monsoon rains, the Third Marine Division (Reinforced), employing courageous ground, heliborne and amphibious assaults, complemented by intense and accurate air, artillery and naval gunfire support, inflicted great losses on the enemy and denied him the political and military victory he sought to achieve at any cost. The outstanding courage, resourcefulness and aggressive fighting spirit of the officers and men of the Third Marine Division (Reinforced) in battle after battle against a well-equipped and well-trained enemy, often numerically superior in strength, and the great humanitarianism constantly shown to the peoples of the Republic of Vietnam, reflected great credit upon the Marine Corps and were in keeping with the highest traditions of the United States Naval Service.

The Author

D R. James Ike Schaap, who likes to be called Jamy, while born in the small town of Haarlem, Holland, grew up in the beach community of Santa Monica, California. He joined the U.S. Marine Corps at the age of 17, where he served from 1964-1967 as a frontline combat warrior and rifleman, with two legendary infantry battalions, and later as a military policeman.

After serving his time in the United States Armed Forces, he attended Santa Monica College and California State University, Northridge, where he earned an undergraduate degree in business. Dr. Schaap went on to earn an MBA at Pepperdine University, Malibu, CA. He later received a second master's degree and a Ph.D. from Fielding Graduate University, Santa Barbara, CA.

After teaching for 24 years at the University of Nevada, Reno, Dr. Schaap is currently an adjunct professor, instructing graduate business courses at California State University, Monterey Bay, California.

Specializing in the managerial sciences field, as a college professor for almost 40 years, Dr. Schaap has published numerous business-related articles in highly respected peer-reviewed academic journals. He has also published his research in three book chapters.

Besides teaching graduate-level business courses and performing research in the business arena, Dr. Schaap is the founder and principal advisor at Schaap Consulting—a consulting firm that specializes in the strategic management business process. As a local professional, he is also a guest speaker/advisor for the award-winning Michael Bosma's radio talk show.

He has been married for thirty-nine years to his wife Marilyn. She passed away on September 22, 2016, due to complications with Parkinson's disease. The two of them have one child, Joshua, who lives in Reno, Nevada (with his wife Jenny). Dr. Schaap also lives in Reno.

71434244R00204

Made in the USA
Columbia, SC
28 May 2017